VIETNAM *BAO CHI*

Warriors of Word and Film

MARC PHILLIP YABLONKA

CASEMATE
Philadelphia & Oxford

Published in the United States of America and Great Britain in 2018 by
CASEMATE PUBLISHERS
1950 Lawrence Road, Havertown, PA 19083, USA
and
The Old Music Hall, 106–108 Cowley Road, Oxford OX4 1JE, UK

Copyright 2018 © Marc Phillip Yablonka

Hardback Edition: ISBN 978-1-61200-687-1
Digital Edition: ISBN 978-1-61200-688-8 (epub)

A CIP record for this book is available from the British Library

Printed and bound in the United States of America

Typeset in India by Versatile PreMedia Services. www.versatilepremedia.com

For a complete list of Casemate titles, please contact:

CASEMATE PUBLISHERS (US)
Telephone (610) 853-9131
Fax (610) 853-9146
Email: casemate@casematepublishers.com
www.casematepublishers.com

CASEMATE PUBLISHERS (UK)
Telephone (01865) 241249
Email: casemate-uk@casematepublishers.co.uk
www.casematepublishers.co.uk

Contents

Preface

I became interested in combat correspondents early in my career as a military journalist. As a writer for *National Amvet* (later *American Veteran* magazine), I wrote pieces on war correspondents Ernie Pyle of the Scripps-Howard News Service, and Andy Rooney of *Stars and Stripes*, later to distinguish himself as a commentator on the CBS-TV news magazine show *60 Minutes*. Plain and simple, I wondered for a long time what it was that would compel a person to want to record action with pen and paper or camera while bullets flew overhead and bombs exploded all around.

Because my reportage for the likes of *American Veteran*, *Stars and Stripes* and *Vietnam* magazine veered toward the war in Indochina, I coincidentally began to befriend combat correspondents who had covered Southeast Asia. One was David DeVoss, whose East–West News Service I contacted after having been a stringer for Reuters and Agence France Presse and looking for more of the same type of wire service work. David had been a reporter for *Time* magazine in Vietnam. He put me in touch with Jim Caccavo. After serving in Germany and on the DMZ in Korea with the 1st Air Cavalry, Jim left the Army and became the chief writer/photographer for the Red Cross in Vietnam during the years 1968–70. He also filed for *Newsweek*. Through Jim I met Nick Ut, Pulitzer Prize winning photojournalist of the famed "Napalm Girl" photo of Phan Thi Kim Phuc, and attended a lecture given by Eddie Adams, who took the equally notable photo of a South Vietnamese general on a Saigon street shooting a Viet Cong in the head. Both photos are often cited as being among those that turned the American public against the war. Indeed some Vietnam veterans are of the opinion that it was photos like these that caused the United States to "lose" the war in Vietnam. I place quotation marks around the word because I am one who, having reported from and about Vietnam, Laos, and Cambodia after the war, and having seen the abject poverty and failure of communism in Indochina after 1975, does not believe we lost it. It's not my place, however, to quibble with Vietnam veterans who feel that way about those photos.

Other introductions to and articles about combat correspondents followed. Famed French photographer Catherine Leroy, whose poignant photographs graced the pages of *Life* and *Look* magazines during the war, was one. Joe Galloway, famous for putting down his camera and picking up a rifle to help troops fight off the enemy in the battle for the Ia Drang Valley, and for co-writing the book *We Were Soldiers Once and Young* with the late General Hal Moore, was another. A third was famed British photographer Tim Page, who I had the pleasure of meeting in the Foreign Correspondents Club in Phnom Penh, Cambodia, in 1996.

Then in 1997 through circumstances I still don't quite understand, I was invited to attend a celebration in Washington, D.C. of the publication of the book *Requiem: By the Photographers Who Died in Vietnam and Indochina*, a project that was the brainchild of Page and German Associated Press photojournalist Horst Faas. I took the red-eye out of LAX with Jim Caccavo and his friend, and very quickly mine, Marine Corps combat correspondent Sergio Ortiz. Sergio was then renowned for taking the last known picture of the four deans of civilian photojournalists—Larry Burrows, Henri Huet, Kent Potter, and Keisaburo Shimamoto—before the South Vietnamese Army Huey helicopter they were flying in to cover 1971's Operation *Lamson 719* crashed in Laos, killing them all.

It was in Washington that I also had the honor of meeting Steve Stibbens, who, as a Marine, was the first combat correspondent that *Stars and Stripes* sent, in 1962, to cover Vietnam. Meeting Sergio and Steve—the first "bao chi" (loosely translated, Vietnamese for journalist) I came to know who reported on and photographed the war in uniform—was the genesis of this book. I went on to write about Steve, our mutual friend Marvin Wolf—the Press Information Officer (PIO) for the 1st Air Cavalry and author of *Buddha's Child: My Fight to Save Vietnam* (written with Premier Nguyen Cao Ky), and many other books—and Frank Lee, who believes that he was the only Chinese-American Marine combat correspondent in Vietnam for the Milspeak Foundation. (Or if not that, Lee believes he was the only Chinese-American Marine combat correspondent from Mississippi in Vietnam, or if not that then the only Chinese-American Marine combat correspondent from Mississippi who graduated from predominantly Jewish Fairfax High School in Los Angeles!) Other articles soon followed, such as the ones I wrote for Sacramento-based *Military Magazine* on 101st Airborne Division combat correspondent John Del Vecchio, author of *The 13th Valley*, and Marine "Snuffie" Bob Bayer, former editor at the San Fernando Valley bureau of the *Los Angeles Times*.

It's in the spirit of honoring these brave chroniclers in uniform who brought the Vietnam War home to us that I offer up this book. For years, there has been a well-deserved plethora of work by and about those who covered the war as civilians, but not enough about the soldiers, sailors, airmen, Marines, and Coast Guardsmen who did so while wearing an American uniform. My hope is that this book will enlighten in some small way those who also honor them.

Author Marc Phillip Yablonka, Chief Warrant Officer-2, California State Military Reserve, ret., with cameras at the ready, prior to a mission at the Joint Forces Training Base, Los Alamitos, California. (Marc Phillip Yablonka collection)

Acknowledgements

For his guidance in unknowingly steering me toward the realization of this book, I offer heartfelt thanks to the former editor-in-chief at both the *National Amvet* and *American Veteran* magazines, Dick Flanagan. In my near 15-year association with both AMVETS' publications, and our friendship, Dick taught me the basics of what it means to write about the US military, past and present. If there were a boot camp for military journalists, Dick would have been its pre-eminent drill instructor. Dick, wherever you are, sir, my hat is off to you. In addition, I'd like to recognize two editors-in-chief of *Vietnam* magazine, for which I also wrote: the late Colonel Harry Summers, and Major General Dave Zabecki, US Army, retired. Both Colonel Summers and Major General Zabecki ran me through their paces and helped me hone my chops as a military journalist. I owe them much. So, too, am I indebted to Tom Skeen, for many years managing editor of *Pacific Stars and Stripes* in Japan, and today the managing editor of content at the *Walla Walla Union Bulletin* newspaper in Washington State. Tom and I share undergrad school alma maters, but far more importantly a long-distance friendship of over 25 years. Last but not least, my heartfelt thanks go to my editor, Brooke C. Stoddard.

Taking on Hollywood: Dale Dye

Writer, actor, director, but above all, Marine Captain Dale Dye put all of his experiences in Vietnam into the film *Platoon*, perhaps the most realistic of all the films about the war in Vietnam. "We wanted to create just one moment for every Vietnam veteran that he would recognize; a moment when he said to himself, 'Yeah, there it is … that's what I remember.'"

In order to do so, Dye put a lot into recreating our enemy, in particular, the North Vietnamese Army, whom Dye himself fought against in Vietnam during three tours of duty between 1965 and 1970.

"The night ambush scene where they emerge from a spooky fog-bank is an example. Been there and seen that … too many times. And I watched a bunch of beleaguered company commanders trying to control chaos on a radio during firefights in Vietnam," he said.

His portrayal of Captain Harris in the film was from Dye's own experiences and remembrances of the war he fought.

"Much of the salty dialogue used by the actors was also from my own personal observations. We wanted the actors to talk like real bush-beasts and not like guys mouthing lines they didn't understand. By the time they finished my training, they spoke the language," he said.

When Dale Dye refers to "my training," he's talking about Warriors, Inc., an actual boot camp-like school he created to teach actors how to best be soldiers, Marines, airmen, and sailors, because the way war was portrayed in Hollywood for so many years really irked the veteran of combat in Vietnam.

"There were a bunch of movies that pissed me off for their cavalier or misguided attitudes about military service, combat, and soldiering in general. The more I saw, the more I became convinced that there was a better way to tell the real story, and telling the real story was usually much more dramatic and exciting than what I was seeing on screen … usually written by people who never served and had rarely even met someone who did."

He is hard-pressed to remember whether there were certain films in particular that pushed him to the point that he knew he had to start Warriors, Inc. and "take on Hollywood" as he called it, but he does remember one.

"It might have been *The Boys of Company C.* I went to see it with a buddy who had served with me in Vietnam, and we were shocked by what we saw. I seem to recall that we repaired to the nearest bar where I declared that I'd had about enough of that kind of thing. Of course, I had no idea what I was letting myself in for and knew very little about the lay of the land in Hollywood. But when you're ignorant you can do a lot of things people tell you that you can't do,"

When asked who his best pupils have been, he alluded to three actors who just so happen to have the first name Tom.

"I'd have to give the nod to guys like Tom Hanks, Tom Berenger, and Tom Cruise (maybe there's something Warrior-like in that first name?) and a few others. I find that the more serious actors are about telling a story credibly—as opposed to becoming a movie star—the better they assimilate my training and the more deeply they understand synergy or playing on a team with a selfless goal in mind."

Dye is hesitant to name off a long list of Hollywood actors he has schooled who have made the grade, but he feels some of them, had they served in the military, would have done it well and done it honorably.

"There is probably a double handful of working-name actors who would have made solid soldiers, airmen, Marines, or sailors of one kind or another. I'm still in contact with most of them, and I never hesitate to point out to them how proud I am of how well they underwent and employed the training I provided. If you want to include the hundreds of lesser-known actors I've trained for movie or TV roles over the years, the number goes up exponentially."

Platoon, the film that he and its director Oliver Stone—himself a soldier with the 25th Infantry Division in Vietnam—are still best known for because of the reality that Dye has been striving for in actors and filmmakers alike, has an interesting history all its own.

"Oliver wrote the original screenplay some 10 years before we actually got the green light to make the film. When it became such a big hit, they wanted a novelization. Oliver knew I was a writer and a published novelist, so he offered me the job of writing a book based on his script. It was a natural choice since I was so close to the story and the characters from the filming and from the character studies we'd done," Dye said.

Stone and Dye connected and formed one of the most powerful and continuous collaborative efforts in the history of Hollywood war films.

"I had been trying for a year or so to convince filmmakers in Hollywood that I had a better idea about how to make credible war movies … without much success. One day I saw a piece in the *Hollywood Reporter* that said a heretofore relatively unknown writer/director named Oliver Stone, who was himself a combat veteran, was going to make a film based on his personal experiences in Vietnam. I knew this was my shot. If anyone would understand my theories about training actors in real field conditions, he would be that guy. I pulled in a bunch of favors and jumped through a bunch of hoops and finally got his phone number. I called him and made my best pitch about what I thought was wrong with most military movies. He got it. We had a few initial meetings during which I told him what I intended, including isolating the actors and making them live like we did as field soldiers in Vietnam. He trusted me and it worked."

And while, so many years after the war ended, it's still an oft told story that Vietnam veterans experience either a cathartic or difficult time when they return to Vietnam, Dye himself has gone through both in the course of working on his Vietnam-related films.

He said: "Two issues to address here: catharsis and flashbacks. I have had, and continue to have, flashbacks when I'm working on military movies. Military service and combat were such big parts of my life that those are unavoidable. It often happens in an unexpected way. There will be something in a scene that I'm helping to stage or watch unfold that just trips a trigger, and I'm frozen for a few moments, back in combat where I watched or experienced something like that for real."

But Dye knows how to cope.

"I've learned to deal with it, and it's not debilitating, but it can haunt me for a few days and those images will be hard to shake. I recall trying to herd cats with some real Vietnamese refugees in the Philippines when we were filming the village scene in *Platoon*. I was surrounded by these folks babbling away at each other in tonal Vietnamese and suddenly, I was back in-country. It hit me so hard, I had to walk off the set and sit down on a rice paddy dike for a little while. Those things happen and they can be distracting, especially when the work evokes something particularly disturbing or gruesome from my personal experiences."

He's had his share of catharses as well.

"I think writing about combat in Vietnam and helping to make movies about it has been a sort of cleansing or healing experience for me. Unlike too many other Vietnam veterans, I chose to deal with my experiences and memories publicly in my creative pursuits rather than suppress them and let them eat away at my mind and guts," he feels. "It was never easy and often painful, but I think it was healthy for me to learn to talk about it; not to fear re-experiencing those times in hopes of helping others understand the experience."

Hollywood's Vietnam aside, Dye actually did return to Vietnam with a group of fellow Marines who had also served with him in Vietnam. Going back was not a decision he made quickly or easily, however.

"It took me a very long time to agree to that return trip, and I don't think I would have ever gone back to Vietnam if it wasn't for guys who were there with me in our outfit agreeing to go also. You don't want to embark on something like that without your real buddies at your side … just like you never wanted to go on patrol or get involved in a firefight without them. Our hosts from The Greatest Generations Foundation were superlative in arranging everything."

Their trip covered a lot of the landscape they once traversed in combat boots and steel cover.

"We got to visit places like An Hoa/Arizona Territory, Hue and Khe Sanh with no prohibitions or restrictions. It was for me much like a Hunter S. Thompson gonzo trip. The stuff I wrote each night while we were there reads much like The Doc's wild-ass first-person reportage. Just spending an hour or so in a hotel room banging out copy with a bottle at hand helped me organize and process the experience. And sharing stories with my buddies while we were standing on the very ground where we fought was an incredible experience. None of us agreed on much. You know, you take two guys who survived a firefight shoulder-to-shoulder in the same hole and they each tell an entirely different story about the experience. That's the nature of that beast, but it was a once-in-a-lifetime trip back down some very emotional paths littered with mines and booby-traps. I'm very glad I went if only to rediscover the fact that combat creates a band of brotherhood that can't be broken."

While he and his fellow Marine combat correspondents formed a band of brotherhood, Dye also formed a band of brotherhood with some of the civilian media who covered the wars in Vietnam, Cambodia, and Laos. He did do despite the fact that the civilians had a far different mission from the combat correspondents and photographers who covered the war in uniform in order to show Americans back home the difficult missions at hand and the brave way the troops in each branch of service went about attempting to complete them.

"I think the big difference in my opinion of the civilian war correspondents I saw in Vietnam runs to the medium for which they were reporting. I had a great deal of respect for many of the print journalists, the 'scribblers' that I saw and got to know. Guys like [Associated Press writer/photographer] Dick Pyle, Al Webb, [author of the Vietnam book *Dispatches*] Mike Herr, Dave Greenway, and a few others come to mind. They got stuck in with an outfit and stayed to observe a day or two rather than dropping in, doing a couple of interviews and catching the first helicopter out of the field," Dye said. "The stuff they wrote had a distinct Ernie Pyle/World War II flavor, and you knew from reading it that they'd seen enough to understand and appreciate what the grunts were going through in that war."

Dye does not hold the same sentiment for those civilian reporters who covered the war for the television networks.

"I had less respect and time for the TV guys who went out just long enough to roll tape, get some whiz-bang footage (usually with no context provided) and then split. That emphasis on eye-popping action, which would garner kudos and guarantee air time on the nightly news, led way too many of them to misreport and misinterpret what was happening in Vietnam," he said.

"The real heroes in my eyes were the photographers (still and motion) who risked life and limb to cover the action. I saw more than one or two of them get hit, but they just took it as part of the job. The safari-suited correspondents got the glory, but the poor lens-fixated shooters got the images that carried the story."

And the story of Dale Dye involved him making a transition from infantryman to Marine Combat Correspondent.

"The transition from infantryman to Marine Corps Combat Correspondent actually came later when I was back serving stateside. I had just about gotten bored with grunt life. All I seemed to be seeing was the back of the guy's pack humping in front of me. I wanted to experience everything the Marine Corps had to offer. I had this abiding appetite to know and understand all there was to the Marine Corps. I love that service, and I wanted to immerse myself in all of it, but that was hard to do when stuck in an infantry battalion. One day I saw an NCO walking along with us in the field—at Camp Pendleton, I think—and he looked a little unusual with a camera around his neck and scribbling in a notebook. I talked to him and he told me he was a Marine Combat Correspondent. I'd never heard of any such thing. He just grinned and told me it was the greatest dodge in the service. He could go anywhere and do anything as long as he managed to churn out a few photos and an interesting little story about what the Marines were doing. I'd been the editor of my high school newspaper and always a storyteller, so this seemed like just the right thing if I was planning on staying around in the Corps.

"The guy hooked me up with an interview at the base Public Affairs Office. They were so starved for talent in such a very small occupational field that I made the cut and got my military occupational specialty changed. Shortly after that I got orders to report to the 1st Marine Division in Vietnam and discovered that the emphasis in the term Combat Correspondent was on the first word."

And in the midst of that combat in Vietnam, being a Marine Corps Combat Correspondent meant that Dye and others in his MOS (Military Occupational Specialty) took on a full load of responsibilities.

"I kind of did it all. I wrote stories, made tape recordings and shot pictures. I wanted to be a jack of all trades so I wouldn't miss a chance at the action or seeing something new. Somehow I maintained that enthusiasm throughout my time at war. I always understood that I was participating in something historical, something larger than any life I'd led up to that time. I was learning from first-hand experience that in combat you can see the entire range of human emotion and behavior ... from the very best to the very worst. That fascinated me and I never lost interest in it."

One of the reasons for his fascination lies in the fact that no two days were ever the same for him or any other Marine Combat Correspondent.

"There was no average day. That's what was so fascinating and alluring about duty as a Combat Correspondent. One day you're out in the field for two or three weeks with a grunt outfit, living just like they had to, and the next you're back in the rear sitting in an office banging out the stories you'd collected on an old Underwood. If we could manage to skate in the rear for a little while before going back out to the field, we raised hell on a large scale."

"We created a little cottage industry trading war souvenirs that we brought in from the field to Air Force types and Seabees for booze. Junior enlisted Marines were not allowed to purchase liquor, but we never let that stop us. There was a kind of desperation in our partying. You know, better let it all hang out now because tomorrow you might be dead," Dye said existentially.

"We had a very small unit in the 1st Marine Division, probably never more than 10 or a dozen enlisted Combat Correspondents that covered every outfit, infantry, armor, artillery, combat support … the whole deal. We spent a lot of time in the field and got in on a lot of action running to the sound of the guns because that's where the stories were. We had all been wounded a time or two and many of us had been decorated for heroism in action. There was a distinct, perverse pride in being a combat correspondent for us. We were combat men and we never let the rear-echelon types forget that."

And often being a combat man meant that Dye and his fellow combat correspondents were required to be chroniclers of the action second and bullet shooters first.

"There were many times when I had to put aside the job in favor of the mission. Most of us became fairly well known in the outfits we covered and they expected us to pack the gear and join the fight when it was on. We did that for the most part. Nothing could get you fired from or disrespected among combat correspondents quicker than not hacking your load or helping out in combat by busting caps at the enemy. There were many times when I was not much more than a glorified rifleman, especially when we were in a really heavy fight. I tried to be a good combat correspondent in the fighting for Hue during the Tet Offensive of 1968, for instance, but that didn't last long. They needed another rifle much more than they needed another correspondent observing the action."

And it was during the Tet Offensive that Dye was wounded, and where the combat he survived stays with him still. The citation that accompanied the Bronze Star with Combat V tells the story.

Here is how Dye himself recalls the incident that garnered him the medal:

"On the north side of Hue, inside the Citadel, I was running with Charlie Company, 1st Battalion, 5th Marines. The camera was in my pack and I'd picked up an M-16 and a couple of bandoliers of ammo from a casualty. I shoot left-handed, so I was the one firing cover from behind a wall while a shot-up squad of infantry tried to cross an intersection. I was exchanging fire with an NVA machine gunner when all of a sudden my rifle seemed to explode in my hands. A sniper on the other side of the street shot at my head and hit the receiver of the M-16 which promptly exploded into a shower of plastic and steel. I got some plastic from the stock and hand guard all over my face, neck, and right hand. I was in shock—really didn't know what had happened—so I just sort of wandered back toward a battalion aid station dripping blood and holding what was left of the rifle. That was it for me in Hue."

But that would not be the last time Dye was wounded.

In March of that year, during what was dubbed Operation *Ford*, Dye, who was with E-2-3, was trapped outside the forward edge of a battle and got hit by shrapnel from an NVA firing a captured M-79 grenade launcher.

But Dye had been wounded even before those occurrences.

"I got hit once before that on a patrol into the DMZ up near Con Thien. The NVA on the other side of the Ben Hai River [the demarcation line between South and North Vietnam] saw us moving through the elephant grass and dropped a bunch of mortars on us. I caught a load of shrapnel in my right leg and right torso," he said.

When asked to reflect on other firefights Dye experienced during his time in Vietnam, he says, "I saw a lot of combat, a lot of firefights, both minor and major, but I can't think of anything in my experience that rose to the level of chaos and sheer bloodiness we experience in Hue during Tet '68."

During the days when Dye was "back in the rear banging out stories," his articles ended up in print in some very important military publications both back home and overseas.

"We wrote for the III Marine Amphibious Force house organ *The Sea Tiger*, *Pacific Stars and Stripes*, and *Navy Times* to name a few military-oriented publications. Those of us who did tape-recorded actualities or interviews also sent them off for rebroadcast on hometown radio stations or on the American Forces Radio & TV Service either in Vietnam or stateside."

Seeing their stories in print was not the only reward that Marine Combat Correspondents received, according to Dye.

"One of the really rewarding aspects of all this was when we'd rejoin one of the outfits we covered, some young PFC or Lance Corporal would show us a clipping from his hometown paper—usually sent from his family—that contained a story we'd written about him. That was a Pulitzer Prize for us. There was usually a lot of harassment about it, but you could see that it really helped morale. That kind of thing shed some long-overdue light on the little guy in the rear-rank with a rusty rifle who was carrying the war to the enemy. No chance for that kind of thing with the civilian correspondents, but it was meat and potatoes for us."

Dye left Vietnam for the last time in May 1970 and was sent to Iwakuni, Japan, to finish his overseas obligation. When he got home, he found the country he'd fought for in a terrible state of turmoil.

"For some reason known only to the Marine Corps, when I finished my time in Vietnam and Japan in 1970, they sent me to Washington, D.C., to work in the American Forces Radio & TV Service. The headquarters was in Arlington, Virginia, right across from Georgetown, and the big anti-war demonstrations were in full swing. My duty station then became the Pentagon, and I regularly had to bull my way, wearing a dress uniform, through throngs of protestors in the parking lot," he remembered.

Dye was not happy about having to do so.

"Frankly, it pissed me off and so I never tried to avoid them. I didn't get into any serious fights, but my attitude told them I was ready for that if they wanted it. I was so immersed in that wild scene in Washington that I didn't contemplate anything about the protestors being ungrateful or anything like that. I just considered them another enemy I had to deal with. It wasn't until later … when there was a little breathing room … and we had clearly given up on ever winning the war that I got depressed about it all."

The seeming shift in the American attitude, shared by many citizens and politicians alike, truly disturbed Dye, who began to wonder what he had been through in Vietnam was all for.

"At that point I was a bit fuzzy on the whole concept of why I had stayed so long and gone through so much for no appreciable reward and so much denigration among my fellow citizens. In fact, for about six or eight years after the war, I mostly avoided going off the base and just stayed among people who understood what I had been through. Later, I got over that, but it was not an easy task to convince myself that not everyone outside the gates was an asshole," he recalled.

For Captain Dale Dye, being able to open that gate eventually meant that he would have something to do with 16 Vietnam-related film and TV projects including: *Platoon, Tropic Thunder, The Music Within, Missing Brendan, Tigerland, Forrest Gump, Heaven & Earth, Dogfight, Cadence, Born of the 4th of July, Casualties of War, 84 Charlie Mopic, Dead Presidents, Air America*, and *Vietnam War Stories*.

His favorites among them are *Platoon, Born on the 4th of July, Forrest Gump, Heaven & Earth*, and *Casualties of War*. "They stick out in my mind as most evocative of the real experience in Vietnam; some more, some less," he feels.

No doubt those both inside and outside the gates of the Vietnam War experience owe Captain Dale Dye a lasting debt of gratitude for enabling us to see the war through the eyes of one who lived it, came home and took on the mission of teaching us what it was truly about.

Marine combat correspondent and future filmmaker Dale Dye, who was wounded during the fighting in Hue during the Tet Offensive in 1968. (Dale Dye collection)

Soldier First, Photog' Second:
John Del Vecchio

Writer/soldier John M. Del Vecchio became an Army combat correspondent (MOS 71Q20) during the Vietnam War because of the influences of five uncles, all World War II vets, an interest in the social sciences, and excellent teachers in high school.

After graduating in 1965 he attended Lafayette College in Easton, PA. Quiet during his first few years, the school, like campuses across the country, succumbed to the turmoil of the 1960s.

"I was a psych major wanting to study the neurological correlates of behavior. I found much of the field to be 'basically soft' or b.s. science, but the physiology of behavior was concrete. It was a nascent field at the time, and the school wasn't equipped for anything more than a surface perusal. This pushed me into courses with 'anti-war' professors and students, because they seemed to be drawn to both the department and to the b.s. I chafed at much of what they said, and many classes were only b.s. discussions on the war."

At least one professor excused this by declaring that he could not teach his students anything, Del Vecchio remembered. They could only learn it on their own.

"Therefore [the professor's] b.s.-ing on the war was justified," Del Vecchio said.

The discussions were always one-sided, nonacademic, and usually either propaganda or whining. Still their skepticism made Del Vecchio want to know what was really happening in Vietnam.

"By 1969 the TV networks of the era [ABC, CBS and NBC] and the government were losing, or had lost, credibility," Del Vecchio felt.

"Three or four months before I graduated, I had my draft physical and was told I'd be called up in June."

However, he wasn't called up in June, and there was no notification all summer. In September he began looking for a job. He wanted to know more about Southeast Asia and the war, so, with that in mind, he began applying for jobs at newspapers with the stipulation that he be sent to Vietnam as a correspondent.

"I was a fair writer, a descent observer, skeptical of all sides, and willing to do the work to find real answers. At the end of October I received a written invitation to interview with the *New York Times*. The interview date was November 8th."

Four days before the interview he received his draft notice to report on December 4th. Thus ended Del Vecchio's civilian job search, but not his desire to learn about the realities of Vietnam.

Before basic training he was given a choice to re-up for three years and be guaranteed a school, so he opted to attend the DINFOS (Defense Information School) journalism course.

"DINFOS was the best school I ever attended. Like any school, you could make of it what you wanted, but the material there was massive. I ate it up; I graduated second in a class of 140."

Del Vecchio's plans for Vietnam were temporarily stymied when he received orders for Okinawa. He had to get the school's master sergeant and his congressman to intervene to get his orders changed for Vietnam.

Once in-country Del Vecchio carried an Army-issued Ashai Pentax 35mm SLR along with steno pads, pencils, and pens.

"I do not have an exact count, but I had maybe 75 photos and 60 stories published in various military and civilian papers or magazines during my tour. Maybe more."

He was assigned to the 101st Airborne Division (Airmobile) Public Information Office (PIO) based at Camp Eagle. From there he was further assigned to the 1st Brigade Public Information Detachment (PID) in "Rocket Alley" on the western side of the camp.

"My orders were to go out with 1st Brigade units and return to the PID office once a week to turn in my film and five stories. I was never assigned anything more specific than that, which was great in some ways, not so great in others."

He had to approach the commander of any unit with which he wanted to travel, and convince the CO to let him accompany them.

"[It was] kind of a weird set up. I spent most of my time with various platoons from different infantry companies of 2/502, but also covered 2/327 and 1/501."

Del Vecchio also covered MEDCAPs (Medical Civic Action Programs) and dust-offs, as well as Engineer and Transportation units.

"On a few occasions, I flew with the 2/17 Cavalry to photograph NVA installations in the A Shau Valley, but this was a very minor part of the job and those photos were not processed via the PIO."

Del Vecchio wanted to know everything, so he spent time each week in the brigade Tactical Operations Center.

"I must have been pretty good at what I was doing. Out of 15 or so writers and photographers for the division, in my first five months I accounted for nearly half of all the photos and articles published outside of the division publications."

SOLDIER FIRST, PHOTOG' SECOND: JOHN DEL VECCHIO • 13

According to Del Vecchio it was routine for his work to run in publications like *Army Reporter*, *Observer*, and *Army Times*.

Overall though, the word "routine" would not apply to Del Vecchio's tour in Vietnam because no two days were the same.

"There was so much variation. A day at Camp Eagle, or out on Firebase Bastogne, or Operation *Checkmate*, was very different from a day on Firebase Zon or Whip. They were different from a day in the bush with a line platoon. Even at Eagle the days were very different up by division headquarters where people were 'strac' (an anachronism for "squared away"), and many worked 8- or 10-hour shifts in offices, versus down at brigade where most everything was aimed at keeping the line companies going and work days could last 24 hours."

The only thing that was constant was writing his stories and turning in his film to the division's Public Information Officer.

The story quota was more important than the film quota, according to Del Vecchio, even though they usually had nearly as many column inches in photos as they did articles. This was much different, he points out, from today's papers where print supports visual images.

"There were no assignments, no orders, just the general 'Go get five stories ...' That left it up to us how we wanted to get them. Some guys never left Camp Eagle. Others went on MEDCAPs or to firebases. Only a few of us spent much time with infantry units. For about half my tour, I spent three to five days per week humping with boonie rats. In 1970, in the 101st, the term 'boonie rat' had supplanted the term 'grunt.' Marines were grunts. We considered ourselves, true or not, more agile than grunts—so boonie rats became the term."

Although each day was a different scenario, he had his preferences, which might come as a surprise to anyone who has not soldiered in the manner that he did.

"This may sound a bit strange, but for me I was usually, mentally, more comfortable in the boonies than back in base camp. Physically, that might not be accurate. Life in the boonies was tough. Carrying a rucksack kicked your ass. Humping the mountains west of Hue in the heat and humidity, or cold monsoons and humidity, was grueling. One might get used to sleeping on the ground, but you never got used to sleeping on the side of a hill where you needed to brace against a tree trunk or rock to keep from sliding out of the NDP [night defensive position]. Oh, and there were opposition forces out there wanting to kill you."

Del Vecchio has a lighter moment when he remembers, "... but in the boonies never once did I have an officer complain about my mustache!"

Then the reality of war sets in again.

"Nor were we ever the target of 122mm rockets, which hit us down in our AO [area of operations] at Eagle four times. I hated 122s. You couldn't fight back. About all you could do was dive in a trench or lay prone on the ground, and hope they fell short or went long, left or right."

Every week Del Vecchio checked the activity reports posted in the 1st Brigade Tactical Operations Center (TOC) to see who was hitting the shit. He also scrounged equipment because brigade did not provide the Public Information Detachment ammo or even C-rats (rations). He usually joined a unit during its op, but sometimes CAed (combat assaulted) with a unit starting a new operation. From there he would do just what those troops were doing—"with the exception that during breaks I'd shift from position to position, introduce myself, often take out my camera and take photos. That established a certain credibility because the most common response from infantrymen was, 'What the fuck are you doing out here if you don't have to be?'"

"Going out with a unit a second time, especially if you had photos you could hand the guys, or if you had a newspaper with a story about them from the last time you'd been there, definitely increased your acceptance."

But a combat correspondent would never gain their respect if he couldn't pull his weight. "Moving, setting up, digging in—you'd better know what you were doing. Very quietly we would talk. Who? What? When? Where? Why? And, occasionally, How? And stories and attitudes would come out. Most stories were in the 'hometown' category." [The "hometowner" was a type of article first popularized by renowned World War II Scripps Howard Newspaper correspondent Ernie Pyle, who would seek out servicemen from all corners of the United States and write their stories in such a way that their hometown newspapers would pick them up and parents and siblings would be able—much to their delight or concern—to read about their son or brother fighting abroad.]

"Guys came from every state in the union; and there were a significant number of non-Americans—Brits, Germans, Nicaraguans. Some were seeking citizenship via the US military. That was always worthy of a story."

Del Vecchio negates the notion that the entire nation was against the war and disdainful of the job our troops were doing.

"Whose mom sent the knitted yellow wool socks? Which sorority, or whose girlfriend, adopted this squad—and sent photos along with care packages. Yes! That did happen. Despite what has come down as 'history,' there was a lot of support for the troops."

Stateside support aside, the humping in the jungle went on.

"Sleep, rise, jam down a C-rat, ruck up, move out, all very quietly, stop, quiet chat, move, stop, talk to the platoon leader or the RTOs [Radio Telephone Operators] who always had the most knowledge of what was happening, monitor the radios with them, ruck up, move … Three or four or five days later, go out on a resupply helicopter, return to Eagle, write up the stories, turn in the film, start the next week." Del Vecchio, who went to Vietnam as a new Spec 4 and left country a Spec 5, then served a tour of duty in Germany.

The mustache that hadn't bothered his superiors in Nam almost got him busted in Germany.

"The regs had changed and didn't permit the hair to fall below a horizontal line drawn across the lower part of the lower lip. So I used to wax up the ends. That brought me very close to being court martialed, but the assistant S-1 tipped me off the night before and I showed up at formation the next morning clean shaven," he said and laughed, "to the obvious displeasure of the company commander."

War is hell, but fear and horror are not necessarily paramount—particularly if the action is of short duration. "This may sound odd, but when you're in it, particularly in flash firefights or single-barrage mortarings, there is no time to feel fear. That may come later upon reflection, but at the moment training kicks in and you react. Your thoughts are not about who has been hit, how horrible it is, etc., but how to fight back, counterattack or disengage, how to care for wounded guys and keep up a defensive perimeter around them. I've often thought over the years that I should have taken a lot more photos of actions, but I was always a soldier first and 'photog' second."

Like many combat correspondents, both civilian and military, Del Vecchio never felt it appropriate to take pictures of wounded or dead, friend or enemy. "If a fellow boonie rat was wounded, taking photos of that, to me, was intrusive and disrespectful. I also felt it disrespectful to take pictures of enemy dead. I know lots of guys did this, but I believed then and still do today that disrespecting a vanquished enemy is one cause of PTSD."

In saying that he doesn't mean he always kept his cool. After the brief firefight that served as the basis for the scene in *The 13th Valley* where Cherry kills his first enemy soldier, Del Vecchio recalled, "Lieutenant Bridges debriefed me. He was doing his best to calm me down because adrenalin must have deluged my entire system. He was telling me to slow down, that my eyes were like saucers, but I do not, repeat do not, recall feeling any horror. That wasn't the emotion. Fear wasn't the emotion either. Excitement doesn't describe it, but it comes closer."

He drew a deeper line between being in the field and being back on post.

"Those experiences were very different than being rocketed back in the rear. [There was] no ability to counter anything once a rocket was in the air. Typically, the enemy would arrange perhaps a dozen 122s with delayed fuses. They'd 'di di' [Vietnamese for 'leave quickly'] from the launch site because counter-battery radar would pinpoint that site and arty [artillery] would immediately begin firing back. But the way the rockets were aimed was virtually always to go off in a sequential row—what we called 'walking.' So if they began to your left and were coming toward you, you knew you were about to be targeted. Once they moved to your right, you knew they were targeting guys further up the line."

Del Vecchio recalls a particular attack, which he rattles off almost like an After Action Report.

"One time I had one go off about 75 feet to my right as they walked left to right. Caught several of us in the open but prone on the ground. Buried itself in the red gravel-sand-clay. Soaked us in a rain of same, but none of us were hurt beyond scratches. Up the line, another one killed the brigade sergeant major, but we didn't know that right away. Instead, as soon as they moved up, we were up searching for canisters that perhaps had not exploded. I hated the rockets. They sounded like freight trains coming in. To me very scary. It was one of the reasons I preferred to be in the boonies rather than back at Eagle."

It was for action in those boonies that Del Vecchio was awarded the Bronze Star, but he shrugs it off. "My role in that firefight was pretty minor. The 11-Bravos [infantry] were the guys that deserved the awards."

Meanwhile, in those boonies he always had two devices at his disposal: his M-16 and his camera. There was never much of a question about which one was more important.

"The camera was secondary to the M-16. When you carry a weapon for a long period of time it becomes kind of an extension of your arm and hand. That's how natural it feels. Being right handed I had my 16 in my right hand on all moves. I kept the Pentax around my neck and often had my left hand on the strap to keep the camera from banging against me and making noise as we moved."

When Del Vecchio got home from Vietnam it was the confluence of the two weapons he held that may have inspired him to write about his experiences in Indochina. His first book was called *The 13th Valley*. He followed that up with a book about Cambodia, *For the Sake of All Living Things*, and then a sequel to *The 13th Valley* called *Carry Me Home*.

"When I was writing *The 13th Valley*, I was writing about the 101st Airborne Division (Airmobile), and my experiences with the division in 1970 and 1971. I knew some of the history of the country, some of the history of the conflict, and a bit about other units, but my knowledge was very limited. A lot of my education into the realities of Vietnam and Southeast Asia came after *13th* was published. That spawned *For The Sake Of All Living Things* and *Carry Me Home*, a veteran's homecoming experience that included dealing with PTSD, the Veterans Administration, and the media.

As with every work of historical fiction there is always the temptation to assume that the writer is somehow embedded in his or her own work. While Del Vecchio admits this, he is careful to delineate the writer from his own writing.

"Like all writers and all writing, parts of the story are autobiographical. There is some of me in Cherry, in Egan, in Brooks. But each character has many elements that are not 'me.' I relied on lots of interviews, lots of 'other voices,' and lots of observations to develop each character."

One of those voices was that of Colonel Harry Brooks under whom Del Vecchio served in Germany.

"I assisted him and his staff with race relations within the 72d Field Artillery Group. Colonel Brooks, who was later promoted to brigadier general, went on to develop and lead the Army's first race relations office. Many of the attitudes and lessons that the character Rufus Brooks has and teaches in *The 13th Valley* are lessons learned from Colonel Brooks in Germany and on later interviews in Washington, D.C."

He also discounts off any comparison between himself and his own soldiering with that of the main character in *The 13th Valley*, RTO James Chelini, who evolves, as reviewers of the book have stated, from being a semi-pacifist to war monger.

"As to pacifist/war monger: I was never either. I was a conscientious participant, as were most Americans who served in Vietnam. We were there to stop the terror war of the communists. It is, of course, much more complex than that statement, but when I hear 'conscientious objectors' talking about their 'anti-war' activities, quite frankly, I vomit inside my throat. The true anti-war crowd was the American and allied (including South Vietnamese and all other Southeast Asian forces) fighting men and women who were doing their best to stop the aggression of the communist North supported by Red China and the Soviet Union."

"Going to Woodstock, smoking joints, getting laid, had no effect on ending the war, and more likely helped extend it. [Secretary of State] John Kerry and the like tossing their medals away, lying about Americans committing atrocities—of the 'Winter Soldiers' whose testimony before Congress he coached, most were not even veterans. Of those who were, most had never been in Vietnam. They have done more to comfort tyrants, terrorists, and murderers than all 'American war mongers' combined."

And while Del Vecchio did not go to Cambodia during his tour of duty in Southeast Asia, he did spend five years researching and writing *For The Sake of All Living Things*.

"I interviewed a number of Cambodian refugees, read many more unedited interviews, got as much Order of Battle (OB) info as I could find. I have had Khmer FANK [Khmer National Armed Forces] soldiers tell me that *For The Sake* is more accurate historically than anything else they've read in their own country."

For Del Vecchio writing is both a teaching and a learning experience.

"With each book I learned more. What passes as conventional history about the war is rather pathetic. There are a number of terrific scholars on the subject; and there are a slew of politically correct professors, teachers, and writers repeating the same orthodox inaccuracies that began in the 1960s."

One of those inaccuracies is that Ho Chi Minh was "a national hero, a nationalist, father of his country." He adds that there was a sentiment, certainly before heavy US involvement began and even more so today, that Ho was someone the US should have embraced in 1945.

"If we had done so," the orthodox view implies, "the entire war in Southeast Asia would have been avoided. A far more realistic view would show Ho as a ruthless tyrant who came to power through brutality, the assassination of other many nationalists, *and* the 'disappearance' of many communists of competing factions. The communists, after brutally coercing the North into submission, secretly declared war, in January

1959, on South Vietnam, Laos, Cambodia, and soon began a terrorist campaign directed from Hanoi that precipitated the events which followed."

As with many veterans, both the war and the country of Vietnam are never far from Del Vecchio's mind.

"I would love to go back to Vietnam. Costs, family obligations … all sorts of things have gotten in the way."

But while he'd love to see the country again, he is not enamored of its politics since the fall of Saigon, which also weighs on his mind.

"One deterrent [to my traveling back to Vietnam] is the communist government that continues to this day to harshly suppress any political descent. Until 1975 there were perhaps a hundred independent newspapers in Vietnam, many of them opposition papers. Today there is only the state press. The Hanoi communists also continue their attacks on religion, much as they did in the North prior to 1954 which caused the migration of nearly a million Catholics to the South (this would be the equivalent of 20 million Americans fleeing the country today). And the government continues its programs of ethnic cleansing and cultural genocide in Laos. To go back as a tourist means to give money to that regime."

Del Vecchio's book *Carry Me Home* deals, in part, with life after Vietnam, something many Vietnam veterans still reflect on today, 39 years after the war's tragic end.

"In late 1974 I was living in northern California next door to a Marine Corps recruiter with whom I became friends. I had written a rough draft of *13th* in Maine two years earlier, but had shelved the work. Gunnery Sergeant LaVere, also a Vietnam vet, was following the communist advances in South Vietnam, down the Song Truong Corridor and the battles in the Central Highlands. I was selling real estate. By December he had me paying attention to this major offensive and the lack of response from Washington. By January we were meeting with other vets about going back as what today might be called civilian contractors," Del Vecchio recalled.

This was a movement that was allegedly supported by Ross Perot, and, according to Del Vecchio, there were reportedly several hundred thousand vets signed up.

But South Vietnam fell more quickly than Del Vecchio, his Marine recruiter neighbor, and the rest of the country expected. Then came the influx of hundreds of thousands of refugees; and with that hundreds of news stories about the fall of Saigon on April 30th, 1975 and a re-visitation of the role the United States, and the troops it sent to fight, had played in the war.

"I didn't recognize the Americans in those stories. I didn't recognize the country, the Republic of Vietnam that they described. But I didn't really know. The impetus to break out my old manuscript was to set the record straight for who we were in the 101st in Vietnam in 1970–71. It was only after *13th* was published that I realized how universal the story was to other American units."

Del Vecchio's realization came in the form of some 6,000 letters between 1982 and 1983.

"Over and over again guys wrote saying they had the same or similar experiences; same or similar conversations; same or similar attitudes. Lots of variations, of course."

The road to finishing the book was a long one. While Del Vecchio continued to sell real estate after the mid-1970s his commitment to that profession was waning. At the same time, to augment memories, he began researching what had actually happened at Firebase Barnett during the battle at Khe Ta Laou.

"By 1977 I was selling off everything I had to work on the manuscript—everything from my Pentax camera system to motorcycles, trucks, and finally my house."

All that he sacrificed paid off, and he continues to write full-time today. He has also gotten involved in a start-up film production company called Charlie Foxtrot Films. "Our films are military related, inspired by heroes," Del Vecchio stated. Perhaps one day, Charlie Foxtrot Films will produce a film about combat correspondents like Del Vecchio who not only brought the war home to those of us stateside, but also who strove their damnedest to show, through their stories and photos, what our soldiers, Marines, airmen, and sailors really went through in Vietnam.

101st Airborne Division combat correspondent John Del Vecchio going over notes for a story. (John Del Vecchio collection)

They Were Marines Like Him:
Steve Stibbens

When Steve Stibbens got to Vietnam in 1962, he had already been a reporter and photographer with *Pacific Stars and Stripes* in Japan. But even before that, as a Marine correspondent (MOS 4312), he had served as the Regimental Correspondent for the 5th Marines, 1st Marine Division, at Camp Pendleton, California. He was no babe in the woods. In fact, he had already jumped off a few choppers. "I was a 26-year-old Marine buck sergeant with eight years in the Corps when I got to *Stripes*. As a Marine Combat Correspondent, I'd been preparing for war all that time."

Stibbens' preparations were about to pay off. The late Al Chang, renowned photographer of the Korean War, had gone on a fact-finding mission to Vietnam quite early on. When he came back, he encouraged Steve to head south to Vietnam himself.

"This is the real one. You need to be there," Chang told Steve.

In the meantime, Stibbens began to bone up on war. He read books about World War II and Korea. He read "all the books," but then a trip to the library introduced him to a book about the French war in Indochina that was to prove insightful to him.

One of the things he realized was that the US Marines were still thinking along the lines of large-unit actions, not the guerilla warfare made popular by Ho Chi Minh's Viet Minh, later Viet Cong, communists. These were large-unit actions, not the war that the French had fought.

"At the time, I just knew it would be great adventure," said Stibbens, and he began working his editors.

When he arrived in Saigon in December 1962, he set up a one-man *Stars and Stripes* bureau. He had an immediate mission: to cover the Christmas visit of Francis Cardinal Spellman, a hawkish supporter of the war in Vietnam.

Once Stibbens was safely in Saigon, he followed Al Chang's advice and headed to the Associated Press's Saigon bureau. It was there that he would meet civilian correspondents Malcolm Browne (who took the famous photo of the Buddhist monk Hoa Thuong Thich Quang Duc immolating himself on the Streets of Saigon), Peter Arnett (later of CNN), and Horst Faas, Saigon photo bureau chief. Coming to Saigon also afforded him the friendship of then *New York Times* reporter the late

David Halberstam, Neil Sheehan (of United Press International), *Life* magazine's Larry Burrows (later to lose his life, along with the Associated Press's Henri Huet, UPI's Kent Potter, and *Newsweek* freelancer Keisaburo Shimamoto, in a helicopter shot down over Laos during Operation *Lamson 719*), and Nick Turner of Reuters.

It is safe to say that his admiration for Horst Faas and his work knows no bounds. Stibbens is quick to point out that by that time, Faas—who in 1997, along with renowned British photojournalist Tim Page, published the book *Requiem: By the Photographers Who Died in Vietnam and Indochina*—had already experienced war when Faas himself had arrived in Vietnam, not only in his native Germany as a lad, but also as an AP reporter in the Congo and Algeria. It was Faas who took Stibbens on his first combat operation.

"It was a dawn H-21 (Piasecki "Flying Banana") helicopter landing in the Mekong Delta south of Saigon. I just wanted not to do something stupid. I tried to hide my apprehension, but I really wondered how I would react to live bullets all around me. After all, I was a Marine."

The bravado that would come with the next several years would develop later, not during that first mission. Stibbens and Faas were the first to jump out of the helicopter into the rice paddy where they immediately began to wade through the paddy's knee-deep water. Jumping out first, Horst taught Stibbens, was always safer because the enemy would not have had time to draw a bead on you.

To Stibbens' relief, no shots were fired on either side. They "sloshed" into the nearest village. But before very long, the first bullets began to kick up the dirt all around him. For some inexplicable reason, Huey gunships were firing at them. Luckily no one was hit, and the Hueys flew away.

"Very quickly, I was feeling like a veteran as we walked and walked and walked. We stopped on the trail for lunch, and Faas somehow located two large bottles of Biere Larue, a popular Vietnamese brew of the era. The South Vietnamese troops they accompanied commandeered some chickens from a local farmer; they ate, drank, and settled down for a siesta. Before the sun went down, they boarded a landing craft and made their way back to an ARVN (Army of the Republic of Vietnam) base. By dark they were back in Saigon.

Said Stibbens, "That's what missions were like in those early days."

But it did not stay like that for long.

He was tasked with reporting on the 16,000 American "advisers" in-country. The Buddhists were already protesting in the streets with banners against the Catholic government of American-supported Ngo Dinh Diem, which was maltreating them, but the editors at *Stars and Stripes* told him to not bother with the Saigon political story. "They'd use AP and UPI stories (and cover their ass with the brass, which looked over their shoulders all the time)."

On January 2, 1963, a rumor went round the press corps about "a big battle" in the Mekong Delta some 70 miles south of Saigon. "I was hanging out at the AP office with Peter Arnett when David Halberstam came in. Peter and David knew I had access to a small Ford Falcon. So, instead of their usual transportation via Saigon taxi or military helicopter, they persuaded me to change into a Marine uniform and drive them to the battle at the village of Ap-Bac. [All *Stars and Stripes* staffers wore civilian clothing and received field-grade privileges just like the civilian media people.] The uniform helped get us past roadblocks and checkpoints on the way to Tan Hiep airstrip, the staging point for the Ap-Bac action.

"At Tan Hiep, we got briefings from Colonel Daniel Boone Porter, senior adviser, and [legendary] Lieutenant Colonel John Paul Vann, 7th ARVN Division adviser. I flew out to Ap Bac on an H-21 with Vann and a group of US Army maintenance people. When we landed at Ap Bac, I got off with the mechanics who were going to repair, if possible, downed aircraft—two H-21s and a Huey. Richard Tregaskis, the World War II writer, was on the H-21 with us and shot a photo of me as I slipped and fell at a paddy dike. He knew who I was but he identified me in his book *Vietnam Diary* as an 'unidentified soldier.'"

Though he may have fallen into a rice paddy, throughout the five years Stibbens spent in Vietnam, he was constantly aware that the bar had been set very high for him, and for other combat correspondents, to represent the GI in the manner of his World War II counterpart Ernie Pyle. Though not a soldier himself, Pyle might as well have been. His acceptance by troops in both the European and Pacific Theaters because of the way he portrayed them for the families back home in his "hometowners," is a testimony to a remarkable war chronicler to this day. In part because of Pyle, and because of his own allegiance to the Marine Corps, Stibbens felt a heavy responsibility to represent the Corps, which he carried with him for three additional years as a reporter in Vietnam for the Marine Corps' publication *Leatherneck Magazine*. In 1967, he felt equally committed to painting a valid picture of the war in Vietnam when he left *Leatherneck* and became a war correspondent for the Associated Press.

During his tenure with *Leatherneck*, Stibbens was interviewed by his friend Bob Schieffer, former anchorman with CBS News, but then a reporter with the *Ft. Worth Star-Telegram* newspaper from their mutual home state of Texas.

"He's one Marine who wasn't sent here to fight the Viet Cong," Schieffer wrote in a 1966 edition of the paper to which they both once contributed. "His instructions were to write about other Marines, but earlier this month when Stibbens arrived for his sixth tour of duty, he had to disobey orders somewhat—he was responsible for the capture of six VC."

Stibbens had been on patrol 15 miles south of the base at Da Nang when he saw something move about 10 feet in front of him, Schieffer wrote in a style of reportage most often associated with Ernie Pyle. Stibbens' attention was immediately drawn to a hole in the ground covered with a lid. Inside were six enemy combatants hiding from the company patrolling the area.

"I looked at them and they looked at me," Stibbens told Schieffer.

The lieutenant who was leading the company pulled the lid back and all at once a hand emerged from the hole with a grenade, pin pulled. The lieutenant slammed the lid down and the concussion killed three of the hidden VC. The other three were forced out with a smoke bomb, Stibbens told Schieffer.

"I always carried the heavy weight of Ernie Pyle. I had read his books before joining the Corps and they stuck with me, especially when I was in journalism school. Even today, I think of Ernie Pyle when I'm writing about military people. He had a knack for placing the reader in the locale of the story … around the campfire, so to speak."

While being around campfires himself and plodding through jungles of Vietnam as a "Striper," Stibbens was always on the lookout for enemy fire.

Stibbens' admiration for his employer was also something he carried into battle.

"*Stars and Stripes* was truly the greatest duty I ever had. In my day, *Pacific Stars and Stripes*, headquartered in Tokyo, was a real newspaper. They published five editions daily for GIs in Korea, Taiwan, Okinawa, Guam, Hawaii, the Philippines, Thailand, and South Vietnam. Daily circulation was 500,000. We had a managing editor, city editor, features editor, Sunday editor, a 10-person art/graphics department, a dozen outstanding Japanese photo lab technicians, our own press, truck drivers, etc.—several hundred people. The only GIs at *Stars & Stripes* were a dozen or so from each of the services. The civilians were top-notch editors from the great newspapers who had taken a couple years' leave of absence for the adventure of Tokyo life. I was the only Marine reporter on staff. There was a staff sergeant in the art department and another staff sergeant in production."

While working for the US military newspaper is today paramount in Stibbens' mind, at the same time working for *Leatherneck* and the AP, three somewhat different assignments during his time in Vietnam, he is ever cognizant of the differences that existed in working for each; the main difference being the audience.

"*Stripes* focuses on the grunt and troop-level action for a generally military audience. AP speaks to the world and told the broad story as well."

Covering events and battles for the AP, Stibbens was usually in a hurry to get information and find a telephone to call Saigon. In fact, he got a cable once from the New York bureau of the AP congratulating him on a nine-minute beat with a story about a B-52 crash. With *Stripes*, Steve knew he could take time to get to know the troops, as he did during one mission in 1963 going on a 10-day mountain patrol with three Special Forces troops and 85 Koho Montagnards.

"*Stars and Stripes* wanted coverage of the GIs for the GIs. The civilian correspondents, of course, had to cover everything, especially the politics … with a coup rumor every day. Horst Faas and I wanted action and we constantly went on adventures while the others had to stay close to Saigon. Afterward, the Saigon-bound newsies treated us like great heroes, buying our dinners and soliciting tales of our adventures in the countryside. It was great!"

How long the war would last was anybody's guess in the early days of Vietnam. But there was a sense of pre-packaged optimism among the brass. In October 1963, Stibbens interviewed the two top American generals, General Paul D. Harkins (MAC-V) and Major General Charles Timmes (MAAG). In almost identical words, they separately told him, "We've done our job here. We've trained the Vietnamese forces." General Timmes said he could see "victory" by the end of the next dry season, about nine months away, barring unforeseen political upheaval.

"Harkins even sent me to talk with his G-1 to verify that 1,000 advisers were going home the next week. Answering my question about the Catholic soldiers brawling with the Buddhist soldiers, Timmes said, 'Just as you and I are loyal to our president whether it's Eisenhower or Kennedy, they are loyal to their government.' My interviews hit the streets in Saigon on November 1st with a bold five-column headline, 'VIET VICTORY NEAR.' It was the very day of the coup that resulted in the murder of President Diem and his hated brother, Ngo Dinh Nhu, head of the secret police."

General Harkins quickly asked Stibbens if he would write a retraction for *Stars and Stripes*, but he declined. Then Harkins claimed he didn't say it. President Kennedy sent Harkins a "cable rocket'" reminding him they'd agreed not to predict the "light at the end of the tunnel." "David Halberstam took the lead and went to bat for me with the generals." Three days later, *Stars and Stripes* arrived in Saigon with a front page box stating, "Our correspondent in Saigon erred in quoting both Timmes and Harkins. Both generals said the South Vietnam armed forces are loyal to their country, not government." As Halberstam wrote in his book, *Making of a Quagmire*, the issue was never in question, said Stibbens.

In a move reminiscent of the fact that in more recent years *Stars and Stripes* has found itself in a tug-of-war with the military over the fact that its reporters endeavored to be free to report the facts as any newspaper staff would, yet being beholden to the US government at the same time with a mission to represent the military, Stibbens took the next plane to Tokyo to protest.

"General Collins, the senior general in the Pacific, flew in from Hawaii to interview me. Then he asked me if he would help the Army save face and return to Saigon. The civilian media suspected I'd been kicked out by Harkins. It turned out that General Harkins' PIO [Public Information Officer], a Colonel Lee Baker, had sent the retraction to *Stripes*, implying that I had written it."

As he looks back on Vietnam today, Steve Stibbens is flooded with the emotions that any combat veteran knows all too well. His time in Vietnam served as a kind of measuring stick against the entirety of a brilliant career in military journalism.

"There was a lot of tragedy in Nam. I especially remember an old man—about 85—who took off running when the Marines landed near his village. About a dozen Marines opened fire and he lay there for a while with his brains oozing into the sand while his family screamed. The Marine lieutenant barely held back the tears when they learned what had happened.

"As an AP correspondent, I covered a lot of tragedy ... like a Braniff plane crash in Dawson, Texas (near Waco) in 1968. I was the first newsman to arrive on the scene and was wandering around the wreckage with the firemen. It had crashed trying to fly through a thunderstorm. Eighty-five dead. There were a lot of body parts in the muck. Arms, legs, a torso or two. The captain's cap. A wallet full of money. Then, there was another crash of a small corporate jet in Dallas, barely missing a school in session. Again, body parts everywhere.

"In Vietnam, I saw a lot of bodies but usually they had been covered and it was hard for me to connect. I can't forget my surprise suddenly confronting the poncho-covered bodies of a half-dozen lifeless Marines. It was during Operation *Orange*, about 1966. I jumped on a H-34 helicopter and realized I was the only [live] passenger with a stack of about ten Marines. They were so big, I thought. It hit me hard. I was accustomed to seeing the relatively small Vietnamese dead. But this was like a slap in the face. I didn't know them but they were Marines, like me."

Stars and Stripes reporter/photographer Steve Stibbens, the first "Striper" in Vietnam as a US Marine, ducking in the bush, camera at the ready, 1963. (Horst Faas, deceased, and Steve Stibbens collection)

Rockin' and Rollin' with the Montagnards: Jim Morris

In his years of soldiering, Major Jim Morris, 1st and 5th Special Forces Groups, perhaps the best-known soldier/writer of the Green Beret experience in Vietnam, was only a PIO for four months for the 5th Special Forces Group (Airborne) and six months as PIO in the 1st Group on Okinawa. Nonetheless, those 10 months were an important time in his Army career.

"All the rest of my time in Vietnam I was an XO or CO of an 'A' Detachment or an S5 staff officer. Most of the photos we shot on a team were either of us with our arms over each other's shoulders or of dead guys. Somewhere in my kit, though, I have a photo of me taking pix during the Tet Offensive with one hand, and my rifle in the other. Once I got my story I put the camera away and settled in to fight for the rest of the night," he said.

"You also have to realize that everybody who worked for me was a better photographer than I was or am. I'm a writer who was put in a position where I had to take pictures."

Indeed Morris is best known for his words. But along with his stories, his photos made print while he was soldiering on in Vietnam.

"For one thing I was editor of a monthly 16-page magazine. Whenever I went out I shot a lot of stuff. I lost the best of it though, when I went out with Operation *Delta* [the precursor to the famed Delta Force]. We went in to take photos of some Russian trucks in the A Shau valley that the Air Force had kindly disabled. My pix were of Delta on an operation, but the S2, who also went in, forgot to take the lens cap off his camera, so Delta confiscated all my footage."

While in Vietnam, he edited *The Green Beret*, the magazine of the 5th SFG-A Detachment, until he was wounded, an occurrence that happened to him four times while in Vietnam and garnered him four Purple Hearts. Before that, for six months he edited *The Liberator*, the monthly magazine of the 1st SFG on Okinawa.

"They ran a lot of my stuff. I also had stories in *Pacific Stars and Stripes*, *Esquire* and the *Saturday Evening Post* during that period, although the latter two were published during a break in service between 1965 and '67," he said. "I was S3 of a reserve 'B' detachment during that period though."

Morris wrote about them in the publications he edited, but also in the first piece he did for *Esquire* and in the *Saturday Evening Post*.

His experience with the *Post* was not what a journalist would call a positive one, however.

"It was one of those 'My Turn' columns in which participants get to mouth off. One of the things I said was that we needed to keep American control over our aid money because too much of it was being stolen, even though we might be accused of 'neo-colonialism.' The editor seized on that and titled the piece 'We Must Colonize Vietnam.' When I saw the proofs I said they had to either change the title or cancel the piece and I'd send them their money back. They agreed to the change, but when it ran, that was the headline."

The experience irked him to say the least, but fortunately he was not out of a job. His expertise as a Green Beret "rocking and rolling with the Montagnards" in the Central Highlands, as he has called the experience, was still very much in demand.

However, there was another scenario for which he did feel unemployed.

When the Cold War ended, Morris said that, as a soldier who had trained all his life to do what he did, it felt like he was "out of a job." That certainly applied to his long tenure in Vietnam, during his two TDYs (temporary duties) and one PCS (Permanent Change of Station) in and out of Vietnam from Okinawa between 1963 and 1968, and as a reporter there in 1973.

"I feel that way now. My old friend, Steve Sherman, was doing a year-by-year history of the war. He asked me to contribute something on Tet '68. During the week I worked on it, I got more and more angry and surly. I've worked for years to get out of that, and there I was, back in it. I doubt if I ever write anything on Vietnam again. It is corrosive to my soul." [Steve Sherman is a Texas-based Vietnam veteran and former Green Beret himself, who has worked for years to chronicle all the Vietnam-related cinema and television programs concerning the war.]

With all those years of combat under his belt, it's no wonder that Morris was wounded several times during his soldiering.

"I made it all the way through the first three and a half months into the second [tour] before I was wounded badly enough to be evacuated, and nine and a half months through the PCS tour before I was wounded badly enough to be evacuated again."

What was it then that compelled Morris to come back to write about the war in 1973?

"I didn't particularly want to be a journalist. I went back to fight with FULRO [United Front for the Liberation of Oppressed Races, also known by its French name, *Front Unifié de Lutte des Races Opprimées*], the Montagnard separatist organization. But when I got there, I found they needed publicity more than they needed another gunslinger, so that's where I directed my efforts," he said.

Morris also filed stories for *Soldier of Fortune* magazine and *Rolling Stone*, through which he obtained his press credentials to report from Vietnam, now as a civilian.

"When I went back in 1973, it was to reconnect with FULRO. I got credentials from *Rolling Stone*, but they never published anything I wrote for them. Not political enough for them. What they wanted was a vet to oppose the war, and I was not that guy. My objective in Vietnam was to get the Vietnamese off the Montagnards' backs. You might say I was fighting in another war in the same country at the same time."

According to Morris, whatever stories *Rolling Stone* didn't publish, they found a home in *Soldier of Fortune*.

As a civilian reporter, Morris was one of many media people sent to cover the war in Vietnam. For the most part, he got along with them though he did harbor some negative feelings about the job they did and how they did it.

"I got along fine with the correspondents themselves. If I have a bone to pick with anybody, it would be the foreign editor of the *New York Times*. I think every other editor in the American media read the *Times* on their way to work and tried to cover the same story a little differently. My problem with war correspondents are two: (1) They live and hang out together and form a consensus story about whatever it is they're covering, and woe to the correspondent who violates that consensus. He will be quickly ostracized. (2) Once the story is set, they never change it. The Vietnamese were lousy soldiers at the start of the war and the press said so. They got better and the press never said so."

It may very well have been that shortcoming that kept Morris from being too friendly with many of the correspondents with the exception of a few, such as the last CBS bureau chief in Vietnam, Haney Howell, professor emeritus of Winthrop University in South Carolina.

"When I went back to Vietnam, we got on fine. Same in Cambodia. I was just one more weird character in the weirdest group of characters I've ever met. Almost all those guys were against the war. I was against pretty much all the parts they were against, but I was for something that was off their radar, to *"De Oppresso Liber"*: to free the Montagnard people from oppression. We were doing a good job of that until we were pulled out."

Like many of his fellow Green Berets, Morris still thinks about that to this day.

"As a soldier I did not want to be part of the first cohort to ever lose a war in the history of the United States. As a journalist I wanted to discover the truth and tell it. Any further elaboration on that would be a book-length manuscript that I do not want to write," he feels. "I left in 1973. I was sick and broke, and deeply, deeply discouraged."

Eventually, journalist Jim Morris turned to writing books, but he traces his beginnings in the medium back to when he was a young boy of 12.

"My degree is in journalism (professional writing), which is part of the curriculum at the University of Oklahoma. The only reason that the program is in the J School is because it was thrown out of the English Department when Dr. Walter S. Campbell, who had founded the program, died. He had a Ph.D. in English, but the other instructors, Foster Harris and Dwight V. Swain, were pulp fiction writers, and the English department did not want them. Dr. Copeland, the chairman of the J School, was a friend of Foster's and took the program on. Foster was a full professor of journalism and he had one degree, a B.S. in geology," Morris said.

And the degree Morris earned at the University of Oklahoma ended up having a direct result on his MOS in the Army.

"I was the only guy in the 1st Special Forces Group with a journalism degree and got shoved into the IO slot. That's how I became a journalist, and the only reason I was a journalist. I'm a novelist, but my day jobs have always been writing or editing," he added.

His Vietnam experiences have played a major role in the writing career of Jim Morris.

"*War Story* is my Vietnam memoir, and *Fighting Men* is a book of stories, mostly about guys in Vietnam who were heroes to me. *The Devil's Secret Name* is mostly about the wars I covered for *Soldier of Fortune*, which include some flashbacks to Vietnam. *Above and Beyond* is a novel set in Vietnam. *Silvernail* was about a fictional war in Central America. I was going to set it in Vietnam, but my agent told me that nobody wanted to read about Vietnam when I started it, so I asked myself where was next and set it in Central America. Again, nobody would publish it until we were already hip deep in Central America, so I lost my chance to go down in history as a prophet. My other four novels are science fiction/fantasy. It is highly unlikely that I will write about Vietnam again."

In addition to writing, Morris has also worked as an editor for many years. His editing career began as a tech writer for the OU Research Institute, as a grad student there. He had a couple of PR jobs in Oklahoma, studied and taught at the University of Arkansas, and worked for two years for *Soldier of Fortune*. Then he moved to New York in 1983, where he worked as the editor for a military magazine called *Eagle* and the Dell and Berkley publishing companies.

"I was 46 when I went to New York, and burnt out from [writing about] six wars in six months for *SOF*. But I did some good work in New York. I left in 1990, when the Berlin Wall fell."

Morris may have left the publishing wing of the writing trade, but his soldiering and those he soldiered on with are never far from him.

"I should like to point out that soldiers neither win nor lose wars. Nations do that. Soldiers either accomplish or fail to accomplish their assigned missions. When you get 100 per cent accomplishment of all missions assigned and lose the war, the place to look is not at the military, but at the civilian leadership."

He quite obviously does not share the same feeling for those who guide nations into wars.

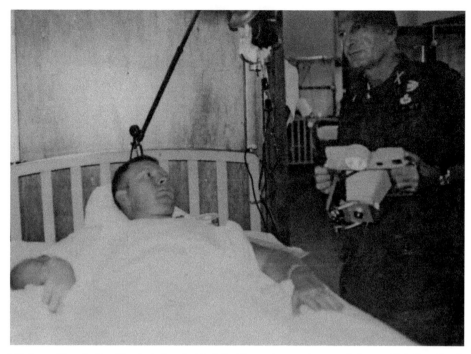

US Army Captain Jim Morris in hospital in Nha Trang about to be awarded one of his four Purple Hearts after being wounded. (Jim Morris collection)

"It's hard to describe the bitterness I feel at America's civilian leadership. You can look at all the literature of the Vietnam War and nowhere will you find a mission statement for the war as a whole. So, why were we there? The only reason I've found is in the papers of President Lyndon Johnson, who said to Senator Richard Russell of the Senate Foreign Affairs Committee, that he could see no strategic stake for the US there, but he had to fight it or 'look soft on communism.'"

Morris came to a discovery in reading further into the exchange between Senator Russell and President Johnson.

"What he meant by that was that he did not want our NATO and SEATO allies to see us wimp out on a treaty we had signed. In that sense, for the Americans, Vietnam was not a war but an infomercial. It worked to the extent that we showed our allies we would expend 59,000 guys and a few nurses on an essentially pointless war. If we'd pushed it further, our allies would not have been reassured, but terrified at how close we'd skirted thermonuclear war. In that sense, we accomplished every goal we had in Vietnam," said Morris. "Too bad for the Viets."

Getting His Knees in
the Breeze: Chip Maury

In 1957, Chip Maury found himself a sailor aboard the aircraft carrier USS *Kearsarge* (CVA-33). Aboard the Midway Class carrier, his routine alternated between mess cooking, photo lab, compartment cleaning, and back to the photo lab again. In fact, he realized that had it not been for the US Navy and photography, he would not be, in words he borrowed from an old folk song by Woody Guthrie, "bound for glory."

"I would secure at 1600, shower, bed down until midnight, get up and fix breakfast, pick up a Speed Graphic camera and go around the ship taking pictures. What distinguished me from the 1st or 2nd Class Petty Officer photographers is that I was able to shoot better pictures," Maury admitted.

Those pictures eventually bought him a one-way ticket in 1960 to *Pacific Stars & Stripes*, Tokyo, where he found out about 35mm cameras, photojournalism, and a TDY tour to Okinawa.

It was on Okinawa that Maury also learned how to jump out of airplanes and capture images as he dropped ever closer to the ground alongside other free-falling troops.

"While doing a story on an airborne exercise by the 2d 503d ABN, I learned how frustrating it was to be left behind in the plane after everyone else goes out the door. The 'rest of the story' is now on the ground, and if you want to cover it, you have to be there with the subjects and continue the story."

At that point, a soldier from 1st Special Forces Group told Maury, "If you think this is fun, we're going sky diving this weekend!"

"I joined the 1st Special Forces Parachute Club so I'd really understand the story I was going to photograph and write about. After many hours of training, I made my first sport parachute jump. By my third jump I was hooked and wanted enough sky diving experience that I could take a free-fall picture to go with my photo story.

"I bought an old surplus military rig and began living for weekends when I could 'get my knees in the breeze' again. Parachuting changed the course of my life and career … almost all for the better!"

He also credits Petty Officer 1st Class Jim Kirby with changing his life as well. "He didn't give me another chance. He gave me another opportunity. He had the King Midas touch in reverse. Jim Kirby was my guiding light. It wasn't a choice. He charged me with an obligation."

Years later he was able to thank Kirby by passing on that obligation to other military photographers and instill in them the drive to shoot the best images they were capable of. When he can, Maury takes off his sailor's cover and switches to the educator's hat that he would wear later as a guest lecturer in the Photography Department at Syracuse University, a school that very actively recruits and trains military photographers.

But that would be in Maury's future.

Maury's knowledge of the various kinds of jumps is most informative, and one gets the strong impression that, in addition to teaching photography, he could also instruct those in uniform how to jump out of an airplane.

Lesson One dealt with High Altitude Low Opening and Airborne Static Line jumps. "There is a difference between an airborne static line jump with full Battle Rattle at 1,250 feet (day or night), a free-fall fun 'Hollywood' jump, demonstration or training, and a HALO jump with full rucksack, weapons, and oxygen," he said. (HALO stands for High Altitude Low Opening.)

"HALO allows troops to exit aircraft up high and away from the intended target. The free-falling parachutist is undetectable by radar. Depending on the equipment load, terminal velocity is about 120–140 miles per hour."

"We also have Stand Off, or HAHO (High Altitude High Opening)," Maury added, "whereby you exit high, pull high and fly overland for long, long distances to the target."

Navy SEALs deployed in parachute insertions to rescue Captain Richard Phillips, whose Maersk freighter had been commandeered by Somali pirates in 2009. They jumped into the ocean, which was a method just being experimented with in the early 1960s when Maury first learned to jump. In the 1960s, it was considered fun, and now it's Standard Operating Procedure. An "op tool," he called it.

"I don't know where this came from, but it says it all … 'If riding in an airplane is flying, then riding in a boat is swimming. If you want to experience the element, then get out of the vehicle.'"

Maury did just that, jumping more than 1,800 times.

"Someone had to be falling with the subjects to record the action," he said.

Maury's HALO training also took place on Okinawa. In that class were 10 other sailors from UDT (Underwater Demolition Team)-11, who wrangled three weeks of R&R, and some soldiers, as Maury put it, fresh from the war in Vietnam to participate in the first Special Forces HALO course.

For that course, Maury was allowed to do free-fall photography, "but I had to wear all the battle rattle, too. Wearing a loaded rucksack, oxygen, and weapon while flying with a camera was like driving a Mack Truck without power steering."

Maury also had multiple deployments on submarines and would "lock out" while underwater, swim to the surface, get in an IBS (Inflatable Boat Small) and then do beach and hydrographic reconnaissance. He did this numerous times in Vietnam with night or limited visibility.

That entailed hydrographic reconnaissance in the water to determine how deep it was, gradients, the nature of the ocean bottom including where coral reefs, rocks, shoals, and manmade obstacles might impede a mission.

Most of the underwater work inVietnam was at night or during grim visibility in the daylight," he added.

He traversed beaches and canals in PBRs (Patrol Boat River), Swift Boats, and APD's, destroyers that had been converted in order to haul troops. He also shot photography in the Mekong Delta, accompanying Alfa Platoon, Seal Team-1, in 1968.

In his time in the Navy, Maury did free-fall camera work as a member of the first Navy Parachute Exhibition Team, the "Chuting Stars" and in 1964 was an original member of the Naval Special Warfare's "Leap Frogs."

"I loved all the different disciplines: working in the sea, in the air, and on land. Each one was a kick in the ass. A much better way of 'earning a living' than being a normal fleet sailor. So often you'd hear guys say, 'I can't believe they are paying me to do this.'"

And they paid him to "swim, dive, parachute, help blow things up, and visit exotic foreign lands," he joked.

"With land and riverine warfare, you were a little more exposed than out in the water," he added. On those missions he did mostly still photography and shot some 16mm footage as well. Video was just beginning then.

As with all photographers in uniform in Vietnam, Maury carried a weapon in addition to his photographic equipment. His protection varied.

"At one time or another, I was tasked with using a grease gun, M-16s, and a 9mm. I carried a CAR-15 on my last tour, which was primarily in the Mekong Delta."

In spite of everything he did with a camera, Maury wants it known that he prefers not to be thought of as a combat cameraman.

"I was never a member of a Navy Combat Camera Group. Therefore, I can't claim to be a combat cameraman even though I did shoot pics under fire. I only shot pictures when shooting a weapon wasn't a higher priority. As long as it didn't compromise a mission," he emphasized.

Combat cameraman or not, there were definitely times when Maury had to put down his camera and pick up one of the several weapons he had occasion to carry. Rather than elaborate on any of those occasions, however, he chose to philosophize.

"There are some guys who swear I was 'just walking around taking pictures' in the middle of a firefight," he said. "Some stories get bolder with time. 'The older we get, the better we were,' it's been said."

When pressed to recall specific incidents when his life was on the line in Vietnam, Maury chose to keep it general.

"I have nothing that stands out. What do they say about combat—'Long periods of boredom punctuated by moments of sheer terror'? The adrenaline rush, sense of purpose, and clear focus when everything was going down was neat."

Maury said sayonara to the possibility of more adrenaline rushes in 1975 when he retired from the Navy. From there he dove into arguably safer waters as a staffer with the Associated Press's Boston bureau.

"My broken body parts began to slow me down, and I gave up shooting and running the bricks," he said. He became director of photography for newspapers in Providence, RI, and Indianapolis. In 2001, he retired to the Adirondack Mountains in upstate New York.

Today Maury continues to visit photography classes at Syracuse University, as well as help to staff numerous story-telling military and civilian workshops around the country, a role that has taken on the special mission of training military photographers. He is also the former National Press Photographers' Association liaison to the Department of Defense.

"That might sound impressive. It ain't," he insists. "It just means I get to go to the Defense Information School at Ft. Meade, Maryland, and work/play with our young military shooters a couple of times each year."

When asked if he regretted anything about his time as a shooter in the Navy, Maury said, "There were a couple of dumb-shit things I regret, but they were done without endangering anyone but me. God protects fools, drunks, and sailors, so I guess I was qualified in at least one category … and had some great luck, too."

Of his fellow Navy photographers, Maury says, "There were so many people who were great leaders and mentored a legion of fine shooters and journalists. One remarkable trait within the Navy is the 'each one teach one' philosophy. Leadership goes beyond accepting responsibility and taking the initiative. Leadership means we pull the younger sailors up to stand on our shoulders. In turn, they do the same during their career. 'Passing it along as freely as you got it' becomes an obligation we all embrace."

Chip Maury (back row, right), free fall and underwater photographer, with SEALS from SEAL Team 1, Alpha Pit, after an operation in the Nam Can Forest, 1968. The team captured a North Vietnamese flag in the op. (Chip Maury collection and courtesy of the National Archives)

Seeing the Action Through the Viewfinder:
Ken Hackman

It is safe to say that Ken Hackman got to Vietnam before many people on this side of the Pacific Ocean even knew of the country's existence—1958. Two years before, he was stationed at Yokota Air Base in Japan as an Airman 2nd Class. At that time, the American presence in Vietnam consisted only of a MAAG—Military Aid & Assistance Group.

"We were there, as I recall, but I frankly can't remember what we photographed of the MAAG," Hackman, a still photographer, said. He was accompanied on that mission by two mopic (motion picture) photographers and their CO, a Major John Murray.

"What I do remember is, at that time I was an A2C, and we had flown to Saigon from Bangkok, where we were also documenting the MAAG in Thailand. Major Murray was an enthusiastic photographer, mostly motion picture, and while we were in Bangkok he tried to talk me into flying to Angkor Wat, Cambodia, with him. It would have been commercial air and cost $50 round trip. I was an A2C and I didn't have the money. In Saigon he asked me if he could get a car and driver out of the embassy, would I go with him to Angkor Wat? Of course, I said yes and very early in a morning we took off in a Ford station wagon for Angkor Wat. I don't know how long it took. All I remember is that the driver put "the pedal to the metal" and only slowed down when we had to take a very small ferry flat boat to cross a river. We spent five or six hours there and then drove back to Saigon."

"My next trip to Saigon was in April 1964. One stop on a round-the-world project photographing the Military Airlift Command mission worldwide. Our stay was very brief."

Two years later, he found himself back in Saigon again.

In August 1966, Hackman's commanding officer at Lookout Mountain Air Force Station (LMAFS), who at that time was in charge of the Air Force documentation mission in Southeast Asia, was taking a lot of heat from the Secretary of the Air Force for Public Affairs for the quality of the color photography being produced by the AAVS (Aerospace Audio Visual Service-Combat Camera) people stationed in Vietnam.

"As a civilian (GS-9), he could not order me, so he asked me if I would go to Vietnam and photograph the Air Force mission there. I asked for how long. He said go, and when I felt I had done enough, to come home. I also asked what specifically I was to photograph. He was not specific. He told me to check with the PAs (Public Affairs Officers) when I got in-country."

Hackman arrived in Vietnam with not much in the way of USAF-provided cameras but rather mostly his own. He was toting a Nikon F with a 50mm lens and a 50–300mm zoom, which he called "a real beast." His personal equipment consisted of a Nikon F, two rangefinder Nikons, an S2 and an SP, with a good selection of lenses from 21mm to 135mm.

Based on Hackman's assertions about the American mission in Vietnam, he came up with about 30 different scenarios that he felt needed exposure and that would provide some imagery of the Air Force mission in Southeast Asia.

Once in Saigon, Hackman made his way to where the 600th Photo Squadron headquarters was located. At that time the 600th had detachments and was operating locations all over Vietnam and Thailand.

"I stayed a brief time in Saigon which, frankly, was a hell hole. I found it impossible to work. I managed to get a vehicle for transportation, but on the first day I had a flat tire, no spare, and hours waiting to get it fixed. The CO of the 600th was planning a staff visit to the detachment at Pleiku Air Base and said I could go along on his small propeller-driven plane. I jumped at the chance to get out of Tan Son Nhut."

Hackman was neither enamored of Tan Son Nhut Air Base nor Saigon itself. For him Saigon was no "Pearl of the Orient," as it was called by some.

"It was awful. Really fucked up," Hackman said. "I never got the sense that there was a war going on other than military vehicles moving about. I was very glad to get out of there. At Pleiku and other bases I was impressed with the professionalism of our troops. It was all very matter of fact. We had a job to do and we were going to do it."

At Pleiku, a Special Operations Wing was flying A1E Skyraiders in support of the Army ground troops. Hackman flew a number of missions photographing air-to-air other A1E Skyraiders, O-1 Bird Dog FAC (Forward Air Control), and U-10 leaflet-dropping aircraft. From there he went to Da Nang, flew aboard F-4 jets and HH-53 Para-rescue helicopters photographing their missions. He covered the ground missions of prepping the aircraft for missions as well as mission briefings.

One memory Hackman can't forget about Da Nang was visiting the base bath/toilet facility.

"I'll never forget walking in to shave and seeing a sign above the mirror: 'Please be neat, 1,500 troops use this facility.' The shower was a 10×10 enclosure with a single pipe going around the room with shower heads every 2–3 feet. You never wanted to be trying to shower at the end of the pipe—you were lucky if you got drops let alone a stream of water," he said with a laugh.

"I did a fair amount of flying. Most of my missions were in the backseat of F4 Phantoms. But I also flew A1Es, A-37 Tweets, U-10s, OV-10 Broncos, O1Es, C-47 gunships, HH-43, and HH-53. I also covered the ground operations, aircraft preps, mission briefings, and other AF activities, even President Johnson in Bangkok," he added.,

Two weeks after one of his flights in an F-4 Phantom, Hackman was in Thailand. He got a message from the F4 Squadron he had flown with at Da Nang.

"They told me that my pilot that day, Captain or Major Bud Flesher and the WSO who had been in the backseat of the other aircraft, had been shot down in a mission over North Vietnam. They said they assumed they were KIA and asked me if I could send some photos I had made to their families. Of course I said yes. In 1973, when the POWs were released, I was delighted to see both of their names show up after almost seven years as prisoners," Hackman happily recalled.

"I remember going to Tuy Hoa Base for Thanksgiving to photograph FAC pilots eating dinner with the Army ground troops. I went to Bangkok to cover the visit of President Johnston to Southeast Asia. I also went to both Ubon and Korat Royal Thai Air Force Bases to cover the flying mission."

When he was not in the air or covering dignitaries, Hackman himself might call his typical day routine.

He would go to the local Public Affairs office, tell them what he wanted to do, and, if he had not been on a particular base before, he would ask to be taken to the flying squadron where introductions could be made. He'd then have a talk to the commanding officer and operations personnel so that he could make known exactly what he was trying to do in the name of the Air Force. In that way, he could get airborne and "show them doing what they do."

It may sound simple, but it was not a piece of cake for Hackman to arrange his daily schedule.

He was not fond of "the inordinate amount of time it took on the telephone between 600th headquarters and me to let them know what I was doing and what my itinerary was. It literally took hours to get a phone call accomplished."

The last thing on his agenda was to "crash at night because there were early morning flight briefings that I wanted to attend."

Once the briefings were over, and Hackman was in the field or in the air, he underwent a mental process he feels common among many photographers. "I think I succumbed to what many photographers do in hazardous situations, namely looking through the viewfinder separates me from what I am photographing. I'm there but not there because I'm seeing the action in my viewfinder."

He recalls one such mission flying backseat in an F-4 jet out of Da Nang.

"It was supposed to be a three-ship, me in one F4 photographing the other two F4s. There was a problem with one of them, so only two of us took off. It was supposed to be an easy mission. Not much happening until we got airborne and the local FAC operations told us we were being sent to support an FAC along the coast. We had weather. Cloudy with a ceiling of only 800 feet. I was in the lead aircraft."

At one point, the pilot of Hackman's plane told his wing man, "We are going out over the ocean. There are no mountains to run into there and then we can drive in and see the target."

The FAC told the pilot that the target was a church at the apex of two rivers that was being used to store ammo, and he didn't want to mark the target with a smoke rocket.

"My pilot said, 'You either mark it or we aren't going in,'" Hackman recalled.

They were carrying 500lb bombs and the pilot of Hackman's jet started heading in at an altitude of less than 800 feet. The pilot told Hackman, "I hate this. They can shoot us down with rifles."

"My silent reaction was, I don't need to know that!"

There were no pictures to be made. Hackman said, "I'm sitting there looking at the bomb on our wing and then it was gone."

Shortly thereafter, according to Hackman, the pilot radioed his wingman and asked, "Where are you?" The wingman answered, "In front of you!" "My pilot says, `What the hell are you doing there? Take heading 90 and I'll take 180 and we'll meet on top!' I was very lucky on the missions I flew. Most went off without a hitch."

And while he got in plenty of flying time, he was never put in a position where he had to carry a firearm … with one exception.

"The only occasion when I was given one was at Pleiku. The A1E Wing was alerted that there were some Army troops pinned down and surrounded by VC and were running out of ammo. In a situation like that, they filled wing tanks with ammunition, and then went in low and slow and dropped the tanks filled with ammo for the troops."

Hackman asked the CO, "Are there any photos I can make?" Hackman explained: "I was never a photographer who wanted to fly for the sake of flying. If there were no pictures to be made either in Vietnam or anywhere during my career, I said, 'I don't want to go. I don't need the flying time!'"

Hackman was told he might be able to get some good images but that he needed to wear a firearm in order to do so.

"So I put on the firearm, and we got in the aircraft. Prior to cranking the engine, we got a radio call, 'Stand down, the Army troop broke out.' So that was my one chance to have a firearm," he said.

But while he stood down on that mission, Hackman made additional trips to Vietnam and Thailand between 1966 and 1972.

Hackman separated from the Air Force in July 1969, but he was far from through with the USAF at that point. Shortly thereafter, he got a civil service job with the Lookout Mountain Air Force Station (LMAFS) in the mountainous Laurel Canyon neighborhood of L.A. Although Los Angeles was half a world away from Saigon, four years later he would find himself in Southeast Asia once again.

He was asked to prepare a training program for Air Force still photographers around the world.

"I came up with a five-day seminar that I taught our troops two or three times in Vietnam and Thailand during those years."

On a 1972 trip to Thailand after the 600th Photo Squadron was deactivated in April of that year, he paid a visit to the new 601st Photo Flight Squadron. That trip took him to Royal Thai bases at Korat, Takhli, Ubon, Udorn, Utapao, Nakhon Phanom, and Bangkok.

"I flew an OV-10 on a four-hour mission from Ubon RTAFB to do some air-to-air of other OV-10s, and then down the Ho Chi Minh Trail in Vietnam and Cambodia. We returned to Ubon in time to get some air-to-air photos of the C-130 gunships as they circled the base calibrating their electronics. I had been told this was the only way I was going to get aerial photos of the gunships."

At Takhli, Hackman observed 12 F-111 "Terrain Tracking" fighter/bombers, which flew night missions over North Vietnam. "The next morning there were 11 on the ramp. One did not make it back," he said.

"They had F-105 Thunderchiefs, better known as "Thuds,' that were flying bombing mission over North and South Vietnam. They were all single seat and I wanted pictures of a flight of them hitting the 'tanker' before continuing on their mission. I talked to a flight lead, Major Bowersox, and asked if he would be willing to take one of my cameras with him and try to get a photo of the refueling of his flight.

The major told Hackman, "No problem, the mission tomorrow is 'easy,'" which was the code word for safe.

"When I showed up at '0 Dark 30' for the morning briefing, there was a palpable sense of tension in the room. I found out the missions had been changed to 'Package Six' which meant downtown Hanoi. Hairy mission."

Hackman told Major Bowersox, "You don't have to take my camera with you."

The major's response was, "I'll take it, if you don't mind losing a camera." The camera was a rangefinder Nikon S2 with a 21mm lens.

"I asked him to be in a position where he could see the other aircraft refueling and hold the camera so that his profile would be in the foreground. He took four or five frames. One was picture perfect."

And while Hackman did not go on the mission over Hanoi, he did go on several others.

During that 1972 Thailand trip, he flew quite a few F4 missions from Thai bases following flights of F4s and F105s out over the sea where they topped off their gas from C-135 tankers before heading to North Vietnam. "I had a couple photos appear on the covers of *Air Force Magazine* that caused some consternation at USAF Public Affairs, which wanted to know why a civilian was flying combat missions."

At Nakhon Phanom, he even flew some Jolly Green rescue HH-53 helicopters over Laos.

After the Thailand missions, Hackman would go on to other assignments that would take him elsewhere in the world. One was to be the official USAF photographer aboard Air Force One, an honor first bestowed upon him when Richard Nixon was President of the United States.

"Nixon was president, and I had told someone that I felt we should get Air Force One flying over Washington, D.C. As I recall, this is when the words 'Spirit of 76' were painted on the nose of the aircraft. I flew chase in an 89th Wing aircraft, probably one of their DC-6s, and we had FAA and Washington National Airport Tower clear the area so we could basically fly against the landing pattern for National," Hackman recalled.

They liked the images, according to Hackman, and picked one that they used as the official photograph of Air Force One until years later when George H. W. Bush was president and the 89th wanted an updated photo.

"We flew a number of missions, one of which was over the Statue of Liberty. Unfortunately this was the time they were doing massive renovation on the statue and surrounding grounds. It was amazing how well that construction showed up. We then discussed possible backgrounds and finally decided on Mt. Vernon. Again they selected that image as the official photo of Air Force One."

In early 1990, Hackman was again contacted by the 89th Wing. They asked him to fly to Wichita for a meeting to discuss a photo of the new 747 presidential aircraft.

"I flew there to the Boeing plant, toured the under-construction aircraft, and then we had our meeting. I had suggested much earlier that our next background should be Mt. Rushmore. They liked the idea and wanted to know if I could work with Clay Lacy (founder of the first executive jet charter service and pioneer of aerial photography) on making the photo."

The plan, Hackman recalled, was for Lacy to fly his specially modified, for photography, Lear Jet when the aircraft flew from the Boeing plant in Seattle to Washington, D.C.

"I was assured I would have a station for my camera in Clay's jet. That never happened. It seemed the pilot from Boeing would be flying the aircraft. The Air Force One pilot said, 'The official photo will be made when I am flying the plane.'"

While on another assignment in D.C., Hackman was approached again by the 89th Wing and asked what he might have planned for the upcoming Sunday. He told them he was free and their response was, "Let's go make the photo of Air Force One in front of Mt. Rushmore."

Hackman invited Nikon rep Ron Thompson along. The pair went out to Andrews Air Force Base and flew the executive jet used by the vice president out to Ellsworth AFB.

"We were treated like VIPs on the plane. Cooked meals, etc. We refueled at Ellsworth and pulled the hatch in front of the rear right engine. I sat in an upholstered seat with a table in front of me and Ron on the other side. He loaded my cameras as I photographed. I told them that we would have to be a distance from the 747 as it flew over Rushmore. Normally when I fly and photograph air-to-air, I like to be close to the plane I am photographing. However, Rushmore is not that large, and I knew if I got close to the 747, I would be using a shorter lens and Rushmore would get smaller."

Hackman selected the 80–200mm lens zoomed to 200mm to try to get some compression and make Rushmore more visible.

"The only problem with that scenario was that the 747 really zipped past Rushmore. I could get one, maybe two images only. We made close to a dozen passes. I said we either have it or we don't. Let's go home. We went back to Ellsworth, topped off the gas, replaced the plane hatch, and flew back to Andrews."

They had departed at 8am and were back by 5pm.

That photo became the Official Air Force One photo until a few years ago when a friend of Hackman's chased Air Force One over the Statue of Liberty in an F-16 and shot an image of the presidential plane. However, that episode created a firestorm.

"I'm not sure if the White House ever has used that image, which was very good. If they haven't, they are still using the one in front of Mt. Rushmore."

Hackman spent 35 years working for the USAF as a civilian. It's safe to say that this allowed him to see a need to train other photographers to do what he had spent a major portion of his life doing. He knew that a lot of revamping was in order.

"When I started out in Air Force photography, still photography and most still photographers were, pardon the expression, shit. In those days, assignments would come down from Headquarters USAF requesting documentation of a particular operation, exercise, event, etc. It would always be one page long dealing with the motion picture coverage they wanted. Usually the last one or two sentences would say, 'Also get some still photography.' That pissed me off, and I determined if I ever had the opportunity to change that thought process, I would do it."

In the late 1960s, the USAF did a study on in-house still photography and determined that it was not "a viable resource," according to Hackman. "Some high-powered friends and I set about to change that situation," he said.

The Navy, Hackman knew, had been going to a one-year program in photojournalism that was developed with Syracuse University. USAF/Public Affairs was an early supporter and negotiated for a slot in the 1971 Navy Syracuse class. In exchange, the Air Force would give the Navy a slot in one of their university-level officers' classes.

"The following year we got two slots, and the next year four slots in the Syracuse class. USAF/PA then said we have validated the need and the results; therefore, USAF Training Command should take over. The only problem was, there had never been a training program in the Air Force where enlisted people spent a year at a university."

After what Hackman termed "some high-powered pressure," Air Training said they would set up their own program at Rochester Institute of Technology, New York, with five students.

"Five students weren't enough to establish a program, so the students were merely placed in existing classes at RIT. We quit that program and went to Syracuse. From 1975 until I retired in 1995, I was the point man on the Air Force program."

He put together the judges who selected the potential students and monitored their progress by making two visits to the school. He worked with USAF Personnel to ensure the students were assigned to billets that he had identified.

"We basically created a cadre of trained, motivated photographers. After my retirement, I kept in contact with Syracuse. Since my retirement we have had some hiccups and lost the program for a few years. Currently it is still going with four students from each of the four services attending the photojournalism and motion-picture media programs at Syracuse."

Along the way, Ken Hackman has won one accolade after another from colleagues and friends who admired his work.

In 1996, he was one of six Air Force civilians who was nominated to receive the Department of Defense Distinguished Civilian Service award. In 2011, he was awarded the DoD's Exceptional Public Service Award for his many years of coordinating, directing, and conducting the Military Photographer, Military Videographer, and Military Graphic Artist of the Year competitions, and for his co-founding and directing of the DoD's Worldwide Military Photography workshop. The latter garnered him the Office of the Secretary of Defense Medal for Exceptional Public Service.

But the accolade that he is most proud of is the Sprague Award given to him by the National Press Photographers Association.

Of that award he says, "To be in the company of people like Eddie Adams (Associated Press photographer and former US Marine who snapped the Pulitzer Prize winning image of Brigadier General Nguyen Ngoc Loan shooting Viet Cong cadre Nguyen Van Lem in the head at point blank range in the streets of Cholon, the Chinese quarter of Saigon), Alfred Eisenstaedt, Ken Burns, David Douglas Duncan, and others is to me a real honor."

No doubt if Eddie Adams were still with us, he would tip his ever-present chapeau Ken's way and say, "Job well done."

US Air Force combat cameraman Ken Hackman loaded down with camera equipment, about to board a flight for photo reconnaissance. (Ken Hackman collection)

He Shot More Photos than Bullets: Marvin Wolf

Marvin J. Wolf, combat correspondent with the 1st Air Cavalry based at An Khe between 1965 and 1966, had already served one tour of duty in Korea as an enlisted infantryman before boarding his first Huey that would take him into the fray in Vietnam. On his way there, the C-130 Hercules he was in had blown an engine and was forced to make an emergency landing on Iwo Jima, where some 7,000 US Marines and 20,000 Japanese soldiers lost their lives a mere 20 years earlier in one of the most decisive battles of World War II, a battle that would help turn the tide of the war toward an Allied victory in the Pacific.

While it certainly did not occur to Wolf at the time, he would admit later there was a similarity between those young Marines about to face an uncertain life-or-death situation and what he faced sitting in the Huey on his flak jacket to protect, first and foremost, his life and, second, as he put it, his family jewels.

"Of course it never occurred to me at the time to make that comparison. I was focused on my own life and what I needed to do. I had a choice to make. Would I stay on this chopper? Would I panic? Was I going to stay on and fly in and out through the flak twice? Was I going to get off? Where would I be safer? Meanwhile my life is flashing before my eyes."

Thinking about it now, Wolf is certain of the parallels between the two experiences. "They couldn't get off until they hit the beach. There were bullets flying everywhere. Since most of those who hit the beach at Iwo were Marines, they were volunteers, so there is a parallel there."

On his first and every chopper ride thereafter, Marv Wolf bore the burden of being extremely weighted down not only with the mandatory gear of every soldier, but with that necessary for a combat correspondent: he carried three M-16 magazines, two in his belt and one locked and loaded. His ammo pouches held either film or extra camera bodies. However, because of the extra camera gear, it made toting an M-16, in his words, "a royal pain in the ass," but obviously a necessary one. He also relished the ability to carry a .38 he had brought with him to Vietnam—though one day that .38 got him in trouble.

"I was accosted by a major who demanded my name and unit. It pissed him off that he had to carry a heavy .45."

By the time Wolf got back to post, his CO, Major Charles Siler, had already been informed and took him aside and questioned him. But instead of a reprimand, Wolf got a trade. His CO offered up his own .45 in exchange for Wolf's .38 and told him, "No one will question you now." He strapped on the .45 whenever he was on post and was tasked with such missions as writing about the ammunition arsenal or interviewing someone at the POL (Preservative, Oil, and Lubricant) Depot.

But when it came to air assaults, Wolf was glad to have had that M-16. "I was a lowly grunt and so it was the M-16. A .45 in an air assault would have been worthless," he admits. "I was trained as a rifleman and knew what to do."

As Wolf looks back on it now, he shot far more photos than bullets and that does not bother him in the least. "I used to tell people that in Vietnam, I shot hundreds, usually at F-11 250."

But all of that would unfold in the future. When he was airborne on that first chopper flight, Wolf didn't think about the grunts he was flying with as he sat on his flak vest. He was, in his words, "completely self- involved." He did, however, think about the pilots and how cool they were. On that day "a Huey 30 seconds in front of mine had been hit and exploded as it left the LZ. They'd seen their buddies roasted alive and to hear them talk they were saying, well if you go in this way, you'll only have a few seconds. I thought they were amazingly detached and cool."

Wolf's time in uniform made him older and far more experienced than most newbies in Vietnam. He knew his mission. "My job was just to take pictures, keep my head up, stay alive. It was no less challenging than any other job in a combat zone. It never dawned on me until that moment that people were going to be shooting at me even though I was holding a camera. I had volunteered to be there and had wanted to find a career in photojournalism. I had wanted to stand at history's elbow as that first draft of history was being written. If I didn't get off the chopper this time, I was never gonna get off the chopper."

Wolf said he understood it intellectually. He just didn't get it in his gut until he jumped off that first Huey.

The soldiers around Wolf had the job of making sure that they killed the enemy before they themselves were killed. Wolf's mission was to make sure that someone knew about it.

Wolf's contemporary, Pulitzer Prize winning AP photographer Eddie Adams often talked about the camera as a weapon and how looking through the viewfinder he somehow felt protected. Wolf feels exactly the same today. "By looking through the viewfinder there is now a barrier to you, everything else is just a distraction and an annoyance."

During the entire time Wolf was in Vietnam, he made it a point to make good mental notes, though he says there's a lot he's probably forgotten. One thing he hasn't forgotten was the job that the 1st Cavalry did at An Khe.

When the Cavalry arrived, the North Vietnamese had infiltrated what Wolf called "very substantial forces into the Highlands. They seemed poised to cut South Vietnam in half." If, Wolf added, "you control the Central Highlands, you control the country, so if you can cut the country at its narrow waist, you can control it. And if the Americans could wrest control from the NVA, they could take the country back from the North Vietnamese Army division-sized main force units.

"The Cavalry arrived. We went looking for the enemy. We found the enemy. We killed the enemy. By the time I left 15 months later, they were no longer a threat. There were still main force units out there, but they were holding. The enemy had depended in large part on the local population to feed them and treat them medically. We found the rice and weapons caches and we denied that to them."

The NVA was also supplying and training the Viet Cong. In spite of that, the 1st Cavalry was able to break the back of the NVA and VC offensive in the Highlands. They were so effective that the Cavalry became General Westmoreland's mop-up firefighters. "You need a brigade? We can get there. You need an airlift? We can get there," Wolf said, recalling too that the 1st Cavalry spearheaded the 1970 assault into Cambodia, though he was long home by then.

On more than one occasion before he rotated out, Wolf had to put down the camera and aim his M-16 even though he had limited ammo. "Once on a company-sized patrol, there was shooting everywhere. My first instinct was to pick up my camera, but then I realized there was nothing to shoot at. Everybody was down on his belly or behind a tree. There were RPG explosions. It was time to fight. I don't think I hit anybody. Seemed like an hour but it was probably ten minutes. They called an airstrike in on them and that was it. I went back to shooting pictures again. I never saw the enemy. Combat in the jungle is often just flashes. You just react on instinct."

Ironically, the scariest experience he had in Vietnam did not involve combat at all. As he recalled it, he was inadvertently left behind on a mountain top in the middle of Indian country.

He was on a Huey headed from one forgotten place to another at night when the chopper he was aboard was diverted to a mountain top to medivac soldiers to a field hospital. That resulted in no room for the Army photographer: Wolf. He was told he would be picked up later. At that point, the acting first sergeant told a corporal to find Wolf a place to bed down for the night.

The place Wolf had to bunk down in was several feet below an ambush site next to a trail with trip wire everywhere and in one of those very typical pouring Vietnam rains. Needless to say, he would get little sleep that night. If his rain-soaked poncho weren't enough, every so often, he would be jarred awake by a battery of 105s firing.

Troops in the battery were firing at locations where the Viet Cong had previously been spotted. At one point during the night, he heard a lot of scurrying around and choppers landing bringing in what he presumed to be ammo and food.

He finally nodded off to sleep and woke up at dawn with, much to his horror, not a solitary American around.

"Oh shit! What do I do?" are the words of disbelief Wolf remembers asking himself at that point 40-plus years later. He quickly scouted around and found some commo wire and pine crates that carried weapons and ammo into an area of operations. There were also some C rats ("Stuff you wouldn't eat if they put a gun to your head"), bug spray ("You'd light it to cook the C rats").

Just in case there were any "bad guys" in the neighborhood, Wolf climbed the tallest tree overlooking the LZ. At one point he heard voices down below. Just whose he never found out, which was probably a good thing in his estimation since the odds were good that they belonged to the Viet Cong.

Taking stock of his available weaponry, in addition to his M-16, "I had carried a grenade since the first day I got to Nam." He then set about camouflaging himself the best he could. "I knew someone would come looking for me because I had called in and told them I was coming back." What Wolf didn't know though was just when that rescue might occur. Of the troops that had left him behind, he said, "They counted noses and I was nobody's nose."

By noon that day, Wolf deemed it safe to come down from the tree, though he never strayed directly into the LZ because he knew that could make him an instant target if VC were in the area.

He took stock of his own belongs: a pocket knife, small Bowie knife, one meal of C rats, iodine tablets, 60 rounds of ammo, a shelter half, two pairs of socks, one change of underwear, a flashlight, and his cameras. "I decided to bury two cameras and keep one." He also decided it would be a good idea to stay where he was for two more nights if necessary, and then try to walk out hoping he could make five miles a day in the mountains, making it a point to stay away from villages.

Fortunately for Wolf, the contingency plan to evacuate his position never had to be put into practice. "About five o'clock in the afternoon, I heard a Huey hovering above. I ran to the middle of the LZ, took off my helmet so that they could see my fair hair. I also showed them my M-16 since it had been a common occurrence for captured GIs to lure helicopters into traps." Wolf knew the sight of the rifle might calm a trigger-happy door gunner.

Wolf got a thumbs-up signal from the pilot that he'd been spotted and he knew then that he had been saved. Moments later three Huey gunships descended down into the LZ "firing like mad. I threw myself into the third chopper belly first."

"I was taken back to Brigade Headquarters 24 hours later. Of course, the sergeant major tore me a new asshole. 'You took three of my choppers that were needed elsewhere to save your sorry ass,'" he had screamed at Wolf.

Wolf had been saved, but the sheer force trauma of Vietnam was not over for him quite yet. Soon thereafter, the battalion commander ordered him on a mission that required him to ride shotgun in a piston-engine two-seater H (Hughes)-13 helicopter to Pleiku.

Midway through the journey, the pilot shouted at Wolf (there was no onboard mics for communication in the H-13), "Look on the floor and see if you can see the cotter pin." (The cotter pin secures the collective, or stick that allows the helicopter to gain or lose altitude to, in this case, linkage under the floor.) Without that pin, Wolf and the pilot would have been destined to fly straight into a mountain on their flight up into the mountainous Central Highlands region of Vietnam.

Wolf spotted the loose pin but was not able to retrieve it. Here is where that hand grenade that he had carried with him since his first day in Vietnam came into play. Wolf decided to remove the pin from his grenade and substitute it for the cotter pin. Situation solved. Well, not exactly!

As Wolf held the spring of the grenade down, the Warrant Officer who was piloting the H-13 yelled for him to toss the grenade out the window.

"It's not safe," Wolf yelled back.

"I'll go higher," the pilot shot back.

"IT'S NOT SAFE!" Wolf emphasized as loudly as he could.

What the pilot was unaware of, but Wolf knew all too well, was that grenades have a five-second fuse, but that you could really only count on three seconds. And that they have a 15-yard lethal radius but can spew fragments out to 50 yards. The H-13's altitude would not have made a difference. If he'd have tossed that grenade out the window, the chopper would have either been blown to bits, or residual effects from the mid-air explosion could have hit the rotor blades or cut the fuel tank causing them to crash.

The way to throw a grenade out of a helicopter, said Wolf, is to put it in a water glass, which will hold down the arming striker and prevent the fuse from starting until the glass breaks. Then, if it were to hit a tree, it would explode after the helo is out of harm's way. But they had no water and no glass on that flight.

When the helicopter landed at Pleiku, Wolf, his hand still firmly on the spring, went in search of an officer. He was screaming at the top of his lungs, "Stay the fuck away from me! Stay the fuck away from me!" Wolf swears that soldiers all around him must have thought he was out of his mind. He finally found an officer who took him to a long-armed Kentucky sergeant who heaved the grenade high into the air above a ravine.

"I counted: one thousand one, one thousand two, one thousand three, one thousand four, BOOM!"

So much for five-second fuses.

While Wolf was not the only Vietnam grunt who experienced the fear that an encroaching jungle full of Viet Cong might have meant his demise, he felt different in other aspects. "I was young but a little different than all the guys I served with … two or three years older than them. I had done three years, two months and one day in the infantry and had a very good idea of how you survive and prosper in the Army."

Wolf sees a marked difference between the people who served then versus those who serve now. Today, he says, it's an all-volunteer army and, with the exception of those in the Officer Corps, the people who are volunteering are not people who got straight As in school. The Army that I was in was a draftee army and you got people from all walks of life. It was a melting pot fairly representative of America. You had people from every state of the union and every economic stratus. Of course the smartest and best connected were able, if they chose to, to stay out of the Army. "The Karl Roves, Dick Cheneys and the likes of President George Bush, who found a niche in the National Guard. The guys I went to high school with at Fairfax High in Los Angeles weren't able to stay out of the service when the Vietnam War came along. If you had money, with a student deferment, you could avoid the draft until the end of the war."

Wolf was cut from a completely different cloth. The Army needed him to tell its Vietnam story, to be sure, but he needed the Army just as much. A history that he did not want to miss and a familial tendency toward short lives connected him with the Army for a lot longer than most. "I came from a long line of ancestors that didn't live past 50." He knew instinctively that the Vietnam War was going to be the defining moment of his generation. "Would I want to look back and miss this? The fact is I didn't have to go. I'd already served three years. I'd already fulfilled my reserve commitment. I was home free. I went back because I wanted to better myself. I didn't know how long the war would last. Who knew? What I thought was, here's a plan." It turned out to be an ill-conceived, cock-eyed plan in Wolf's estimation, but it worked.

Wolf went on to shoot photos and write stories that would, as his MOS required, tell the Army's story in Vietnam. One assignment took him to Qui Nhon to cover the flamboyant, scarf-wearing Premier Nguyen Cao Ky and his wife Mai, a former stewardess for the country's national carrier, Air Vietnam. They both had come for a "Meet and Greet" of the Air Cavalry. "I was struck by how young he was and how attractive and lively his wife was," Wolf recalled. "I knew I was in the presence of a big shot. I'd never really been awed by big shots, but he was an important guy at a moment in history, and it never dawned on me that we would meet again and under different circumstances."

Years later, Wolf would team up with Ky to write what was Ky's second book: *Buddha's Child: My Fight to Save Vietnam.* By total coincidence, a writer who lived in his west Los Angeles neighborhood relayed a message that "some Asian general with a name she couldn't pronounce was looking for someone to help write his book, and it really wasn't her cup of tea, would it be something I'd be interested in?"

At the time, Wolf never thought that 30 or 40 years after what he went through as an Army combat correspondent would manifest itself in one published book about Vietnam with Nguyen Cao Ky, with another—rich with his Army memoirs—offered to bids by publishers. "I made it a point to make mental notes as things happened; I've always had a pretty good memory."

Ky and Wolf had to fight to get their book published. Twenty-six publishers turned it down, Wolf thinks in part because they confused Ky with the corrupt South Vietnamese President Nguyen Van Thieu. Wolf doesn't know why but hazards the following guess: "The people running the publishing houses in New York during the war had served in the peace movement, gone to Canada, gotten umpteen deferments, gone to divinity school. This is not a knock on the whole New York liberal establishment, but that's who these people were. As far as they were concerned, the whole South Vietnamese government was a bunch of corrupt crooks. Since Ky's family name was Nguyen, like Thieu's, they figured they must be birds of a feather. There was a certain amount of guilt in the liberal establishment, and they didn't want anything to remind them of their own cowardice."

When Wolf got back from Vietnam, the story of the war was just beginning to unfold in movies. As luck would have it, while Wolf was stationed at Ft. Benning, Georgia, John Wayne's production company had pulled up to film *The Green Berets*, a film originally on the schedule of documentarian David L. Wolper. Wolper was forced to give up the project when the United States government deemed dialogue in the film relating to the Central Highlands and the Montagnard warriors, who embraced our cause and fought alongside us, should be classified. Wolf was then a 2nd lieutenant working in the Public Information Office living in an apartment off post surrounded by neighbors who basically ignored him. "I wasn't a local guy. I was an Army guy who came and went in uniform. Nobody paid the least bit of attention to me." His apartment was right across the street from where Wayne's company was filming.

In his capacity as a PIO at Ft. Benning, Wolf was often the go-to guy for the Public Affairs Office. In modern military terms, he was the "POC" (Person of Contact). "If they needed two hundred Asian girls between the ages of 12 and 99 or a 'mad minute' (when an artillery company expends all of its ammo, five seconds of which usually ends up in the film), they came to me," he said. At one point, John Wayne's company approached the PAO for a vantage point overlooking scenes they were shooting, what Wolf called a nearby antebellum plantation house, residue of an American Civil War-era estate. They also needed a place where the director, Wayne, and other staff could rest between takes. Wolf had just the place in mind: his apartment.

"I slept on the floor of my apartment. I gave the first assistant director my bed; somebody else had my couch. While I was there, neighbors who never paid me any mind because I was just a guy in uniform not from there, started coming around. 'Do you happen to have a cup of salt? Do you have a measuring cup? I'm fresh outa orange juice. Do you have any?' Everybody wanted to come by and meet John Wayne because he was in and out of the apartment."

Fast forward to 1977, 10 years later, Wolf, who had continued to write about his Vietnam experience in, among other publications, the Time-Life Books series on Vietnam, was checking out equipment at Cal's Camera in Costa Mesa, California. He hadn't noticed the tall man at the counter whose back was to Wolf. He came up and asked a salesgirl for his film. The lady behind the counter motioned with her eyes toward the gentleman now beside Wolf. It was John Wayne, who until his death called nearby Newport Beach his home. When Wolf said hello to him, the Duke looked him right in the eyes and said, "*Green Berets*," and walked out the door.

"What are the odds of that?" Wolf mused.

US Army combat correspondent Marvin Wolf double-timing it on the DMZ in Korea. (Marvin Wolf collection)

He Had Survived: Frank Lee

Frank Lee's interest in photography began when he was in junior high school in Mississippi, and for reasons other than just liking photography. Being Chinese-American in the Deep South, and in spite of the fact that the girls wanted to go out with him when he reached the dating age, it was hard for him to ask girls out without causing embarrassment and discomfort—the social mores of the South in the mid-1950s tending to forbid inter-racial dating—so he chose photography as a way to make friends. "It was my free pass to be with all the stars of the school: the jocks and the cheerleaders. Everybody wanted their picture taken and I was the go-to guy," he said.

This was a strategy that also worked well for him when he moved west to Los Angeles and attended largely Jewish Fairfax High School, where he became editor-in-chief of the high-school yearbook.

When, in his senior year, Lee was tasked with selling the yearbook, he went from class to class donning a Jewish *yarmulke* (skull cap). "It busted all the students up, and I sold more yearbooks that year than had been sold in any year in Fairfax High's history," he said with a laugh.

For Lee, the early years behind the camera and what he called "breathing noxious chemicals" were his ticket to becoming a Marine Corps Combat Correspondent. When he was in boot camp being tested for various MOSs, he informed his drill instructor that he was a photographer. The next thing he knew, he was hustled over to a corner desk and given an aptitude test. He not only passed photography, he found that he had an aptitude for electronics and audiovisual as well. "What surprised me even more was when they *asked* me what specialty I wanted! That, I believe, was a first in the Marine Corps. I chose photography."

Soon he was off to Vietnam, though he did not fly a direct route. His trek into the fray took him first to the Marine Corps Air Station in El Toro, California, and then on to Okinawa, Japan, where he reported with two junior enlisted photographers to the 2d Battalion, 4th Marine Regiment.

"2/4 was in a horrific battle at the Rock Pile that fall, suffered heavy casualties and was in Okinawa to pick up troop replacements. While the grunts trained in the hills and mountains, we were at the base post office shuffling and sorting mail. My first hint of a war was when I had to stamp "Return to Sender. Deceased" on a copy of *Playboy*."

On New Year's Eve 1966, Lee boarded the USS *Bexar* (pronounced "Bear") along with the men from 2/4. The following day at 1600 hours, the ship slipped quietly out of Kin Bay, leaving behind a panoramic backdrop of fertile green mountains, untouched sand dunes, and colorful peaked roofs scaling up the hillsides, all lit bright by the setting sun.

"5 January 1967. Land ahoy! Instead of a blast of heat engulfing me as it did to others when stepping off an aircraft, I stood on the deck of the *Bexar* and sailed against a cool breeze into Da Nang Harbor. The scene resembled the Kin Bay I left behind: Thin slips of sand marked the border of the sea; a multitude of trees fell in line behind the sand creating a solid green curtain. As the ship coasted near the shoreline, birds appeared and cross-hatched the sky."

Lee didn't expect this. He fully thought he would be met by the sounds of artillery or gunfire, not such a tranquil and tropical setting as this.

"At that moment it would have been impossible to convince me there was a war. And it wasn't too long before that thought vanished.

"My first encounter with the Vietnamese was probably like that of the other new arrivals. It was a shock. I had never met a Vietnamese before; I didn't understand their language, culture, or food except what little I read about Vietnam from a pamphlet issued by the Marine Corps that listed verbal orders in Vietnamese: to say stop, go away, or don't move. The most common phrase everyone knew was, "Number Ten" or "Number One," the latter meaning "good." As I spent more time in Vietnam, I became confused about America's role. One day we'd be at a civic action camp protecting the Vietnamese villagers from VC attack; the next time we'd be destroying the village ridding it of the enemy. Sadly, the Vietnamese all looked the same to me. I can still recall my mother crying in the driveway asking me why I wanted to kill 'our people.

"My simple answer then: I was an American first regardless of my ethnicity. One day in the DMZ, I watched a young NVA soldier—no more than 15 years old—lay dying under the hot sun after being shot by his superior for surrendering. The Marines brought him back and as the medical doctor worked on him I looked into the teenager's face as he gasped like a fish for air, his chest heaving. I realized that he and I were the same, not just the same skin color but of the same species. I felt ashamed."

But one gets the feeling that that shame did not last all that long in Vietnam. Being Asian and a Marine in Vietnam had some obvious drawbacks, such as getting killed by friendly fire. In the heat of combat Lee could easily be mistaken for the enemy. To minimize this risk, he always tried to meet and introduce himself to whomever he was linking up with. "Look. Me Marine. See?" And being from Mississippi added credibility since many of the Marines were from the South. The standing joke, according to Lee, was that there were very few if any North or South Vietnamese who talked with a southern accent. "I readily spoke with a Mississippi Delta drawl," he said.

While in camp, Lee was relegated to the most mundane of duties—cleaning his living quarters, doing laundry, organizing combat gear, cleaning cameras, or raking the dirt around the hooch. For Lee, it felt like they were always cleaning something because of the wind, sand, rain, and mud. On duty, he sequestered himself inside the air-conditioned comfort of the photo lab, a mobile darkroom. There, he processed film and printed the pictures. Some evenings when it was particularly hot, he stood night duty and slept underneath the processing sinks where it was really cool. Off duty evenings, he went with the other photographers to the enlisted club and sucked up "near beer until we looked like bloated rubber fuel bladders."

A standing routine every morning after breakfast was to report at the Admin Hut and look for your name on the field assignment board. If it was there, the details of the assignment followed, perhaps matching you with a platoon patrol in the DMZ or participating in a major combat search-and-destroy operation involving thousands of Marines, in which case the entire photo section was there. The first thing Lee noticed inside the Admin Hut was a plaque with several rows and columns of Purple Heart ribbons, with one empty spot at the bottom right edge. One of the NCOs told Lee the ribbons represented how many photo people had been killed and wounded since 1966. "It was a little disturbing to wonder if that spot was for me," Lee remembers worrying at the time.

Lee enjoyed going into the field if for no other reason than what he felt was his personal freedom.

"In the rear, every senior office pogue demanded our uniforms be starched and crisp; you had to salute every officer in front, behind or beside you, or draw duty that was totally alien to your occupational specialty."

Being in the field was always preferred—even if it was dangerous. A typical day on a combat assignment might involve humping up a gorge, down a hill following the Marine in front of you, constantly reminding yourself what the gunnery sergeant said: "Stay at least five meters behind the man in front of you. One round will get you both."

Lee recalled that the gunny never mentioned what to do if a grenade landed among the troops. Its killing radius was 15 meters. "If you are lucky (as a photographer), or unlucky as a grunt, you make contact with the enemy and your instincts spring into action. Both of us run toward the gunfire, I behind a viewfinder with a false sense of safety, and the rifleman with his weapon on automatic, sweeping the foliage with bullets."

During the first half of Lee's first January in-country, the countryside was under water from the monsoon rains. During the second half the Vietnamese began preparing for Tet, their New Year. As would happen more than once in the Vietnam War, North and South Vietnam struck an informal truce to last through Tet. For the Marines it was an opportunity to reconnoiter the area. Lee had not yet had the chance to go into the bush since arriving in Vietnam, so he petitioned and was granted permission to join and document a recon team in action. His gunnery sergeant heard about it, however, and tried to convince him not to go out.

"At the time, few if any photographers had been out with a recon team because of the extreme danger that usually follows them. Instead of having 100 Marines sweep an area with some personal protection, recon teams of ten or fewer Marines are often dropped smack in the middle of Indian country. I appreciated gunny's warnings but joined a squad from 1st Platoon, Alpha Company, 3d Recon., led by Lieutenant Richard Piatt, an enlisted 'Mustang' Marine sent earlier by the Marine Corps to the US Naval Academy, where he became an officer. Piatt was a leader among leaders, and very much admired by his men."

Lieutenant Piatt introduced the squad with a cheerful welcome. Among handshakes, howls of laughter, and giggles they proceeded to try and transform Lee into a Recon Marine—first dumping all his gear in the rucksack onto the floor, then removing his C-ration cans from the boxes and shoving them into two pairs of socks. While his pack was being reorganized, someone collected three extra water canteens and hung them with the two already on his web belt ("making me feel more like a water buffalo.") Next, a clutch of grenades was handed to Lee, but not before they taught him how to protect against the safety the pins accidently coming off. Utility covers were the headgear instead of helmets. And the final makeup of a Recon Marine, Lee said, was applying camouflage grease on his face to become "a new human species."

After a couple of days of bad weather which kept Lee's unit grounded, they boarded two helicopters. An hour later, they landed on a small plateau high in the mountains. They quickly off-loaded from the aircraft and ran into the tall elephant grass.

"Before the last man vanished into the thicket, the aircraft were already flying down the mountain slope, quickly disappearing around a bend," Lee recalled.

He remembered the area being incredibly quiet. There were no sounds at all except for the breeze moving the grass. The lieutenant gave a hand signal and the circle of Marines contracted into a small group with Piatt at the center. Willie Acosta, who, according to Lee, was an easy-going Hispanic who always had a quick smile, was the point man. Armed with a machete and rifle slung across his chest, he began whacking at the heavy foliage, creating an opening for the unit to pass through. This went on for an hour or more until the sun began to set and they dropped their gear for the night. For the next two days, they humped up and down the mountains setting up different observation posts, watching the enemy below them move about. On the fourth day, while Willie was scanning the terrain with his binoculars, a rustling of grass on a nearby trail gave away the VC's position. AK-47 rifles rang out.

"We started running up the hill, returning fire, trying to encircle them. The firefight escalated. Bullets sounding like angry wasps snapped around us. I started taking photos of the fighting when a cry broke through the noise, 'Doc! Doc! Tex (our radioman) is hit! Corpsman up!' Tex was slumped over in the grass a few meters behind me. I thought for sure he was dead. The bullets were still dancing around us when Doc reached Tex. As he rolled the radioman over, his arm began to move, then the rest of him. We later saw where a round hit the metal buckle on his shoulder harness and ricocheted past his chest. It barely missed his heart."

Lee marvels now about how, apparently, the VC "didn't get the word" about the "mutually agreed upon" Tet truce because they kept shooting at the Marines. Lieutenant Piatt then led them further downhill across to another knoll and called up a fire mission on the radio. In less than 10 minutes Lee's unit heard a "Whump, whump" sound overhead and then the loudest boom he ever heard. That explosion was followed by another series of explosions with dirt, rocks, and tree branches showering them from every direction. Afraid that the VC was still there, they stayed in position for almost another hour. No one moved.

"Our legs ached and the muscles in our arms cramped in pain. As if that wasn't enough, the rain started, first with a few drops that increased into a steady heavy downpour. Under the noise of the rain we climbed back to the ambush area to assess the battle damage. The artillery apparently did its job very well; tunnels and trenches were unearthed, but no VC, not even blood trails or spent brass.

"Willie found some enemy documents and collected them for the lieutenant. Not finding anything else, we humped for another hour to the razorback of another hill and set in for the night. Even though the rain receded, we were soaked and cold. No fire was permitted so the C-rations were eaten cold. Everyone paired up and erected two-man shelters. Willie and I partnered together. As they said in boot camp, it was a 'hole to belly button tight' trying to stay warm. We all shivered in unison, too tired to worry about the VC, the cold, or the rain. Sleep was the elixir."

The next day Lee's unit ran into the VC again and another firefight broke out. In spite of the bullets flying, Lee was able to maneuver around taking pictures, this time standing only briefly because, as he was later told, the bullets were hitting all around him.

"My sense of invincibility almost got me killed. When the fighting stopped, the lieutenant ordered a headcount and we responded by shouting our last name. When Corporal Dray didn't answer, everyone panicked and started searching, only to find him behind a huge boulder spooning fruit cocktail from the can into his mouth. 'I was hungry,' Dray protested."

Covering combat never got easier, but it did become what Lee termed more routine.

"Once you can manage the initial paralyzing fear and exposure to the blood, guts, and death—on both sides—you go about filming without so much as a wince from a decaying body. The worse for me was finding women and children grievously wounded or dead, which kept me asking, 'Why, why?' The emotional pain can be intense. We had a saying at the press center: 'God protected drunks and fools.' We got and stayed drunk after coming off the line, and were fools for going out there with only a camera. Taking new photographers into the field was also a heavy responsibility."

Along with the relationships Lee forged with new combat correspondents in uniform, there were also those he and others in uniform forged with the civilian media.

Civilian journalists going north to cover the war were billeted at the Da Nang Press Center. The Marine correspondents and civilian press had a cordial relationship, not the competitive friction one might expect. Where some chafing appeared was when a civilian journalist attempted to order the enlisted photographers around in the compound. Most often it came from "celebrity" journalists or the first-time-in-Vietnam guys who concealed their discomfort and innocence by being pushy.

"Veteran journalists like Jim Lucas, Joseph Alsop, Henry Huet, and Larry Burrows—to name those I came to know—were always kind and interacted with us. The Marines particularly liked Dana Stone, the redheaded photographer who thoroughly enjoyed being in the bush with us." (Stone disappeared with fellow shooter Sean Flynn, son of actor Erol Flynn, when the two of them headed down the road in Cambodia in 1971 never to be seen or heard from again.)

Overall, the military and civilian press worked comfortably together. On one occasion bad weather kept Lee's unit from being extracted for two days.

"By the last day a CBS news crew ran short on food, so I shared the goodies from home, a can of pâté, beef jerky, soda crackers under the shelter of our assembled ponchos. 'It's not Paris, but it beats being hungry,'" Lee told them.

Lee feels he owes one of those civilian correspondents a heartfelt apology, which he offers here:

"In the summer of 1967, Ted Koppel, his ABC film crew, other journalists and I were in the Con Thien area covering the Marines recovering the bodies of fellow Marines. The dead had been killed earlier by NVA artillery and rocket attacks and had to be left behind as the battle became intense. Only after the United States retaliated with air strikes and artillery did the enemy stop. Ted and his people were behind me as we walked alongside tanks accompanying the Marines when suddenly the NVA began a rocket attack. Everyone ran looking for cover or a hole, the deeper the better. Ted was running and I was following behind him as the rockets exploded around us. As he dived into a nearby bomb crater, I noticed something falling out of his pocket and quickly picked it up as I went head first into another crater. The attack lasted for another five minutes and ceased. I sat up and immediately saw that it was a Gossen photo light meter. I was preparing to give it back to him when selfish thoughts got the best of me. I had an old General Electric photometer that was on its last leg of life and here was a top-of-the-line meter. I guess necessity can distort rational thought, (Koppel could always obtain another one, whereas we didn't have any spares). So I kept it. Ted was searching the area asking if anyone had seen it; I even pretended to assist in the search but to no avail.

"I have been living with this guilt for 50 years. It's about time I fess up and publicly confess and apologize to Mr. Koppel for this terrible error in judgment. No excuses except to say that Marines—including Marine combat photographers—when desperate will do questionable things to get the job done. So, Mr. Koppel, I trust you will understand. I gave your light meter to another Marine photographer when I left Vietnam. I still have the General Electric meter, however. It only works if pointed directly at the sun. Thank you for your contribution. Semper Fi."

Lee said that there were two times when the odds were against a Marine walking away alive: (1) When he's new in-country and not familiar to the sounds and sights of combat, and (2) during his last month in combat when he's distracted thinking about going home.

"These moments have killed many. And the last thing I wanted was to have a Marine killed on my watch."

Of all Lee's memorable assignments, one that stands out was a trip to the 2d Korean Marine "Blue Dragon" Brigade south of Chu Lai. The Blue Dragons were fearless warriors and notorious fighters who neither the VC nor NVA wanted to engage in combat. With a three-man photo/sound team led by a Lieutenant Carpenter, Lee's unit shot a film story of that brigade. As guests of a General Kim, they were treated like "VIP's attending an officers' mess" that evening. After two days of filming, Lee and the unit bid farewell to the ROK brigade and boarded a Huey back to Da Nang.

"The highlight of this trip for me was actually flying the Huey back as co-pilot. I was surprised the captain invited me to take the controls, especially with General Kim in the back. I must have done okay; the general fell asleep during the rest of the trip."

If asked, Lee would probably clarify that particular mission a rarity. Others more like … Vietnam, were the norm.

"At the DMZ, both Con Thien and Khe Sanh were subjected to some of the worse artillery and rocket attacks. At times the shelling would last for hours, stop, and resume at another unannounced time. One early evening before it became ink dark, a group of Marines and I assembled on top of the sandbag bunkers to watch the B-52s drop their ordnance on the other side of the DMZ. It was a spectacular show of fireworks as one explosion followed another. They lit up the horizon like a string of flashbulbs followed by thumps of sound. We were pretty engrossed in the action, standing up, yelling and cheering as if at a football game when an explosion erupted nearby. Like a cluster of prairie dogs we scattered in all directions, some literally flying into the trenches while others ran over each other searching for cover. When the excitement was over, we got up, looked around and started laughing. All of us were covered in mud. We obviously forgot about the rain early that day that turned the trenches into thick rivers of red clay mud."

But by far the worse experience was far less congenial than even that.

"The worse firefight I encountered was getting ambushed and wounded while on a combat patrol. It was about 1400 hours when I was called to the Admin Hut to suit up and go on a Sparrow Hawk with Lima Company, 3/4. A Sparrow Hawk is simply this: we Marines think bad guys are in this area but are not sure. So go out there with only a smattering of questionable intel and verify the situation. The helicopters inserted us outside the Gio Linh District in Quang Tri Province. The absence of males—only women and children—was the first clue that something was very wrong. Even yard animals and dogs were not seen or heard. After passing through the village all hell broke out. This time the North Vietnamese Army—not the VC—engaged and pinned the entire platoon down. I was behind the lieutenant when he and the machine gunner rushed forward to the point man who was already killed. I was filming when a round pierced my canteen. I immediately felt wetness and thought I was surely hit. A second round followed, hit my helmet and grazed my forehead before the bullet spun to a stop on the ground. Because the capillaries are so close to the surface of the skin, I bled profusely, making my head wound look worse than it was. I called for cover fire to a group of Marines at a hooch nearby. As they started shooting, I raced to them. Then a young corporal came from nowhere and asked, `What are we going to do now sergeant?' The lieutenant and platoon sergeant were gravely wounded and here I was, the next senior Marine. The Marine Corps command structure is very specific: if a senior Marine is incapacitated and cannot command, the next senior in rank takes over regardless of whether he is a cook, clerk or, in my case, a photographer. 'All Marines are riflemen first,' I could hear my DI bark. I put my camera down and picked up the M-14 rifle."

"A quick assessment was not encouraging. The lieutenant was pinned down about 20 meters in front of us. Those near him, including the Marine who ran up with more ammunition for the M60 machine gun, were dead. All three squads were rendered immoveable by the NVA, now trying to outflank and envelop us. I had two radiomen with me, one on the platoon/battalion frequency, the other in radio contact with several Huey gunships. I popped a green smoke grenade marking our position while the radioman directed the flight parallel to our position. A helicopter made an initial pass. We by then were inside the hooch and observed the action through peep holes. Other Hueys followed and opened fire, launching a volley of M-79 grenades from the belt-fed grenade racks while the crew chiefs strafed the tree line with their M-60s. The three flybys slowed but did not halt the advancing enemy.

"Sensing we were about to be overrun, I decided that with three remaining rounds in my pistol, I would take out two NVAs and save the last for myself. As an Asian, I wasn't about to be captured. Then a flight of F-4 Phantoms returning from an aborted mission came up on frequency and asked if we needed help. The radioman couldn't key the microphone fast enough to respond. As the fighters were lining up, the other radio operator made contact with battalion headquarters for me. The colonel asked if we could be the blocking force, because they were sending a rifle company to our rescue. I told the colonel that we had about 60 percent killed and wounded and would try and hold our position as best we could.

"As the Phantoms began their air assault, we shouted to the lieutenant to keep his head down and to tell us how close to bring in the fighters. Napalm exploded about 100 meters from us. The lieutenant shouted back, 'Closer! Closer!' The radioman called in the adjustment. The jets realigned and came in screaming. It was a scene right out of the movie *Apocalypse Now* as a huge wall of napalm exploded and rolled across the rice fields, destroying the entire village, vaporizing everything in its path. Debris, shrapnel, and the overwhelming heat from the napalm sucked the air out of our lungs. I could hear cries of women and children and the fire still raging from the bombing. Nothing else moved. When night fell we crawled to the lieutenant, lifted him on our backs and crawled to safety.

"Hearing us in the dark calling out, Kilo Company found us at around 2100 hours. Medevac helicopters airlifted the severely wounded—including the lieutenant—that night, their flights occasionally interrupted by sporadic gunfire which Kilo Company quickly suppressed with every weapon on hand. I got tagged to be extracted for the next morning ... not before finding my camera and finishing filming."

Lee was awarded the Bronze Star with Valor (V) for calling in the air strike that kept his unit from being overrun. He had no idea that was going to happen to him until the colonel at the Da Nang Press Center called and told him to report to General Cushman, commanding general of 3d Marine Amphibious Force, the counterpart of MACV, and General William Westmoreland in Saigon.

Lieutenant George Sullivan, the platoon commander, survived; however, he lost both legs because of his severe wounds. Sullivan himself received the Navy Cross and put Lee in for his Bronze Star.

There were other times when Lee put his camera down as well. Once, he didn't pick up a weapon; instead he helped a corpsman try to save a wounded Marine during a search-and-destroy mission in Helicopter Valley when a fierce firefight erupted. Lee was with the main squad when a rifleman nearby was hit. He spun around screaming in pain. The doc appeared and immediately opened his jacket and saw that he had a severe chest wound and was going into shock. Lee, being the closest, stopped filming and held the Marine down as the doc tried to find a vein in his arm to insert an IV. "The Marine kept thrashing uncontrollably, making it all but impossible for the doc to insert a line. Suddenly he stopped fighting and relaxed. He looked up to the sky as if he saw something in the far distance. As his eyes began to close he called out for his mother with his last breath. Doc dropped the IV to his side and I gently placed the Marine's head on the ground."

Today, when he thinks back to his time in-country the words bravery, courage, honor, loyalty, discipline, dedication, and commitment come to his mind.

"Those words are forever embedded in me after being in Vietnam. Today, I could not be prouder than to say I was with the finest company of those Marines and Navy corpsmen, and thank them for giving me the rare privilege to bear witness to their efforts and sacrifices. I wish all the images in my mind could be reproduced because they are far exceptional than the images I captured on film as a photographer."

These days, thousands of Vietnam veterans are returning to the scenes of transference from youth to manhood, Lee is not one of them.

"I thought about going back but didn't see any value to retrace that time in hell. The only place I have often visited is the Vietnam Memorial. Enough memories were there to remind me of Vietnam, much less than having to kick red clay for emphasis."

Lee's thoughts now turn to what was going through his mind the day he left Vietnam forever.

"As the plane climbed from Da Nang airfield, I felt both tremendous guilt and relief. Guilt that I was leaving behind my photo colleagues and the grunts I accompanied into the bush and became close to, and an overwhelming feeling of disappointment that my intentions to do my part to rescue the Vietnamese from Communism were very naive. I was going to be the knight on the white horse and save the oppressed. But the white horse died. Progress in combat once measured by securing objectives morphed into daily body counts to justify our presence in Vietnam. That mentality was pervasive in the command, while far down the chain the grunts were defining progress as surviving another day. Saddest of all, I was leaving behind the ghosts of men I knew who died in combat: Lieutenant Piatt and Corporal Dray, killed in action; senior NCO Gunny Highland and Bernard Fall [French journalist and historian whose books *Street Without Joy* and *Hell in a Very High Place* helped define the French experience in Indochina] killed when he stepped on a landmine; and Corporal Bill Perkins, who threw himself on a grenade and was posthumously awarded the Medal of Honor. He was the first combat correspondent in US military history to receive it. And Tex, the recon radioman went home never mentally the same, according to his mother to whom I briefly spoke in 1992. The list of the dead rolls past like ending film credits in my mind. As the last sight of Vietnam disappeared underneath us, I sighed a breath of relief. I had survived."

Marine mopic cameraman Frank Lee on patrol, signaling to a still photographer to slate a photo for film roll # 2. (Frank Lee collection)

Connected with Vietnamese
Refugees from Home: John Taylor

By the time Saigon fell on April 30, 1975, the unit known as DASPO (Department of the Army Special Photographic Office) had changed its name to ASOPD (Army Special Operations Pictorial Department). John Taylor was assigned to the CONUS (in the Continental United States) detachment located at Ft. Bragg, North Carolina, where he was tasked with very special Department of the Army photo/film documentation missions. His work with ASOPD was mostly TDY which often took him far afield of Ft. Bragg.

"In April 1975, I had a film crew in Ft. Richardson, Alaska, shooting a Department of the Army-scripted film entitled *Helicopter Icing*. The film was intended to inform flight crews about the dangers of aircraft icing and preventive measures," he recalled.

Though Taylor did not get to Vietnam, it was not for lack of trying.

"While dining one night at the Elmendorf Air Force Base Officer's Club, I met some of the Air Force flight crews who were involved in Operation *Baby Lift*. We got to talking about what our film crew was doing, and they suggested we come with them on the next flight back to Vietnam to document it. I checked with my CO, and he checked with the Department of the Army, but the final word was no go. One of the flight crew later sent me some photographs of babies in boxes in the aircraft hold."

Operation *Baby Lift*, which occurred during April 3–26, 1975, saved the lives of over 10,300 infants and children and helped resettle them in the United States, Canada, France, and Australia. Sadly, it is also known for the crash of one of the evacuating aircraft, a C-5A Galaxy, which on April 4 came down 12 minutes after take-off from Tan Son Nhut Air Base in Saigon. Killed were 138 people, including 78 children and 35 persons from the Defense Attaché Office of the US embassy in Saigon.

In spite of not making it to Vietnam, Taylor did have a connection to the people of that country.

"Later in 1975, I was assigned a project to take a film crew to Ft. Chaffee, Arkansas, and Ft. Indiantown Gap, Pennsylvania, to document the US Army's Vietnamese Refugee Resettlement program known as Operation *New Life*."

Operation *New Life*, which spanned late April to November 1975, oversaw the care and processing of 111,000 of 130,000 Vietnamese refugees on the island of Guam as a result of Operation *Frequent Wind*, the name given the evacuation of Vietnamese from Saigon on April 30. While on Guam, the refugees lived in tent cities for several weeks before being processed for resettlement, mainly in the United States, but in other countries as well.

"We spent about two weeks at each location documenting the process from arrival through departure," Taylor said. The footage was then sent to the Tobyhanna, Pennsylvania Depot for storage.

Taylor's team consisted of himself, the project officer/director/2nd camera, the director of photography, a soundman, and a still photographer.

With an Arriflex BL, Arriflex S, Nagra III, and a Hasselblad still camera, they "documented thousands of Vietnamese refugees arriving, being processed, and living their lives in the barracks. We even befriended one family and shared dinner with them one night at Ft. Chaffee. The husband was an American missionary with a Vietnamese family," Taylor recalled, wishing today that he had kept in touch with them.

Taylor had been well-suited for the work he did with ASOPD, to which he was assigned after the Signal Officer's Basic Course training at Ft. Gordon, Georgia, in 1974. The military tradition ran through his family. His father, at only 16 years old, had served in the Merchant Marine during World War II, and, later in the US Army, from which he retired as an artillery officer at Ft. Bliss, Texas.

After high school, Taylor went on to earn a bachelor's degree in radio/TV/film from the University of Texas at El Paso. Even while still in college, he went to work in the production department of KDBC-TV El Paso, the local CBS affiliate.

For Taylor, it was not a case of going after a particular MOS when he joined the Army. It was more a case of an MOS (8511 Motion Picture & TV Director) finding him.

"It was pretty much fate and luck," he recalled. "After completing the Signal Officer's Basic Course at Ft. Gordon, I was offered two jobs by personnel. One was a traditional Signal Corps type job and the other ASOPD. The advisor/captain did not know much about either position but thought the Ft. Bragg job involved taking pictures and travel. That seemed closest to my goals, so I went with that and reported for duty around December of that year. That's when I learned it was a dream job for me. We traveled around the world making movies. It was paid graduate school."

There was also a lot of "OJT" (on-the-job training) with the unit, according to Taylor.

Army Special Operations Pictorial Department mopic photographer John Taylor's TDY in Alaska in April 1975, just as Saigon was falling. (John Taylor collection)

"I learned a lot from fellow officers and NCOs. I knew a bit about TV studio production but nothing about location film production. I bought a few books about the technical and creative aspects of filmmaking, and the rest was learning in the field, producing around 20 projects during my tenure there," said Taylor, who ETS'd [Expiration Term of Service] out of the Army in September 1976.

"I really enjoyed my work and considered staying, but the likelihood of remaining with ASOPD was not good because I was due next for a more traditional Signal Corps officer's job. So I left."

Taylor was, unfortunately, never privy to knowing whether or not his work on the Vietnamese Refugee Resettlement program ever came to fruition.

"I don't know if an edited version of the project was ever released," he told me. "If, in your research, you find out anything, please let me know."

Learned How to Deal with the Danger: Bob Bayer

Bob Bayer had no idea that the journalism classes he took in high school and junior college would one day propel him, a camera-toting Marine with the MOS 4312 (public affairs specialist), onto the battlefields of Vietnam, in 1967. The way he figures, it was just fate that right out of boot camp at Marine Corps Recruit Depot San Diego, some 4,312 billets arrived at Headquarters Marine Corps on the same day.

El Toro Marine Corps Air Station in Orange County, California provided the seeds of the "OJT" Bayer would need in military public affairs, or Informational Services Office in Marine parlance. But just when he thought he was bound for DINFOS (Defense Information School then at Ft. Benjamin Harrison, Indiana) for further ISO training, his orders came through for Fleet Marine Corps-Pacific. "Meaning I was on my way to 'scenic Viet Nam'," Bayer said with a laugh.

A C-130 out of Okinawa was Bayer's lift into Da Nang Air Base, through which most Marines passed en route to Vietnam.

While sitting on a bench at the Marine air terminal, waiting to catch a ride to the 1st Marine Division ISO office, he pulled out a copy of *Track and Field News*.

"The guy next to me sees what I'm reading and strikes up a conversation about being a runner in high school in L.A. It turns out we had competed in some of the same track meets. His name was Wade Early and we're still in occasional contact," said Bayer.

Early was an 0311 (rifleman) with the 3d Battalion, 1st Marine Regiment, and, when he met Bayer, he had just returned from R&R. He described to Bayer how his platoon had been overrun a few weeks earlier.

"I remember thinking that although we were both 20, he looked a hell of a lot older than me. After he left to catch a ride back to the 3/1, I found a copy of *Stars and Stripes*. As I was reading it, I came across a list of those who had been killed in action and the name Farrell Hummingbird (KIA, January 14, 1967). Farrell had been a bunkmate of mine in boot camp.

"I now had lots to think and worry about, and I'd only been on the ground in Vietnam about an hour and hadn't even come under fire from the enemy yet."

Once with his unit, Bayer settled into the routine of a Marine Corps Combat Correspondent. Mornings, he would get up with his fellow combat correspondents and trudge up the hill from the hooches that served as their barracks to the ISO office, a Quonset hut in the 1st Marine Division's headquarters compound on a hillside northwest of the Da Nang Air Base.

Those who were assigned jobs in the office would start their daily tasks, while those who were in from the field would write and file their stories, after which they would eventually be ordered back out in the field to cover an operation or do a specific story. Whenever Bayer was assigned to a particular unit, he would report to the operations office to find out what was happening and see if there were incidents that deserved coverage, or he would talk to various troops in the unit to, in his words, "ferret out stories."

"If it was a battalion embarking on an operation, I would go out with it and look for stories. If we had lots of contact with the enemy, it was easy to come up with them."

Bayer would then either go back to the ISO to write and file, "or I would find a spare typewriter at the battalion's command post, write and then send the stories to the rear on the mail and courier run truck."

One such story came about the same month he arrived at the 3/1 in February 1967. His battalion was operating along the coast south of Da Nang and the Marble Mountains. The latter was an infamous clandestine Viet Cong stronghold deep within its cavernous environs, unbeknownst to the Marines who manned a lookout post atop one of the mountains.

"I was on patrol with a squad when we started taking sniper fire from a nearby leper colony. We were ordered not to shoot back because the leper colony was considered a no-fire zone. The VC in the area knew this and would do some sniping at us from the compound."

Bayer's squad left the area and he filed a story on this incident. Somewhere up the chain of command, however, the story was killed. Bayer never found out why.

Although there were VC units where the 3/1 operated, the area according to Bayer had become fairly pacified. Even today he speaks highly of the battalion's intelligence staff and how the information gathered would be the impetus for company- or platoon-size sweeps where they would be looking for, "and frequently finding" specific individuals suspected of being Viet Cong.

On one sweep, the unit he was with encountered stronger than anticipated resistance.

"We ended up capturing a half dozen NVA regulars with their 82mm mortar and ammunition. They told us they'd come down the Ho Chi Minh Trail, and then worked their way over to the area south of Da Nang. The NVA told us that they had been escorted by local VC units and that their mission was to start hitting targets around the Da Nang Air Base. To my knowledge, this was one of the first elements of what was to be a major thrust into the Da Nang area in 1967 by the 2d NVA Division."

Major battles between the Marines and the 2d NVA Division started in April 1967 and continued into 1968.

"I went out with the 3/1 on the first day of Operation *Union* on April 21 and was wounded," Bayer recalled.

"That day really sticks out in my mind. I flew in with one of two companies from 3/1 that were sent into the Que Son Valley to reinforce a company from 2/1 that had been decimated after running into a large element of the 2d NVA Division. We were pinned down by heavy fire most of the afternoon and casualties were quickly mounting among the two companies from 3/1."

Numerous air strikes and a large amount of artillery support temporarily helped thwart the NVA attack on the Marines.

"I was in the process of helping move our dead and wounded from the front lines to positions inside our perimeter late in the afternoon when I spotted a radio operator I knew. I was leaning over to ask if he had seen where I'd left my camera and other gear when there was a boom from a mortar round that impacted 10 feet behind him. I got knocked back on my butt from the explosion," said Bayer, who neither felt immediate pain nor realized he'd been hit.

"I saw the radio operator in front of me and I jumped up to help him. That's when I felt warm liquid running down the front of me. I put my hands there and realized it was my own blood."

Bayer was quickly attended to by a corpsman who checked him over and wrapped a battle dressing about his chin and head. He'd been hit just below the left side of his jaw, and a piece of shrapnel had "sliced down through my neck and lodged under my right collarbone," Bayer was told by the doctor who operated on him the next day at the 1st Hospital Company in Chu Lai. A number of pin-sized pieces of shrapnel had also pierced his body, particularly his chest. Shortly after being treated by the corpsman, Bayer passed out from shock and loss of blood.

When he came to, he found himself in a heavily damaged brick building with many others around him likewise being attended by corpsmen. Wounded or not, that same night he volunteered to man the lines to help guard against NVA probes against the Marines' perimeter.

"I got my rifle and spent the rest of the night on the line. He was medivac'd out the next morning. I believe the radio operator survived. He was lucky because the radio, which was still on his back when the round hit, absorbed most of the blast from the mortar round. This probably also shielded me from sustaining more serious wounds," said Bayer, who received a Purple Heart.

September 1967 saw another incident that Bayer will likely never forget. Fellow combat correspondent Gordon Fowler was with the 5th Marines at the beginning of

Operation *Swift*, yet another battle in the Que Son Valley between the 1st Marine Division and the 2d NVA Division.

"A few days later, Fowler was back in his hooch late at night describing what happened. He was normally a laid back Texan, but after the first day of *Swift*, Gordon was as wired as I'd ever seen him. He described how the unit he was with had been overrun, how there had been NVA all over the place, how the Marines had taken very heavy casualties, how a chaplain, Father Vincent Capadanno, had been killed while doing heroic deeds (for which he would eventually be awarded the Medal of Honor), and how Gordon himself had received shrapnel wounds."

The next day, Bayer and an ISO newbie named Tom Donlon were ordered out on that same operation. They got to the Que Son Valley about mid-afternoon on a resupply chopper. And no sooner had they reported in than an order came down for the company to move out ASAP to help another company that was heavily engaged.

"We could hear the battle in the distance," Bayer said. "We double timed it over and linked up with them and spent a tense night fighting and getting mortared."

The next morning Bayer and Donlon went with the company a short distance to retrieve the bodies of about a half dozen Marines who had been killed the day before.

"They were lying out in a rice paddy. But instead of moving out into the open from the cover of the tree line we were in, it was decided to call in Marine jets to drop tear gas in the rice paddy to screen our attempt to get the KIAs. Everyone was told to put on gas masks and soon jets made their bombing runs; we were able to pull the KIAs back to our lines without the NVA being able to see what was going on through the cloud of tear gas. This was the only time in a year and a half in Vietnam that I saw anything like that," Bayer said.

Bayer also encountered the weirdness for which the Vietnam War was well known. One night he and other lower-ranked ISO enlisted men (referred to as the Snuffies) were staggering down a hillside from the enlisted men's watering hole called the Thunderbird Club to their hooches where they lived when they weren't out in the field when the NVA started raining rockets down on the Da Nang Air Base, a couple of miles away.

"We looked up to see bright flashes coming from the air base. It didn't take us long, even in our somewhat besotted states, to figure out what was happening. Our hooches were situated on pads that had been cut into the hillside, built a couple feet off the ground with plywood floors and sheet-metal roofs. You could step off the hillside and onto the roof," Bayer said.

"Someone yells, 'Let's get on the roof and watch the fireworks show!' Another shouts, 'Grab the beer and the beach chairs!' A third Snuffie screams out, 'Get naked!' So before long, you have about 10 stark-naked Marines sitting on the roof of a hooch in beach chairs and drinking beer while the air base is getting blasted. It was about as surreal a scene as one can envision. I don't make this stuff up."

Bayer's MOS sometimes required him to serve as press escort for the civilian media in Vietnam, thereby causing him to intermingle with some very well-known and respected reporters and photographers. One of those was UPI photographer Kent Potter, later killed when the ARVN helicopter he was flying in took a round and crashed in Laos during 1971's Operation *Lam Son 719*, which was launched to cut off the part of the Ho Chi Minh Trail which wove its way through Laos, down into Cambodia and on into South Vietnam. Killed along with Potter were *Life Magazine* photographer extraordinaire, Larry Burrows, the AP's beloved French-Vietnamese photographer, Henri Huet, and Keisaburo Shimamoto, a Japanese freelancer on assignment for *Newsweek*.

In the summer of 1968, Bayer had escorted Potter out to the scene of Operation *Allen Brook*. They landed in a hot LZ aboard a helicopter that was sent in to evacuate casualties.

"Things were pretty chaotic and there was lots of firing. I told Potter to stay put while I went over to a small command unit nearby to try and get a handle on the situation. When I returned to where Potter had been, he was nowhere to be found. He had taken off toward the tree line about 100 meters away at what seemed to be the focal point of the fighting. The open area surrounding the LZ was a sea of tall elephant grass, and all I could see were the tops of those trees. I worked my way over there and found him after what was probably a half hour," Bayer recalled.

"By then the fighting had deescalated. Potter already had lots of good shots and wanted to get back to Da Nang to get his film processed. We went back to the LZ. There were a number of casualties who had been moved there. I told Potter we wouldn't be getting on any helicopter out until the WIAs had been flown out."

The two eventually got out on the helicopter that had been sent in to carry out those killed in action.

Bayer said that after being in Vietnam a few months "learning the ropes," and despite the serious wounds he had received in April 1967, he felt he knew how to conduct himself while out in the field and get the stories his job required. "The danger element was always there, but I learned how to deal with it."

After leaving the Marine Corps in October 1968, Bayer earned a degree from California State University at Northridge, then went on to a career as a journalist in Southern California. He retired in 2009 from the *Los Angeles Times,* where he worked for 24 years.[1]

---

[1] Author's note: Dale Dye contributed to this chapter.

Marine combat correspondent Bob Bayer in between firefights taking notes for a story. (Bob Bayer collection)

Covering Operation *Homecoming*: Tom Lincoln

Stars and Stripes reporter/photographer Tom Lincoln was at Clark Air Base in the Philippines a full month before the culmination for Operation *Homecoming*, the release of American prisoners of war by communist North Vietnam in February 1973. He was not alone, however. There were some 300 other reporters, photographers, and staff from all over the world who had descended on Clark AB before the arrival of the first planeload of POWs in the Philippines. *Stars and Stripes* alone sent Tom, photojournalists Paul Harrington and Chip Maury, and longtime "Striper" Hal Drake down from Tokyo to cover this event of monumental importance.

"No one knew for certain when the first releases would occur because even though the Paris Peace Accords had been signed in late January, negotiations were still underway on the timing and manner by which the prisoner swaps would occur," Lincoln said.

He remembers a lot of frustration on the part of the seasoned correspondents who were forced in to that uncomfortable experience with virtually nothing to do but attend the military's daily briefings. "Nobody wanted to venture too far from the base for fear of missing the first release. We didn't know if we'd get 30 minutes' or three days' notice."

With all that time on his hands, Lincoln could not help but notice the reason for choosing Clark as the point of disembarkation. "It had the best-equipped hospital within reasonable flight distance of Hanoi, and all the military efforts were concentrated there. They had assembled all medical specialties in anticipation of receiving the POWs who might be suffering from any number of medical conditions. There were dieticians, physical therapists, surgeons, orthopedists, and psychologists waiting to deal with whatever presented itself.

The day that the hundreds of uniformed and civilian correspondents had been waiting for finally arrived late in the afternoon of Monday, February 11, 1973, according to "Striper" Tom Lincoln; the most detailed stories and photos were transmitted by teletype from the Philippines to the *Stripes* Tokyo bureau two days later.

"I remember working through the entire night of the 11th to write and file stories, and we all waited with great anticipation for the arrival of *Stripes'* Wednesday edition to see which pictures had been selected and which stories ran," Lincoln recalled.

Though he was at Clark Air Force Base for the return of the POWs, he knew full well what his colleagues back at the Tokyo bureau of *Stars and Stripes* were going through to get the stories of the POWs out to the military and its dependents. The sight and sound of the bureau are with him to this day. And he prefaces his remarks noting that faxes were only in their bourgeoning days and that emails, PDF attachments, and electronic transmission of documents were not even a gleam in anyone's eye.

"The sound in the typesetting room at the paper was deafening. The paper was the real deal—cigarette smoke drifted in the air in all spaces of the paper. The teletype room clattered and bells rang with arriving stories. You could hear the typesetting machines clanging away a full two stories below, sounding much like a Tokyo Pachinko Parlor," he said, referring to the Japanese form of gambling that involves machines that constantly shoot steel marbles at such a volume that participants often plug their ears to salvage whatever hearing they have left.

Lincoln found other parallels between the United States and Japan besides the way a newspaper was run at the time. "The sentiment of the Japanese people was much like that of the Americans. There were those who were supportive of the war and those who were opposed, vehemently opposed," he said.

Tom Lincoln has a vivid memory of his arrival at *Stars and Stripes* in November, 1971.

"I was driven into downtown Tokyo in a *Stars and Stripes* staff vehicle. It was a Sunday about 1pm. As we approached the front gate of the *Stars and Stripes* compound, I remember wondering why there were Japanese military guards posted at the gate. Later that day, I found out.

For Lincoln, the moment that POW Jeremiah Denton—later an Admiral and Senator from Alabama—deplaned at Clark and uttered his now famous first three words, "God Bless America," is forever imprinted on his mind and in his heart.

"I have always been one to get chills down my spine when our national anthem is played, so the feeling I had when Denton delivered his remarks was no different," Lincoln remembered. Those same three words made the banner headline of the lead story for *Stars and Stripes* on February 13.

"Three words said it all: 'God Bless America,'" said Lincoln, whose memories of the first planeload of POWs arriving at the air base remain exceptionally vivid.

"There was a large assemblage of military personnel and dependents behind a rope line that had been strung alongside the tarmac. The press corps was situated along that line as well as at a separate vantage point that had been reserved for us [military journalists]. I was lucky enough to get one of the two seats in a lift truck with a bucket that elevated Paul Harrington and me about 20 feet above the crowd, right at the rope line. We had the best view of anyone."

Of the mood of the crowd waiting for the first plane, Lincoln said it was "anxious and anticipatory. Photographers were jockeying for position. A red carpet had been laid on the tarmac and spanned the distance from where the exit of the plane would be to military buses that were waiting. Someone announced over a loud speaker that the first C-141 was in range and preparing for its final approach. A big cheer went up at the announcement and you could feel the tension in the air. No one knew what to expect. Would these men walk off the plane? Would they be carried off? Would they appear emaciated? Would they be wearing prison garb or American uniforms? So many unanswered questions."

Another cheer went up the moment the plane landed. Even though it was daytime, Lincoln remembers the landing lights glistening in the distance. "I could feel my heart pounding in anticipation. I checked and rechecked my two cameras to make sure they had film and were set to the proper exposures. Paul [Harrington] did the same."

The runway was a long distance from where the military reporters and photographers were assembled, but as soon as the plane touched down the crowd let out yet another loud cheer that "rang along the rope line," according to Lincoln.

"As the plane taxied from the runway and approached the tarmac, I remember how proud I felt to be an American. As the plane turned in front of the rope line, I remember the scream of the engines and the great welling up of emotion in me as it turned in front of the crowd and came to a halt. I had a lump in my throat as big as a tennis ball. As the jet engines spooled down, I looked at those gathered behind the rope line and I saw men in uniform, women, children, all with tears in their eyes, some weeping openly. It was a very moving sight."

For Lincoln, it seemed like a lifetime before the plane door opened. When it finally did, Jeremiah Denton was the first to exit. He gave his famous remarks, then shook hands with Admiral Noel Gayler of CINCPAC and Air Force Lieutenant General William Moore, commander of the 13th Air Force, and a representative of the Philippine government.

Next off the plane was Lieutenant Commander Everett Alvarez, the first and longest-held POW during the Vietnam War. "I remember reflecting over the realization that when he was shot down and captured, I was barely 14 years old and entering high school. I was now taking this man's picture as a 23-year-old Army Spec-4. It really brought into focus for me the enormity of what was happening. He had been held so long that his wife, whom he had married shortly before he deployed to the theater, divorced him while [he was] in captivity allegedly because she gave up hope that he would ever be released. I never learned if he was made aware of the divorce by his captors, or if it was revealed to him upon his arrival at Clark."

When the rest of the POWs on that first of what would be several planes arriving over a period of a few days deplaned that day, Lincoln recalled that several of the men walked off the plane with noticeable limps. Many were gaunt and malnourished, but others were so happy they ignored protocol and simply relished the moment. "Some kneeled down and kissed the tarmac, and several had scrawled personal messages on different items to show their appreciation for having been freed. One held up a cloth on which he had written 'GOD BLESS AMERICA & NIXON.' Another had taped the inscription 'God Bless Nixon' on his jacket breast pocket."

Those jackets, grey windbreakers all, black trousers and black Oxford shoes had been issued to them by the North Vietnamese before their departure from points of captivity, most notably the Hoa Lo Prison, forever dubbed the "Hanoi Hilton."

"The ones who were too weak or injured to walk from the plane were carried down the back ramp in litters and placed directly on buses outfitted as stretcher carriers. But many of them rose on their elbows and acknowledged the crowd's affections. They were in poor shape, but they were very happy men."

While happy is the word that Lincoln used to describe the released POWs, lucky is the word he would apply to himself whenever he thinks about the assignment to cover Operation *Homecoming*, which is frequently.

"What comes to mind is how lucky I was not only to get assigned to *Stars and Stripes* but also to be given the opportunity by the paper to be part of the team that was selected to cover the first releases."

Of Hal Drake, Lincoln recalls that he helped compile a book published in 1985 called *Pacific Stars and Stripes: The First 40 Years 1945–1985*, in which he included a copy of the lead *Stars and Stripes* story, which he attributed to Lincoln as the sole author. In actuality Drake and Lincoln had collaborated on the piece, but in what Lincoln called "typical Drake fashion," he attributed the story only to Lincoln, who called Drake, "one of the most brilliant reporters I have ever met and one of the few mentors in my life."

Tom also spoke highly of photographers Chip Maury and Paul Harrington. Maury had been a "superb photojournalist," who, along with Harrington, won many awards for his photography of Operation *Homecoming*. Harrington went on to a multi-year career with the Associated Press's Los Angeles bureau from which he recently retired.

"I remember that Paul and Chip went everywhere loaded down with extra film and multiple cameras, some with motor drives and others with long and short lenses, prepared for both color and black-and-white shooting."

In the meantime, Drake and Lincoln made sure their tape recorders had extra batteries. "We had each purchased a set of field glasses just in case we were kept at a distance and needed a closer perspective. I carried a couple of cameras as well," Lincoln recalled.

Lincoln, who had gone from graduating from the military's Defense Information School (DINFOS) at Ft. Benjamin Harris in Indianapolis to *Stars and Stripes*, gives talks from time to time about his experiences covering Operation *Homecoming*.

"I still get a little choked up when I get to the point where I describe the arrival of the first plane," he said. "It was emotional for me then, and it is still emotional. I realize now that I was a witness to one of the great events in our country's history, and I feel enormously privileged to have been a part of it. The men who were imprisoned by the North Vietnamese and the Viet Cong endured things that none of us can begin to imagine. Not only the torture, which has become legend, but also that fact that none of these men had any idea if they would ever be released, ever see their loved ones again, or even survive to the day of release if it ever came. A number of them did not. And those men and the ones who returned deserve our lifelong gratitude, no matter what our opinions of the war."

Stars and Stripes reporter/photographers Paul Harrington and Tom Lincoln in the Philippines to cover the return of the POWs from Hanoi in 1973. (Tom Lincoln collection)

So That Others May Live:
Rick Fuller

Before retired Air Force Colonel Rick Fuller served as a Public Affairs Staff Officer for the 3d Aerospace Rescue and Recovery Group (AARG), Tan Son Nhut Air Base in Saigon in 1971, he had already served in several other capacities: Public Information Officer with the British Royal Air Force in Mildenhall, England (1963–64); Commander of the Armed Forces Radio Spain–Morocco Network of five stations headquartered at Torrejon Air Base, Spain (1964–67); and Public Affairs Staff Officer for the Secretary of the Air Force in the USAF's Public Affairs Office in New York City (1967–71).

Of his assignment to the 3d ARRG, Fuller said, "It was very rewarding. During my year assignment, the crew members again and again risked their lives and showed amazing courage. They rescued some 365 aircrew members during my tour, many under horrific battle conditions."

Assigned to what he termed a "one-man public information office," he wrote and released hundreds of news releases and articles for both public release and internal military outlets.

"Some of the more memorable ones included New Year's Eve 1971, when ARRG saved the crew of a C-130 Spector Gunship. The Spector crew was spread over the Ho Chi Minh Trail and presented one of the greatest challenges the rescue forces faced. There were lots of NVA units around and the fast movers, the Sandys [A-1Es] and the helicopters, executed a classic operation. Morale of the gunship crews took a 'Great Leap Forward' when it became known that every one of the crew members was saved.

"We had installed a belly camera on the HH-53s in the fall in order to film the PJs [pararescue specialists] and jungle penetrators during rescues. I sat in the Rescue Coordination Center (Joker) and wrote the story as I heard the radio calls."

The film was flown to Tan Son Nhut via what Fuller termed a "Scatback" (T-39), and he finished the news release while the film was being processed by the 600th Photo Squadron, USAF.

"The Commander of 3d ARRG and the 7th Air Force approved the release, and it was sent to both the print media and to the pool TV network (CBS that week). It was shipped by them to Japan and all the networks used it. The system in those days was for one network to function as the pool network, duplicate the film, release and provide it to the other networks. We provided the material to the media in time for them to make the New Year's Day stateside broadcasts. The rescue forces had done the impossible again."

For Fuller another memorable mission was the rescue of Bat 21 Bravo, call sign for downed USAF Lieutenant Colonel Iceal E. "Gene" Hambleton, a signals intelligence expert and navigator aboard an EB-66 aircraft that was shot down behind enemy lines in Vietnam. The mission took 11 days. All told, six Americans lost their lives attempting to rescue Hambleton. The North Vietnamese attempted to capture him as well, but he was finally rescued in a land operation by US Navy SEAL Lieutenant J.G. Thomas R. Norris and South Vietnamese Navy Petty Officer Third Class Nguyen Van Kiet.

"I was in Joker for many hours during the rescue efforts," Fuller said. "The final news release was a 7th Air Force product because of the massive effort to rescue Hambleton."

A Hollywood production of the incident, entitled *Bat 21*, released in 1988, starring Gene Hackman, Danny Glover, and country music singer Jerry Reed, was "not a true telling" of the rescue mission, Fuller believes. "While the movie was accurate in some areas, it wasn't the real story."

"My tour involved visiting all of our rescue units, flying with them, writing articles and news releases, and arranging for news media and members of Combat Camera to sit alert and fly missions with the crews. The normal mission for the Local Base Rescue units who flew HH-43 Pedro helicopters involved scrambling when an inbound flight declared an emergency, rescuing the crew if they punched out, or helping to extract them if they crashed. Several times I was flying training missions when an inflight emergency was declared and I would be dropped wherever we were while the rescue crew responded to the emergency. Weight was an issue," he said.

One such time, in Da Nang, Fuller was within a kilometer of Marble Mountain, a US Marine stronghold by day but, it was learned after the war, controlled by the North Vietnamese by night.

Fuller remembers the situational details for Air Force Search and Rescue Missions to this day.

"The HH-53 Super Jolly Green helicopters normally stood alert and flew orbits near where the strike aircraft were operating. If a fighter went down, the fast movers (usually F-4s) Sandys and Super Jollies worked closely together to try to extract the crew members as soon as possible. The fighters would try to keep the Viet Cong and North Vietnamese forces away by dropping bombs, strafing and attacking them with everything they had. The Sandys had great loiter time and they would fly slow and continue to attack the enemy on the ground. The Super Jollies had mini guns, a .50-caliber machine gun, and [troops aboard would have] M-16s and .45-caliber sidearms."

For their part, any pilots who were downed had a protocol to follow as well.

"The survivors would call on guard channel and would follow instructions about when to release 'smoke' to help guide the rescue forces. They would either talk to them as soon as they went down or when directed to do so. All crew members were equipped with locator beacons which directed rescue forces to them. The helicopters would have a 'high bird' and a 'low bird'. The low bird would be the primary rescue bird, and would hover over the survivor(s) and would lower a jungle penetrator for the survivor(s) if they were not injured, or pararescue specialist (PJ) on a jungle penetrator, who would be lowered into the jungle to help an injured survivor and fight off any Viet Cong or North Vietnamese."

The high bird was designated as the responsible aircraft should the crew of the low bird need extraction along with the survivors.

"I flew orbits with the Jollys but was only on one actual successful rescue. I was in the high bird and the Army helicopter crew was successfully extracted by the low bird. When we dropped them back at their unit, there was a great celebration (and a case of champagne). And when we returned to Da Nang there was another wonderful celebration."

On those flights, Fuller was not a fully-fledged crew member, having flown far fewer flight hours than the regular USAF crews. Technically, he was classified as an observer, though he is quick to point out, "I did fire the mini-guns in anger a few times."

When he thinks about the 3d ARRG, Fuller said, "I never knew such dedicated individuals. They truly believed in their mission and all were willing to go into the valley of death to save a downed brother in combat."

It's no wonder then that the pararescuers' motto is "So that others may live."

Fuller's thoughts then turned to Armed Forces Radio and TV Service. Though he was the CO for the bureau in Spain years before arriving in Vietnam, and would be assigned Commander of the AFRTS Broadcast Center in Los Angeles (Sun Valley) between 1989 and 1993, as what he called being a "customer" of AFRTS, he cannot sing its praises enough for what AFRTS meant to our troops in Vietnam.

"It was a real morale booster for those of us who had access. It provided news that was uncensored, sports, entertainment, and information. TV network news and sports came days after original airing in the States. It seemed strange to watch football games days after you had heard the results on AFRTS or read accounts in *Stars and Stripes*.

During Fuller's tour in Vietnam, one of the AFRTS Saigon bureau's mainstays was "The Weather Girl," Jane Lewis, the attractive wife of former NBC Correspondent, George Lewis, whom Fuller called "truly professional."

"She brought class and beauty to the audience. The staff at the TV and radio networks were important to all of us. A touch of home was true because they provided a valuable bridge to home and family."

While the troops within ear or eye shot got their taste of home through the radio and TV services, the loved ones back home got a taste for what their men and women in uniform were going through via cassette tapes, according to Fuller.

"The soldiers in the field were pretty much separated from those great services, except when on home bases. The tapes were very important to me, too," he admitted.

Fuller's thoughts, when he thinks about Vietnam today, are many. "I always thought Vietnam would be a beautiful place if there wasn't a war going on. I was usually the 'guide' for our unit members visiting the headquarters because I knew the good restaurants, the parts of Saigon to avoid, and the way to stay reasonably safe in the city," Fuller said.

According to him, those rules were: "That there was safety in numbers. We tried to always be with several others in town. Always make sure at least one member of the group stayed sober. Keep aware of your surroundings. Don't go looking for trouble."

And it was only if trouble came to the headquarters in what Fuller described as "an expected or on-going Viet Cong or NVA attack" that weapons were dispersed.

"When there was an attack on the base, the duty officer would issue weapons and ammunition from a con-ex at our headquarters. During mortar/rocket attacks on the base you never knew where the shells or warheads were going."

No doubt the South Vietnamese soldiers on base felt the same way; however, according to Fuller, there was limited contact with the ARVN troops there. "Vietnamese Bachelor Officers' Quarters were next to our quarters, but we were separated by barbed wire. But from time to time, there was communication," he said.

One such time was when the Americans helped their South Vietnamese counterparts catch eels during a rain storm. "One night we invited them to a barbeque, but language was a big impediment," Fuller remembered.

He also remembers those who cleaned up their quarters: a young maid and her mother. "The mother was 'Mama-San' and the daughter was 'Baby-San.' During the World Series we had a pool with each square being 10 dollars. When everyone in our headquarters had picked our squares we still had one empty, so several of us put in the money and made it Baby-San's square. She won. Probably a year's wages. We had a presentation ceremony where she was given the money. We had an interpreter who tried to explain to her that the money was hers and that there was no ulterior motive involved."

When Baby-San didn't show up for work for several days, Fuller and others in his unit were worried that she somehow did not understand.

"When she finally returned and smiled when we greeted her, we saw she had had all of her teeth removed and replaced with gold teeth. We learned later that having gold teeth was a way for her to save the money we had given her. Hopefully she never smiled after the fall of Saigon," Fuller said.

In addition to the honorarium given to Baby-San, there were also celebrations for those in the unit who received orders for home or were "hailed," as Fuller put it, for jobs well done.

"We all had 'party suits' made with our names, rank, unit insignia and embroideries of our aircraft. Colors were based on the aircraft we flew. Since I was not aircrew but flew in all of our aircraft, I was unwilling to have green (Jolly Green HH-53), blue (HH-43 Pedro), or yellow (HC-130 King), or a rescue coordination center suit. So I had a purple suit with an HH-43 on the front and an HC-130 refueling an HH-53 on the back."

He also had the public affairs patch (a pen, a martini, a typewriter) with the motto "The last to know, the first to go" on it.

"These Hail and Farewells were huge for maintaining unit morale and a good way to say good-bye and welcome to our [new] teammates," he added.

During morning staff meetings, one of Fuller's roles was to provide news media briefings regarding what *Stars and Stripes* and the civilian media were reporting. "It was a check on our intelligence briefing and provided a look at how the war was perceived by the media," Fuller said. He became his unit's historian for the last three-quarters of his assignment in Vietnam.

Fuller's time in-country allowed him time to do a lot of humanitarian work off base. He was the liaison for a nearby Catholic orphanage.

"We loaded a pick-up truck cab and bed or two with our people, food, and toys and drove to the orphanage. I met with the Mother Superior and several nuns along with our other officer and enlisted and enjoyed wonderful iced tea and a fried banana."

But that was not all that occurred at the orphanage.

"I would teach the nuns English while the others went and played with the kids. After the English lessons, I would join in playing with the kids. It was a break from the war for us and fun for the kids. When I was not there, we had others who would drive to the orphanage, but they usually did not try teaching English."

At Christmas time Fuller and the others provided a toy for each child as well as several for them to share.

"We also collected enough money to buy hams, and canned food from the commissary (which we could not normally use since it was there 'for embassy personnel,' and we had to have special permission for a 'unit function' to be able to use it). The nuns told us what they wanted in the way of food. We then gave them several hundred dollars as well. We normally gave them upwards of $100 in Vietnamese currency each week, collected at headquarters."

In spite of being inundated with mission after mission both on post and in the field, throughout his tour in Vietnam, Rick Fuller was able to establish an exercise routine that he religiously carried out.

"I ran almost every day for the year. We had a five-laps-to-the-mile track at Tan Son Nhut, and I would run at lunch time. When visiting units or flying missions, I always made time to run at whatever base on which I was sleeping. One time we flew a night orbit and I ended up at Nakhon Phanom [Thailand] at about 4am I was too stoked to sleep, so I jogged to the track and was running laps to dissipate the adrenaline. On one lap, I jumped over a branch on the track. Another jogger started running on the opposite side. As he got to where I had jumped over the branch, he let out a blood-curdling scream. I yelled to ask him what was wrong. He replied he had just jumped over a cobra. We both sped off the track and I went to bed."

Thankfully, that was the only time Rick Fuller had to ponder the possibility of being struck by a cobra. He retired after a career that spanned 30 years in the Air Force, taught for most of a year at Hollywood High School in Los Angeles, and served 11 years as the Director of Communications for various organizations within McDonnell Douglas (later Boeing) from which he retired in 2005.

Captain Rick Fuller, US Air Force Public Affairs Staff Officer, 3d Aerospace Rescue and Recovery Group, Tan Son Nhut Air Base, Saigon, (right) with his brother-in-law, Airman Don Bolduc. (Rick Fuller collection)

Memorializing the Troops: Roger Hawkins

The opening scenes of the first film to deal seriously with the Vietnam War, *The Deer Hunter*, could very well have paralleled to the young life of Roger Hawkins, who wielded cameras as a trooper in the 221st Signal Company Pictorial. Roger is from "Steelertown. Pittsburgh, PA," as he called it. His father worked in a steel mill right next to the Allegheny River, and Roger did what many young men were doing in 1967: he entered the service. One year later, in June of 1968, having completed Army boot camp, he found himself in the Republic of South Vietnam. It was *The Deer Hunter* redux.

But his introduction to the military actually preceded the Army. As a graduate of the Valley Forge Military Academy in Wayne, Pennsylvania, he walked the same halls as the likes of author J. D. "Catcher in the Rye" Salinger, playwright Edward Albee, and General "Stormin' Norman Schwarzkopf, commander of the Armed Forces during Gulf War I. From there, Roger earned a Bachelor of Fine Arts degree from Carnegie Mellon University.

"At the beginning of my junior year it was apparent that, as a male of my age, I was likely to end up in Vietnam, so I applied to the ROTC program. I was given credit for two years of ROTC for my Valley Forge experience. At the end of my senior year, I was commissioned a 2d lieutenant in the US Army Signal Corps."

But it was the BFA that Roger had earned from Carnegie Melon that predicated his assignment to the Photo Officers Course at Ft. Monmouth, New Jersey.

"I still know the difference between Frequency Division Multiplexing and Time Division Multiplexing," he said. "Photo school at Ft. Monmouth was far more to my liking. The warrant officer in charge of housing could be bribed into saying there were no more quarters at the fort, so I was able to move off base."

That, too, was to Hawkins' liking because there was a private women's college nearby, and the Officers Club at Monmouth was a private golf course that had been sold to the Army during the Depression.

Needless to say, Hawkins "thrived in that environment. I left Ft. Monmouth with a 8500/8511 MOS, which meant I was theoretically a pictorial unit commander and motion picture director. I took an introduction to photography course at Carnegie Mellon University, and the Army put me through the Photo Unit Commanders/Motion Picture Directors Course in which I worked with a wide range of still and motion picture cameras."

From there, Hawkins received orders assigning him to the Department of the Army Special Photographic Office (DASPO) at the Pentagon.

"I have a neighbor who is a well-known Air Force major general. His dad was the second director of the CIA. I reminded him that he spent his long career working his way up to the Pentagon while I started my Army experience and rapidly worked my way down to Vietnam," Hawkins joked.

For Hawkins, the DASPO experience was interesting,

When he wasn't making long chains out of paper clips, he "critiqued film from DASPO teams around the world. I led film teams in the streets of Washington, D.C. when it was under siege from anti-war protestors and during the Poor Peoples March. Martin Luther King had been killed, and Bobby Kennedy had been killed. Parts of D.C. were on fire. There were sandbagged bunkers near the White House, and you could see smoke rising all over the city. I led my team of short-haired photojournalists all over the city looking for hot spots."

Hawkins noted that there were no cell phones and no GPS in the 1960s. "I was issued a bag of dimes to call into HQ from public phone booths. We had a helicopter team testing a live airborne TV link to the Army chiefs of staff at the Pentagon."

When the generals wanted to see a location on the ground, they would look it up in a Thomas Guide map book and have a conversation with the aircraft commander that probably went something, Hawkins recalled, like this: "Your photographers on the ground say they are hearing gunfire near their location, so fly over to page 35 column C row 7." The aircraft commander would look that up in his own copy of the Thomas Guide and point the pilot in the right direction.

"And to mix things up a bit, I was asked to volunteer for two secret missions. But neither ever came to fruition, and I was never told where, when, or what the mission was."

For one mission, Hawkins was asked if he could set up a darkroom in the bathroom of a civilian hotel somewhere in Central America or the Caribbean. Nothing ever came of the assignment, but shortly afterward there were newspaper headlines about the dictator Omar Torrijos being deposed.

On another occasion, he was asked if he could operate a motion picture camera in a waterproof housing. Hawkins was very interested in diving at the time and had dived on an old Spanish wreck in the Caribbean, the *El Infante* from a 1733 pirate fleet. However, he demurred because he wasn't actually a certified scuba diver.

"The answer was, 'No worries L-T. This is not an underwater assignment. You will be wearing a chemical, biological, and radiological suit, and the camera will be in the underwater housing just so we can wash the housing and decontaminate it.'"

Hawkins almost turned down the assignment, but his curiosity was aroused and he agreed.

"No one told me any secrets, and I was never called on to perform the mission, whatever it might have been. Still it wasn't long before the media was screaming about a chemical warfare test going wrong at the Dugway Proving Grounds in Utah. Of course, it's pure speculation on my part about either of those events being related to the requests for a volunteer. Anyway that was my prelude to Vietnam.

"One day I was returning to the DASPO office from lunch in the Pentagon and the E7 who was in charge of getting things done stopped me and said, 'have new orders for you. How would you like to go to the jungle?' Being a strong advocate of wishful thinking, I was sure he was referring to DASPO's Panama detachment. Of course not; I was on my way to Vietnam and the 221st.

Once in Vietnam, Hawkins went straight to the headquarters of the 221st Signal Company (Pictorial) and SEAPC (Southeast Asia Pictorial Center).

"The 221st was an administrative unit dedicated to supplying photographers with food, pay, and discipline," Hawkins recalled.

"SEAPC handed out photographic assignments because there needed to be a buffer between colonels, generals, and the sweaty masses of raw talent in the form of young inexperienced officers, the enlisted photographers and artists."

Hawkins' first stop was the office of a young Intelligence Branch major who was running SEAPC.

"Little did I know that many years later, he would go to the dark side. This was Halen V. Peake, who would leave the Army to work in both the operations and the technical directorates of the CIA. But that was to be far in the future. At the time, he just wanted to know 'What would you like to do in Vietnam, Lieutenant?'

"I was surprised. The Army usually told rather than asked. I didn't even know what was on the menu. I was told I could be in charge of a photo lab or the graphics shop and stay in the safety of Long Binh, or I could be sent up country as a Detachment Commander. We had a brief conversation about life expediencies. That did not go well. He thought I was trying to be funny, but for him it was an important issue."

Hawkins' Pentagon experience convinced him that he wanted to be as far from headquarters as possible. He opted for the command of Detachment A at An Khe. While he was waiting for orders to be cut and processed, Peake gave him two assignments: One was to take a motion-picture cameraman and photograph the testing of VC weapons that ARVN had captured.

"A somewhat functioning alcoholic and I went over to an ARVN facility where they had built test bunkers and were firing captured RPGs at various protective walls like brick, concrete, sandbags, and mud filled drums."

Fifty years later, someone looked at Hawkins' photos of the black drums with an orange stripe around them and exclaimed, "Did you know those were Agent Orange drums?"

"In the intervening years, a cancer grew in the back of my leg until it was the size of a large orange. It was a mixed soft tissue sarcoma and the VA would not give me disability, but that's another story."

The second probationary assignment was photographing the testing of fighting fires with buckets of water (large buckets of water slung under helicopters). That done, it was off to An Khe and rebuilding a somewhat abandoned detachment there. That was followed by moving the detachment to Pleiku. After being in Pleiku for a while, he was reassigned to a small roving combat photo team that would operate in all four corps.

According to Hawkins, officers were supposed to lead and not photograph. But a lot of what went on in Vietnam did not go by the book.

Hawkins operated both still- and motion-picture cameras on many occasions. And the list of the equipment he and other soldiers with the 221st took with them into battle could fill the walls of a camera store.

"The Bell and Howell Film weighs approximately 4.739939lb. Ten 100-foot film rolls is about another 5lb. Throw in a copy of the American Cinematographers manual, some filters, lens cleaner, wipes, and a light meter, and you are probably close to 12lb," Hawkins joked. "The Bell and Howell was spring wound. The other two cameras required battery belts and there were no recharging stations out in the jungle.

"I much preferred the German Arriflex but could not get my hands on one in Vietnam. There was also a Beckman and Whitley, which was a piece of crap. The humidity in Vietnam caused the film emulsion to swell and stick in the film gate of their CM-16. They had to ship technicians to Vietnam because of the problem," he said.

"The still cameras many of us used were our own equipment. I used a Yashicamat 120 Twin Lens Reflex, a Yashica 35mm, a 35mm Pentax Spotmatic, and a 4×5 press camera. The Army supplied Graphlex XLs, Leica 35mm rangefinders, Cambo 4×5 studio cameras, and a Besseler Topcon (a Japanese 35mm camera marketed by the Amerilab company to get around the Buy America Act). There were probably others that I have forgotten."

With all that imposing equipment the photographer/soldiers carried in order to record the war for the Army itself as well as the American public back home, Hawkins is nonetheless of the opinion that troops from the 221st did not get in the way of the missions of the troops photographed, and that there was no ill will between them and those troops.

"There was never animosity. The troops seemed to know they could die at any minute and appreciated being memorialized. There was one Intel major who said we couldn't photograph some busted PT76 tanks. He was so pissed at me for insisting we were authorized that he did not realize that, while he was berating me, one of my photographers continued to photograph. The photographer finished his job and put in a fresh roll of film. And when the major asked for his film, the photographer took the film out without rewinding it and held the raw film up to the sun and handed him the fully over-exposed roll."

While Hawkins was not particularly afraid of the encounter with the angry officer it did not mean that fear was not lurking around the next bend. It was never far from anyone who lived the Vietnam experience, Hawkins feels.

"Fear is an interesting phenomenon. It's a good thing if you can manage it and a destructive thing if it manages you. There is the 'fright or flight concept'. If a deer runs from a hunter, it is generally good for the deer. But if a deer crossing a road freezes in your headlights, he gets wounded or killed.

"One thing I can tell you is that the anticipation of combat is stronger and more protracted than what happens in combat itself. That is fear minus the adrenalin. It gives you time to rehearse all the many terrible ways to die. Once in the field, there is a level of exhaustion and discomfort that takes over your mind. Your thinking is reduced to left foot right foot, left foot right foot, left foot right foot, swat that mosquito, left foot right foot, ad infinitum.

"Then there is the 'holy shit we are being shot at' phase when your body itself goes on full auto and your brain goes into hyper-drive. I struggle to describe what happens."

But he does not struggle long.

"You consider fewer options than you would in normal times because you are constrained by reaction time. Leisurely contemplation is a luxury. You are actually driven to a level above fear. I don't know what to call it. You can still think, but you can no longer stop to think. The imperative to take an action, any action, overtakes pondering about death and dismemberment.

"You might freeze, curl up in a fetal position, run away, stand and fight, or charge the enemy. Much depends on how you have been trained or conditioned by all your life's experience up to the current moment.

"But adrenaline only takes you so far. You can only produce and absorb so much. Battles are definitely physical, but the decisive moment is mental when one side or the other believes all options are exhausted."

Hawkins feels that it is somewhat of a different scenario for the combat photographer, however.

"A photographer is somewhat distracted from these emotions by the art and technical decision-making of photographs. But as soon as you take your eye from the viewfinder you are back in the violence of the real world. Your brain can only do so much. To the extent you are concerned with photography, you are distracted from the physical conflict. It is the impending danger that plays more with your mind than real danger. Once you start to go over the falls, you just grab the sides of the boat and hang on. After it is over, and the adrenaline is gone, you shake like a leaf."

Hawkins would "shake like a leaf" many times during his tour of duty in Vietnam, occasionally having to choose between his cameras and his weapon. It was no different for other troops in the 221st. However, the mission the photographers went out on determined the weaponry they toted into battle. Photographers were issued .45-caliber semi-automatic pistols.

"I was also issued an M-14 that rotted away in a wall locker for a year. When I turned it in before going home there was green mold growing on the stock. On other operations, I borrowed M-16s and a pump shot gun."

The conversation turned to *Stars and Stripes* photographer Al Rockoff, who gained notoriety as a civilian journalist by the film *The Killing Fields*, which gut-wrenchingly detailed the genocide suffered by the Cambodian people at the hands of despot Pol Pot and his Khmer Rouge cadres. Estimates range from one to three million Cambodians tortured to death.

"Rockoff got a hold of a Swedish K submachine gun which got his OIC [Officer-in-Charge] reamed by a general. Most people were confused by the sudden appearance of unannounced military photographers, and we could get away with more questionable actions than most soldiers.

Another civilian photographer in Vietnam whom Hawkins remembered well interacting with was the legendary British "snapper," as he calls himself, Tim Page.

"While my sergeant, Darryl Arizo, and I were away photographing a Mike Force, Page came by my photo lab in Pleiku and asked my lab techs to do a snip test. When I got back, the lab tech was all excited because Page was one of the big names among civilian photographers. I've since had a chance to talk to Page, who does not remember our earlier encounter."

But Hawkins is quick to point out that Page suffered a serious head wound that affects him to this day. It was the result of friendly fire while Page was aboard a US Coast Guard vessel off the coast of South Vietnam.

"Page gave me a photo of his friend Sean [son of actor Errol] Flynn, who had come to Vietnam to pose as a model in a photo shoot for *Paris Match* as if he were a photojournalist. Flynn ended up staying and becoming one of the most renowned photographers of the war. That was shortly before Flynn disappeared along with fellow journalist Dana Stone in Cambodia. That photo was in return for a photo of a Montagnard chief smoking a pipe and wearing a blue velour sweater," Hawkins recalls.

Sometime in 2004, he also communicated with the late diminutive French photojournalist Catherine Leroy, who had come to Vietnam with a Leica and $100, having never photographed anything other than her cats in her Paris apartment. Hawkins got her to donate a copy of her book *Under Fire: Great Photographers and Writers in Vietnam* to the now defunct International Combat Camera Association. The book contained many of her most haunting photos, which graced the pages of both *Life* and *Look* magazines for which she filed.

Relations with media while Hawkins was attached to DASPO in Washington, D.C., was quite a different story.

"We rubbed shoulders with media people in the streets all the time but avoided interpersonal contact because we were dressed as civilians and didn't want to answer any difficult questions."

Vietnam was the exact opposite. There was an abundance of interpersonal contact with people. Especially the enemy.

In the early part of 1969, Hawkins' team was on Operation *Lamar Plains* with a unit of the 101st Airborne Division. He later heard it described as one of the largest "least reported" operations in Vietnam. In other words, it was a hard-fought operation that garnered very little press coverage in proportion to the fierceness and size of the struggle.

The first day they choppered into a battle in progress. It was over a hundred degrees and near 95 percent humidity, according to Hawkins. The fighting was in pretty close. Due to mental and physical strain, Hawkins passed out. He was given salt pills and water by a medic and continued to function somewhat normally.

"Well enough to take a photo used by the *Washington Post* 40 years later," he remembered.

The second day Hawkins and his team started to move off a hilltop when they received artillery fire.

"We had just got that mess cleared up and begun to move when we received stiff enemy resistance. My three photographers and I became separated in the action. After a while, I had shot all of my motion-picture film and switched to a waterproof Nikonos still-photograph diving camera that could be operated one-handed and could be cleaned by dunking it into a stream."

Before long, Hawkins had shot the last of his still film. With no film left, he decided to "temporarily join the Infantry."

"I checked my M-16 (borrowed and untested) and stood up behind the berm of the rice paddy where our infantry was online. I expected to see the enemy but could only hear a massive volume of small-arms fire and see a tree line in front of me. I clicked the selector on the M-16 to full auto and planned to spray the whole tree line. Pop, one shot was all I got. I jumped down behind the berm and popped the magazine out. It was full except for the one round.

"I jammed the mag back in and pulled the receiver back and looked in the chamber. The brass from my first round was still there. I jacked the receiver several more times and the shell casing would not come out. I asked the guy next to me what to do. He suggested I crawl down the line to the machine gunner who had a cleaning rod.

"I did that and knocked the spent brass out. I thought, 'Problem solved.'"

Hawkins crawled back and tried again, but had the same result.

"Now I had fired two rounds down range and at an enemy I could not see. This time I asked where the platoon leader was. I went in the direction indicated and found him. At this point, he was not even aware he had a photographer with him. I explained I was out of film and without a functioning weapon and asked if there was anything I could do for him.

He asked Hawkins, "Are you willing to take some walking and crawling wounded back to the rear?" Hawkins answered in the affirmative.

"I fell to the end of the group to help a guy that was shot in the ass. At some point, he expressed concern about his family jewels. Since much of the back of his pants had been shot or cut away, and I was crawling behind him, I was able to assure him that everything was hanging normal."

Hawkins and the rest of the "Screamin' Eagles" had to crawl through an irrigation canal to avoid enemy fire. Water leaked into ten cans of motion-picture film, and he lost 1,000 feet of prime combat footage. They arrived at the rear, whereupon Hawkins found his face covered with blood from the wounded trooper in front of him.

A medic ran up and wanted to examine Hawkins for a head wound, which he didn't have.

"I'd been deafened by artillery and aerial bombing and could not understand that I was okay, but I got the medic pointed toward the butt-hurt trooper."

That would not be the last of Hawkins' unit missions during which decisions had to be made whether to snap a photo or pull the trigger.

In the jungles west of the Central Highlands city of Ban Me Thuot in 1969, they were operating with a Mike Force out of Pleiku.

"I'm not sure what we were accomplishing, but I did learn many years later that we had a couple of Army Security Agency people with us talking to EC47 electronic warfare planes flying overhead with Vietnamese speakers aboard, listening to enemy unencrypted radio transmissions on the ground. Those translators could tell us in real time what the enemy was doing and saying, and they sent it to us in real time via a secret voice encrypted radio handset."

Hawkins and his unit also patrolled with the mechanized infantry of the Big Red One (1st Infantry Division) through the Michelin Rubber Plantation called "Terre Rouge" (Red Earth) near An Loc northwest of Saigon.

"We saw signs of activity and were able to take pot shots at a few of them, but they were a ghostly presence that managed to stay just ahead of us."

They also picked up a lot of ARVN wounded flying with the Air Ambulances of the 82d Medical Detachment stationed in Can Tho in the Mekong Delta.

Hawkins personally patrolled with LRRPs from the 173d Airborne.

"Those were six-man patrols, so generally it would have been a failure on our part if we got in a firefight with the enemy. Not something you want to do when there are only six on a team," he stressed.

In 1968, they were patrolling west of An Khe. "It was a black night, and we were watching from a hilltop when we spotted about 50 flashlights in the jungle below us. We did not have our fingers on any triggers, but we had maps and radios and called in an artillery mission on the group. In spite of that, some got through and mounted a short mortar attack on An Khe."

Thinking back 48 years, it becomes easy for Hawkins to philosophize about the war. "This may sound stupid, but finding the war was the hardest part. US dominance was peaking in 1968 and 1969. This was post-Tet, and the enemy was still recovering. You would hear about something happening and by the time you arrived, it was all over. This was also compounded by my own inexperience," he admitted.

Among the upsides to Hawkins' time in Vietnam was his interaction with the people most affected by the tragedy of the war: the people of Vietnam.

"The easiest thing was documenting positive aspects of Vietnamese culture. A Vietnamese friend here in the US once called me the most Third World American he has ever known. I think this was a comment about my appreciating Vietnamese culture, but I am not sure. Rather than asking, I just decided to take it as a compliment."

Roger Hawkins' work and connection to Vietnam as a still and mopic (motion picture) photographer did not end when he left Vietnam.

Long after Hawkins retired from the Army as a captain in the US Army Reserves, his Vietnam film was used in several History Channel documentaries and a Discovery Channel Wings documentary. His still photography appeared on the cover of the *Washington Post Book Review*, and in a Spear Point Publishing book called *The 101st Airborne: The Screaming Eagles*. At least six of his photos are in a show at the Pritzker Military Museum in Chicago. They also appeared in a show in the Cardinal Stritch University Art Museum. The Art of the American Soldier at the Constitutional Center in Philadelphia also accepted his work. One photo has appeared in an old copy of the Vietnam Veterans of America publication *VVA Veteran*.

"I'm sure some are in other places I don't know about," he said.

Hawkins has worked for civilian photo studios and for 16 years at Hitachi Data Systems, where he was editor and designer of the corporate magazine. He was also a volunteer editor/designer/webmaster for the International Combat Camera Association. "I've done perhaps 15 assignments for prestigious college and university alumni magazines," he said. In addition, he was the Communications Director and Photographer for Boyle Engineering Corporation, formerly one of the top consulting engineers and architects on the *Engineering News Record* list. "Now that I'm retired, I do what I want when I want, but it does not pay very well," he joked.

When asked to reflect on the 221st Signal Company Pictorial, Hawkins had this to say: "You would be surprised what I don't know about the 221st. I left the HQ within about a week of arriving in Vietnam and returned there about two weeks before heading back to the States. Contact with HQ was extremely sparse. I was wandering along undirected in the middle of arguably America's most contentious war."

Contentious for many, but the contention is not what he thinks about today. "In spite of the poor pay and danger, it was the best job and most fun I ever had."

But that does not mean that his MOS came without anything to complain about! "My biggest objection to the 221st was the lack of a feedback loop, especially in film. We never saw what we did until perhaps 30 to 40 year later when bits and pieces started appearing on TV. We didn't know our film was precooked in hot conex containers. We were unaware of camera malfunctions. We didn't know when our framing or exposure was off."

Today the new generation of military photographers is sent to Syracuse University for journalism classes, says Hawkins. They digitally edit and produce their own work and instantly see the successes and failures, he said. "But we paid the price for being pioneers," Hawkins feels.

When Roger reflects back to his time in Vietnam, he is able now to put things in a more proper perspective.

"Active combat was only one part of the story. People died there. Some of us got married there. We had many rich cross-cultural experiences. I have a photo of a butt-naked Montagnard right out of the jungle being trained to use an M-16. Years later a Montagnard woman contacted one of my photographers to thank him for the visual history he did of the Montagnard people. It turned out that she was working on Wall Street as a stock broker. Jungle to stock broker in one generation," he said.

Illinois Farm Boy Thrust into a Different World: Mike Boggs

Mike Boggs enlisted in the Marine Corps right out of high school in 1958 and after boot camp was assigned to the Air Wing at Marine Corps Air Station El Toro in Orange County, California. Fairly soon the Illinois farm boy found himself thrust into the completely different world of Iwakuni, Japan, where he arrived as a lance corporal with VCMJ-1, Marine Composite Reconnaissance Squadron.

Iwakuni was also his baptism into the world of military photography.

"Most of the work was in the photo lab using 4×5 speed graphic cameras," he said. Not only was Boggs hooked on Marine Corps photography, but like many young people who find themselves in the Orient at a young age, he was hooked on Japan.

"I would have stayed in Iwakuni for 20 years," he said. "I had responsibilities there. I was a 19-year-old kid supporting two bars downtown and one 200cc Martin motorbike on $80 a month."

In those days, there were 360 yen to the dollar, he remembers. "Beer was 200 yen, girls were a thousand yen, and it cost me US15 cents a gallon to fill up my bike."

But it wasn't all just riding, drinking, and girls for Mike Boggs.

"We did a lot of classified work, too," said Boggs, who had top-secret clearance at the time. He said he was also posted to Okinawa and Taiwan during an operation called *Blue Star* at Kang Shang, Taiwan, in March of 1960 when communist China began shelling Taiwan's inland territory.

Boggs rotated back to Marine Corps Air Station Cherry Point in North Carolina the night John F. Kennedy was elected president and remembers clandestine reconnaissance flights over Cuba at the time. His job was to take the film magazines out of the F-8U-1P Crusader aircraft that had been doing the fly overs and, owing to the top-secret nature of the flights, process the film himself.

Rather uncommonly for Marines, whose mantra is always "Once a Marine, always a Marine," in June of 1961 after mustering out of the Corps once his three-year enlistment was up, Boggs joined the Army in October that same year. With the photographic experience under his belt, and the rank of Spec-6, he hooked up with the 221st Signal Company Photographic (SEAPC) in June 1967 at its headquarters in Long Binh.

As Boggs reflects back on his service in Vietnam, it seems to him almost like a series of memoirs, many horrific, some comedic, as Boggs can be himself.

"I always carried a pound of C-4 to cook with," he laughed. "If you wanted to heat up a can of beans, a little C-4 will do it."

But it was no laughing matter when he was tasked with photographing Ambassador Ellsworth Bunker inspecting the American embassy in Saigon after it was overrun by the Viet Cong during the Tet Offensive of 1968—dead bodies were strewn about the compound.

Two months before, Boggs was ordered to get a Beckman and Whitley camera to film "some guy named George H. W. Bush" at Tan Son Nhut Air Base. "I didn't know who he was," said Boggs.

Representative Bush had come to Vietnam to pose for "Support Vietnam" statements. In some, he stood in foxholes. In others, he stood in front of barbed wire.

The climate really tested the limits of Beckman and Whitley cameras.

"It was a sound-on-film camera, and in the humidity and the weather we had in Vietnam, sometimes you had to keep your fingers crossed that the darn thing would work okay."

As it turned out, the day that Bush was paired with Boggs and Spec-4 Marty Neff, it didn't work.

"I received a letter from him stating that the film had skipped though the sound and exposure were good," Boggs remembered. He also recalls how, when first introduced to the man who would become the 41st president of the United States, Bush wondered where the film crew and the lighting were.

I told him, "No. it's just me, Spec-4 Neff, and our cameras."

George Bush was not the only president Boggs would come into contact with.

"I was also at Cam Ranh Bay with President Johnson and also at Vung Tau with Vice-President Hubert H. Humphrey. After I listened to Humphrey, I had a feeling that we had lost the war," Boggs said.

Nonetheless, the war, and one mission after another continued for Boggs.

On one such mission, he with out with the 4th Infantry Division near Pleiku out of LZ Oasa. "They were calling in Air Force 104 jets to make bombing runs on Charlie," Boggs said, using the nick name for Viet Cong cadres. "After about a week in the bush, I told our lieutenant it would be great to get some aerial shots of the jets making their runs."

Boggs' lieutenant gave him his approval and Boggs hooked up with an Air Force Bird Dog unit with call sign "Whiskey Cider." One week later, when Boggs returned to the LZ and told his superior that he'd spent a week with a nice bed, showers, and good food courtesy of the USAF, the lieutenant told him, "Next time, I'll do the aerial work."

Another operation with the 4th ID out of LZ Oasa put him with Echo Team. They moved in armored personnel carriers to a Montagnard village. After some time in the APCs they dismounted and walked a few miles through the darkness. Boggs turned to a Spec-4 on the march and whispered, "Yea, though we walk through the Valley of Death, my hand grenade comforts me."

Boggs just happened to be in Saigon during the Tet Offensive in 1968, but he didn't have much time for any New Year's celebrations. He was at BOQ [Bachelor Officer Quarters] #3 near Tan Son Nhut Air Base where a truckload of troops from the 716th Military Police Company had been ambushed and killed. There was a track vehicle that they wanted to go down the alley behind the BOQ.

"The track would not go because of a dead MP lying near the truck that had been ambushed. Charlie was still putting up a good fight for the area when an MP said he would go if someone else would go with him. I said, 'Let's go.'"

When they got to the dead MP, the man Boggs was with said, "He may be booby trapped." Boggs responded, "A grenade takes five seconds to go off and by that time, we'll be behind the truck."

The two of them picked up the dead MP then ran back to an armored personnel carrier and laid the body on top of it.

When they returned to the BOQ, Boggs was asked what the "hell" they had done. "Didn't you see all those bullets hitting around you?" the other troop asked. Boggs hadn't.

By coincidence, two months later, Boggs drew an assignment to film the same MP with whom he'd rescued the dead body receiving the Silver Star for his actions that day. He was given accolades for "going forward under fire and retrieving a dead MP so a tank could move down the alley behind BOQ #3."

Boggs, on the other hand, got an "Atta Boy" for that action and one paragraph at the bottom of a request for a Bronze Star written by a Lieutenant Bostrum.

Boggs got more than an "Atta Boy" for filming the 1/10 Air Cavalry in action though he remembers his first flight with a good deal of jocularity.

"We were flying along when I heard over my headset, 'There he goes! Get him!' At the same time the crew chief opened up with his M-60 machine gun. I also had an M-60 across my lap and didn't know whether to grab my camera or the M-60. I was looking around but could not see anything to shoot at … either with my camera or the 60."

Boggs came to find out that they were shooting at a deer to take back to a barbeque that night. He did eventually fire both his camera and the machine gun in the line of duty, but his humor prevails.

"I still think of the time that I could have gotten three NVA if I had just been fast enough with that M-60," he laughs. The humor stops, however, when he remembers a night operation when the Air Cavalry was fired upon by a ChiCom (Chinese Communist) .50-caliber machine gun.

"At the gun, it looked like it was shooting little green sparks, but when the bullets came by the helicopter, they looked like large green bowling balls," he said.

And that would not be the last time he was in the crosshairs of the enemy. During the 1968 Tet Offensive, Viet Cong cadres took what he called "a few pot shots" at him and a fellow troop from the 221st.

"I returned fire after a while. Until Spec-4 Neff said to me, 'I wish you would quit shooting at that guy. All you're doing is pissing him off.' So we proceeded to get up and get the hell out of there."

As he reflects back on his service in Vietnam, he thinks somewhat whimsically. "I always thought that some VC was sitting in the weeds, thinking, 'Look at that dummy. He brought a camera to a gun fight,'" he joked.

US Marine Corps combat correspondent Michael Boggs checking his camera as the bullets fly overhead, Phuoc Loc, Vietnam, 1967. (Michael Boggs collection)

From the Peace Corps to the Coast Guard, San Francisco to Vietnam: Donn Fry

After graduating from Denison University in Granville, Ohio, with a BA in English in June 1964, Donn Fry joined the Peace Corps and taught English and history for two years at a secondary school for boys in Tanzania, returning to the United States in December 1966.

"My draft board was waiting for me with open arms," Fry joked.

The reason being that, at that time, the Peace Corps was not a substitute for military service. Instead young men received deferments much the same as they did for college.

"I didn't want to be drafted. I might get sent to Vietnam, after all!" he added, "So I investigated the various branches—enlistment in the Coast Guard, Navy or Air Force meant four years of service—and I chose the Coast Guard. It had the redeeming feature, I felt, of being a military service primarily concerned with saving lives, not taking them."

Fry opted to join the Coast Guard in February 1967, and, quite ironically, the country that he wasn't very keen on going to, Vietnam became his duty station from January to August 1970, when the USCG turned over the last 82-foot patrol boat to the Vietnamese Navy at Cat Lo. This was a joint Navy/Coast Guard base at the top of the Mekong Delta, a few miles from Vung Tau, the old French colonial town formerly known as Cap St. Jacques, an in-country R&R site during the American tenure in Vietnam.

Before being sent to Vietnam, Fry had hopes of going to Officer Candidate School.

"I wanted to go to OCS, but the Coast Guard, being a small military service, had only two OCS classes a year: one was already selected and ready to begin, the other was a number of months away, and my draft board wouldn't wait."

Fry also had been accepted to graduate school at Indiana University, "but the board wouldn't defer me until I had 'done something about my military obligation to my country'—a view with which I profoundly disagreed. I don't believe that one has a *military* obligation to our country, though I wouldn't mind seeing a one- or two-year national service requirement with a wide range of options and something akin to the GI Bill for all participants," he believes today.

"Naive as I was at that time, I let the Coast Guard recruiter convince me that I could easily enter the next OCS class after enlisting and passing the exam. I'm still kicking myself for that one."

Fry took the test at Ft. Macon, North Carolina, passed it, and was sent to Norfolk, Virginia, for an interview before a board of officers.

"They clearly were suspicious of someone with a Peace Corps background, and when I truthfully indicated that I had serious reservations about American policy in Vietnam, I felt the door to OCS clanging shut."

Fry became a radio distress-call watch-stander at Ft. Macon, subsequently applied to JO school and was assigned to DINFOS (Defense Information School), then at Ft. Benjamin Harrison, Indiana, in the summer of 1968. Before that, the only journalism training he'd had was writing for his high-school newspaper.

"Being stationed at DINFOS was an odd coincidence: Indianapolis is my hometown, so I was able to live at home with my family during the three-month school. I never thought I'd ever live in Indianapolis during Coast Guard service," he said.

"Though I was not a willing participant in military service, I thought the training at DINFOS was generally first-rate, especially the training in straight news writing. It served me well in my later career."

After completing DINFOS training in early December 1968, Fry received orders to San Francisco and was stationed there at the district office downtown in the US government building on Sansome Street. He was there throughout 1969.

"As military duty goes, I can't complain. I lived in an apartment, first on Nob Hill, then in Pacific Heights. My main social outlet was playing rugby, which I had learned in Tanzania, for the San Francisco Rugby Club with all the beer-drinking and carousing that that entailed. I generally had a good time. My bosses in the public information office were JO1 Larry Nelson and Lieutenant Gil Shaw, two men I liked and respected."

Though it was a full two years past San Francisco's "Summer of Love" during which popular rock bands like the Grateful Dead, Jefferson Airplane, and Quicksilver Messenger Service regularly converged on Golden Gate Park along with thousands of hippies, the city's political ambiance was not antithetical to Fry's convictions on the Vietnam War.

"Throughout that year in San Francisco, my strong sympathies were with the anti-war movement. San Francisco, you may recall, was ground zero for resistance to the war, and there were many demonstrations and marches; I participated in a number of them, at least once in uniform to show that not all military personnel supported our Vietnam policy."

Ironic it was then that Fry should receive orders for Vietnam, though this did not come as a total shock to him as—according to Fry's fellow Coast Guard journalist, Commander Bob Douville—it did to other Coast Guardsmen who were stationed in San Francisco.

"I was somewhat surprised, though I knew it was a possibility. There was a billet for one journalist in the Coast Guard in Vietnam, a JO1 (E-6). By this time, I was a JO2 (E-5), but apparently I was the only journalist of a high-enough rating who still had at least one year remaining in his enlistment, so they chose me. I attempted to have the orders changed. I wrote a frank letter to the district legal officer and Coast Guard personnel outlining my feelings about the war and my desire for a different assignment. I was turned down, and in early January 1970 I was sent with a contingent of boatswain's mates and enginemen for a couple weeks of weapons training at Coronado and Camp Pendleton. Before the end of the month, we were in Saigon."

His impressions of "the Paris of the Orient," as Saigon was long known, are with him even today, 47 years after his service there.

"I was struck by the dilapidated beauty of the city, especially the old French colonial neighborhoods. But I was tense at first, and I actually remember the first time I touched a Vietnamese person–paying a cyclo driver on my first day in Saigon and feeling as if a small electric shock had gone through me. It wasn't fear; rather, it was like a concrete acknowledgement that I had finally arrived in a place and a situation that I had long resisted."

"Saigon had its charms. It was also crowded, chaotic, and filled with the tinny snarls of a zillion motorbikes. It often felt impossible to breathe because of the gasoline fumes. But I'd brought some civilian clothes, and I would often go out bar-hopping at night after curfew. If I was ever stopped by MPs or the Shore Patrol, I was prepared to adopt an Aussie accent and claim to be a civilian contractor and tell them to bugger off. Fortunately, I never had to perform that charade. I also liked to sit in the open-air lounge of the Continental Hotel and pretend I was in a Graham Greene novel."

The famed Continental was the locale of Greene's novel *The Quiet American* and two movies that sprang from his classic anti-American work about the waning days of French Indochina and the United States' early involvement in Southeast Asia. The likes of civilian journalists, secret agents, and ladies of the night frequented the hotel and told tales from true to tall, but this was not, unfortunately, where Fry was billeted.

"In Saigon, we lived in hotels taken over by the military, though I had no fixed bunk there because I was soon commuting back and forth to Cat Lo. I had to return to Saigon to develop my film and print my pictures in a Navy darkroom across the street from the building housing the Coast Guard's Saigon office, which was about an eight-story walkup in deep humidity. At night, if I wasn't cruising around downtown, we were smoking dope on the roof of the hotel. Or, if I had a hotel roommate I could trust, I'd be smoking weed with headphones on, listening to Cream or Donovan."

For many servicemen based or on R&R in Saigon, making the bar scene was common during the war. Donn Fry was no exception.

"One interesting experience I remember in Saigon, particularly in light of military developments during the Obama administration, was with my buddy Rick Martin, a yeoman at Cat Lo. He and I went to the bar at the Eden Roc Hotel on Tu Do Street. We were there early, and the bar was only gradually filling up. Usually a swarm of bar girls would descend on you, bargaining for a drink or a 'short-time,' but this bar was different. There were only about three women there, and they didn't give us the time of day," Fry recalled.

"As we drank our beers, and as the bar filled up, we gradually realized we were in a US military gay bar. Rick and I were sitting near the door, but there was a large, horseshoe-shaped bar where all the action was. Most surprising, it was totally mixed rank-wise: officers, petty officers, seamen—no rank was unwelcome, and everyone was on first-name terms. I saw Navy guys I knew, both officers and enlisted men, and I realized what dual, stressful lives they must have been living. My own brother was gay, and I could easily imagine him in such a setting. These were all good men in uniform, and I was profoundly happy when Obama did away with Clinton's cowardly Don't Ask, Don't Tell policy."

About half-way through the eight months Fry spent in-country, he was transferred to the joint US Navy/Coast Guard base at Cat Lo. But he also covered a good deal of other territory in-country.

"I was also sent on a couple trips to do hometown news stories on Coast Guardsmen elsewhere. One of those times I was on a USCG buoy tender along the coast, and we stopped at Qui Nhon up the coast, eventually reaching the base outside Da Nang, where a few Coasties were stationed. Another time I spent a few days at Cam Ranh Bay, where a number of the bosons I trained with were stationed, supervising and keeping watch over ammunition off-loading operations."

Fry also made one trip aboard one of the Coast Guard's 82-foot cutters, otherwise known as "WPBs" into the Mekong Delta combat zone.

"The Cat Lo commander had taken a dislike to me, and he sent me along on patrol up some rivers in the Delta. There was absolutely no reason for me to be there. 'News' was unlikely to be made, no matter what happened, and no hometowners were to be written. I didn't even carry a weapon, and I remember sitting on the foredeck, between a couple of 50-calibers as we cruised down a river.

"'Listen for a gunshot from that tall tree down there,' said the chief (second in command, after a lieutenant CO). 'He's warning his men further down the river.' It happened just as the chief said. I felt supremely stupid sitting there in my flak jacket.

I was nothing but a target. I had been told that if the boat were hit, it would come from the side, amidships, at water level, so below deck in the galley wasn't a great place to be. But I eventually went down and stretched out on a bench. I thought, 'If I'm going to get it today, I don't want to see it coming, and I sure as hell don't want to just make myself a bullseye above deck,'" Fry said.

"Later, we ruined the day for some Vietnamese in their dugout, confiscating their cargo—food—and lashing the dugout alongside the 82. We also picked up a contingent of the so-called Kit Carson Scouts, Vietnamese commandos who would go where no one else would go. We dropped them off in the jungle."

Fry states that there was a prelude to the Cat Lo Coast Guard commander's decision to send him on that patrol. That happened when Fry drew Shore Patrol duty, which, says he, "amounted to checking out the string of shanties and lean-to bars across the road from the base.

"I had already determined that I was not going to carry, or use, a weapon in Vietnam. I was not going to shoot anyone for any reason. Of course, you were expected to carry a rifle or sidearm on SP duty. I told the chief I would be happy to take SP that night, but I wouldn't carry a weapon. The chief, to his credit, was okay with that, but word apparently got upstairs. I remember the XO berating me for taking such a stand; he noted that he had looked into my record and read my exchanges with the legal office in San Francisco. He fumed a bit, and that was it. I went on SP duty unarmed."

It is safe to say that Fry much preferred the confines of his work station at Cat Lo on the ground floor of a two-story frame building to Shore Patrol. At Cat Lo, the only thing he had to be mindful of was the office upstairs from his, where the CO, the yeomen, and storekeepers were quartered.

"Mercifully his office was air conditioned. A couple of other guys had desks near me, and I don't recall any large output of 'work' from any of us. We had a fridge for old rusty cans of Carling Black Label and a TV. I remember watching the Knicks win the 1970 NBA championship while we were allegedly working. Basically, it was a case of out-of-sight, out-of-mind as far as our officers were concerned, and we took royal advantage of that fact. I don't think any of my commanders in Vietnam had a clue as to what I was supposed to be doing there."

"Allegedly working" is not exactly accurate, however, as Fry daily wrote "home-towners," the type of journalism created and honed by Ernie Pyle

"I probably turned out one or two hometowners a day," Fry said. "The stories were basically glorified captions for the photos I took, probably not much more than one typewritten page, double-spaced. I would have to wait until I got up to Saigon to develop and print the photos, then match them up with the stories.

"They were always something like: 'Engineman 2nd Class John Smith, of Nevada City, California, shows Vietnamese Navy man Trung Ho Dao how to service the pressure valve on a diesel engine powering their 82-foot Coast Guard patrol boat.

Smith, a 1968 graduate of Nevada City High School, is serving with Coast Guard Division 13 at a naval base in Cat Lo, South Vietnam. He expects to return to the US in the late summer, after his patrol boat is decommissioned by the Coast Guard and recommissioned as a vessel in the Vietnamese Navy … blah, blah, blah.'"

Fry further defines the day-to-day missions of a Coast Guard JO as "nuts and bolts stuff, but I had to gather information and backgrounds on each of my fellow Coasties. After printing the photos and attaching the stories in Saigon, I generally consulted *Ayres Directory* to find any applicable local papers. It was my habit to mail the stories/photos directly to the editors of the hometown papers, though I was supposed to channel them through the Great Lakes Naval Base in Chicago. I had a higher success rate in placing stories directly than if I had done it as I was supposed to," he said.

On weekends, Fry was able to let the hometowners sit for a couple days.

"We frequently took a truck into Vung Tau and spent the day on the R&R beach. Sometimes we went surfing, or tried to, since we were generally wrecked by mid-afternoon. So we spent our time listening to Filipino rock bands doing Trini Lopez covers."

When the weekend and Vung Tau were behind him, Fry was not always stuck at a desk knocking out stories in Cat Lo, however.

"I traveled back and forth frequently, sometimes catching rides on a military chopper, sometimes in Coast Guard vehicles going in either direction. Once I rode up to Saigon on a Thai Navy ship, and the Thais treated me like an officer. We had a great evening at a couple of Thai restaurants in Saigon, and they wouldn't let me pay for a thing."

Sometimes Fry was tasked with work that was not a part of his Coast Guard rating. "Besides my work in the Navy darkroom and mailing off hometowners, I sometimes would be assigned menial office tasks by the XO. I remember the CO once assigning me to be a bartender and waiter at a cocktail party he was having at his quarters, a nice old French colonial townhouse. It was a sort of fraternal gathering, on a first-name basis (just for the occasion) between officers and my fellow enlisted men."

It was not uncommon in Vietnam for the civilian media covering the war to mingle with uniformed combat correspondents, photographers, and public-affairs officers like Fry and end up bringing a service member's story to national attention back in the United States. That very well may have happened to Fry.

"A few months before the turnover of the last [WPB] 82 in Cat Lo, I sent out a press release to all the US media in Saigon, noting the impending wrap-up of the USCG mission in Vietnam. I provided facts and statistics and descriptions of the Coast Guard's various jobs in-country. ABC News bit on it, and I subsequently arranged to accompany a reporter and his crew to Cat Lo, where he interviewed the CO—the one who didn't like me and had ordered me on Shore Patrol—and cruised around the river with him as he explained the Guard's mission at the base. It was supposed to appear in Sam Donaldson's newscast the following Saturday evening, and I sent a message to Coast Guard HQ in Washington, asking them to monitor the program in case the story was included. I never learned if it was, but you might find it in ABC's archives, probably from June or July 1970."

Overall, when Fry compares his duties in Saigon and Cat Lo, he feels there was not too much difference.

"The work was pretty routine in both places, but I developed more friends among my fellow Coasties in Cat Lo, and even among Vietnamese people. However, Saigon had plenty of massage parlors and steam-bath joints, something Cat Lo lacked," he says.

And while the CO who ordered Fry aboard the WPB 82 for Shore Patrol was not one of his favorite human beings, he had nothing but praise for another one.

"The last CO at Cat Lo for the final three or four three months was a man I already knew: Commander Louis Gatto, who, in one of those coincidences that often happened in a service branch as small as the Coast Guard, was also the last CO I had had at Ft. Macon. He was a good man whom I liked and respected," Fry said.

When his tour in Vietnam ended, Fry preferred to return to San Francisco, but he was ordered to Governors Island, New York.

"I enjoyed Governors Island for that brief period. My best friend and his wife lived in Manhattan and I saw them often. Also, I had made JO1 (E-6) while in Vietnam, so that allowed me to see a bit of the Guard I hadn't seen before, like the inside of the Chief's Club, where 1st Class was welcome. I mainly spent my days drinking coffee in the public information office and working, somewhat half-heartedly, on a script for a film about the Coast Guard's role in that particular district.

Fry does not remember the film being completed, but he does remember his direct superior, Chief Larry Worth, whom he called "a kind and thoughtful man" and liked a lot.

Donn Fry served four years in the Coast Guard and rose to the rank of Journalist, 1st Class. "I was rather proud of that; people didn't normally make E-6 in their first enlistment," he said.

After Fry left the Coast Guard in 1971, he was able to follow through on his deferred plan to attend graduate school at Indiana University, from which he earned an MA in English in 1973. It was there that he also met his wife Diane, who was finishing up her Ph.D. in English when Fry was just beginning graduate studies.

He did not stay away from journalism for long, however. He took a job as a news reporter, first at a small-town daily near Indianapolis, then at the *Indianapolis Star*, where he became the art critic and book editor. He also spent three years with the Associated Press at its Indianapolis bureau. In 1982, he received a job offer from the *Seattle Times* and went there as the arts and entertainment editor. Later, Fry became the book editor for many years and retired when he was 56, in 1998, after calling Seattle home for 30 years, 16 of which Fry filed as a writer, columnist, and editor at the *Times*.

"After retiring, I studied drawing and painting at a small art academy in Seattle. We also owned a country music radio station in the North Cascades mountains for a few years. But that's another story."

Requested Vietnam Duty on Friday, the 13th: Chris Jensen

In November 1968, Chris Jensen was living a typical 1960s life—at home in Columbus, Ohio, attending Ohio State University and majoring in photojournalism.

"I loved photojournalism but wasn't paying attention to other classes. In one of those 'less-than-brilliant' teenage moves, I decided to enlist in the US Army so that I could return as a more mature and serious student," he said.

In order for that to happen, Chris went down to the Army recruiter and signed up for 36 months of wearing the uniform so he was guaranteed a job as a photographer.

Chris thought it was the logical move. His parents, however, didn't quite see it the same way. "You will break your mother's heart," his father told him.

"My mother drove me to the enlistment center and on the way offered to drive me to Canada if I wanted to change my mind."

Canada was not in the cards for Jensen. He did basic training at Ft. Jackson, South Carolina, and then photo school at Ft. Monmouth, New Jersey, which he termed "a pretty good school and easy assignment."

Upon graduation, most of Jensen's class got orders for Vietnam. He and another graduate got orders for Ft. Hood, Texas.

"The only thing we could figure out was that we were supposed to photograph some unit probably getting ready to go to Vietnam. If I'd known I was going to be struck at Ft. Hood, I would have volunteered for Vietnam," Jensen said.

"I got to Ft. Hood and was told the Army didn't care about my training. They needed armored recon scouts and that was my new job. I found out there was a post newspaper and went to the lieutenant colonel running it and told him I was a photojournalism major. He got me assigned to the newspaper, which really pissed off the commanding officer of the armored cav troop."

Furthermore, Jensen got to move to a barracks with the other soldiers from Headquarters Company, including those working on the newspaper. Other than coping with the Texas heat, Jensen called it an "easy duty."

Easy duty or not, he got bored with Ft. Hood and after less than a year decided to request Vietnam.

"I was waiting to do that on a Friday the 13th. Morbid humor. But a week before the 13th I got my orders. They simply told me to report to the 221st Signal Company by the middle of April 1970."

The headquarters of the 221st and the Southeast Asia Pictorial Center were at Long Binh, where Jensen scored a bunk and a locker in a small area shared with another photographer, Dennis Lasby.

"It was part of a one-story barracks known as a 'hooch'. Tin roof, plenty of roaches, and even a few rats. But it was home. Bunk beds and a tiny bit of privacy," Jensen recalled.

The 221st had a mess hall and showers, outhouses for latrines. Long Binh was a huge post with a restaurant serving Chinese food. It had a huge PX and, in 1970, was quite secure.

"Every once in a while we'd take some incoming, and guys in our team typically didn't bother to take cover unless we were ordered. The base was so big and the chance of getting hit was so small that it just seemed silly."

There were people at other detachments, such as Phu Bai or Pleiku, who had specific AOs (Areas of Operation). But the 221st was free range. The photographers could go anywhere they wanted.

"That was also nice because there would be monsoons in the north while the south was dry, and then it would switch. So we could go wherever it was dry because of the camera gear. If you were in an AO, and it was raining in your AO …"

It was simple. Anyone who has ever operated a camera in a tropical war zone would know that, with days and days of heavy rain, the gear would just not work for long.

Officers at the 221st often had information about where something exciting was likely to happen or important operations, and the three-person team that Jensen was on sought those out. There was no designated leader on the team because they rarely had an officer with them. The three of them would just discuss things and decide what to do.

"We had an amazing amount of latitude. We just packed our rucksacks and took off. We had these cards that said we were Department of the Army and please assist us. We had travel orders that helped us get a bit of priority hitching rides on planes and helicopters," Jensen remembered. People weren't sure what the 221st was, so the photographers were typically left alone.

"I can only remember being bugged once. We were in line for chow someplace and had just come back from the bush and were filthy. Some sergeant thought we should go get cleaned up before eating. But he couldn't convince a nearby officer to order us to do so."

The troops of the 221st were usually smelly and dirty en route to their HQ at Long Binh as well.

"Sometimes we'd catch a flight from Da Nang to Bien Hoa or somewhere. I used to love trying to find a seat next to some pristine officer. I was such a dope, being the stinky guy some officer had to endure. Looking back, I see what a jerk I was. Too late," he realizes.

When the photographers got back to Long Binh, they would turn in their film and write captions, and then would have three or four days "to just goof off," Jensen said. "We were exempt from company duties like picking up trash or burning shit because we went into the bush."

"I used to climb up into my bunk, read paperbacks, and listen to Peter, Paul and Mary in my headphones. My favorites were 'Leavin' on a Jet Plane' and 'Early Morning Rain.' I often ate an entire 1lb bag of M&Ms at a time."

Then the cycle would repeat itself. The team would head out into the bush. Jensen carried a 16mm Bell and Howell Filmo on a strap over his left shoulder.

"If it was dusty because I was riding on top of an armored personnel carrier, or if it might rain, I'd put the Bell and Howell inside a plastic bag. I also had two Nikons hanging from my neck. One was a Nikon F. The other a Nikkormat. One had a 28mm lens and the other a 105mm lens. The Filmo shot Ektachrome color. I shot black and white—Tri-X—with my Nikons for reasons I no longer remember, but color would have been much smarter."

It was an exciting and fascinating time, he recalls, particularly if there was a combat assault with a dozen helicopters landing troops.

"I never landed in a hot LZ," he is happy to report. "But once we landed we'd settle in with the grunts or cav and just do what they did. Slogging along or riding atop an APC [Armored Personnel Carrier] or flying in a Huey," he related.

"I recognized there was a chance people would get hurt or killed, but I just never imagined it would happen to me. So much for self-preservation instincts. And to be honest, things in 1970 and 1971 were not as active as in the earlier years."

The Americans were slowly pulling out and the huge, aggressive operations of previous years were gone, with the exception of Cambodia, and then early in 1971, *Lam Son 719.* "And that was mostly ARVNs in Laos with our support," he recalled.

Nevertheless, the 221st had five photographers killed when their slick (UH-1 helicopter) was shot down heading back to Pleiku as part of the unit's coverage of the 1970 Cambodian invasion. One of the team members, Jim Saller, an "intrepid still photographer," according to Jensen, was wounded by shrapnel at Fire Support Base Ripcord.

"And we were with [other] units where people were hurt or killed."

Like many war photographers, Jensen said there is a feeling of being apart and insulated while filming.

"It was illusory and not indicative of a good sense of self-preservation, but it was there," he feels.

"The other thing was when we were with grunts, the commanding officer inevitably put us with the so-called command element. That was basically with the commanding officer, usually a captain, and his RTO [Radio Telephone Operator]. That put us towards the middle of the unit, so we were less likely to get caught in an ambush. That made humping along, following the guy in front less nerve-wracking than if we had been near the point. I always figured they wanted us with the command element so we would be out of the way and not filming the guys on point who shouldn't be distracted. Often we just humped and humped and nothing happened."

When Jensen and other shooters in the 221st were in the bush, their routine was to be up early and quickly eat some C-rations. "A good breakfast for me would be pound cake, fruit cocktail, or peaches and some coffee. Then we'd quickly pack up our stuff and 'saddle up,' which meant putting on our rucksacks and heading off. We'd spend the day moving through the jungle. It was flat and not too hard in III Corps."

However, I Corps was mountainous and really rough, according to Jensen.

"All this weight and then pulling yourself up and around and through vegetation, often when it was quite steep. If the company happened to cross a stream before heading up, there would be a good chance the equipment would get wet and slippery."

Whenever something looked good, Jensen would shoot some film.

"But the trick was not to take so long that I fell behind. Plus, there was always a balancing act. Shoot some film but be sure to have plenty left if something big happened."

The routine would include a few breaks during the day, and then they would settle on a night defensive position. Soldiers would put out claymores. They were never with a unit that dug fighting positions for a one-night stand, which always surprised Jensen.

They would then pull out C-rations and have those for dinner. Sometimes they were heated with a heat-tab which they lit. Some soldiers would use a bit of C-4, the plastic explosive, because it burned much hotter. It was safe unless you stomped on it while it was burning.

"Heat and pressure: Ka-boom!" Jensen said.

The insects in the jungles were such that Jensen always carried extra insect repellent and would put a small trail around his air mattress to try to dissuade what he referred to as "small, biting things."

When it came time to sack out, he would put his head on part of his rucksack and often used a poncho liner in case it got cool.

"And I always slept with my boots and glasses on. My weapon would be nearby. Keeping my glasses on was important because my vision was horrible. About 20/400. So, without glasses I could see at 20 feet what somebody with normal vision could see at 400. This was a disadvantage in a war zone."

Ironically, when Jensen enlisted, not one doctor or anyone else suggested he might be unfit for service.

"The only one who cared was a guy when we were processing in, getting jungle fatigues and junk. One stop was an optical dispensary. The guy took my glasses to check them, came back saying something like 'Holy shit. You can't see anything.' He made me wait and then in a huge rush job made me another pair of glasses which I carried in my left, top pocket. And I had one of the straps to hold my regular glasses on my dumb, young head."

If asked, they would pull guard duty in the bush, but normally the unit wanted its own guys, people they knew and trusted.

Overall, Jensen was happy with what he was doing.

"It was a big, deadly adventure with tanks and guns and helicopters, and you never knew what would happen. I was 21 years old. Only as I got much older would I realize how sad it was. All those young men trying to kill each other for no good reason because of old men who were politicians."

Perhaps more well-known to those back home were the civilian reporters and photographers who were bringing the war home. They sometimes were covering the same thing or simply crossed paths with civilian photographers, some of whom were held in very high esteem for the stories they wrote and the images they made.

"The most notable was covering *Lam Son 719* when we were based at Khe Sanh early in 1971. There was a big press tent with cots where we all stayed and shared it with Larry Burrows of *Life*, Henri Huet of AP, and Kent Potter of UPI. John Saar, a reporter for *Life*, was also there. It was damp and cold and somehow we had managed to get real sleeping bags from the Army, so we gave those guys some of our gear, like poncho liners, to try and stay warm."

"Even though they were civilian photographic gods, they were very nice to us. There was a feeling we were all doing the same thing. I never sensed any condescension. One morning we were all having C-rations for breakfast, joking around and getting our stuff together. I remember Huet saying it was his lucky day because he had pound cake in his box of C-rations.

Burrows, who was British, Huet, half French, half Vietnamese, Potter, who took a leave of absence from his National Guard unit to photograph Vietnam for UPI, and Japanese freelancer Keisaburo Shimamoto, on assignment for *Newsweek* magazine, decided to try and get the ARVNs to fly them into Laos, something the Americans wouldn't and couldn't do based on the 1962 Geneva Accords forbidding the American military from crossing into Laos.

"We decided to go out. I don't remember where. When we got back that night we were told they were all dead. Their ARVN Huey was shot down. It was pretty stunning," Jensen said.

"Another time we were with a unit on Route Nine during *Lam Son 719* with an armored cavalry unit that had been ambushed.

"The decision was made to do what is called a 'thunder run', which basically meant going as fast as the APCs could go down the road, shooting the shit out of everything on either side of the road. This is sometimes known as 'recon by fire'. Shoot and see if anything shoots back," he said.

Shortly after the thunder run, an officer ordered troops to go back down and secure a Huey shot down nearby so the NVA wouldn't get the radios.

"People were willing to go back to rescue their friends, but nobody was willing to die for a radio. The slick could easily be blown up by a Cobra. Everybody refused. A real mutiny."

The officer, according to Jensen, went down the roster and asked one person after another whether he was refusing a direct order. They all were. However, Jensen's team was not part of the unit, so they were not asked.

"I took a couple of photos with my Nikons but made a conscious decision not to do any motion picture because I didn't want to do the slightest thing to help make a case against these guys."

The next morning Jensen's team arrived back at Khe Sanh as quickly as possible to find a civilian reporter because they figured some attention to such a stupid order would make the Army back off. The first journalist they encountered was H. D. S. Greenway, who was reporting for *Time*.

"He did indeed do a story called 'Incident on Route Nine'. I've since been in touch with those troops and [found out that] the commander was replaced, but no action was taken against them. I hope our contacting Greenway played a part in that.

"I think they were interested in us being there because we were something new, a novelty. I also think they might have been a little flattered that we were recording what they were doing.

As for being accepted among those troops for not being a new guy, one sign of a GI who spent time in the bush was scuffed-up jungle boots.

"I made sure never to polish my jungle boots. Troops in the rear had to have their boots polished and shiny. So, ratty-looking boots with a dog tag in the laces was a signal to the guys in the bush that you were not a rear echelon guy. I don't remember anyone showing the least bit of animosity. More often they wondered why we were out in the bush if we didn't have to be there," Jensen said.

"There was a sense that we were all in it together and we tried to be part of the team. I remember once in I Corps the logistics bird (resupply) couldn't reach us because of bad weather, so it was going to be two or three more days until we could get C-rations. I had a bunch of Knorr soups my family sent, so we all shared them. One night I dreamt I was being stabbed in the stomach and woke up. Hunger pains," he said.

"We were also in good shape, so we could keep up and not cause problems. We worked pretty hard not to get in the way or do anything dumb. In fairness, we also carried lighter rucks than the grunts. I probably carried 50lb in my ruck, including water, film, food, some ammunition, poncho liner, air mattress, etc. Grunts, I think, often carried at least 20 if not 30lb more because they had to hump stuff like extra batteries for the radios, ammo for the M-60, LAWs, etc."

In the years since the war, Jensen has been in touch with some of the soldiers his unit photographed. He has often reached them through Facebook pages, posting a link to video and photos and then hearing from them.

In spite of the 15 months he was in-country and in the bush photographing the troops, he only fired a weapon twice.

"Photographers were supposed to carry a .45. I did a couple of times, but a couple of grunts made jokes about it and I decided to upgrade. The question was: to what? An M-16 was too bulky. I wanted something that would leave me free to photograph but would allow me to make a meaningful contribution if things got out of hand. I was not a first responder, as it were, so the weapon didn't have to be handy.

The first time Jensen fired a weapon was just before dawn when sappers attacked the troops he was with at a small base called Kham Duc in August 1970.

"It was dark, so no photos and shooting seemed appropriate. In addition, we had sappers inside the wire running around, rudely blowing up shit and shooting at people. When it got light I filmed the aftermath. You can find my film on YouTube by searching for 'Jensen-Vietnam War' and 'Kham Duc'.

"Not very pretty. At that time I was using a Thompson submachine gun."

The other time he used a weapon was in 1971 on Route Nine during *Lam Son 719*. His team joined an armored cavalry unit just after they had been ambushed.

It is here that Jensen's involvement with weaponry took on a life of its own.

"A guy in our hooch offered to sell me a Thompson he bought on the black market. I did. The stock unscrewed so it was not too big. I carried it maybe three times to the bush. It looked great, but I was once told by some ARVNs that it sucked compared to the accuracy of the M-16. Probably right.

"The last time I carried it was when the sappers attacked at Kham Duc. At that point, I came to the conclusion that it had style but that was all. Among other things, it used .45 ammo, and if I ever ran out, no grunts carried .45. The M-16s used .223/5.56 and the M-60 7.62. I forgot who I sold it to, but I think it was somebody with the armored cavalry because they could carry boxes of .45."

Jensen went back to the guy who sold him the Thompson, who told him he could get Jensen a grenade launcher, also known as an M-79, or "Thumper."

"Bought it. Borrowed a saw and cut down the stock and barrel, so it was a pistol. I was able to hook it onto my rucksack so it could be retrieved in a few minutes, but it didn't hamper me. The first time I took it to the bush and came back to Long Binh, I went to turn it into the company armorer. He brought it to the attention of the company commander, who said, 'Do you know how dangerous this is?'"

Jensen thought that was exactly the point, but he didn't say anything and the armorer confiscated it.

"No punishment and the captain did not ask where I got it. Good guy."

So Jensen bought another one and just kept it in his wall locker along with the ammo. "Not too safe," he admits today.

The second time he fired was with the cavalry troop on Route Nine, the guys that mutinied. They had been ambushed maybe 30 minutes before Jensen, Jim Saller, and Denny Jones came upon them and asked to join them.

Several guys had been left behind and the discussion was what to do? The answer was the thunder run.

"It was late afternoon and everyone figured when it got dark the NVA would get them. The hope was to get down, grab those guys and get back before the NVA could react. I don't think anybody thought it would work very well."

The flaw in the plan was that there was only one way down and they then had to return on the same road.

"This tends to eliminate the always desirable element of surprise. Plus, the NVA knew those guys were there and must have figured somebody would try and save them."

Jensen referred to the plan as "kinda sketchy" because the North Vietnamese troops were still in the area.

"There was a call for volunteers, and I said I'd go. They needed help and I thought it would be interesting. There was barely enough light, so I could have shot motion picture, but they needed people who were shooting [weapons], not tourists. So, I grabbed my sawed-off M-79 and fired HE rounds as quickly as I could into the bushes and trees alongside Route Nine."

They got down there, picked the troops up and headed back. The APCs had a big open hatch, so a soldier could stand up with half his body inside.

"I was standing up firing. Somebody yelled that I was standing on a wounded guy, which seemed rude on my part," he recalled.

"There was a huge racket with everybody firing and all sorts of dust in the air from the tracks. I remember hearing a whoosh behind me. I figured it was a rocket-propelled grenade and later asked the guys on the APC behind us. They said it was an RPG and it just missed. Amazingly we got back without anybody being hurt, something nobody could quite figure out."

In spite of the APC incident, when asked to recall the greatest horrors of the war he fought, Jensen was hard put to answer.

"I wouldn't describe anything I was in as being a classic battle. In fact, I don't remember seeing a muzzle flash or hearing a bullet pass me. But my memory isn't great. I was at a reunion a year or so ago and a guy on our team mentioned being heavily mortared and losing part of his hearing. I didn't remember that at all."

He does remember Kham Duc in August 1970, however.

"There were four of us: me, Jim Saller, John Luckey, and John Brock. We shared a fighting position between the wire with a 105mm battery behind us. That's where the arty guys told us to set up and, being relatively new in-country, we were too dumb to realize that they put us in a dangerous position so their guys wouldn't have to man it. We took turns on watch. Two watching, two sleeping. I was really dumb.

I was using a flashlight to quickly scan the barbed wire. I knew it would give away our position but thought it might also catch somebody in the wire."

Jensen and Saller's watch was over and they were trying to sleep when, suddenly, there were explosions and people were yelling, "Gooks in the wire."

The North Vietnamese had snuck through off to the right, a little bit away from their position. "I always wondered if they went that way because the flashlight showed them where we were," Jensen said.

"The sappers were not just in the wire, but inside our base running around throwing satchel charges, shooting. We were down behind some sandbags and shooting when one of the artillery guys ran up and said we needed to hunker down because there were lowering the barrel of the 105mm to fire a flechette round over our heads. That was an anti-personnel round that would send out thousands of tiny, metal darts. We got down. There was this huge explosion behind us. I remember seeing a huge ripple of dust going out. An arty guy later told me he was watching and saw a sapper outside the wire simply disintegrate. The whole place was lit up with flares and it was right up there on the surreal scale."

After the flechette rounds were fired, Jensen and the others decided to quickly scatter from their position.

"I jumped into a fighting position occupied by a guy with an M-60 machine gun. It was a metal culvert with sandbags on top. It was incredibly loud as this guy fired. I fired the Thompson but really didn't have a target. I just shot out into the jungle because everyone was worried there would be an additional ground attack.

I looked off to what would have been about a 2 o'clock position and there were three sappers on the ground. I guess they could have just been wounded. Somebody ran up to them and sprayed them with an M-16 to make sure they were dead."

Then, the gunner that Jensen was with suggested he try to shoot other sappers who were also either dead or wounded. They were on the ground in another area and Jensen guesses today that the gunner was concerned that the more powerful M-60 rounds might ricochet and hit their fellow soldiers.

"So, I tried to hit them with the Thompson. Couldn't really tell to be honest.

Things were so chaotic nobody was taking chances. There wasn't any thought of prisoners although sappers were not likely to surrender. They were brave, hardcore guys," Jensen believes.

After some time, Jensen couldn't stand the loud gunfire and left no matter if he ended up safe or not.

He doesn't recall where he wound up, but the fighting was soon over at that point and the sun rose. A large-scale ground attack did not materialize on that occasion, so he put away his Thompson submachine gun and began shooting motion-picture film of the destroyed bunkers, damaged artillery pieces, and the dead sappers.

"We still took a little bit of incoming and I remember getting a couple of still photos of guys running for cover."

Three Americans died. One was a medic tending a wounded soldier. Sixteen sappers died. They also had some other wounded GIs.

"A little bit later a general and a few officers came in on a slick to see what had happened. I remember seeing some officer take out his .45 and shoot dead bodies in a pit. Very heroic," Jensen states bitterly.

Thanks to the marvel of today's social media, Jensen has actually been contacted by people in Vietnam who recognized a family member through the photographs he has posted on YouTube.

"I was very surprised to see comments from people in Vietnam who said they recognized a husband or father or son, and they begged to know where we buried the bodies. I also got an email from a guy who claimed he was a high-ranking officer who used binoculars and watched me filming that morning from a nearby mountain."

One of those who contacted Jensen was Pham Cong Huong, who sent a photo of himself in uniform and said he was a scout with the 404th Sapper Battalion, the unit that attacked the unit Jensen was with.

"I began trying to find guys from the artillery unit who might know where the sappers were buried. Randy Fleetwood, then a sergeant, was in charge of security for the burial detail. He got back to me, and that began more than a year of trying to put memories together with what Kham Duc looks like today."

A lot of digging occurred, but the grave was never found. Pham Cong Huong was planning another effort in March 2017.

Pham and Jensen are now Facebook friends, and Vietnamese television has done some stories on the efforts to find the bodies.

For now though, Jensen's thoughts shift from his friendship with Cong to another battle still etched in his memory 46 years later.

In July 1970 still photographer Jim Saller, mopic shooter Jerry Dubro, and Jensen heard there was a firebase in I Corps called "Ripcord" that was under siege, and they headed up there. It was a 101st Airborne Division base, so they went to the PIO at Camp Eagle and told him that they wanted to get out to the firebase. The PIO told them no photographers, not even Army, were being allowed.

"I suggested we go to the dust-off pad and see about getting a ride out to Ripcord on the next medevac. The pilots thought it was weird but they basically didn't give a shit if we wanted to go, so we just waited. Sure enough they got a call and off we went."

"We jumped out of the dust-off with our rucksacks and cameras, and there was Lieutenant Colonel Andre Lucas looking at us. He wanted to know what we were doing. I told him we were with the 221st Signal/Southeast Asia Pictorial Center and wanted to get out with the grunts on the surrounding mountains."

Lucas told the photographers that there was no way that he would allow that to happen, but they were welcome to stay at the firebase.

"He ordered somebody to get us helmets (which we normally never wore) and flak jackets. Then, they told us we could stay in an empty bunker."

The firebase itself was never under ground attack when they were there, but it did take a lot of incoming.

"We ran around filming the artillery guys responding, the dust-offs landing, and Phantoms bombing the surrounding mountainside in support of the grunts out there."

Things at Ripcord would soon heat up, however.

"One morning I was filming and Saller was up and behind me. Suddenly there was a huge 'crump', the sound of a mortar exploding, and the back of my neck was covered with something warm and goopy. My instant thought was that the mortar hit where Saller was, and I was covered with Saller. It turned out Saller had moved and the mortars blew up Mermite containers which were insulated metal containers designed to keep food warm. The goop was Spanish rice," Jensen said.

"A day or so later, Saller was not so lucky. We were standing next to each other at the end of a trench that led down to our bunker. I jumped down to get something from the bunker and just as I hit the ground there was an explosion and Saller yelled, 'I'm hit.' He was peppered up the side by shrapnel."

Dubro and Jensen took him over to the command post, where he was told to go out on the next dust-off.

"We agreed Dubro should go with him to make sure he was okay, and I would stay a while longer since I still had film. If SEAPC wanted more coverage, they could send a team back up and bring me film," Jensen said.

He stayed three or four more days. But by then, Jensen was out of film.

"The NVA started dropping 120mm mortars on us. Those were much bigger than anything before. They could go right through a bunker that would stop the smaller stuff. That struck me as a compelling reason to take off. I jumped on a slick going back to Camp Eagle and quickly ran into John Luckey and a few other guys who had just arrived to go out to Ripcord. I told them it was just the same stuff day after day, and I thought we'd covered it. I was wrong."

Soon after Jensen left, a Chinook bringing in supplies was shot down, crashed on the firebase not far from where Jensen's bunker was located and burned. One crewman was trapped and burned to death.

"It also set all sorts of ammunition and shit on fire, so there were all these explosions," he said.

Eventually, the firebase was evacuated under threat of a ground attack and intense fire. Lieutenant Colonel Lucas and others were killed.

"We missed the chance to film an amazing chapter of the Vietnam War. On the other hand, some of us could easily have been killed," Jensen admitted.

"Years later I read a book by Keith Nolan about Ripcord. He'd contacted me for photos. It made clear how tough the fighting was in the bush around Ripcord and there's a good chance Lieutenant Colonel Lucas saved our lives by not allowing us out there. Another example of being careful what you ask for."

The first time Jensen went to the bush was in May 1970 when Cambodia was invaded. That's when he met legendary still photographer Al Rockoff, then a photographer with SEAPC.

"I was new in-country while Rockoff was a veteran, highly respected, and gung-ho still photographer. The first time I went to the bush—into Cambodia—it was with Rockoff and a lieutenant. We were back in Long Binh and there were news reports of ethnic Vietnamese being killed by Cambodians and their bodies floating down the Mekong River. Rockoff said he also heard the ethnic Vietnamese were being put in concentration camps in Phnom Penh, so he said we should go."

The problem was that the Cambodian invasion was supposed to be strictly limited to the border areas and Phnom Penh was beyond that. It was clearly in the interior. But Rockoff convinced Jensen that it was a good idea.

"He tended to have the attitude 'What are they going to do, send me to Vietnam?'"

They persuaded the company clerk to type up travel orders that just read "Cambodia" instead of a specific area or unit, and they never told anybody what they were doing.

As if it were a scene out of the film *Apocalypse Now*, the two hitched a ride up the Mekong on a PBR (Patrol Boat River) and got off at Neak Luong, on the Cambodian border. They spent the night with some Americans stationed there and then took a civilian ferry across the river. From there, they bargained for two seats in a civilian taxi by paying with a carton of Kool cigarettes for the ride to Phnom Penh, about 45 miles down the road.

"I was in the front seat next to the driver when these guys wearing black pajamas came out of the rice paddies and the car slowed. I unholstered my .45. Figured I would shoot through the door if needed."

It turned out that the cadres were local Cambodian militia and no threat.

"Rockoff was really scared I would shoot unnecessarily," Jensen recalled. "Hard to blame him."

Jensen and Rockoff, who, years later would see his life immortalized in the film *The Killing Fields*, a docudrama about the late Cambodian journalist Dith Pran, made their way to the American embassy in Phnom Penh.

Somebody lent Rockoff some local currency because they only had military scrip that didn't work in Cambodia. They got a room at the Hotel Mondial and went to the government press office. Personnel looked at their IDs and gave them press passes.

"We spent three or four days wandering around and found the ethnic Vietnamese who had been rounded up and were being kept in a compound. Not quite a concentration camp, but they were not free to leave. We shot film of them living there, cooking, etc.

"All this time we are walking around the streets of Phnom Penh in jungle fatigues. It could not have been clearer that we were GIs. We kept waiting for some Western reporter to see us and make a big deal out of American soldiers being much farther in Cambodia than President Nixon had promised."

"One afternoon we were sitting around having a beer at a sidewalk café when a big black American sedan with an American flag flying pulled up. It was the military attaché from our embassy, and he wanted to know what we were doing in Phnom Penh. We showed him our orders saying 'Cambodia.' He shook his head and told us to get out of town."

So Jensen and Rockoff checked out, took their rucksacks and made their way back to Long Binh.

"The officers couldn't believe we'd been so dumb. There was even a discussion about whether to admit where we'd been."

Luckily, they did not get into trouble and their film was sent up the chain of command. Jensen knows because he found it in the National Archives and has a copy.

"Only later did I realize how dangerous that was. We could have been grabbed anywhere, especially on the road to and from Phnom Penh, and nobody would have ever known what happened to Jensen and Rockoff. We would have just disappeared."

Jensen is quick to point out that, in fact, two civilian photographers, actor Errol Flynn's son Sean and Dana Stone, disappeared traveling on motorbikes in Cambodia in April 1970.

"Captured and killed," Jensen adds.

Jensen's luck brought him back from Cambodia, but that did not mean the plod through the jungles of Vietnam were over for him.

"At times it was pretty rough physically although we were in good shape. The worst was walking off Firebase O'Reilly, a companion base to FSB Ripcord. We'd gone up there after Ripcord because it, too, was supposed to be under siege."

When they got to O'Reilly, they found it occupied by ARVN soldiers.

"We got up there and filmed for a day, and then a pair of advisors told us the plan was to quickly abandon the base because the NVA were closing in. Indeed the plan was for all the grunts to simply leave early the next morning by walking off the base and trying to cover ground so quickly that the NVA couldn't react."

Their destination was a distant mountain where the helicopters could pick the ARVN up the next day.

"That was a hard hump. We really moved. I shot a tiny bit of film in the jungle. We kept thinking it would be over, but we kept going."

The plan worked, according to Jensen. The NVA never got to the firebase in time to attack the ARVN before all the troops lifted off.

Jensen considered staying in Vietnam as a civilian. But the war was winding down and there seemed to be less and less interest from the press. He went home and graduated from George Washington University, and worked for 30 years as a reporter for the Cleveland *Plain Dealer*. Since 2006 he has freelanced on automotive and consumer safety issues for the *New York Times*, and done general assignment reporting for New Hampshire Public Radio. He has no complaints about what he did in Vietnam.

"Most of it was easy. Nobody messed with us. I really liked what I was doing. It was interesting and exciting and seemed important, although I didn't think at the time that one day people would view it as historic footage. In my wall locker I had a note to my family if I got killed. It basically said I'd had some bad luck but really liked what I was doing and don't blame the war."

221st, Unique by Any Definition of the Word: Frank Lepore

Lieutenant Colonel Frank Lepore referred to himself as "a charter member" of the 221st Signal Company Pictorial because he was among the first to report to the unit when it was constituted at Ft. Monmouth, New Jersey in June 1966. He also called the unit "unique by any definition of the word." He was among 26 officers and 218 enlisted men. Since then, he has been a voice for the unit and its official historian.

"You might say I was a charter member of the 221st Signal Company (Pictorial), being among the first to report in June 1966 to Ft. Monmouth, New Jersey (World War II home of the US Army Signal Corps).

"The 221st was 'authorized' a total of 26 officers and 218 enlisted men. I was one of 24 lieutenants. The 221st was designed and organized to be deployed in detachments throughout the Vietnam theater. Span of control over such a large area is one reason for the number of officers required. The 221st was about one-quarter the size of a typical 1,000-man Signal Battalion in Vietnam. There were 22 signal battalions, group and brigade headquarters in Vietnam, numbering 23,000 in total.

"The number of officers actually 'assigned' varied over the 221st's history, occasioned by normal DEROS (Date Expected Rotation Overseas)—back home to the Land of the Big PX (Post Exchange)—reassignments, wounded, and attrition over the duration of the war. The actual distribution by ranks were: one major (O-4) commanding officer; one captain, who served as OIC, or detachment commander, 'AB Detachment,' the largest of three platoon-sized company elements, and/or alternately as company executive officer); 24 lieutenants; and most important, 218 enlisted men.

"The 221st was designed to function as a theater-level 'combat service support' organization. It was one of many 'tails' in the frequently mentioned expression: 'tooth-to-tail ratio'—the actual ratio in Vietnam in 1968 was approximately one combat to two support. Support organizations provided direct and indirect support and sustainment, without which the war fighter (the 'teeth') could not function (or for very long), said the Army.

"Signals and logistics are two examples of the 'tail' part of the equation. One wag thoughtfully observed the relationship between the 'tooth and the tail'—Infantry and Signal Corps—suggesting that our motto be: 'When you're out of commo, you're outta beer.' Or 'Call us when you get there.'

"True, the 221st served in a support capacity. But to provide that support, they had to go where the action was. If the guy they were supporting was a 'moving target that attracts the eye,' then the men of the 221st also were going to be an equally inviting target. Telephoto lenses, of course, were a possibility, but these could only make for slightly smaller targets.

"If you've ever witnessed a pole lineman stringing multi-pair cable atop a 30-foot pole as the bullets fly, you may appreciate the blurry relationship between 'tail' and 'tooth.' Combat photographers' direct contributions ranged somewhere between the immediate and the sublime. For example, thousands of 221st photo-prints were made and distributed Vietnam-wide. They made real the latest Viet Cong improvised weapon, a do-it-yourself Claymore Mine fashioned entirely from discarded GI beer cans, salvaged explosives, nuts, bolts, and nails. Did a photograph save allied lives? Perhaps. It certainly raised awareness.

"In the longer perspective, the photographers 'immortalized in celluloid' the history of the Vietnam conflict and what United States and Allied men and women accomplished there. Historians and countless documentaries use this pictorial evidence to this day.

"The number, specialization, and dispersal of the unit's many audiovisual missions accounted for the large number of officers and NCOs. The 221st was authorized 16 Photo Assignment Teams (PAT), each with a 2nd lieutenant, and senior NCO (E-5/6). Color and black-and-white (still and mopic) processing laboratories, equipment maintenance, supply and logistics all required unique management and skill sets.

"The 221st employed modular, mobile (four-wheeled trailer-mounted), processing vans which could be arranged like so many dominoes. These were deployed in mobile, or fixed-position (using jack stands) to provide laboratory processing of black-and-white and color mopic and still photo prints and negatives as well as equipment maintenance. They were self-powered (when connected to diesel generators) and air-conditioned (four-wheel) vans, manufactured by Kellert Aircraft Co. They could be geographically dispersed to locations within corps-level areas of operation.

"The unit's first Table of Organization and Equipment (TO&E) 11–500 initially included photo equipment in vogue during World War II and the Korean conflict. Venerable still-camera classics included the 4x5-inch Combat Graphic (Speed Graphic) camera (cut sheet holder) introduced to the Pacific war in 1944, and its companion 'Combat 70mm' Signal Corps KE-4 (1). This was a motor-driven still camera that looked like an olive drab Contax II on steroids and was about the same size and weight as a 5lb red clay brick. Motion cameras included the hand-held/ hand-cranked 16/35mm Bell and Howell Filmo/Eyemo (three-lens turret) cameras, and a Newsreel Cine Camera 'Wall 35mm,' which would have taken a crane, two men and a boy to lift and mount on a tripod, These relics rounded-out the original TO&E.

"Fortunately most of this original TO&E equipment was never delivered or uncrated. The Department of the Army's senior visual information official, Charles Beresford, astutely realized they needed to work on an updated, or (modified) MTOE (Modified Table of Organization & Equipment) for the 221st. The MTO&E 11–500D resulted. As a French statesman, Georges Clemenceau, famously remarked, 'Generals always fight the last war.' The same could be said for photography in Vietnam.

"As I recall, the updated MTOE 500D for still photo included standard issue 35mm single-lens reflex Canon Topcon (United States marketed by Bessler), an aluminum brick with a lens, and the Graflex XL with 120mm roll film back. Mopic equipment included the Bell and Howell (hand-cranked) 16mm Filmo and the Beckman and Whitley CM-16 (Sound-on-mag-stripe-film-co-axial feed-400 load).

"The in-country elements of the 221st Signal Company Pictorial continued their mission of providing photographic and audiovisual support to the US armed forces and other US government activities throughout Southeast Asia. Photographic operations during the first six months included film coverage of the 4th Infantry Division, 9th Infantry Division, Task Force Oregon, 11th Armored Cavalry, Queens Cobras from Thailand, land-clearing operations, and other combat and combat support activities in Vietnam. Three photographic teams covered Vice President Humphrey's visit to Vietnam during the period 28 October–1 November 1967.

"On August 20, 1967, the 221st began field testing of the Beckman and Whitley CM-16 single-system motion-picture camera. Testing was completed on September 19, 1967. Extensive major mechanical problems were encountered during the test, rendering the equipment unacceptable for use in Vietnam without modification by the manufacturer. An Equipment Improvement Recommendation (EIR) (DA Form 2407) was submitted and a factory representative arrived in-country on October 23, 1967 to begin making the necessary modifications. We were told, 'When this work is completed, the camera will be retested.'

"In short, the CM-16 cameras—particularly their rotating mirror-shutters— were not designed to function in the heat, humidity, dust, dirt, and crud of a tropical environment. As several mopic shooters discovered, exposed film needed frequent inspection upon processing. One sanity-saver was any excuse to personally visit the air conditioned Kellett (Aircraft Co.) mobile vans where their film was processed."

Lepore also describes what was involved in putting the unit together in Vietnam, how the men were organized, and how many photographers the 221st had at its high point.

"Beginning in June 1966, most of the 221st enlisted and officer cadre arrived at Ft. Monmouth, New Jersey. The group had an eclectic mix of skill sets—there were enlisted still- and motion-picture photographers, laboratory technicians, mechanics, power generator operators, and administrative personnel.

"Officers were recent college graduates of ROTC (Reserved Officers Training Corps) or OCS (Officer Candidate School) having Basic Signal Officers MOSs (0215). All completed or monitored training in motion-picture and still photography MOS courses at Ft. Monmouth, or they received training directly from manufacturers providing new state-of-the-art photo technology. A few officers were MOS qualified with specialization as 8500-Pictorial Unit Commander, 8510-Pictorial Officer, or 851-Motion Picture and Television Director.

"All personnel were drawn from units and schools from around the world. Some officers and enlisted men were re-assigned (some would argue Shanghaied) from existing Signal Battalions with photo MOSs, for example the 69th Signal Battalion, RVN, while other 'inductees' had recently completed their MOS training at the US Army Signal School at Ft. Monmouth. The challenge for both officer and enlisted in the early months of the unit's organization was gaining technical 'facility'—ease in using the newly issued camera and processing gear to the point where it became instinctive—strike the patella tendon, get a knee jerk.

"Much like infantry weapons qualification—readily acquiring a site picture, and squeezing the trigger—the photographer (new or seasoned) had to exercise their 'photo-reflexes' to the point where using the newly issued camera gear or film processors could be applied in a field environment and be automatic in doing it—often by touch only. This was challenging because new state-of-the -art equipment arrived in late fall 1966, months after the troops. Improvisation and sharing what was available, plus added bench-time in a classroom, filled the void until each 'camera shooter' or lab tech had his own issued 'kit.'

"Each PAT (Photo Assignment Team) had its own way of achieving proficiency. Field training in a variety of environments in different scenarios sharpened mind–body coordination. Skills sharpened, such as recognizing and acquiring a 'subject', long shot, medium shot, and close-up composition, changing camera lenses, or adjusting an aperture ring and focus by feel—all became automatic. This type of hands-on training was of the 'use it, or lose it' or 'When you're without, practice within' category of skill enhancement. Even infrequently used skills were included and rehearsed; for example, loading a 400-foot mopic magazine, cutting film or bulk 35mm film inside a cloth changing bag.

"Most of 221st cadre (officers and enlisted personnel) reported to the unit on or about June 1 to August 1966. The unit's MTO&E 11–500D 'authorized' 28 officers and, I believe, 143 enlisted men. The 'end strength' (officer and enlisted) actually 'assigned' at any given time in the unit's early history (1966–68), varied between 200 and 244.

"The entire company might appear top-heavy in officer 'management' with 28 officers. Packet #1 included eight Photo Assignment Teams each led by a lieutenant. The company was authorized 16 such PATs. The PATs were generally eight-man teams: one officer/team leader (2nd or 1st lieutenant), two or three senior NCOs (still and mopic), and specialists (grade SP-5 or SP-6), the balance being (E-4) still and mopic cameramen.

"Teams operated independently, usually attached to combat units in order to document specific operations or subjects of command interest. The team's (mix 'n match) composition was 'weighted' or tailored to the mission and need for still photography, silent or mopic sound-on-film, or combination.

"Headquarters 221st consisted of admin, supply, and motor pool. The 'AB Detachment,' located at Long Binh, included an operations officer and operations NCO, a Photo Branch (still/mopic teams), and graphic arts, audiovisual, laboratory and photo maintenance. The AB Detachment was an eclectic mix of technical skills: enlisted ranks, still photographers, motion-picture photographers, audio specialists, still photographic lab specialists, motion-picture lab specialists—affectionately known as 'Lab Rats'—audiovisual equipment repair specialists, power generator operators, vehicle mechanics, admin and supply specialists.

"In the officer ranks, most were newly minted 2nd lieutenants—roughly half being either recent OCS or ROTC grads. There were, one or two 1st lieutenants, one captain executive officer, and Captain (later Major) Thomas A. DeYoung, commanding officer.

"Photo assignments supporting PIO still- and motion-picture requirements varied in volume and type throughout the 221st's deployment. The ratio was driven largely by the availability of 221st in photographers ('shooters') not otherwise documenting field combat operations or fulfilling 'direct tasking.' The protocol guiding priority—who comes first—was driven by the seniority of the requesting headquarters.

"The empirical method for presenting how much PIO work we did for any given period of time was to count the total number of 'work order requests' sorted into two stacks: (1) command directed—tasking from HQ, Department of the Army, HQ, USARV, and HQ MAC-V); (2) soft subjects (every unit level below command headquarters)—targets of opportunity that smile and shake hands.

"Our priority was to support those in our chain of command who controlled everything. As the guy who often stretched resources to cover all contingencies, I don't recall an occasion, even the Tet Offensive in 1968, where we couldn't find the talent to do our job.

"This does not understate the important role of public affairs or diminish the value of 'grip and grins,' or informing the troops and families back home. Photography helped local public affairs officers highlight individual lives in a distant war, or inform a nation via syndicated television series such as the 'Army's Big Picture.'

"One recognizes that few of us in uniform will ever have a statue erected in our honor. The practical part of any legacy lies within family and colleagues. If our guys somehow provided one old soldier, sailor, airman, Marine, or 'Coastie', or their families, a view of what they contributed—then we honor those men and their legacy. We also covered most all of the dignitaries and icons of the Vietnam era 1967–68 with the same fervor.

"By November 1967, the 221st's remaining four packets brought an additional eight photo assignment teams. The 221st total complement then was 16 photo assignment teams, so a total 64 'shooters.'

"In March 1968, the 221st 'end strength' increased dramatically from 244 to 328 with the reassignment of 94 personnel from the 69th Signal Battalion's Photo Element in the period June 1, 1967 to March 25, 1968. While I have been unable to locate a record of the MOSs involved in this consolidation/reassignment, it's likely that at least a third of the 94 (or 30) transferred MOSs were photographers. This would place a total of approximately 90 still and mopic shooters under the control of a newly created (on April 1, 1968) Southeast Asia Pictorial Center (SEAPC). SEAPC, served as a 'clearinghouse' for both coordinating the 'front-end' of assigning Photo Assignment Teams and the 'backend' of processing and distributing their audiovisual products."

What about the men attached to 221st and the challenges they faced?

"Reporting for duty—and assignment with the 221st—was an 'incongruity' of sorts. How else could one explain instantly having 23 brother officers, all lieutenants, working side-by-side in the same unit?

"The explanation, we later discovered, was the highly modular nature of the 221st. We were separate teams working independently—but as one—to serve an entire Army theater of operations. This gaggle of officers may have arrived at their commissions and leadership skills by separate paths, but we were alike in many ways. Give or take, about 50 percent were OCS graduates, products of Signal Corps OCS at Ft. Gordon, Georgia. The balance were ROTC. Mercifully, there was so much to do in getting the unit and ourselves prepared for deployment that we seldom got in each other's way. For the physics-minded, our interactions were something akin to subatomic electrons, each in its respective path, orbiting around a nucleus.

"Most OCS officers had prior enlisted experience (E4–E8), or were civilian college graduates who enlisted for the 'OCS Option' after completing basic combat training. ROTC officers graduated from both private and state universities. On the surface, there was very little to distinguish us one from the other. You would find similar education, life experience, managing people, problem solving, and moral resolve in getting a job—any job—done. The OCS officers, having just completed a rigorous six-month course of instruction, tested both academically and physically, were—putting it mildly—'gung ho' and 'full of piss 'n vinegar.' Many topped-off their OCS training, accepting 'walk-on offers' to gain airborne qualification. While OCS-ers were a competitive lot, routinely setting standards of physical fitness for the entire company, they willingly shared their 'school of the soldier' knowledge and 'tricks-of-the-trade.' They were uniformly 'salt-of-the-earth' leaders both with their fellow officers and enlisted men.

"Whether OCS or ROTC, they all brought some skill, trait, or aptitude to our endeavors. The mix of brainpower, creativity and testosterone made the 221st a very dynamic and stimulating place. Believe me, no one (officer or enlisted) could rest on the laurels for very long before some new, better application or higher standard appeared."

"On May 3, 1967, nine officers and 44 enlisted men—officially Packet #1 of the 221st—arrived in the Republic of Vietnam. Any lofty illusions we may have had about being 'pioneers,' 'first- on-the- beach,' 'spearhead,' or 'choosers-of-the-short-straw,' quickly devolved into just saying 'Advanced Party.'

"You can go through all of the POR (Preparation for Overseas Redeployment) training, and the rigors of 9,000 miles of travel, and still wonder what it's going to be like once you arrive in a war zone. No storming the beaches, just an unceremonial 9,000-mile cruise on a World War II troop transport, transfer to a Landing Craft Utility (LCU), short flight on a C-123 and bumpy ride in a 'deuce and half.' My read of the furled, facial expressions of almost everyone assembled that very bright and hot day in Long Binh, Vietnam, was one of puzzlement and being 'letdown.' Your mind wanders.

"Somebody's got to go first, you reckon. Someone has to be first to survey the scene, provide shelter, and guide those that follow. The experience was something like a mission to another planet—make that a galaxy—far, far away. The feeling becomes a strange mix: uncertainty because you're on your own, occasionally offset by the great comfort in just calling our home base 'Ft. Monmouth' for moral support. Simple enough. We shared the same discomforts and uncertainties with at least half a million fellow GIs, similarly dispatched beginning in the fall of 1966 as part of President Lyndon Johnson's troop surge.

"The 221st needed the fundamentals: food, shelter from the elements, bullets and film. If you don't like being wet in monsoon rains, pitching a tent; if you don't like rolling out of your cot in the dark and stepping into a 'river,' then you would scrounge wooden pallets and put them end-to-end until you have a 'floor.' How about cold showers in the morning? Then figure a way to place a trailer-mounted 400-gallon water tank, weighing 1–1½ tons atop a tower and heat it. (A tank retriever crane and mess-hall immersion heaters work nicely).

"Packet #1 didn't have 'problems' back in the day. We may have been puzzled, pissed-off and/or pissed on like everyone else. Thankfully we had no problems that couldn't be resolved—just an unending series of multiple 'challenges.'

"It would take us collectively—officer and EM alike—to accomplish all the things that had to be done. For openers there was no shelter on our new home site. No one complained, though some grumbled. Here were leaders and skilled technicians whom we 'turned-to.' There were no 'yes-men' or 'straw men' just a serendipitous collection of multiple skill sets. Call it 'Yankee ingenuity' or guys with a lot of 'do-it-yourself' time and experience. There seemed to be no construction, general contractor, or skilled building trade that was not covered by someone's experience. And there was little discussion. It was a group-think, problem-prioritizing, results-achieving almost by osmosis series of end-to-end 'Kodak Moments.' In the final measure the 'needs' were so many that you could put your shoulder to any challenge, resolve it and there'd be something else right behind it.

"Sociologists call it a 'need hierarchy,' a theoretical pyramid—or hierarchy of must haves—air, food (beans), and safety (bullets) at the pyramid's base. Any of the troop's higher needs, above the basic physiological and safety, were on temporary hold. Oh, we could dream and speculate. But as mother used to say: 'resolving your current challenge ain't going to happen by magic.'

"You could just look in any direction and something needed to be done. Needs were self-evident and required little explanation or motivation to address … though necessitating prioritization in a war zone.

"Our first challenges upon arrival at Long Binh Post were self-evident. We were standing on a barren piece of real estate roughly a city block in size. Combat engineers (or contractor Brown & Root) had wrested this landscape from jungle and swamp—now neatly graded, with compacted crushed rock (called Laterite), eerily terraced to resemble an abandoned 12th-century Inca burial ground. It was prime real estate, (location, location, location) about a mile down the road from a sprawling building complex called Headquarters, US Army Vietnam.

"Our assigned 'home' had only the most rudimentary form of shelter available. General-purpose medium tents lay in a neat heap to be erected before twilight of 'day one' in-country. The large tents, of course, beat sleeping in two-man pup tents. Somewhere between pragmatism and skepticism one got to think: roughing-it might have been appropriate for the Roman Legions subduing Germania. But Packet #1 had an entire company—192 troopers with about $4 million in equipment—expecting to join us in the following six months. By November 1967, literally several cargo ships loaded with our motor vehicles, vans, CONEX containers, reefer refrigerators, and tractor-trailer loads of film would occupy the same one-city block. We and the equipment all needed permanent sheltering.

"We weren't unique in solving such challenges. It may be arguable, but Packet #1 had more talent and ideas for innovation man-for- man than any similar group of 'dog robbers'—those who make problems disappear by whatever means necessary. Call it a 'collective creativity.' Imagine the synergy when you plunk down 500,000 similarly creative GIs and insert them into a country which charitably could be called an 'opportunity-rich environment.' Solutions become exponential. There were many 'moments' when you just had to shake your head and marvel at what had been accomplished by so few with so little.

"They say you can buy a man's labor by the hour, or by the job; what you can't buy is enthusiasm. And this was long before Eastman ever coined the notion of the 'Kodak Moment.' Both officers and NCOs shared in the construction effort led by lieutenants Ed Herrneckar, Jim Phelps, Ralph Smith, Bruce Wesson, Ken Wingender, and many others.

"Our 'sheltering' challenge would be solved by the Army thoughtfully providing pre-fabricated 20 foot × 60 foot aluminum buildings—'Adams Huts.' These were 'D.I.Y.G.I.' (Do-It-Yourself GI) 'Erector Sets' on steroids, made more challenging in a host of ways, not the least of them missing parts.

"All construction was scheduled around our daily photo assignments and 'other duties as assigned'—base perimeter defense and manpower levies—to support two senior neighboring Signal Corps headquarters. These were the 160th Signal Group and 69th Signal Battalion, both located across the street, within the shadow of their flagpoles, and a microwave tower, known to be a Viet Cong mortar aiming stake.

"The first step in construction required pouring a 20 foot × 60 foot concrete pad. Given the volume of concrete required, we had to borrow, beg and, yes, bribe a neighboring Engineer Construction Battalion for their commercial cement mixer. These mixers were in high demand, so they said, given the half-million troops soon facing the same housing issues across Vietnam, 'The Land of the Smaller Dragon.' We could borrow the mixer for use, but often only at night. This 'wrinkle' meant construction in spooky darkness, illuminated by several jeep headlights. Just to complicate matters, concrete pouring and construction occurred during Southeast Asia's monsoon season (May to November). There were times (it seemed every night at the same hour) when the monsoonal downpour was so heavy, it would literally wash the newly poured concrete out of the steel retaining forms surrounding the pad. Symbolically, it was enough to bring a tear to the eye. (Actually, you wouldn't have noticed tears because you'd be as tired as the next guy and soaking wet—either by sweat or rain.) After this first rain-soaked encounter, someone thoughtfully suggested spreading burlap sandbags over the setting concrete to reduce the rain's impact on the setting concrete. Overnight, the carefully placed burlap bags became an integrated mosaic-burlap pattern. There was much discussion about keeping this unique and highly original design, eventually saving for another night the task of re-troweling the surface.

"You could almost hear an audible, collective sigh of relief as additional personnel joined the Packet. We all had jobs to do, and an extra set of any new hands and/or eyeballs were always welcome and put to good purpose. We were very 'democratic' in placing individuals where they were needed at the moment, whether pouring concrete, or documenting a combat mission.

"There was not much pre-verification, justification or pre-sale explanation required. There was just a lot of work to do. Simply sweeping one's arm majestically in the general direction of unfinished buildings knee deep in mud, or a ¾-ton truck, impatiently revving its engine to take a PAT team—one man short—to the helipad became a self-evident explanation.

"One the most important challenges for each 'tail' was earning the trust of the units we supported. I think it fair to say that all team leaders and shooters arrived at the formula early on: 'you carry your own weight' and 'help lessen the burden upon all concerned.' You listen. You heed. You survive. You win each day anew. Do these things consistently, and you earn a place among the trusted … and you all get to go home at night."

Lepore also reflects on the relationship between the 221st and the Department of the Army Special Photographic Office (DASPO) and other units.

"While the two organizations shared the same skill sets for (still and mopic) photographers, sound recordists, officer and NCO managers, and some over-lap in equipment capability, DASPO and the 221st had similar missions and served different 'masters.' Both units had the same goal: provide still- and motion-picture documentation of the war for their respective command channels and users.

"DASPO was created in 1962 to provide documentary film and still photography for use by senior officials of the national command authority: Department of the Army, Secretary of Defense, the Joint Chiefs of Staff and the Executive Branch (White House). DASPO operated three detachments: DASPO CONUS (Continental United States), DASPO Panama, and DASPO Pacific. Each detachment reported directly to, and received tasking assignments from the Office, Chief of Staff, US Army. DASPO Pacific, based at Ft. Shafter, Hawaii, rotated teams in and out of Vietnam generally on three-month rotations.

"DASPO's still- and motion-picture products served multiple purposes, for example, senior officials requiring coverage of specific subjects, combat operational and historical record, broadcast news (or B-roll) clips, or public information forums, such as 'The (Army's) Big Picture,' a TV series that aired as the Vietnam War progressed. The US Navy, Air Force and Marine Corps also deployed photo teams to document their role in combat operations and service unique branch requirements.

"The advance elements of the 221st arrived in Vietnam in May 1967. Here we reported to the Photo Officer, Headquarters, USARV (US Army Vietnam). The Photo Officer position was later 'dual-hatted' as Photo Officer, USARV and OIC, Southeast Asia Pictorial Center (SEAPC). SEAPC was a 'one-stop clearinghouse' for coordinating photo assignments throughout Vietnam, scheduling lab processing, and assuring quality control of both equipment and post-production before, during and after photographic material returned from the field. As a theater-level organization, the 221st supported USARV, MACV, and combat Divisional units in the Southeast Asia Theater of Operations.

"The personnel relationship between the two units might be labeled 'incestuous' given the relatively small demographic of Army officers, NCOs, and enlisted personnel with photo MOSs. It was not uncommon for personnel assigned to the 221st to later gravitate to DASPO, or vice versa. As in most professions, the word gets around if one is a 'rising star,' 'rocket-in-the-pocket,' 'requested-by-name' individual who adds quality to whatever he touches. You might imagine a two-star general on the Department of Army staff directing a by-name request for the photographer who just took the Army's Photo of the Year. Then too, there's 'the grass is always greener phenomena.'

"DASPO frequently swept Defense Department awards for photography. Their shooters were mostly senior NCOs with well-deserved reputations for excellence. They used 'high end' commercial photographic equipment, such as the Arriflex 'S' (Silent) and Arriflex 'BL' (Bulk Load 400/1200 foot) synchronous sound 16mm cameras and Nikon 35mm still cameras.

"DASPO personnel enjoyed additional benefits such as living on the 'civilian economy' wherever assigned. They had unfettered access to just about anything in a combat zone. Their entrée, if you will, might suggest—with all the subtlety of a falling redwood—that the current 'Army Chief of Staff has asked that we cover your operation, 'Sir.' They were diplomats and gentlemen, and gracious to their peers. When in their presence their modus operandi always brought a smile to my face, for bureaucratic inertia would evaporate like the morning fog.

"Having worked with, and for, both organizations, I believe DASPO did enjoy a certain cachet—a prestige and admiration amongst its peers. A 'tip-o-the-hat,' though, to both organizations for the soldier-photographers and those that supported them in getting the job done, be it big or small, hazardous or happenstance. Great photography doesn't depend on equipment, for iconic photos have been taken with a Kodak Brownie Hawkeye camera. Nor does it matter who defined the need. Rather, it is a keen eye in finding meaning, and sheer doggedness in getting the perfect shot—especially when your subject is 'shooting' back at you.

"We all aspired to meet the standards of those who came before us—the Lions—Matthew Brady, Robert Capa and W. Eugene Smith, come to mind. Both organizations upheld whatever legacy we may have occasioned for those who followed us. The measure of each organization's success is part of our nation's history now residing at the National Archives and Records Service.

"In general, we were 'attached' to the units we supported. By Army definition 'attached' is a relatively temporary placement of personnel and equipment required to accomplish a specific mission. Additionally, the field commander that receives the 'attachment' is responsible for the logistical support (primarily food, shelter, medical) of the personnel who are attached.

"The 221st was permanently 'assigned' to 160th Signal Group (a component of the 1st Signal Brigade). The Commander of the 160th Signal Group had OPCON

(Operational Control) over both the 221st and later the Southeast Asia Pictorial Center (SEAPC). OPCON gave the 160th Commander authority over all subordinate elements assigned to him. In this case, SEAPC managed, assigned tasks, and allocated assets to accomplish Headquarters Military Assistance Command (MACV), or Headquarters, US Army Vietnam (USARV) Theater-wide photo missions.

"Signal Corps OPCON commanders logistical assets were provided from (or through) their subordinate battalions. For example, the 69th Signal Battalion provided logistical support including laboratory processing to the 221st in the early weeks of Packet #1 deployment to Vietnam. In 1968 all 69th photo personnel and equipment were integrated with the 221st.

"I don't recall specific field assignments designated as 'joint operations' with Navy, Air Force, Marine Corps, or Coast Guard photographers, though it is highly likely we may have been working the same operation or story each from a unique branch perspective.

"We did support Allied forces in historical record documentation of operations for the Royal Thai Army (Queens Cobras), Australian Task Force and Republic of Korea (ROK) 'White Horse' and 'Tiger' Divisions."

Lepore went on to describe the weaponry that the soldiers deployed with the 221st carried.

"The standard MTO&E issue was the Colt M16A1 assault rifle with 5.56mm ammo, several 20–30 round magazines (a combined weight of nearly 8lb) and the .45-caliber M1911A1 pistol, for which the combined weight of pistol and one loaded magazine was about 3lb).

"The choice of weapons actually carried in the field depended on several things: the mission, whether we were going by foot or by chopper, and likelihood of exposure to direct contact with the enemy between points A and B.

"There's an unwritten rule, not often expressed. It's essentially the principle of not imposing on your infantry/armor/artillery host, who is, after all, allowing you to tag along. The host command defines whether you bring a bat or a bazooka to a potential gunfight. Once you've left the relative safety of the 'wire' surrounding a forward operating base, prudence and self-preservation dictated that you be able to go it on your own … or, at least, fire in common defense of everyone else.

"Once on the dusty trail—say supporting 'friendlies' in the bush—most of the hosting commanders 'appreciated' having we 'support strap-hangers' pulling our own weight. While our primary mission was photography, 'there is a tide in the affairs of men' … if someone shot at the collective 'we': 'Ya'll-best-be-engagin' the enemy.'

"Most of our photogs and team leaders recognized the pressure and burden placed on their brothers-in-combat arms in baby-sitting 'us.' It was not a war fighter's 'collateral' duty to do so. Most of the PAT members carried the .45-caliber pistol at minimum—plus, ammo cans, and whatever else might ingratiate 'us' with our infantry, armor, artillery, or aviation hosts—in mutual survival.

"The real issue was not the weapons that the photographer carried. It was the combined weight of everything else we lugged around. If we could manage it, and take pictures at the same time, we'd all be carrying M60 machine guns.

"Consider the weight-poundage of their 'survival' gear: flak jacket (body armor), roughly weighing 10lb; pistol and ammo; and one (or more) canteens of water. A photog would be lugging about 20lb total, plus C-rations, just for starters.

"Now, add the weight of the cameras (plural): the Bell and Howell hand-cranked 16mm Filmo camera weighed-in at about 6lb; or the 'light-weight' Beckman and Whitley CM-16 camera at 15lb. Additionally, each photog had to carry an expendable film supply (called a Prescribed Load List or 'PLL'). The quantity and type PLL varied by mission and how long and far afield they travelled before returning to re-supply. A mopic photog, 'Day-Tripper,' with a 'round trip ticket' might carry a Bell and Howell Filmo: basic load of roughly ten 100-foot film reels for the mopic Filmo, each weighing about ½lb, so 5lb total. The Beckman and Whitley CM-16's 400-foot loads each weighed about 2½lb, so for a basic load of three reels—7.5lb total. Still camera shooters equipped with the 120mm Graflex XL or 35mm Topcon and a load of 120mm/35mm roll film might add 7lb.

"A pound here, a pound there, and the total equipment load (film and camera) for a mopic or still photog's 'walk-on-the-wild-side-stompin' through the bush' might add an extra 31–42lb, give or take. Add the 'survival' gear of 20lb plus equipment/PLL for a combined load of 50–60lb."

What about contact with the enemy?

"Clearly the battle of Dak To (November 11, 1967) and the Tet Offensive (January 1968) were pivotal events, both as turning-points in the war, and as a revelation of how truly dangerous combat photography can be. These engagements are cited in detail both in *The History of the 221st Signal Company (Pictorial) 1 Jun 1966–25 March 1968*, and in numerous motion-picture documentaries, such as *Raw War: The Lost Film of Dak To*, and Ken Burns' *The 10,000 Day War*.

"Numerical measures alone cannot begin to describe the sacrifice by US and Allied forces engaged with an intractable enemy. Whether measured in the numbers of men-at-arms engaged by both sides, the cost in blood and injury, or citations for conspicuous valor while doing so, the legacy of those events lingers in the heart, and the images recorded there became enduring testaments to what occurred."

"I vaguely recall a statistic that somehow stuck with me over the years. The gist of it was the likelihood of a US platoon-sized contact and engagement with an opposing enemy force of the same size was about 1 in 23 sweeps. While trying to affirm this, I stumbled upon a 1967 CIA report in a book entitled *The Cold War in Asia 1945–93* by Vivienne Sanders that reported, 'Under 1 percent of nearly two million small-unit operations conducted between 1965 and 1967 resulted in contact with the enemy.'

"Given the CIA numbers, if you work through the math, one percent of nearly two million contacts (2,000,000 × 1% = 20,000) with the enemy over a span of two years, would be 10,000 enemy contacts per year, assuming (a) an equal frequency distribution of contacts on a daily basis, theater-wide (which of course there were not) at 27.4/day (10,000/365); and (b) Packet #1 was fielding eight PATs, each divided into two sections, or effectively 16 sets of shooters. Realistically we rarely had all eight or later 16 sub teams in the field at the same time, given the need for rest, refit, leave, medical, etc. Thus the odds would be pretty long at being in the 'right place' at the 'right (or wrong) time.'

"This back-of-the-envelope calculation ignores intelligence input that at least would hint at the concentration of bad actors in or near a given operation, thereby increasing the odds of raw, visceral imagery.

"Of course cameras give way to firearms at some point in coverage of a firefight, even if our mission was primarily photography, as indicated in the Unit History chronicle of events.

"There is often a supposition that some officers or enlisted men never ventured off the reservation, but rather stayed snugly on Long Binh Post. If you review the unit's development, equipping, deployment and what it took to get into the 'fight,' this supposition doesn't entirely fit.

"The 221st deployed to Vietnam in small groups (or 'packets') of 30 to 40 personnel, roughly at intervals of one to two months. Effectively from May 3, 1967 when Packet #1 arrived, until November 15, when the company's command element landed, all officers and NCOs served in double-, even triple-duty capacities. Any notion of staying on the 'reservation' for any prolonged period was a non-starter, and occurred only in rare circumstances.

"Those officers and NCOs, collectively the 'we,' led PATs in the field during the day. And when not in the field, all served as general contractors, foremen, and swing shift supervisors (often at night) to build a base camp of prefabricated Adams Huts. In the rare 'meantime' everyone performed 'other duties (motor pool, supply officer, perimeter defense etc.) as assigned.

"It was either 'all the above' or have an 'alphabet-numerical soup' of headquarter echelons above us wondering what the hell was the pay-off in sending photographers—and about $8 million dollars in equipment—to a war zone?

"It wasn't uncommon for officers and enlisted men to serve in all capacities in the same day, if not 'up-country' and too far afield. And they multi-tasked like this day after day, night after night, largely without grumbling.

"Every swinging 'Harry' (pardon the pun) had to multi-task, and this was before the term multi-task was but a twinkle in the eye of some business school professor's lecture on the military industrial complex.

"We simply didn't have the luxury of a stay-at-home Hobbit, of 'small size and hairy feet,' officer or enlisted, The reason was simple: As mother used to say, 'It don't happen by magic.' The 'it' in this case were mission objectives, be they photography, constructing buildings, standing guard, or supporting the manpower needs of the two Signal Headquarters across the street. Mother was right. Everyone in Packet #1, and later arrivals, pulled his weight because he had to. There was no one else to do what needed doing.

"We may not have had a complete complement of TO&E photographic equipment early on, but we had enough to assign Photo Assignment Teams with ongoing combat missions, and have that still photography processed by a 'sister unit' in the 69th Signal Battalion until our lab equipment arrived in July 1967.

"We all served double and triple duty in the first months (May–November 1967). All in all, the officers and NCOs were very tight with their enlisted team members. Remember, these teams often operated independently throughout the theater of operations. Once attached to a combat outfit, each team might be further divided into two or three pairs (still- and motion-picture photographers) to cover action from several vantage points.

"To lead effectively, officer and NCO PAT leaders had to think independently and lead by example. By its very nature, the Vietnam War either came to you, or you went to it. You could not look through the 'wrong end' of the binoculars and expect to see what you needed to record on film. Granted, you could use telephoto lenses with some subjects and situations, but you had to go where the action was. You had to see, feel, and understand the sweat and anxiety to record its enduring image. They had to be with their people.

"I served as OIC (Officer in Charge) (Acting Company Commander) of the 221st elements in Vietnam from May 3 to November 15, 1967. As elements of the 221st deployed from Ft. Monmouth to Vietnam in 'Packet' groups (# 2 through 5), effectively another 177 (14 officers and 163 NCOs) would be added to the total number of personnel in-country.

"This additional manpower becomes relevant when you consider that when first assigned to the 221st I was responsible for a Photo Assignment Team, PAT, with (then) six cameramen. I was in my element, doing what I loved. I could look through the viewfinder as I had always done, at least since the age of 13.

"I don't know if having responsibility for 243 others six months later qualifies as an overdrawn example of 'fleeting glory thrust upon you,' but command responsibility certainly distanced me from hands-on, looking through the viewfinder and working individually with my PAT.

"As the troop numbers under my care increased, my 'inner voice' reminded me, 'Lead, follow or get out of the way.' I deliberately made a point of sneaking away at the slightest excuse to 'check on my guys in the field.' I even took on assignments along the way. 'How else could I have realistically assessed what's really going on, unless I'm on the ground with them, much less ask them to do more than I, myself, was willing to do?

"The Army in August 1967 was keenly interested in demonstrating the role of armed gunships in air-to-ground support. The thrust of their requirement would highlight the effect of aerial-delivered 2.75-inch rockets before the insertion of troops into a hot LZ. Additional funding was required, apparently to increase the number of existing helicopter gunships and develop future generations of these unique airborne platforms. The air mobility folks had orchestrated a potent tactic. Prepping an LZ with suppressive fire was proving increasingly effective in reducing Allied casualties while increasing pressure on the Viet Cong.

"How best to demonstrate the effect of aerial-delivered fire on the enemy? There were numerous point-of-view (POV) shots taken from the perspective of the helicopter—through helo-mounted gun cameras, cockpit windshields, and helo to helo. While dramatic and visual, what we were missing was the POV from the ground perspective of gunships tearing up the real estate. Obviously, we could not provide an absolute POV of the Viet Cong, as death and destruction rained down from the skies. But we could show a POV as close as two antagonists could get and not become mutual casualties. The run-down went something like this during the 9th Infantry Division's (I believe) Operation *Coronado II*, a joint US–Vietnamese operation in Rung Sac Swamp of the Mekong Delta. Our 'slick' and team would parallel the first run of gunships to an LZ. As the gunships commenced the first of several suppressive-fire gun runs against a perimeter tree line we would slow hover, nap-of-earth [low altitude flight course], almost to the deck to get a 'standing man's eye view' just outside the footprint where the trailing troop transports were slated to touch down on a bone dry LZ about half a mile in diameter.

"From that vantage point, smoke and dust filled the air, punctuated by round impacts beyond. Blast pressure waves from these explosions were palpable to the body and ears. What one could *not* see beyond the smoke and flashes one only imagines.

"Two thoughts came to mind. It seemed time was in slow motion, moments at most, in the transition from hover to forward flight and climb-out. I wondered, 'Doesn't this thing move any faster?' I rocked back and forth in my bucket seat, as if creating an 'oomph-assisted take off' might help our bird get off the deck. We all began breathing again when it did.

"I pitied the VC present that day. No one could have survived that assault, even if bunkered. From time to time I re-imagine what it must have been like for them—perhaps a prairie dog witnessing the final minute of Macy's Fourth of July fireworks.

"There is an epilogue to this event, an ironic twist. About a year later, I was assigned to the Pentagon-based Army Photographic Agency (APA), as chief of production services. APA had its own motion-picture editors and we were frequently tasked by the Army staff to edit Vietnam-era motion picture footage for use in briefing Congress.

"I noticed in the booking for one of our mini-screening rooms that the Army DCS Operations had scheduled a showing of a film on Army Aviation in Vietnam. Curious, I monitored the proceedings in the standing-room-only 28-seat theater. It was a short 10-minute review of Army Aviation's use of gunships and development since the mid-1960s. One could speculate at that point that it would be used for briefing Congress appropriations committees to sustain development of future attack helicopters. The building storyline included the evolution of ever more violent and lethal applications of Aerial Rocket Artillery. Sure enough, there was our footage. The irony is that I had never seen the rushes from this particular assignment. But I knew it was ours—a shoot-'em-up finale to this film. The point was well made—airborne assault by rocket and machine gun was devastatingly lethal.

"As dimmer lights brightened, the three-star general host asked, 'Any comments? Suggestions?' There was a very, very pregnant pause. One full bird colonel just pursed his lips, slowly letting exhaled air form a 'W-o-o-o-ho-o-o.' Then came the 'rain-on-the-parade' punch line: 'Just too Hollywood,' opined some eager-beaver, grand-standing lieutenant colonel.

"The three-star purposefully asked, 'Whatdya mean?'

"The light colonel responded. 'Well, Sir, how did they get there first? I mean the camera.'

"At that juncture I was tempted to scream, 'Ya dummy! Among the first, if not *the* first people on that LZ were photographers.'

"In later re-thinking this encounter, it's a wonder that I didn't climb over the seats and, eyeball to eyeball, get in the face of this posey. Prudence, thoughtful reflection, divine providence, and probably my career prevailed. I just bit my tongue. Such are the vicissitudes of doing your job in war."

The award of the Meritorious Unit Commendation recognized only those who served with the Southeast Asia Pictorial Center (SEAPC) and the 221st from July 1, 1969 to March 31, 1970. Such citations were usually initiated by the commander of the unit, in this case SEAPC, bounded by an inclusive from-to date range, or specific, noteworthy contributions.

"Unfortunately, a petition to redress, or amend the commendation to include all members of the 221st having served just as diligently, effectively, and honorably had to be made through the Secretary of the Army to the Board for the Correction of Military Records within two years of its original submission date. Such a request for redress was not made. Had I personally known of this oversight, I would have written the petition myself and requested the commander, Major Thomas A. DeYoung, to serve as its sponsor. Certainly all members of the unit were equally deserving of recognition for their contributions. In this regard, all those not so recognized are diminished. But in our heart of hearts we know what we contributed."

But it wasn't all action, as Lepore makes clear.

"The 221st, as a subordinate unit of the 160th Signal Group, essentially provided still photographic support for the 40th and 44th Signal Battalion units also under the 160th Signal Group. Civic Action initiatives undertaken by the 221st in the fall of 1967 included visits to a Catholic Orphans Home in Bien Hoa and support for a sister Vietnamese photo unit, which provided audiovisual support to regional ARVN."

Finally Lepore talked about the relationship the troops had with the civilian press and joint missions with it.

"Early in the war, the civilian press had unfettered access to just about everything. They could go practically anywhere, any time. There was no PIO supervision to speak of, though later in the war as media bias became more obvious, commanders might be more circumspect about having media embedded within their operations.

"Print and electronic media's only real impediment was waiting for helo transport from location to location. Here we could be of some assistance, for example offering a spare seat on a Huey hauling us. Along the way, if we were headed to the same destination, they would usually 'pump' us for insight: Where was the action likely to be? Which was the more aggressive airborne unit? They might ask if we had contacts with the destination unit that might put them up for the night. They usually had these livability conditions worked-out in far more detail than we. But there was no harm in asking the question and helping push back the frontiers of the mutually possible. It might give all a competitive edge, or something more than C-rations for dinner.

"Basically, our interactions were congenial. Civilian and military photographers alike shared common objectives. We all had to get to the action to record it, usually by way of helicopter. It was a give-and-take proposition. They'd run out of film, we needed a cigarette and a light, we envied their equipment and wondered what it was like to stay at Saigon's Caravelle Hotel.

"Two memorable names come to mind, both brief, chance encounters. One was Oriana Fellaci, a delightful Italian journalist, who talked a mile a minute. She was very frank and direct, adept at covering wars and revolutions and tough as nails. The other was Peter Arnett of the Associated Press. His persona was right out of central casting for a war correspondent of the old school, and he had a lot of mileage and experience under his belt. It has been so long ago that I don't remember the precise location of our meetings though I think it might have been the Michelin Rubber Plantation in late 1967 with the 25th Infantry Division during Operation *Diamond Head*."

After leaving Vietnam, Lieutenant Colonel Frank Lepore continued to make contributions to public affairs at U.S. government level, including working for Secretaries of Defense James Schlesinger and Caspar Weinberger, and in several different capacities at the Pentagon. He also served in public affairs capacities for NATO, the National Oceanic and Atmospheric Administration, the National Hurricane Center in Miami and FEMA. Early in his life, he vowed to 'do his part for God and Country.' He most certainly has.

Lieutenant Frank Lepore at his desk mapping out the work of photographic "packets" (team operations) at the headquarters of the 221st Signal Pictorial Company, US Army, Long Binh, Vietnam. (Frank Lepore collection)

The Country Needed to Know: Chuck Abbott

Lansing, Illinois, native Chuck Abbott worked as a union projectionist in a movie house before joining the Army at age 25. As a projectionist, he was already familiar with splicing both 16 and 35mm film, so it was natural that, since Abbott had just graduated from the Army's Motion Picture School at Ft. Monmouth, New Jersey, and was still awaiting orders, several NCOs suggested he try being assigned to the Motion Picture section of DASPO. He hadn't heard of the unit up until then but soon discovered that the mopic office needed someone to assist instructors who were charged with preparing daily itineraries.

"I was told the new CO of the Photo School had just been the CO of DASPO/Panama, so I made an appointment to speak to him. He was very kind. We spent several hours talking about DASPO. He called someone, who I later learned was the sergeant major of DASPO located at DASPO HQ at the Pentagon.

"The CO gave the sergeant major my background and ID number, and told him that I'd just graduated from the mopic school." One week later, Abbott had orders for DASPO Pacific.

Abbott said, "When talking to the CO, I noticed he smoked House of Windsor cigars. I returned to his office with a box, and showed him my orders, with a great deal of thanks."

Before that, being involved with motion pictures was a hobby for Abbott.

"I had purchased a Bolex H 16mm camera, and shot family and friends. On occasion, I would film some newsworthy subjects. I attended a few mopic courses at Columbia College in Chicago. Being involved with theater projection of 35mm film, mopic was a real interest of mine."

Abbott also remembers why he wanted to take his hobby further and what he wanted to do with it.

"The reason I joined the Army was because of the Vietnam War. I wanted to pursue my Interest in mopic photography."

Before signing up for the Army, he'd made the rounds at different service organizations' recruiting offices, but he inked with the Army.

"Of all the recruiters, the Army one was most helpful in getting me into the Army Photo School," he recalls. And Abbott has high praise for the training the Army afforded him as well.

"Training at Ft. Monmouth was awesome. Between lectures on basic story-telling, camera operation, creating a script, writing captions, the hands on of performing these skills was unbelievable. The first few weeks outdid the several semesters I paid for at Columbia. Several trips outside the fort took us to Ft. Dix, where we photographed guys going through basic training, which was neat since we had already been through basic."

Another trip Abbott and his classmates took was to Lakehurst Naval Air Station, where the German airship Hindenburg crashed in 1937.

"We were flown around in a helicopter to get a feel of shooting aerial footage," he said.

His classmates then took a trip to the Army Pictorial Center (APC), in New York City to familiarize themselves with studio cameras and the procedures to set-up for shooting on a stage.

Back at Ft. Monmouth, they were taught the use of the 16mm Bell and Howell camera known as the Filmo, and the similar 35mm B & H camera known as the Eyemo.

"When I was assigned to DASPO Pacific, I was using the 35mm B & H camera, and a few months later, we started shooting everything in 16mm. So we did most of the shooting with the 16mm B & H camera. Sometime in late 1967 or early 1968 we began to use the Arriflex camera with a 100-foot spool load or with the 400-foot magazine, to which the Arriflex could adapt. We did use the Arriflex 35 on occasion. For my personal use, I carried a Nikonus by Nikon. It was a waterproof camera and ideal when traveling during the monsoon season, or on an assignment that took us through wet terrain."

Abbott's Pacific Theater résumé remains impressive. He served three 90-day TDY assignments in Vietnam, one 90-day TDY assignment in Thailand, one 90-day TDY assignment in Korea, and a 40-day TDY assignment that took him to Taiwan, Okinawa, and southern Japan.

"I was assigned a few days to travel to the big Island of Hawaii to cover a firing of a Davy-Crocket missile. This was located at the Pohacaloa Training area, where it is the only place it snows in Hawaii. I can tell you for sure that it does get cold there, and it does snow!"

His feelings run deep for the combination of TDYs he was ordered on.

"I loved all the places my assignments took me to. Vietnam had some good experiences, and certainly some bad ones. The Viet Cong and NVA troops were killing their own people to prove that they were in charge, and the locals were not to side with the ARVN or American troops. Most of the guys that I photographed were certainly all out to aid the South Vietnamese People, but it just became a chase from one area to another rather than some front. When the troops moved forward, the people behind should have been able to collect themselves and get back to a normal way of life. But, without a front, you gain no ground. I believe that is what disgusted the American troops most. It just seemed like the local people did not want our assistance. Of course in their defense, when we came by during the day and discovered enemy presence, no one wanted to say anything because the bad guys would come back at night and kill a few of the villagers."

Vietnam still seems to be at the forefront of his memories so many years later.

"One operation I was on with two other guys was a bad one that I continue to recall at times. We were filming a device called the "People Sniffer." It was about shoebox size and strapped to the floor of a helicopter. A hose was plugged into the sniffer, and the other end dangled from beneath the chopper. It measured the ammonia scent of the human body and was best used in early morning daylight as the dew rose from the ground carrying the human scent.

We had two mopic guys, Rick Rein and me, and "Frenchy," a still photographer. Frenchy and I took the first flight with the sniffer, and Rick covered us with air-to-air shots from one of the two trailing gunships [helicopters with heavy armament]. When we returned to base, I was really sick, and Rick was joking about how we looked so good sailing across the treetops. I didn't eat that night, and we were up early to do it all over again. Rick was joking and wanted to fly in the sniffer. He reminded me that I didn't look well enough to fly [in the sniffer] again. We had a few laughs and I agreed." Abbott remembered.

In the chase ship, which Rein had been in the day before, Abbott could see and photograph them easily by placing one foot out the door on the left landing pad of the helicopter. He was secured to the chopper with a harness which was hooked to a "D" ring mounted on the floor of the chopper.

"The sight was awesome," Abbott enthused. "The sniffer looked like a dragonfly looking for its morning meal. Back and forth and up and down over the treetops. I had earphones on, so I could hear what the flight crew was saying."

He heard that the sniffer had taken a hit from ground fire and was going down.

"As I looked at Frenchy, I don't recall if he pulled me back into the chopper or the gunner at the door, but we took a steep climb and as we banked into a dive, I was trying to right myself. I could see the other chase ship climb into the same dive that we were in. Machine guns were firing and rockets being shot into the area that was believed to be where the ground fire came from."

They made several passes and then climbed to a height just over the area where they could see the crashed sniffer through the heavy covered terrain.

"We hovered there for quite some time. I could hear in the earphones that troops were landing just outside that heavy terrain. But it would be a while before the troops could reach the crash site. As two other gunships hovered next to us, we returned to base. Frenchy and I stayed in the command center hoping to hear some good news, but about midnight word came through that the troops had reached the crash site and all aboard, including his friend Rick Rein, were dead. I have never forgotten Rein."

Frenchy and Abbott called the team office in Saigon and reported what happened. They were told to take our time and return when they could.

"That was the worst of my experiences," Abbott recalled.

Abbott's other experiences involve traveling throughout the country documenting U.S. Army activities. He was assigned several subjects to cover in the Mekong Delta, which took him near the Cambodia border. One interesting assignment was the move of an orphanage run by Catholic priests and nuns.

"The Viet Cong were robbing the head priest of rations and money that the South Vietnamese government gave him to operate the orphanage. The VC would come at night to take what he had and leave little for his staff and the orphans. He was afraid to bring this to the local government representative, believing that it would get back to the communist guerillas."

The priest was finally able to meet with the American general in charge of this area to discuss his situation. The general assured him that he would see what he could do and was able to obtain another location for the orphanage through the South Vietnamese government a good distance from the Cambodian border. U.S. Army trucks and two "Flying Crane" helicopters were sent in to effect the move.

Several DASPO teams were sent to cover the packing and moving of the orphans and orphanage staff, then film the arrival at the new location.

"We slated our film 'Operation Little Lift.' It was quite interesting and very touching to see everyone so cheerful. A still photographer and I boarded one chopper and another DASPO team boarded the second chopper. We met the other DASPO teams covering our arrival."

While covering Army activities, new weapons were introduced into the war effort—Hueys, Cobras, and tanks were the norm. But Abbott took special interest in an out-of-the-ordinary story concerning the Veterinary Corps. This unit oversaw the dogs assigned to dog handlers with whom they guarded base perimeters, sniffed out and pointed to Viet Cong cadres hiding in the bush, and the like.

"I traveled with a veterinarian to the Marine Corps base in Hue. He performed a follow-up on a dog that had been wounded," Abbott said.

An added interesting responsibility of the Veterinary Corps, according to Abbott, was that it was responsible for was the inspection of meat products. When entering Vietnam by air or ship, the vets would inspect the products for any meat that may have spoiled, or was incorrectly packaged.

Once out of Vietnam, Abbott's mopic work no longer included the possibility of combat lurking in the tree lines.

"The teams in Thailand and Korea did not have combat to cover. While in Thailand, there were encampments for civilians coming across the Cambodia and

Thailand borders. The U.S. and Thai Armies had encampments as well, because [Khmer Rouge] snipers from the Cambodia side would take shots at the civilians. Most coverage in Thailand was of the assistance the American and Thai troops gave to local villages."

While Abbott was in Korea, he journeyed to the DMZ to cover the troops a few times.

"The Korea team was first on sight regarding the Pueblo incident," he said. "DASPO was the only photo group allowed to cover the exchange of prisoners."

He also remembered "one big coverage, an exercise that brought troops and equipment from Ft. Bragg, North Carolina, directly to Korea." The operation, which was called Operation *Redifreeze*, brought "everything and went on non-stop," Abbott said.

"What a sight that was," he added. "I was on the ground covering men and equipment being dropped by parachute. I had to stay alert or I could have had a tank, truck, jeep, or troops landing on me. The sky was loaded with parachutes. A beautiful, awesome sight."

All told, Chuck Abbott shot mopic for DASPO Pacific from May 1967 to July 1969. After his discharge from the Army, he returned to the Chicago area and spent a few years covering the news, mostly as a freelance photographer for a local TV station.

Today, Chuck Abbott calls Macungie, Pennsylvania, home, but his thoughts are never far from his time filming the troops for the Army, and for a country that needed to know how our troops were faring in Asia.

MoPic Photog' Wearing the Blue:
Joe Montgomery

Joe Montgomery graduated from Philadelphia's West Catholic High School in June of 1955 and immediately tried to join the US Air Force. But there were so many enlistees trying to do the same that even his having been in the Air National Guard since his junior year in high school, he was not able to wear the blue until September of that year; he was sent to Sampson Air Force Base in upstate New York for basic training.

In addition to being surprised that he was not able to enlist in the USAF immediately after graduation, he was further surprised when he received orders to be trained as a motion-picture photographer. It was something he had absolutely no experience in.

"I was assigned to Eglin AFB Air Force," he said. "The Air Force had no school for motion-picture photographers at that time. All my training was On the Job Training (OJT). I always seemed to be in the wrong place for advanced courses like those they offered at Syracuse University and other colleges. However, the OJT provided training in studio work, animation, documentary, and engineering photography,"

Being a mopic photographer in the Air Force carried with it a lot of different responsibilities, according to Montgomery, who pointed out that the term MOS does not apply in the USAF, which uses AFSC (Air Force Specialty Code) instead. He further stated that up until the Vietnam War, if you were a motion-picture photographer, there was an invisible line separating documentary mopic and technical mopic.

"My Eglin and Edwards assignments meant I fell under the technical side. I was in Systems Command and most of our photography was done with high-speed cameras (200 to 1000fps). At Eglin they primarily tested weapons and ordnance, and how these worked from different aircraft."

There, they photographed cold-weather testing in the climatic hangar at temperatures as low as -40. At Edwards, Montgomery primarily photographed flight testing of experimental airplanes such as the X-15, XB-70, SR-71, and others.

"So, I did a lot of flying at both bases," Montgomery said. "I witnessed the testing of a missile called Bomarc, which was designed to intercept enemy aircraft—for which we used a series of remote cameras. I also filmed numerous drops of an X-15 from a B-52, the rollout and testing of the XB-70, and the testing of using a C-130 for picking up a man from the ground who was tethered to a balloon."

"One of our photo chase pilots at Edwards, Joe Engle, became an astronaut. Flying with him in a jet was like being with a kid in a hot rod."

Montgomery is quick to point out that when the Vietnam War took over the news, things changed for Air Force still- and motion-picture photographers.

"Due to Vietnam, in 1965, the line between technical and documentary disappeared. From that point I was strictly documenting the Air Force at Ubon, Thailand, Vandenberg Air Force Base, Hickam Army Air Field, and Norton AFB in San Bernardino, California."

But Montgomery's missions as an Air Force photographer were far from mundane.

"Aside from Ubon, two of the many of the interesting projects I covered were President Nixon greeting returning astronauts at Johnson Island in the Pacific, and my final assignment as a photographer covering the Thunderbirds tour of South and Central America in 1973. I even got to fly with them," he recalls.

Montgomery's detachment at Ubon had just been established when he arrived in October 1966. Before that, he was what he referred to as "mal-assigned" to the Philippines in July of that year.

"There were no slots for a motion-picture photographer, and I spent four months waiting for the Air Force to do something with me. Finally, I just volunteered for Southeast Asia."

Ubon had the 8th Tactical Fight Wing, flying F-4s, led by Colonels Robin Olds and Chappie James. Montgomery was supposed to fly backseat F-4 missions, but the brass at Ubon wasn't thrilled about that, so they initially had the pilot in the backseat carry a camera. After he had been there almost a month, however, a mission order came from South Vietnam specifying a backseat photographer.

"I flew my first mission [over North Vietnam] escorting F-105s from Takhli. Nothing spectacular. The weather was bad in the north, so they just radar dropped bombs on a suspected truck park," he said.

When they got ready to land, they had to use the cable system on the runway—similar to cables used on carriers—because the cockpit lights indicated one landing gear was not down.

"I flew seven more F-4 and two Blind Bat—C-130 dropping flares—missions, though initially, I could not photograph F-4s if there were Thai Air Force aircraft in the shot, because we weren't really in Thailand."

A normal day for Montgomery was often just coming up with his own ideas just to stay busy.

"In a lot of ways, it was a strange war experience. For example, our security police could not openly display weapons while guarding entrance locations since it was a Thai base. NCOs lived off base. I lived in a house with five other NCOs from our detachment. Most of the time we would not realize a war was taking place. It was the downing of an aircraft and loss of a pilot that brought home the realities," he remembers.

And the day-to-day routine of Ubon was interrupted once when Montgomery received orders to return to the Philippines.

"There appeared to be problems with F-4 and Sidewinder missiles. They wanted coverage of test missile firings from an F-4."

The only other unusual events at Ubon happened on the day of the "Great MiG Hunt," and coverage of pilot Robin Olds returning from missions after having downed MiG fighters.

"His fourth MiG was a big celebration with champagne," Montgomery remembered. "They anticipated he was going to become an ace for the second time." (His first time was during World War II.)

Olds never did get the fifth MiG, however.

"Ubon became much more involved in combat operations after I left in 1967."

Joe Montgomery retired from the Air Force nine years later as a master sergeant. In 1986, he received his master's degree in education from the University of Houston (having received his bachelor's from Chaminade University in Hawaii while in the Air Force). He taught middle school social studies for 17 years in Houston and retired from teaching in 2003.

"I believe I had one the greatest jobs in the Air Force. Every day was something different, sometimes exciting, sometimes boring, but different, and I was on flying status. Can you imagine, being 18 years old and breaking the sound barrier in an F-100 fighter jet? Or flying at Edwards with your pilot who is a future astronaut, and a couple days before he might have piloted the X-15 rocket plane? What more could you ask for? I went to various places in the world and in the United States, either for a long stay or a short TDY. Great friends were made, and some were lost in combat or accidents. A great time all in all. Actually, I was sorry I retired when I did.

Part of that great time included the fact that he met and married his wife Judy, who was also in the Air Force, at Eglin AFB in 1960.

"It was probably fate. I was from Philadelphia, and she was from a Philly suburb. Our two daughters were born at Eglin, and my son was born at Edwards. My Air Force career meant a lot of suffering for them. Essentially, Judy raised the three kids. And the children had to put up with constantly changing schools. I could not have made it without their help. Judy and I just celebrated our 56th anniversary. Not an easy 56 years for any of us, but we made it."

US Air Force mopic cameraman Joe Montgomery (crouching lower right) at the ceremony at Ubon Air Base, Thailand, for World War II ace Colonel Robin Olds after the colonel downed his fourth North Vietnamese MiG fighter jet. (Joe Montgomery collection)

From Hot Rod Comics and Hemingway... to Vietnam: Dennis "Bao Chi Mac" McCloskey

Dennis McCloskey grew up in a small western Montana town in the 1950s and early 1960s. It was not an experience that could be described as sophisticated, according to the Montana lad who would one day go by the nickname "Bao Chi (Vietnamese for journalist) Mac."

"We had two local TV channels, and the neighborhood parents had an agreement that no one would cave in and subscribe to cable. It wasn't Mayberry, but it sure wasn't *West Side Story*, either. I grew up hunting, fishing, camping ... and reading. I enjoyed everything from Hot Rod Comics to Hemingway, and dreamed of adventure."

Adventure would come McCloskey's way eventually but that would be a few years down the road.

"I was shy, not particularly interested in team sports, and did fairly well in school ... academically rather than socially." He credits his mother with introducing him to the hobby that would carry him through his enlistment in the United States Navy.

"My mother—as a teenager during World War II—had used a Kodak Brownie and developed her own film, contact-printing her snapshots. She mentioned casually that it had worked fairly well as a ploy to meet people—an idea that I grabbed and decided could be applied easily to my situation. I read a couple of photo magazines to be able to throw out words like f-stop, depth-of-field, and film speed, then bought an off-brand 35mm SLR with two lenses from a newspaper classified ad and started convincing cute classmates I could take their portfolio pictures."

When he thinks back on it now, he says, "My photographic efforts were probably slightly better than their dad's snapshot, but I did get to spend some time alone with a few cute girls."

McCloskey's father had spent most of World War II aboard ship in the Pacific, "dodging kamikazes at most of the island-hopping major invasions," McCloskey said.

"Despite my curiosity, he rarely shared memories or stories, and I was left to speculate. I found myself digging into *Encyclopedia Britannica* looking up odd place names I occasionally overheard—Iwo Jima, Saipan, Tarawa, Ulithi ... Brisbane, the Shanghai Bund."

McCloskey graduated from high school in 1966 and didn't have enough money to go on to college. He went to work at an auto parts store for the next year and a half, still living at home. His mother, however, very much wanted her son to attend university, but sending him there would have been difficult on the family.

McCloskey had never seen the exact dollar amount that was available to him if he enlisted, but he realized that if he were to enlist, he would be able to go to college on the GI Bill after his time in the service was up.

"Vietnam was starting to appear regularly in the nightly news, while local university students began trying to get their names in the paper, protesting the war.

"I had a couple of friends who had already enrolled at the University of Montana, and were parroting their knowledge of what-the-Vietnamese-people-really-wanted. I wasn't buying into the narrative. It occurred to me that not a single pundit my age had ever been closer to Vietnam than Spokane, and none had ever even met a Vietnamese."

The draft was hanging over McCloskey's head, and at the same time, perhaps influenced by the writing of the likes of the Ernest Hemingway he was first exposed to as a younger lad, he was desperate for a taste of adventure.

"Leon Uris' *Battle Cry* was my favorite book, so the Marine Corps was on the table, but I thought my father would be proud of me if I joined the Navy. I talked to the recruiter, got a bus ticket to Butte, took a physical and written test, and raised my hand to take the oath," he recalled.

There were 17 or 18 sailors in the Navy contingent, and McCloskey overheard one of the recruiters discussing splitting up the group. Only six were to go to San Diego and the rest were to be sent to Great Lakes.

"It was February 1968, and I broke into their conversation. I knew I'd rather be in California than Illinois during the winter. It worked, and I found myself carrying six sets of records and 'in charge' of a detail en route to the Recruit Training Center in San Diego."

When he got to boot camp, more comprehensive physical exams awaited him, as well as shaved heads, hours-long written tests, and a "classification interview."

"I had filled out my 'dream sheet' and only remember that I had photographer's mate as my first choice. The personnel man on the other side of the desk tried to tell me that it was ridiculously unlikely that I could get Photo School, but that with my scores, almost anything else was a possibility. I didn't bite, and explained that I had interned with a local photographer, assisted in the darkroom at the newspaper, and had years of photo hobby experience. I was lying through my teeth … and confident that there was no way my claims would be investigated. I just needed to convince one guy I deserved a photo school slot if one was available.

"When the last week of boot camp rolled around, I heard my name and 'Naval Air Technical Training Unit, Photo "A" School, Pensacola, Florida.' My company commander snagged me after the announcements were complete and congratulated me on being the first boot he had ever seen actually get photo school."

When McCloskey got to the Photography School complex at Naval Air Station Pensacola, it seemed to predate World War II. It consisted of "A" School, which entailed teaching basic photography, including aerial, architectural, studio, scientific, motion picture, photojournalism, darkroom techniques, and chemistry, and both "B" and "C" Schools for more advanced and specialized study.

"I believe it was rare for Navy photographers to make E-4 without going to 'A' School, but it was possible," McCloskey said.

All Navy rates—or job specialties—are sub-groups of broader classifications, McCloskey explained. Photographers were an aviation specialty, so only "airmen" (E-3) were eligible to strike for photographer's mate. By the same token, journalists were "seamen," and any Seabee specialty became "construction men." Hull and propulsion specialties are "firemen," and so on.

Before a sailor volunteers for a specialty, McCloskey said, he or she must first qualify as an airman, seaman, or whatever. Out in the fleet, or at a shore establishment, an unrated sailor can apply to work in a particular area, get OJT, and study for rating tests. His photo school class included WAVES, Coast Guard, Marines, Reservists, one UDT (Underwater Demolition Team), and a couple of Photographer's Mates Third Class petty officers from the fleet.

"All the members of my class were probably 18 to 22 years old, and certainly included a wide variety of personalities and backgrounds. I remember one actually had a degree from Rochester Institute of Technology in photo science, and we had a couple of GEDs. Most of the rest had at least a year or two of college. During the first week of class, except for a few students sent by their parent commands, we were again filling out our dream sheets for assignment after graduation. There was a tradition that the top-scoring student got his choice of available assignments … and, oddly enough, the most requested duty was shore-duty Vietnam. In fact, an incredibly high percentage of photographer's mates in the Navy were trying to get to Vietnam. That was my first choice, and I knew I had to graduate at the top of my class or it just wasn't going to happen. I coasted through high school … but now I really had some incentive to study."

At the end of the three-month class, assignments were again handed out, and the tension was pretty high. McCloskey got a slip of paper that simply said, "COMSEVENTHFLT DETACHMENT CHARLIE." Everyone else's orders either had a ship name and fleet, base and location, or squadron and air station.

"I approached one of the instructors and asked, "What and where is COMSEVENTHFLT DETACHMENT CHARLIE?" His response was, 'You gotta be shittin' me!' He called over two of the other instructors. I was standing there, an 18-year-old E-3, and two E-7 Chiefs and an E-6 First Class were enviously staring at my orders. The Chief quietly said, 'You've got the best orders in the Navy,' and walked away."

McCloskey and two other classmates were still waiting for travel orders when the rest of the class had already flown out, and he had what he called "a greatly expanded list of inoculations" on his shot card.

"I was headed for Saigon and the other two were going to Hawaii and Guam or Okinawa. I had been warned that I was probably going to have to go through SERE [Survival, Evasion, Rescue and Escape] school, but they just routed me to Great Circle from Travis AFB into Japan and that was one of the cracks I fell through."

McCloskey flew into Tachikawa Air Force Base and was bussed to Yokota AFB transient quarters.

"There I was, a 19-year-old kid who had never been out of a highly regimented training command, and told to 'hang loose' in Japan. I was terrified. An alcoholic E-6 stew burner (ship's cook) on the third floor took pity on me. He had been in Florida and got orders back to where his wife lived in Georgia and then somehow managed to get all the way to Japan, knowing that it would be easier and cheaper for the Navy to change his orders to the Western Pacific than fly him back to the States. He and I lived in the Enlisted Men's Club until I got called for a flight into Saigon."

Although McCloskey was Vietnam-bound, the inner workings of the Command Seventh Fleet Detachment Charlie Public Affairs Office were not explained to him before his arrival in Vietnam and even during his time in-country.

"None of this was told to me at the time. I learned most of what follows after I did some research decades later. The chain of command for the Navy ran from the Chief of Naval Operations (CNO) to Commander in Chief Pacific (CINCPAC) in Pearl Harbor, and then split into Commander Naval Forces Vietnam (COMNAVFORV), subordinate to MACV in Saigon, and Commander Seventh Fleet (COMSEVENTHFLT) aboard the flagship in WESTPAC.

COMNAVFORV commanded almost all Navy units based in Vietnam—Naval Support Activities (NSAs) for logistics, Navy Construction Battalions (SeaBees), smaller boat units including PBRs, Swift Boats, and a variety of LSTs and LSMs. Naval Advisory Groups—advisors to the Vietnamese Navy—Naval Special Operations units such as UDT and SEALs, and the only Navy Attack Helicopter squadron (HAL-3) were also assigned to COMNAVFORV. To the best of McCloskey's knowledge, DET CHARLIE was the only Navy unit in Vietnam not subordinate to NAVFORV."

"This division was actually important to what I was assigned to cover because the rest of the Navy presence in or offshore Vietnam consisted of the 'blue water Navy,' or the Seventh Fleet. All the ships off the coast of Vietnam were part of the Seventh Fleet, from nuclear submarines and aircraft carriers through a battleship and heavy cruiser, then continuing through destroyers and minesweepers, all the way down to fuel and ammo replenishment ships. Even a couple of hospital ships.

"Almost all of them pulled a WESTPAC Cruise, visiting Japan and Taiwan and making port calls in Hong Kong, Manila, or Singapore, as well as duty off Vietnam.

"I don't believe the Navy was unique in the tendency of middle- and upper-level 'management' to engage in 'turf wars.' Competing for publicity, and available funding, between NAVFORV and Seventh Fleet was an unfortunate reality. A few unaligned Navy units, such as Combat Camera Group Pacific, that flew in and out of the hostile fire zone, additionally muddied the waters," he added.

In 1965, Vietnam seemed to be heating up and a couple of Navy Public Affairs Officers, who were on what McCloskey called "limited duty not eligible for ship command," suggested that there was a need for Fleet Public Affairs to be available in Vietnam for handling civilian press inquiries and generating features and press releases about fleet contributions to the war effort. COMSEVENTHFLT DETACHMENT CHARLIE had been established and headquartered at Tan Son Nhut Air Base in Saigon to coordinate air strikes between Seventh Air Force and Seventh Fleet, after some near dogfights when both Air Force and Navy aircraft were striking targets in close proximity.

"Because DET CHARLIE already existed, along with an administrative and communications capability and even had its own C-1A courier aircraft, it was relatively simple to attach a PAO component with photographers, journalists, and public-affairs officers in downtown Saigon. DET CHARLIE became an opportunity to shine for rising-star PAOs, and it rapidly expanded from a few TAD/TDY personnel to a more formal unit with established billets for specific rates, ratings, and PAOs.

"When I arrived in September 1968, there were about a dozen each of PAOs, journalists, and photographers. PAOs handled press inquiries, briefed the media daily at the Five O'clock Follies, and escorted news media groups visiting ships. Journalists and photographers formed teams embarking with Seventh Fleet units to generate features and 'hometowners' afloat, while our elite photographers and journalists (8148s—graduates of the Syracuse University Military Photojournalist program) were allowed to embark alone and create their own stories. There was a tendency for DET CHARLIE officers to arrange embarks aboard specific ships with the journalists leading the team and photographers supporting the journalists' efforts."

Photographers who wanted to write their own stories, and journalists who wanted to take pictures, were actually encouraged to do so," McCloskey remembered.

DET CHARLIE was unlike any other public-affairs unit in the Navy at that time, McCloskey said, because it was free to distribute photo features to any outlets that men in the unit thought might be interested.

"After my second or third centerspread in *Pacific Stars and Stripes*, I was allowed to embark as a solo act, effectively becoming a designated photojournalist."

For sailors, Vietnam tours were classified as "sea duty" even though they were rotated between sea duty and shore duty for a 12-month period. What were known as "Critical Ratings" were allowed with approval from a sailor's command and the Pentagon to voluntarily extend their tour for six months.

"I managed to get approval to extend my tour four times until I ran into the troop withdrawal political move from Washington. (DET CHARLIE had been authorized four 8,148 billets, and I held one of those designated slots for more than a year and a half, despite having never been formally classified as a photojournalist," McCloskey said.

In 1969, DET CHARLIE established a satellite office at Subic Bay in the Philippines.

"Because a majority of our stories were aboard ship, and almost all Seventh Fleet ships called in at Subic frequently, it was easier to go aboard there than trying to arrange helicopter or high-line transfers at sea to reach a ship."

McCloskey remembers a "minor turf battle" over permission for him to use the base photo lab, a problem that was solved by his unit's possession of the Fleet Air Photo Lab at Cubi Point during the night shift. "Problem solved … FAPL used it during the day, and we used it at night," he said.

As part of the "troop withdrawal" from Vietnam, DET CHARLIE PAO was decommissioned as a unit on June 30, 1970, and immediately renamed CINCPACLFT PAO Det Westpac. "Same people, same mission, but no longer in Vietnam."

During the following 11 months until McCloskey's discharge from active duty, he still qualified for and received hostile-fire pay. And he actually encountered more actual hostile fire than he had while he was officially stationed in Vietnam.

"Because I was from a fleet command, there was always a struggle to get permission from the appropriate command to do features on ground combat units. Those of us dedicated to the idea of getting the story of Vietnam in the media were pawns in the turf battles of career Navy and Marine officers. Our problem was actually one of overcoming the popular idea that combat was restricted to muddy boots and ejected brass. Very few people were aware of the often fatal dangers of working on an aircraft carrier flight deck, or pumping jet fuel across a narrow gap between two ships steaming side-by-side at 20 knots. Medevac choppers often delivered casualties direct from the bush to one of the hospital ships in Da Nang Harbor … and in some cases, the casualties included helicopter crew members."

During his over 32 months in the detachments, he embarked for more than two weeks at a time aboard a battleship, two destroyers, a hospital ship, a nuclear attack submarine, two oilers, two helicopter squadrons, an ammo replenishment ship, a UDT detachment in Da Nang, and a Naval Advisory Group north of Qui Nhon on Yabuta junks. He wrote stories about fleet tugboats, logistic support ships, and a Marine medium helicopter squadron.

"I was also caught in the middle of a turf war concerning who got to ride with a PBR River Division," he said.

He was heavily involved with the *Evans–Melbourne* collision court of inquiry, which concerned a collision of the Royal Australian Navy light carrier the HMAS *Melbourne* and the US Navy destroyer USS *Frank E. Evans* in early June 1969. Both ships were participating in the SEATO exercise *Sea Spirit* in the South China Sea. At 3 o'clock in the morning, the *Evans* sailed under the *Melbourne*'s bow after being ordered to a new escort station. The collision cut the *Evans* in two, killing 74 of her crew.

The inquiry found that both ships were at fault for the collision. Four officers, all captains on the *Evans* and the *Melbourne*, and two junior officers in control of the *Evans* at the time of the collision, were court-martialed. While the Australians believe the joint inquiry to have been biased against them, three US Navy officers were charged, but the Royal Australian Navy officer was cleared of wrongdoing.

Suffice to say, for all of his work as a public-affairs officer, writer, and photographer, Dennis McCloskey definitely earned the nick name "Bao Chi" many times over.

Played an Invaluable Part in Training New Army Photographers: Stanton Pratt

Stanton Pratt became interested in photography at a young age. The Honesdale, Pennsylvanian's father, whom he called "an advanced amateur," assisted him as much as he could by introducing his son, not only to photography, but also to the essentials of film processing and printing. Knowing these basics propelled the younger Pratt into becoming the head student photographer in high school.

In fact, photography was so much a part of Pratt's life by then that, when he enlisted in the Army in September 1964, he did so with a guarantee from the recruiter of photo school, which took him to Ft. Monmouth, New Jersey. He graduated first in his class of 18.

With graduation under his helmet, so to speak, June 1965 would find Pratt looking through his viewfinder in Vietnam for the 593d Signal Company, 2d Signal Group (later part of the 69th Signal Battalion) at Tan Son Nhut Air Base, Saigon.

"My first combat assignment was with the 101st Airborne. We departed Cam Ranh Bay by truck convoy for Nha Trang, where we boarded two LSTs to Qui Nhon. Arriving at the beach off that city was a little strange. The LSTs came in and dropped their ramps. The troops charged off to be greeted by GIs and beautiful young Vietnamese women. Once together we walked or were transported to a patch of desert-like country a short distance inland to set up camp for the night. Many of us went into town for some excitement for the evening. In the morning we formed up in a large dry rice paddy area awaiting the arrival of the Hueys that were going to take us on an assault on Deo Mang Pass, which we were to clear for the arrival of the 1st Cavalry Division in-country. I was accompanied on this mission by a long-time veteran, Sergeant First Class DASPO, motion-picture photographer Thomas Shiro, who my CO, then Captain (later Major) Charles Beresford, was tasked to show me the ropes on how to stay alive and get my photographs. Tom was a World War II veteran. He gave me lots of great advice, which I will never forget."

He won't forget New Year's Day 1966 either, but not because of choruses of "Auld Lang Syne" or champagne corks being popped.

"I was with the 173d Airborne Brigade in a company-size unit. We were in the field north of Bien Hoa in an area called the Iron Triangle. We had been proceeding through a relatively open rice paddy moving along the dikes when we suddenly came under heavy fire and were pinned down in the paddy. Artillery and reinforcements were called in as the battle raged in front and to the left of our position. We took some casualties. Once the reinforcements started coming up from behind us, the enemy force was thrown back and broke off the engagement."

On another engagement, Pratt was with A Battery, 3d Battalion, 319th Artillery, 173d Airborne Brigade, on a joint operation with the 2d Brigade, 1st Infantry Division.

"It was around lunch time and there were no immediate fire missions, so everyone was taking a brief break when we were all of a sudden confronted with a barrage of small-arms fire from the rear. The sound reminded me of popcorn popping in a corn popper. Everyone grabbed his weapon and took cover while the gun crews turned their 105s around and prepared to fire in the direction of the assault. One shot was fired from the 105s and the attacking force broke off. It seems that a company from the 1st Division was lost and thought they were coming up on an enemy position and opened fire. Once the artillery fired, they quickly realized that it was not the enemy but their own forces that they had engaged. Fortunately no one was injured during the brief encounter."

As was the case with many combat photographers who saw action in Vietnam, there came a time for Pratt when he had to make a decision whether to shoot film or bullets.

"The first time was during that operation with the 101st. It was during the night out on the end of our lines. The second time was on a night patrol with the 173d. There was not enough light to take pictures and everyone else was firing at the enemy who had walked into our ambush," Pratt recalls.

As also was the case, there was often the opportunity for combat correspondents in uniform to interact with their fellow shooters and reporters who worked for the civilian media in Indochina. Pratt was fortunate enough to have some interaction with some of most renowned civilian journalists in Vietnam, including the Associated Press's noted German photographer Horst Faas, Joe Galloway, and Jack Foisie of the *Los Angeles Times*.

"I am quite certain that Joe would not remember meeting me because I was just another one of those military photographers. I clearly remember meeting Horst as Tan Son Nhut was being attacked by mortar fire. This was likely one of the most frightening times of my tour because I was with troops who, for the most part, had no idea what to do in a combat situation. Being in the field with experienced troopers had a completely different feel. Anyway, another photographer, who just happened to be in from the field, believed that it was more important for us to document what was happening than to hunker down in some bunker. So I managed to grab us a jeep with a driver along with our photo equipment and film and head across the airfield to where the action was. Coming out of one large smoke cloud was Horst looking for a ride in the direction we were headed. Aside from nearly getting run over by a flight of Douglas A1E Sky Raiders getting off the field while they could, and us nearly being shot by a very nervous MP on the field, our trip to the burning fuel farm was uneventful. Our driver parked the jeep and we all headed out to do our jobs. Horst said, 'Thanks for the Lift fellows,' and went about his business."

Pratt remembers *Los Angeles Times* photographer Jack Foisie fondly as well.

"I don't remember the reason why, but Jack treated my photo team member, mopic photographer Paul Updike, Vincent Calarco and me to François' French Restaurant in Nha Trang for the best lobster dinner I have ever had. I see that it is still rated the best restaurant in Nha Trang today," he says.

Pratt also met one of the doyens of Vietnam photojournalists, Larry Burrows, in Vietnam. Burrows lost his life when the South Vietnamese Army helicopter he took off in was shot down over Laos during Operation *Lamson 719* in 1971. Killed along with him were three other renowned photojournalists: Henri Huet, Kent Potter, and Keisaburo Shimamoto.

Ironically, a few years after Vietnam, Pratt was helping Paul Updike, both of them by then civilians, take photographs for the Centenary University yearbook in Hackettstown, New Jersey. As it turned out, they photographed Burrow's daughter, who was a student there.

Thoughts of Larry Burrows' daughter returned Pratt to the battlefield and the day-to-day routine of a uniformed combat photographer.

"There really was no such thing as an average day. One day you were in the field. The next you were photographing a promotion, or covering a VIP tour, or photographing equipment to document issues with it. Then it started all over again. We worked with American, Vietnamese, Korean, Australian, and New Zealand units in the field. As the first military photo unit to arrive in-country, if a unit needed its photograph taken, we were charged with providing it. I even photographed a wedding at one point as part of my official duties."

But photographing a wedding was far from the norm.

"I saw some pretty bad things over there that I have tried to get out of my mind without a lot of success. Among the worst were how the Viet Cong and North Vietnamese treated villagers who had befriended Americans or were loyal to the Saigon government. As a 19-year-old kid from a small town in northeastern Pennsylvania, I just could not believe that one human being could do such things to another."

By June 1966, Pratt was done with Vietnam but not the Army.

"When my time in Vietnam drew to a close, I was on orders to the Army Pictorial Center in Long Island, New York. Two people thought I would be of more value teaching new photographers who would likely be headed to Vietnam. My then commanding officer, Captain Carl Conn (later Lieutenant Colonel) retired, and Major General John Norton contacted the commandant of Ft. Monmouth, General Rienzi, and suggested he should bring me there as instructor. Two weeks before I left Vietnam my orders came down changed to VOCG [Verbal Order of the Commanding General] Ft. Monmouth to report there as an instructor."

Pratt has no doubt that the change in orders meant a great deal to all parties concerned.

"I believe that, as the only instructor there at the time with Vietnam experience, I played an invaluable part in the education of many of the new students soon to be Army combat photographers."

When he looks back at his time as a combat photographer and teacher, his hat is off to two of his commanding officers and the DASPO unit they served in.

"Army Photography, particularly early on, was a rather close-knit small organization. My first CO, Major Charles Beresford, had a strong connection to many of the DASPO photographers. For example, he teamed me up with a DASPO mopic photographer for my first mission in the field. My final CO in-country, Lieutenant Colonel Carl Conn, was at some time in his career a DASPO photographer. Finally during my time teaching at Ft. Monmouth I taught many future DASPO team members," he said.

Pratt, who ran a successful photo studio in his hometown for nearly 30 years after leaving the service, points to one happenstance that had a profound effect on him as a photography teacher at Ft. Monmouth as well as in civilian life.

"About a month and a half before returning to the States a failed photo assignment to take official portraits of then Brigadier General John Norton by one of our photographers completely changed that last month and a half [in Vietnam] for me. I retook the general's portraits, and he was very pleased with the result. So much so that he recommended me to his boss, Lieutenant General Jean E. Engler. From that time on for the next month or so, all I did was create official portraits for nearly every Army general in-country at the time. This experience was invaluable to one who at 20 years of age would soon be teaching future military photographers and later needed to be able to work with all sorts of people in the civilian sector."

Stanton Pratt, combat still and mopic photographer with DASPO, during a break with his carbine and cameras ever ready for action. (Stanton Pratt collection)

A Rifle and a Hard Time:
Bill Christofferson

Minnesota-born, Wisconsin-raised Bill Christofferson enlisted in the Marine Corps just before his 22nd birthday after he lost his II-S deferment when he dropped out of college at the University of Wisconsin-Eau Claire.

"I was a reporter making the rounds of the federal building in Council Bluffs, Iowa, when a woman working there said, 'I don't have anything for the paper, but I have some news for you,'" he recalled. He was in the next batch to be inducted.

"I hoped to get a journalism assignment in the Marine Corps, but had no guarantees. The Army had guaranteed me, in writing, that they would send me to the Defense Information School and make me a journalist. The Marine recruiter said all he could promise me was a rifle and a hard time (and the Marines made good on both.) But they had a 120-delay program, which meant I could defer reporting for four months after I enlisted. That's what I did, enlisting in December 1964 and going on active duty in April 1965. I also had the idea that if I wanted to be a writer, which I did, I would get more unique experiences in the Marine Corps than in the Army. At least that was part of my rationale. But it was really the 120-day reprieve, which I spent getting into even worse physical shape than I was before," he joked.

Christofferson went through boot camp at Marine Corps Recruit Depot (MCRD) San Diego, from April 16 to July 8, 1965, then in infantry training at Camp Pendleton, California, until August 19, 1965. Unlike some who cut their journalistic teeth in the armed forces, he came to the Corps with newspaper experience under his belt.

"I had worked as a newspaper reporter for about two years before I went in, in Red Wing, Minnesota, and Council Bluffs, Iowa. When they asked during boot camp whether anyone had any journalism experience, I raised my hand and was interviewed by some PFC who asked me some inane questions from a sheet of paper. I was a lowly recruit, a private, but I showed my irritation, and that probably doomed my chances. At the end of boot camp, the MOS I was assigned was 2500, communications. I thought I would end up as a radio operator. But when I reported to my first unit after infantry training, the company officer looked at my record book and decided that if I had been a reporter, I must know how to type, so they made me a company clerk."

So much for being a Marine journalist … at least for the time being.

The unit Christofferson was with, 2d Battalion, 5th Marines (2/5), had been the first to land at Da Nang in March 1965 to guard the airfield. The battalion had rotated to Camp Pendleton and was in the process of being reformed to go back to the Pacific, and clearly destined for Vietnam. The Marines who had returned were being transferred to other units and replaced by others to form an all-new battalion.

"I joined 2/5 in September 1965, and it took a few months to get the unit to full strength. We left by troop ship on January 10, 1966 from Long Beach, California, and arrived February 2, three weeks later, on Okinawa for jungle training. In April we went by ship from Okinawa to Chu Lai, Vietnam, then the 1st Marine Division headquarters, landing on April 13, 1966. 2/5 was based on a hill south of Chu Lai," he remembered.

Before arriving in Vietnam, while still on Okinawa, Christofferson had applied for a transfer to Informational Services to be a combat correspondent, but his commanding officer turned down the request, saying he was too valuable in the company office. When Christofferson got to Vietnam, his MOS was, as yet, a clerk, but he would soon be transferred to another unit.

"I was transferred in July 1966 to 2d Battalion, 1st Marine Regiment (2/1), who were near Phu Bai, and asked again for a transfer to ISO. But this time I did it as a 'request mast.'"

Headquarters Marine Corps explains the specifics of a Request Mast as follows:

"A Request Mast includes both the right of the member to personally talk to the commanding officer, normally in person, and the requirement that the commanding officer consider the matter and personally respond to the member's requesting mast. It provides a member the opportunity to communicate not only with his or her immediate CO, but also with any superior CO in the chain of command up to and including the member's immediate commanding general. Request Mast also provides commanding officers with firsthand knowledge of the morale and general welfare of the command."

"I started with my company commander, a captain, who once again denied my request," recalled Christofferson. "So I asked to see the battalion commander, a lieutenant colonel, who backed the company commander's decision. Next I went to the regimental commander, a full colonel, who did the same. I ended up in front of the 1st Marine Division commanding officer, Major General Herman Nickerson, Jr. By this time I was armed with a scrapbook of clippings of articles I had written as a reporter, and letters of recommendation from editors I had worked for. I told the general I thought the Marine Corps was not making the best use of me by keeping me a clerk, and I could contribute more as a combat correspondent. He listened but made no commitment.".

He went back to his unit, but the clippings and letters worked. He got orders to ISO about 10 days later.

"I was apparently too naive to realize that almost no one takes it all the way up the chain of command. But it worked, and I finally got to ISO as a combat correspondent in November 1966."

Christofferson was due to rotate stateside in February 1967, 13 months after leaving Long Beach, but he extended his tour for six months once he had been in ISO for a while.

"After fighting that hard to get there and feeling like I was doing something that actually made a contribution, I didn't want to leave after three months in ISO. So I rotated in September 1967 instead."

Christofferson spent his last six months at 4th Marine Corps District Headquarters in Philadelphia, editing a monthly magazine and trying to keep his sergeant stripes until his discharge date. It was not a very pleasant experience.

"It was quite an adjustment, after 17 months in Nam, to have people telling you on the elevator that your belt buckle wasn't shiny enough. I wished I had extended once more in Vietnam; stateside duty was unbearable. When I got to Philadelphia, I was issued dress blues for the first time ... for a reason. We provided funeral details for Marines from several states who were killed in action, and during the Tet Offensive there were lots of funerals."

Thoughts of the funeral details he was tasked with usher up his memory of Vietnam.

"While I was in-country, I was first stationed near Chu Lai with 2/5, then near Phu Bai with 2/1, and near Da Nang with the 1st Marine Division when I was with ISO. I did not get north of Phu Bai, to Hue or the DMZ, but saw a lot of the rest of I Corps with various units on combat operations. We were short-handed in ISO, so I was not assigned to a specific unit (or embedded, as they now say). Rather, I worked out of the ISO office at division headquarters and would be assigned to various units when they were going on combat operations."

He was chiefly a writer and not a photographer, but that did not mean he did not carry a camera slung about his neck. He did. His was his personal 35mm Pentax, but the slides he has today are mostly of people and scenic shots, not Marines in the field.

"Much of the time when I was on an operation I had a still or movie photographer, or both, with me. I carried an M-14 the entire time I was in- country, although M-16s were issued to the troops while I was there. I was comfortable with the M-14, even though it was heavier, and saw no need to change. I never felt the need to engage in a firefight. Nor was I in a situation where I thought using my rifle would make a difference.

"Every Marine is a rifleman, but that wasn't my job. We did try to pull our share of the load when in the field, whether it was standing radio watch in the middle of the night, humping some extra gear, or helping the wounded. We were all Marines, helping one another."

Christofferson and his fellow Marine combat correspondents sometimes wore no rank insignia in the field, but their uniforms did have patches made for their jungle utilities saying "1stMarDiv Correspondent," so, given the fact that civilian correspondents often wore fatigues, helmets and combat boots for their own protection while accompanying a unit, it wasn't always immediately clear whether Marine combat correspondents were military or civilian.

"Although the weapons we carried should have been a giveaway," he said.

And of all his time in the field, there is one day that he will never forget.

"The day I remember most vividly is the first day of Operation *Union II*, in late May 1967 in the Que Son Valley south of Da Nang. I landed with a company of 3/5 in a hot LZ, and we were pinned down in a rice paddy in scorching heat for most of the day, unable to move. A helicopter was downed by enemy fire, and we were mortared. At one point, I was behind a dike when a lieutenant looked at me, unsure who I was or what I was doing there with his platoon. 'Are you a Marine?' he asked. When I confirmed that, he sent me and another Marine to recover the body of a Marine killed by sniper fire, perhaps 20 or 25 meters in front of us, in the open. We went in under some covering fire and retrieved the body, one of us on each arm. He had been shot in the throat. I had seen dead Marines before and had helped load the dead and wounded onto helicopters, but this experience has stuck with me. There's nothing heroic about it; I cite it because it is an example of how we were all just Marines in the field."

Another memory that Christofferson called "terrifying," and that remains with him to this day happened in the Hai Van Pass between Da Nang and the imperial capital of Hue. Luckily, he made it out alive.

It was "on a night you couldn't see your hand in front of your face. We were halfway up a steep mountain before realizing there were only five or six of us, and that the rest of the column had lost contact with us. Our small group made it safely down and reconnected with the unit, but I was fully prepared to be ambushed at any moment since we were on patrol and because intelligence reports said there was a VC company operating in the area."

In all his time in-country Christofferson was never wounded, which he called a "distinction that makes me almost the only one without a Purple Heart at Snuffies [the nickname Marine Corps Combat Correspondents call one another] get togethers. I credit that to chance, not any particular skill on my part."

But that is not meant to imply that Christofferson or any other Snuffies had an easy go of it.

"A lot of the time we were in the field, it would end up being a long hot walk in the sun with little enemy contact. It's hard for people to understand, but Marines wanted contact. It was very frustrating to hump and sweat for a week and lose some casualties to snipers without ever actually engaging the enemy. Grunts used to call the tactic 'walk around till ambushed.'"

And the challenge that had been a part of Christofferson's pre-Marine days as a reporter in the Midwest followed him into the jungles of Vietnam.

"For us correspondents, the challenge was to find some stories to write even when nothing much happened. The Snuffies adopted the idea that every Marine was a story, and that you should be able to write a feature about any one of them if you spent a little time asking questions. I remember writing about telephone operators back at the base camp, and even a story about someone working in graves registration, the euphemism for the in-country morgue where KIAs were processed. The graves registration guy told me proudly about a new system he had invented to be able to stack more dead bodies in the cooler, but that didn't make my story," he said.

Christofferson rates the job the Snuffies did very highly.

"In general, I thought what we did was about 80 percent journalism and 20 percent PR. There were guidelines, like how to report on Marine casualties (never worse than "moderate" and usually "light"). And there was a certain amount of self-censorship. Most of what we wrote were feature stories; even the hard news from an operation needed what the newspapers call a second-day lead because we had no way to get stories into print in any timely way."

But when their stories did make print, they ended up in some substantial publications. Many, according to Christofferson, appeared in the *Sea Tiger*, the Marine Corps in-country paper, and some even were published in *Pacific Stars and Stripes*.

"They also were released to Marine Corps publications in the States, to base papers and *Leatherneck Magazine*. Many found their way to the hometown newspapers of individual Marines. Civilian correspondents working out of the Da Nang Press Center also got copies of our stories, and once in a while we could see some familiar language in a story one of them filed, or they would use them as tips for stories of their own. We were just happy to get the word out."

Like many Vietnam veterans, Christofferson has returned to Vietnam to visit the place many who were there call "the place they came of age." For him, the opportunity came in 2000. He spent three weeks in Vietnam with two other Marines, his best friend and fellow correspondent Gordon Fowler and Dave Cutaia, a friend from boot camp.

"We only spent one day in the Que Son area, where we all had spent quite a bit of time and saw a lot of action. We didn't go to tour battlefields or relive our days in Nam, but to experience the country and the people. Dave was a scout-interpreter for the Marines, with 1/5, and is pretty fluent in the language. He had been back a number of times before we went and has a Vietnamese wife, so it was like having our own guide. We flew into Hanoi and made our way down to Ho Chi Minh City [formerly Saigon]. It's a beautiful country, as we remembered, and the people are gentle, patient, industrious, and uncomplaining. They were very friendly to us. When

Americans think of Vietnam, we think of the war, but to the Vietnamese, what they call the 'American War' is only a blip on their [radar] screen," Christofferson said.

During their time back in Vietnam, the three met former Viet Cong, and even befriended a former North Vietnamese Army soldier in Hanoi who had been in much the same parts of the I Corps as they had.

"He's an artist, as is Gordon Fowler, and our new friend, Dinh Luc, visited the US later and even had an art show in Austin, where Gordon lives. It was a real reconciliation tour for us. Eighty percent of what we saw was new to us, including the world-class beach at Nha Trang, Hue, the Perfume River, and the two big cities [Hanoi and Ho Chi Minh City]," Christofferson recalled.

He reflects on Vietnam then and now further:

"When we were in-country as Marines, it was almost impossible to interact with any Vietnamese people or learn anything about the culture. I didn't experience Vietnamese food until I was back in the States. During the war, everything was off limits, at least for Marines, and fraternization was not allowed. A few found ways around it, but those were the exceptions. So our trip was an eye opener. I doubt I will get back again, but would love to."

He didn't always feel that way, though. When he came home from Vietnam four and a half months before the 1968 Tet Offensive, he very much wanted to put his experience there behind him.

"When I was discharged, I was purposely out of touch with everyone I served with for 25 years, although I knew where a few of them were. It wasn't that the experience was too bad or painful. But I didn't want my service time to define my identity. I didn't want Vietnam to be the most important thing that ever happened to me. I saw too many vets dressing, acting, and talking like they were still in Nam. I wanted to move on," he said.

Christofferson was indeed able to move on until his fellow Snuffies tracked him down in 1992. That came in the form of a call from his friend Gordon Fowler, who told him they'd been looking for him for 10 years, and had been holding reunions every two years. Fowler invited him to a reunion later that year in Reno.

"I was ambivalent about it but wanted to see Gordon and others I was close to in Nam, so I decided to go. It's one of the best decisions I've made. Gordon and I are best friends, spend a lot of time together, have traveled to Nam, France, Mexico, and Ireland and know we can count on one another, whatever may happen. Steve Berntson is another I was delighted to reconnect with, although we don't see each other as much," he said. "When we do, it's like family. We just pick up where we left off."

"It's an interesting bunch, to say the least. In general, we were a little older, more educated, and more creative than your average Marine … and a lot wilder and crazier. I always say that when we were together back at division headquarters for a few days it was like *M*A*S*H* to the 10th power."

But Christofferson's connection to Vietnam wasn't always filled with positive memories. Back at home, he, like most Americans, couldn't help be made aware of the anti-war sentiment that began to envelop the nation in the late 1960s.

"Not long after my discharge, while working in Illinois, another ex-ISO correspondent, Mike McCusker, called me to tell me he was part of a new organization called Vietnam Veterans Against the War [VVAW] and asked me to add my name to a newspaper ad opposing the war. I begged off, saying I couldn't do it because of my job as a newspaper editor. Not long after, I covered the 1968 Democratic National Convention in Chicago. It was a time you had to take sides, and I came down on the anti-war side. I began writing columns about the war in Vietnam and the struggle in the streets, but didn't join VVAW. I was a Vietnam vet against the war, but not a member of anything. It wasn't until I retired that I decided to devote more time to promoting peace, and belatedly joined VVAW and Veterans for Peace in time to try, unsuccessfully, to prevent the war in Iraq, and later to try to end it. Having seen what war does to human beings—both to the innocent and those who go into battle—I want to do whatever I can to try to convince our government that war should not be an instrument of our foreign policy, as Veterans for Peace puts it."

"I joke that when I came home we were still winning, that the guys who came later screwed it up. In fact, we *thought* we were winning. I recall writing any number of stories about the success of 'pacification' efforts, how you could drive Highway 1 now, how many villages were pacified, and more. So I was stunned when, back in Philadelphia, I read about the places battles were going on during Tet. It really changed my thinking about what we were doing," he added.

When Christofferson was discharged from the Marines, he went right back to the profession he had worked in prior to enlisting. He took a job as the editor of a small daily newspaper in Belvidere, Illinois, which he then parlayed into a job as the city editor of the *Champaign-Urbana News-Gazette*. After that, he worked as the editor of the *Loves Park Post*, a small tabloid. His last job in journalism, after a move back to Wisconsin in 1973, was as a political reporter for the *Wisconsin State Journal* in Madison. But things in Madison did not turn out the way he had thought they would.

"In 1977 I became involved in a strike against Madison Newspapers, Inc., which resulted in a career change after we lost the strike and our jobs," he said.

That career change catapulted him into the world of politics Wisconsin style. He became a consultant working for Democratic candidates in the state, which he did for about 20 years until he retired in 2007.

That included running successful campaigns for the US Senate, governor, attorney general, mayors of Milwaukee and Madison, a state supreme court justice, a state school superintendent and others.

Since retiring, Bill Christofferson's main focus—aside from being a grandpa to two young boys—has been working with the Homeless Veterans Initiative in Milwaukee, where he has lived since 1996. It was begun by his local Veterans for Peace chapter in 2008 and since has become an independent non-profit agency, serving thousands of veterans.

"I've served as board president, development chair and in other capacities. Last year, we launched a new initiative, the Wisconsin Veterans Network (VetsNet), a collaborative effort of 30-plus agencies that will help anyone who served and their families, without a lot of bureaucracy or red tape. If you took the oath and wore the uniform, VetsNet will help, including those who served in the National Guard or Reserves. Too many veterans are still literally out in the cold. That's simply unacceptable. Vietnam Veterans Against the War say, 'Honor the Warrior, Not The War,' and that's what I've tried to do in some small way."

Marine combat correspondent Bill Christofferson taking notes for a future story in the all too infrequent calm of Vietnam. (Bill Christofferson collection)

Chronicler of the Coast Guard
Experience in Vietnam: Paul Scotti

Although Paul Scotti was not a Coast Guard combat correspondent or public affairs officer in Vietnam, he did do a tour as a gunner's mate aboard a Coast Guard patrol boat in the Vietnam. Fifteen years after he rotated back home, he began writing about his fellow Coast Guardsmen's experiences in Southeast Asia during the Vietnam War, all of which is revealed in his book *Coast Guard Action in Vietnam* (Hellgate Press). In addition, he eventually did change hats, once CONUS (Outside the Continental United States), to serve as a public-affairs officer in the USCG. Today, Paul serves as the historian for the United States Coast Guard Combat Veterans Association.

"I was not at all shocked at being sent to Vietnam. I grew up watching war movies such as *The Fighting Coast Guard* and *Onionhead* and knew the Coast Guard had been in all the country's wars. When I was in the Air Force, in the medical field, there was a bulletin board notice from the Army soliciting airmen to apply for helicopter training that would lead to assignment in Vietnam. I would have applied but I could not meet the no-eyeglasses vision requirement. I was out of the Air Force when I learned that the Coast Guard would be deploying to Vietnam. I joined the Coast Guard with the goal of becoming a gunner's mate and going to Vietnam. I volunteered for duty in Vietnam at my first opportunity.

"I landed in Saigon on May 1, 1967 as a member of Coast Guard Squadron One. Saigon was headquarters for Coast Guard Activities, Vietnam. From here the 15 men in my group were assigned to one of three divisions. I was sent to Division Twelve, Da Nang. There I was assigned to the 82-foot cutter *Point Dume* (WPB-82325). I was on the *Dume* for 10½ months. When she went to Japan for yard overhaul I was put on the *Point Comfort* (WPB-82317) for a month. The final two weeks in-country I spent ashore and left for the United States on April 29, 1968. Because 1968 was a leap year I spent a full year (365 days) in Vietnam.

"Before deploying to Vietnam I reported to the Coast Guard base in Alameda, California, the administrative unit for Squadron One, to begin five weeks of training, orientation, and putting legal affairs in order. The first week was spent at the Navy facility at Treasure Island for refresher training in shipboard damage control and chemical and biological warfare.

"There were 15 men in my group: two lieutenants (junior grade), one ensign, and 12 enlisted men. Of the 12, 10 of us were gunner's mates. The other two were a fireman and a fireman apprentice.

"The second week we joined other Navy sailors going to Vietnam at the Navy amphibious base in Coronado where we underwent a series of lectures on what we were doing in Vietnam and the nature of the enemy. The third week put us with the Marines at Camp Pendleton for physical fitness and firearms training.

"The fourth week we underwent COIN-SERE (counterinsurgency, survival, evasion, resistance to interrogation). The first day we spent on the beach learning to live off the sea. The next three days we were in the mountains living off the land. The final day, after a week of little food and in a weakened physical condition, our Navy-Coast Guard group of 115 men was released into 'enemy territory' to evade capture. That exercise lasted the morning. Those of us not yet captured during that phase had to surrender to begin the prisoner of war/interrogation phase. When it ended around three o'clock in the morning we were given oatmeal and an apple because that was all our shrunken stomach could handle. I lost 7lb that week.

"The fifth week was back at Alameda for familiarization with the 82-foot cutter and to handle our legal affairs (wills, allotments, power of attorney and such).

"Twenty-six Coast Guard 82-foot patrol boats with crews were sent to Vietnam in the summer of 1965. The cutters were split into three divisions: Division Eleven was at An Thoi, in the south, in the Gulf of Thailand, Division Twelve was out of Da Nang to cover the northern part of the country, and Division Thirteen was at Cat Lo to cover the middle of the country.

"The cutters carried an 11-man crew: two officers and nine enlisted men. When on patrol a South Vietnamese Navy man joined us as liaison and interpreter. Our patrol boats had an 81mm mortar on the bow with a 50-caliber machine gun mounted on top. Behind the deckhouse we had two 50-caliber machine guns amidships and two 50-caliber machine guns at the stern.

"In 1967, Coast Guard Squadron Three came into being. Based in Subic Bay, Philippines, five ocean-going cutters ranging in size from 255 feet to 378 feet were on a 10-month deployment. When their deployment ended another five Coast Guard cutters replaced them. They patrolled the deep water off Vietnam looking for infiltrators. They also provided naval gunfire support to land units.

"There were five Coast Guard Explosive Loading Detachments, each consisting of one officer and seven enlisted men: ELD 1—Nha Be/Cat Lai; ELD 2—Cam Ranh Bay; ELD 3—Qui Nhon; ELD 4—Da Nang; ELD 5—Vung Tau.

"The three-man Ports & Waterway Detail was in Saigon. The three-man Aids to Navigation Team was in Saigon. The Coast Guard pilots who flew combat search-and-rescue for the Air Force were out of Da Nang. The Merchant Marine

Detail was in Saigon. The Coast Guard LORAN (Electronic Navigation) Stations in Vietnam were at Con Son Island and Tan My; in Thailand they were at Sattahip, Udorn, and Lampang. Buoy tenders were sent to Vietnam periodically to install and maintain navigational aids. Squadron Three high-endurance cutters that patrolled the Vietnam coast were based in Subic Bay, Philippines.

"In total 61 cutters made their way to Vietnam: 26 WPBs, 30 HECs, four WLBs (buoy tenders), and one supply vessel. None were lost, although seven USCG names are on the Vietnam Memorial Wall in Washington.

"In addition, Coast Guard combat search-and-rescue pilots may have done some rescue work in Cambodia, but I have no information in that regard.

"In general, although the Navy, Army, and Air Force had significant missions in Vietnam, they found gaps in their ability to fully carry them out.

"I can envision underlings making excuses to admirals and generals why they could not complete certain tasks because they did not have the resources or expertise. I can imagine those admirals and generals in their wisdom saying, 'Well, then, *somebody, get the Coast Guard!*'

"Essentially, that is what happened. The Navy lacked shallow draft patrol boats to work inshore to interdict the enemy moving men, equipment, and materials close to the beach. So it asked for patrol boats to cover inshore.

"South Vietnam had little in the way of commercial ports. With the massive American buildup many new ports were opened. The Army had no navigational aids capability. So the Coast Guard was called to install and maintain buoys, range markers, and other such aids.

"The Army was responsible for the security and safety of ports from sabotage and fire. It lacked the expertise. The Coast Guard was called and sent in a Ports & Waterways Detail to advise in these matters.

"Ammunition and other hazardous cargo needed to be safely offloaded from ships and barges. Again, this was something the Coast Guard did by assigning five Explosive Loading Detachments with the Army.

"Ships under contract with the Military Sea Transportation Service (MSTS) brought into Vietnam 98 percent of the materials needed to support the war. Any interruption in this massive flow of supplies could impact the forces fighting in the field. Problems with captains and crewmembers could hinder a ship from sailing. Here was another area of Coast Guard business because it licensed mariners. The shipping industry clamored for Coast Guard help. In foreign ports the American embassy is responsible for American seaman conduct. The embassy in South Vietnam was overburdened in dealing with merchant marine problems; yet, it ignored the clamor for calling in the Coast Guard. Consequently, MSTS, called the Coast Guard directly and brought in a Coast Guard officer to bring order and mete out punishment, if necessary, with troublesome seamen. He was given the title of Shipping Advisor that in time evolved into a three-man Merchant Marine Detail.

"Meanwhile, the Air Force had the task of rescuing downed fliers in and around Vietnam. This task exceeded the number of qualified rescue pilots. It was short of helicopter pilots, so much so, that it was converting its bomber pilots into helicopter pilots. This still did not solve the rescue problem. As a consequence it called the Coast Guard. An exchange agreement was made by which the Coast Guard would send helicopter pilots to fly with the Air Force in Vietnam and the Air Force would replace those pilots by sending Air Force pilots to Coast Guard Air Stations in the United States.

"The Air Force had another problem. There was no accurate means of navigation in Southeast Asia for pinpointing enemy targets. Again, the Coast Guard was called upon, this time to install and operate a long-range navigation (LORAN) network in Southeast Asia. The result was two Coast Guard stations in South Vietnam and three in Thailand.

"When the Navy's destroyer escorts were pulled off Vietnam patrols because they were needed elsewhere in the world, the Navy requested ships from the Coast Guard to replace them. This is how Coast Guard Squadron Three came into being."

Scotti went on to describe the activities of USCG journalists in Vietnam.

"In my time in Vietnam, I was underway 77 percent of the time. I made 58 combat patrols. During non-monsoon season we were on patrol six days straight. On the seventh day we were relieved but it took half a day or longer to get back to Da Nang. Our in-port period that was supposed to last two days for maintenance and replenishment of stores and ammunition was actually a day and a half. During monsoon season the patrols were cut back to four days, but still only two in-port days.

"The only journalist I was aware of was Woody Dickerman, a reporter for *Newsday*, the newspaper for Long Island in New York. He came aboard to interview the skipper about an all-night action we had against the North Vietnamese Navy above the DMZ. The only reason he came to us was that before going to Vietnam, *Point Dume* had been stationed at Fire Island on Long Island.

"As I recollect, the Coast Guard had only one journalist in-country each year and he worked out of Saigon. So, the likelihood of seeing one was remote; after all, he had to cover Coast Guard units the entire length of the country, with finding transportation being his biggest obstacle. Nonetheless, he did his best. The other Coast Guard journalist was assigned to Squadron Three covering the activities of its five cutters.

"The Coast Guard journalist had the entire country of scattered Coast Guard units to cover. He did his best to get information but the task was overwhelming for one person. He wrote news releases and feature stories. He photographed activities. Because we operated under the Navy it was unlikely that the Navy would give credit to what the Coast Guard was accomplishing. When Coast Guard 82-footers intercepted the first two armed North Vietnamese trawlers since the Coast Guard had come on scene—the trawlers were trying to smuggle tons of supplies, weapons, and ammunition into South Vietnam—I am sure the Navy reported it as 'Naval forces today ...' So it is not surprising that the general public was largely unaware of what we did in the war.

"My job as a gunner's mate was to maintain, repair, and operate ordnance. The comparison between a journalist and a gunner's mate was this: a gunner's mate makes the news and the journalist promulgates it."

Scotti switched specialties from gunner's mate to journalist once he got home.

"Coast Guardsmen who served in Vietnam were given their assignment of choice if it was available. I was given my first choice, Coast Guard Base, Sault Ste Marie, Michigan, on the Canadian border. The snow fell as early as October and did not melt until April. This winter wonderland was a great place to raise a family (my wife and two young children).

"I was there three years as the base gunner's mate. In my last year there I applied for the Famous Writer's School correspondence course in fiction writing. My intention was to eventually write novels. The school was sending a representative to interview me as a credible prospective student. It was funny, but on the day he headed north a major snowstorm struck, blocking roads and closing the bridge connecting the lower and upper peninsulas. The gentleman, along with other stranded travelers in Gaylord, ended up sleeping overnight in the town jail.

"Life is a rhythm of cause and effect. To get the Veterans Administration to pay for the course I had to get approval and validation from my commanding officer. The cause was the writing course; the effect was my being made command's collateral duty journalist. I put out a monthly newsletter, writing features that went out to the multiple units under the Group Sault Ste Marie command.

"My next assignment was that of pre-commissioning crewmember of a new Coast Guard cutter under construction. The 378-foot cutter was comparable to a Navy frigate or destroyer escort. The ship was put in commission—special, in New Orleans. That day, before we got underway to the Coast Guard Yard in Baltimore for further outfitting, I spoke to my wife in the Boston area (where the cutter would be home ported). She told me that she read in *Navy Times* that the commandant had issued a notice seeking applications from first and second-class petty officers in any specialty to switch to journalist. The Coast Guard found itself short of journalists, as a number of them unexpectedly were not re-enlisting. A board would convene in the future to review the applications and select from them the numbers needed.

"The cause: my writing background, my public affairs duties in Sault Ste Marie, and favorable recommendations from my former commanding officer and executive officer. The effect: my being selected to become a journalist.

"Hence, one day in 1972, I walked up the gangway of the ship a gunner's mate first class to pick up my orders. When I walked back down the gangway I was a journalist first class.

"Why did I make the switch? In considering life after the Coast Guard I knew that people did not have naval deck guns on their lawn that needed servicing. So job opportunities as a gunner's mate were not promising. However, as a writer my jobs opportunities would be broad. As well, writing was my pleasure.

"In the Coast Guard the journalist is a spokesperson, a writer, and a photographer. My first assignment was Third Coast Guard District headquarters, public affairs office, on Governors Island in New York City. I was sent to this tough news media town to learn my trade fast under a senior chief journalist (E-8) taskmaster who was one of the Coast Guard's best. I wrote my first news releases like I was writing a novel. Wrong: just the facts please—who, what, when, why, and how.

"Six months into my new field the Coast Guard merged the journalist and photographer's mate specialties into one—photojournalist (eventually renamed Public Affairs Specialist). It was a harder transition for photographer's mates because they had no interest in writing. When their enlistments ended a good number of them got out of the Coast Guard.

"An oddity developed in my new career. It happened that whenever I was on-call, during either the week or weekend, major news stories occurred. There would be ship collisions, sinkings at sea, large oil spills, foreign fishing vessel seizures, and on and on. My reputation for handling major news events had begun. I had become a journalist in the summer of 1972 and in summer of 1974 I was promoted to chief photojournalist (E-7)

"In the summer of 1976, I was transferred to the Thirteenth Coast Guard District public-affairs office in Seattle, Washington. The Pacific Northwest was relatively quiet until I arrived. After three years I was transferred to the Seventh District public-affairs office in Miami, Florida. That was a 22-month tour of near daily trouble: thousands of Cubans fleeing Cuba during the Mariel Boatlift, the Coast Guard buoy tender *Blackthorn* sinking after colliding with a tanker in Tampa Bay, the collapse of a thousand-foot span of the Sunshine Skyway Bridge over Tampa Bay after being hit by a ship, endless drug seizures, and more.

"I had taken the promotion examination for E-8 and for chief warrant officer. I came out on top on both of them. I opted to take chief warrant officer. With that came orders to Coast Guard Headquarters in Washington, D.C., as a staff officer in the public-affairs program.

"What could go wrong in that job? For one, the Coast Guard lost a third of its photojournalist billets. It fell to me to come up with a total reorganizational billet structure. Twice I was sent on temporary duty into the field. Once was to handle public affairs in Seattle during the absence of a district public-affairs officer for the arrival of the USS *Ohio*, the first operational Trident missile submarine to its homeport in Bremerton, Washington. Heavy anti-war protests were expected and it was the Coast Guard's task to keep them away from the submarine by means of a floating security zone. The other was going to Kennedy Space Center to handle public information in the Coast Guard's search and salvage effort during the aftermath of the Space Shuttle *Challenger* disaster."

A typical day as a USCG journalist was January 8, 1980, in Miami, as Scotti recorded in his log:

"Busy day on the telephone and in the photo lab: seizure of F/V *Lucky Louise* with 15 tons of marijuana; two Marine jets collide in the air; bomb threat aboard M/V *Louise Jones*; 117 Haitians in a 50-foot sail boat; 20th Century Fox scriptwriter in for an interview on drug smuggling techniques; Channel 7 wanted an interview with someone so they could do a film report on the Seventh Coast Guard District; a rush order by Coast Guard Headquarters for portraits of certain captains."

But not all calls were in the nature of hard news.

"When citizens called for information I always tried to help them. These examples came from my time in the Third District public affairs office. I answered the telephone and a tugboat captain was on the line. He told me he was towing a barge out of Holland, Michigan, when the barge caught fire. The Coast Guard put out the fire and saved the barge. He wanted to write a letter of appreciation to the Coast Guard but he was not a writer. Would I write the letter for him? I gathered the information, wrote the letter and delivered it to him at the Seaman's Church Institute in Manhattan.

"I remember another call in which a man wanted to verify if Louis Beck was drowned when the schooner *A.B. Goodman* sank off Cape Hatteras—in 1881! I said that I would see if I could find out. We happened to have a collection of annual reports of the Life Saving Service. I found one for 1881. I could not believe what I read. I called the man back and told him that Beck did indeed drown but four others were saved. He was ecstatic. Those two efforts only elevated the good reputation of the Coast Guard in the public's eye."

Scotti was on duty on Friday, October 6, 1972, when there was a war protest outside his station.

"To get to Governors Island you have to catch a Coast Guard ferry on the Manhattan side. The trip across is seven and a half minutes. We were passed a report in the public affairs office that there was a small group of anti-war protesters at the ferry terminal. They had green sheets they were passing out calling for the Coast Guard to get out of the 'death business.'

"Somehow they learned that the Coast Guard operated electronic navigation stations in Vietnam and Thailand that guided our bombers to enemy targets.

"My reaction was amazement about how they discovered that obscure information. As a Vietnam veteran my only thought was how misguided they were. Security Coast Guardsmen man the ferry terminal and the protest did not last long. I do not remember that the public-affairs office had any media inquiries about the incident. After all, what is newsworthy about a protest in New York City?

"My final assignment came in 1988 when I was sent to Los Angeles to be the Motion Picture/Television liaison officer to the entertainment industry. After three years there I retired on October 1, 1991.

"All this happened because I took out the Famous Writer's School correspondence course."

Scotti then had a career as a book writer.

"While in Vietnam, I kept a daily log of doings, but I did not start working on *Coast Guard Action in Vietnam* until 1982, 15 years later.

"I was proud of the perseverance, initiative, and dedication that my fellow Coast Guardsmen pursued to accomplish our missions. Military readiness is only one of the Coast Guard's multiple missions, but the way Coast Guardsmen performed in Vietnam one would have thought that all we did was train for war.

"For years I had been expecting someone to write a book chronicling what the Coast Guard did in the Vietnam War. When I was assigned to the Public Affairs Division at Coast Guard Headquarters I mentioned to my commander my disappointment that no one had written a book on the subject. His response, 'Why don't you write it?'

"From that point I began my research. Trying to write an accurate military history with all that goes on in one's life—job, family, new assignment, retirement—made it slow going for me. From when I began my research to when it was ready for publication, 16½ years had passed.

"I finished my manuscript before seeking a publisher. I did not want to be contract bound to deliver the manuscript by a certain date because I did not know when I would finish. I submitted the manuscript proposal to a handful of publishers and received two acceptances. The fact that I had books previously published showed publishers I had the writing credentials to produce a quality manuscript. If it had been my first book I would have likely had a harder time finding a publisher."

Finally, Scotti broached the subject of whether feels the USCG received enough recognition from the country, or perhaps from the other service branches, for the job it did in Vietnam.

"Because the Coast Guard carries out a disparate range of missions (polar and domestic icebreaking, boating safety, marine law enforcement, search-and-rescue, military readiness, environmental protection, port security, and so much more), the public cannot grasp in a few words what the Coast Guard does.

"Its military role is among the least known because the Coast Guard does not fall under the Department of Defense. Often in recruiting commercials and in military musical salutes the Coast Guard is left out (to the ire of any Coast Guardsmen or family members present). So informing the public about the Coast Guard's military role is a constant chore. One of the reasons I wrote my book on what the Coast Guard did in Vietnam was to let people know what we did there and that they should be proud of that accomplishment. It is not written as dry history but as a fast-paced narrative of heroism and valor.

"In 1985, I founded, along with several other Coast Guard combat veterans, The Coast Guard Combat Veterans Association. One of its purposes is to let Americans know of the sacrifices Coast Guardsmen have made in protecting our country against foes.

"My wife once attended a Washington, D.C., event of military wives from all branches of the armed forces. Learning that I was in the Coast Guard, one snooty wife of a member of another service said to Liz, 'Your husband did not have to go to Vietnam.' To which Liz replied, 'No, he didn't. He volunteered.'"

On a Special Purpose Mission: Sonny Craven

Sonny Craven was a radio-TV-motion picture officer assigned to the Pentagon's US Army Mobile Television Detachment, based at Tobyhanna Army Depot, Pennsylvania, and was the officer-in-charge of one of two of the mobile television units at Ft. Sam Houston, Texas, in 1967. The one for which he was OIC was deployed by request to design, install and begin start-up operations of an on-base television production studio at Ft. Sam. But Vietnam would soon be added to Sonny's résumé.

"While at Ft. Sam Houston, I received assignment orders attaching me to the 90th Replacement Battalion, a processing center in Long Binh that managed open vacancies for Army skills in-theater."

After he arrived in June 1967 and was in-processed, Craven was sent to the 69th Signal Battalion in Saigon. At the 69th, he found it had recently eliminated most of its photo-officer positions, which left the newly arrived in-theater 221st Signal Company as the only alternative assignment.

"When I arrived back at Long Binh, I met with 1st Lieutenant Frank Lepore, the officer-in-charge of the element which he had recently brought into theater a month earlier," Craven said.

According to Craven, the living quarters of the 221st Signal Company were not exactly ideal but typical of the US Army bases in the rear.

"The 44 enlisted members and nine officers of the first packet lived in tents in the hottest part of summer, with some relief provided by rolling up the tent sides, and at least one large industrial-size fan per tent to circulate hot air. The unit was located in a city-block-size vacant lot, assigned by Long Binh post officials."

"During my initial in-briefing, Lieutenant Lepore explained his drive for better accommodations and facilities rather than rely on the general-purpose medium tent city and mortar-round sleeves (tubes) used as latrines, affectionately dubbed, 'piss tubes.'"

Not only was 1st Lieutenant Lepore not enamored of the living conditions of his men, but he was also not the happiest about the photographic equipment the "packet" had to use.

"Lepore explained that despite limited photographic equipment—much of it vintage equipment harking back to World War II and Korea—he was struggling to meet mission operation requests soon after arriving."

Other members of the 221st also struggled with being able to complete the missions with the equipment the unit had at its disposal.

"I heard most of the conversations with unit members who were a part of the early struggles to stand-up an operational unit with almost no equipment, seasoning, or experience documenting images for history in peace or war. There was no documented 'how-to' formula or guides, and no preexisting organizational document developed to realistically prepare a unit to take on a theater-wide combat photography mission in Vietnam," Craven said.

"Pressures from press and public were building on the Army. The press and public wanted more information on the expanding military involvement in Vietnam. The press ultimately wanted access to still and moving images from the combat zone.

"Once again, history repeated itself. As happened in previous conflicts, at the time the Army wasn't far-sighted enough to realize the need for a seasoned, ready-to-deploy unit that would document Army ground combat operations for military visual information history archives."

According to Craven, the 221st was once rumored to have been a deactivated signal supply unit that was reactivated and then given a newly designated special-purpose mission. The first table of organization (TO&E), the official document authorizing unit manpower, was developed by what Craven called "well-meaning bureaucrats with no real combat expertise in the types of equipment suited for tropical jungle conditions." Readily available personnel for immediate assignment or imminent deployment matched to the unit mission did not exist.

"Manning a new unit requires a few years to access new recruits and train them through the Army school system. New graduates usually had no experience or seasoning, and were led by junior and mid-level noncommissioned officers with only stateside audiovisual experience, because combat veterans were scarce.

"These NCOs were cadre, yet were unable to begin training for new arrivals because there was little actual photographic equipment on-hand, and new equipment orders consisted mostly of off-the-shelf equipment from the private sector that didn't begin arriving until the first packets neared deployment, leaving little time to train and familiarize."

At that point, the Pentagon entered the picture when assignment specialists sent Army-wide messages to field units, authorizing still photographers, motion picture cameramen, sound-audio specialists, photographic laboratory operations, and camera-repair specialists to be released from the units in which they were previously serving in order to, as Craven put it, "swell" the ranks of the 221st. In so doing, smart commanders swept their units of disciplinary problems.

"A few 221st officers weren't career-minded or enthusiastic soldiers but were willing to serve their obligation, if only to avoid the draft," he said.

These challenges not only affected the unit in Long Binh but also back at Ft. Monmouth, New Jersey, where the 221st was formed, its soldiers trained, and equipment was issued for deployment.

In spite of all the problems facing the unit, once the soldiers got to Vietnam, even with their inexperience, they understood the importance of the mission and what had to be accomplished.

"They met every challenge and more," Craven said.

"Absence of an active-duty, large-scale photo unit for wartime was not an unfamiliar circumstance in the Army Signal Corps. It has never regarded audiovisual services as an essential part of the signal mission. The Signal Corps is steeped in traditional tactical and strategic communications-electronics for peacetime and in battlefield environments. Combat photography units, after serving their purpose in conflicts, are resources for the taking in peacetime to meet ever-changing manpower needs for new Signal Corps requirements.

"Lieutenant Lepore and his first packet faced a Herculean task when it arrived in Long Binh. The small number of men were the advance element meant to prepare a base for follow-on packets. There were no pre-prepared facilities for them, yet although troops lived in tents in sweltering-heat, they began conducting limited operational missions and at the same time building an operational base camp. Tent-city living quarters and offices during the early summer of 1967 can only be described as 'primitive.'"

If the MOSs of carpenter or construction worker existed, the first packet of soldiers of the 221st might have qualified for them in addition to that of Army photographer.

"Building permanent facilities relied on manual labor using simple tools on-hand, 'scrounged' locally or from those brought with the packet. Troops battled scorching hot weather and the effects of anti-malaria pills, affectionately dubbed 'Brown Bombers' due to near-instant impact on soldiers' alimentary tract," according to Craven.

"In around-the-clock shifts, unit troops leveled large expanses of ground made of tough red clay, used bags of concrete mix to pour dozens of large foundation pads on which big aluminum buildings were erected. No heavy equipment, engineer units, or extra labor were available from the main base garrison to help.

"Construction crews were mixed-rank and worked side-by-side. Our numbers were too small and deadlines too tight to observe strict military formalities, yet courtesy was observed. Contrary to expectations, it was a bonding, morale-boosting effort, as everyone wanted better quarters and pitched in. Construction continued even as the four remaining packets arrived."

Once the 221st's headquarters was completed, training became the order of the day.

"Official training was a function of the duty day for all personnel in garrison as called for by a training schedule posted weekly. Sessions were mandatory and instruction was assigned or delegated to team and section leaders. Army subjects were mandated for safety, escape and evasion; black market fraud; host nation customs and courtesies; and hygiene, health and welfare subjects. Lessons learned and quality assurance feedback of visual information products from completed projects were discussed in informal team meetings," said Craven.

Although some in both the enlisted and officer ranks who were assigned to the 221st had practical experience in photography from college courses and the like, Craven was mindful that most of the men assigned to the 221st cut their photographic teeth at Ft. Monmouth.

"I can personally attest to the quality of the Army course training in lab and still photography operations, and although short (around 8–10 weeks), the training was comprehensive. Learning outcomes were formally and individually evaluated and tested. The course was a mix of theory and practical hands-on. Group and team exercises and individual assignments reinforced classroom curricula. The course used mixed film formats, and tactical mobile photo labs were used for processing by hand," he said.

In addition to the missions the 221st's troops would undertake in the field, they also had their share of what Craven called "Grip 'n' Grin" photography.

"The unit had a mission to provide audiovisual equipment loan, repair, and maintenance; small camera 35mm processing and printing; visual graphic transparency production; and 35mm transparency slides for briefings to large units and commands in USAR-V. The 221st was staffed and equipped for that mission, and major headquarters used the service, especially equipment loans (slide projectors for briefings, and motion-film projectors for Army library training films). Another support mission was walk-in photo studio services for full-length and head-and-shoulders shots for promotion packages and career files. Copy services were also available, as well as draftsmen or graphic illustrators."

However, the 221st's main mission was to be out in the field recording the Army's operations.

The Grip 'n' Grin functions "rarely, if ever interfered with field combat-mission assignments, because the 221st had a large garrison industrial support operation capable of processing and printing the visual products of the returning teams for inspection, review, and ultimately, transport to Army archives," Craven said.

"The other support to in-theater 'brass' was photo support, and 'coverage' for various headquarters commands and our own Army archives: visiting VIPs from Congress, the Pentagon, and the State Department, assessment visits of President Lyndon Johnson, Vice-President Hubert Humphrey, chief of staff of the Army, the chairman of the joint chiefs—all guests of General Westmoreland or Ambassador Ellsworth Bunker," he added.

"In-country US press bureaus and the *Pacific Stars and Stripes* newspaper photographed their visits extensively, but the 221st, including my team, were frequently at Saigon's Tan Son Nhut Airfield to document arrivals of dignitaries."

The 221st was sometimes tasked with PR duties as well. These involved 221st field team photo opportunities incidental to the combat that the unit photographed.

"There were the Army's humanitarian programs, such as MEDCAP (Medical Civic Action Programs) and school assistance programs (distribution of prodigious amounts of books, uniforms, and school supplies by stateside charities, religious groups, churches, organized school efforts, and civic clubs such as Lion's Club, Rotarians, etc.)," Craven said.

The unit also filmed a mission that Craven likened to Doctors Without Borders when his team photographed a surgery performed by an American doctor in a remote Montagnard village in the Central Highlands region of Vietnam.

"My experiences came from observing and documenting the variety of missions conducted by brigade and division-level organizations to show our forces were challenged to help indigenous citizens who never had any level of formal medical healthcare, dentistry, pre- and post-natal care, vaccines, immunizations, and minor surgery. Army combat unit medical teams were superb in providing the first American contact for most of these patients and a level of compassionate care."

Other public relations-related missions that Craven recalls the 221st field teams covering in 1967–68 included the South Vietnam presidential inauguration ceremony, the Emancipation Proclamation of Montagnard tribes people—Vietnam's indigenous minority—officiated by President Nguyen Van Thieu and Vice-President Nguyen Cao Ky, and the official celebration ceremony preceding Tet 1968.

The task at hand, from combat to PR, would always determine the size of the teams and the ratio of still cameras to mopic cameras.

"Team leaders added members with skills as dictated by the mission type, nature, and character. If more motion-picture film was needed, an additional mopic cinematographer could be borrowed from a companion team," according to Craven.

"In my experience, each team often had at least three to four members, plus an officer team leader. The actual configuration called for a Specialist/6 senior mopic photographer who functioned as the team noncommissioned officer, a silent mopic photographer, a soundman, one senior still photographer, and a still photographer, plus a lieutenant team leader. Typically, the teams experienced shortages and some members were cross-trained to perform dual roles. It seems to me we combined some teams to achieve full strength and capabilities."

Whatever their mission as soldiers in the 221st Signal Company, Craven holds them in the highest regard.

"With few exceptions, morale and discipline was good, and in 1967 we had not yet been infused with soldiers later recruited with strong anti-war sentiments. The key was we had a mission bigger and tougher than any of us, a historical legacy, and jobs carrying sizeable inherent risks. The industrial functions and technologies required to create, process, and produce our visual information products kept everyone 'leaning forward.' There weren't significant mission lulls long enough for boredom to set in, and too few PAT teams to meet an increasing number of combat mission requests."

"Over my 13 months, normal end-of-tour rotations of team members, various distractions, mission peculiarities, and in some cases, medical problems changed team composition at random intervals, but troops learned to be flexible and absorb personnel changes."

Craven well remembers one mission his team was tasked with that exemplifies the pride he still has for the unit 50 years later.

"The team with me during the battle of Widow's Village was hastily thrown together that morning from photographers near the company headquarters eager and ready to move out. All displayed courage, bravery and intrepidity, and I'm proud to have been associated with them."

Another mission that stands out for Craven he refers to as "the implausible but true story of the Texas Tree-Crusher."

"Along the Cambodian border, the enemy used the dense jungles and forests as cover for irregular forces to launch raids and skirmishes, then withdraw back to safety. US forces were intent on eliminating these enemy sanctuaries. The Army and Air Force were already engaged in trials to defoliate wide-areas of jungle which concealed networks of paths and narrow roads which formed the infamous Ho Chi Minh Trail," he said, pausing to reflect upon the Agent Orange that was used to achieve that goal.

"Agent Orange is an herbicide and defoliant chemical used by the USAF as part of its herbicidal warfare program, Operation *Ranch Hand*, in Vietnam from 1961 to 1971. Air Force and Army helicopters sprayed herbicides and dropped fire bombs to clear away the foliage.

"It was effective in turning large swaths of jungle into barren wasteland, but when sprayed from large Air Force aircraft, it was indiscriminate, and lacked pinpoint accuracy. Any human life in the area of spraying became potential collateral targets and aerosol mists drifted anywhere the wind blew. Further, the mists landed on foliage in droplets, which dried and was reactivated by moisture and humidity for long periods after spray operations."

Unfortunately, Agent Orange's being indiscriminant also meant that it affected American ground troops.

"Unsuspecting US ground forces moving through the sprayed areas often came in contact with the deadly chemicals," Craven said, "causing health consequences lasting for life. This may have included 221st teams accompanying ground patrols."

In the summer of 1967, the 221st was tasked by Military Assistance Command, Vietnam [MAC-V] to test equipment that was undoubtedly less detrimental to the health of American troops and Vietnamese nationals.

"It would potentially help US forces deny Viet Cong hiding spots in jungles and forests around the Long Binh and Bearcat areas. Bearcat was a nearby operational home of the 9th Infantry Division."

The equipment was called a Rome Plow. It was a large, armored, specially modified bulldozer used in III Corps for major land clearing operations. The plows equipped with a sharp two-ton "stinger blade" were able to cut down trees and brush which were then burned.

But the US military needed a better instrument to level Vietnamese forests. The monstrous Tree Crusher was thought to be the answer. In 1968, the Army leased two of these vehicles from the Le Tourneau company and sent them to South Vietnam."

And Craven went even further by echoing the sentiment of Major General Robert Ploger in the work *Vietnam Studies: U. S. Army Engineers, 1965–1970.*

"US military leaders had recognized early on the tremendous advantage the jungle offered the Viet Cong and North Vietnamese Army in terms of limiting the movement of modern military equipment and in protecting their bases, their lines of communication, and their arsenals," Major General Ploger wrote. "As early as November 1965 General Westmoreland put his staff to work looking for means of jungle clearing."

Army commanders were eager for new, faster ways to clear away the jungle but MAC-V thought the Tree Crusher might be too heavy and cumbersome for ground clearing operations in jungles, according to Craven.

"My photo assignment team set out to document the test. It came at a time when we were performing our own equipment test to determine the feasibility of using the unit's large, double-system (sound and picture recorded together on the same film) motion-picture cameras in Vietnam. The Beckman and Whitley CM-16 camera was heavy, and although it could be shoulder-mounted, when it was equipped with large film magazines, it was too heavy for work over long periods, and was best used with a tripod."

"The camera had never been tested in humid, tropical environments and if film wasn't exposed shortly after being threaded, heat and moisture rendered it unusable. Heat-struck film changes color properties, and the camera was limited to 50-foot loads of film to prevent film-gate cinching and gear stoppages caused by gelatin-like swollen film emulsion. It was virtually impossible to operate the camera in jungle conditions with 400 foot film magazines because of high tropical humidity.

"Soon, the CM-16 was limited to garrison and indoor use," Craven said. "The camera gear for long field missions was simply too heavy to be easily transported and a hassle to load onto helicopters and fixed-winged aircraft shared with other passengers."

The camera was not a viable choice for certain other missions.

"It couldn't be used in stealthy combat search-and-destroy operations because of its bulk and its relatively insensitive 80 ASA color film in low-light triple-canopy jungles. It required multiple steps to setup and operate the camera system, and the weight of film required to sustain multi-day operations was also a big factor," said Craven.

The 221st did not give up on the camera, however, and decided to test it in action.

"We decided to give the camera system with all its gear, a fair trial by filming the slow-moving Tree Crusher in jungle-clearing operations within a range of 20 miles of

Bearcat, reachable by our unit jeeps. With four crew, and all our photo equipment, we were an attractive target, and engineer soldiers smiled when they saw us for the first time. Fully loaded we were a pretty pitiful sight. By the time we began filming, the Tree Crusher required a trailing tank retriever and a squad of mechanized infantry for protection. The crusher's cab was equipped with bulletproof green-tinted glass, a whip antenna connected to a standard series Army radio, and a public address system to permit the operator to communicate with supporting ground crew. We had to use hand signals if we needed the operator to stop or perform a maneuver for our cameras."

Eventually, the distance between where the 221st was filming the Tree Crusher operation and Bearcat AO became a concern because the two were too far apart to guarantee the unit's safety.

"We needed aerial footage to show the effect it had on jungle clearings. This mission justified use of helicopter transportation for the rest of our documentary project. Pilots needed almost no bearings to find the Tree Crusher. They just closed in on a last reported position, and followed the spoon-shaped curvatures dug by the blades in the cleared wide swaths. It was an impressive sight resembling Mars's craggy surface," Craven remembered.

"Near the end of the Tree Crusher operational test, we were contacted by the engineer unit, alerting us to a new development. We ordered local helicopter support, loaded up and flew to the coordinates. They took us over a river tributary leading to the South China Sea. After a short search, we found the Tree Crusher. In about 30 feet of crystal-clear water. We filmed the beast from the helicopter as it circled. The Tree Crusher had settled to the bottom of the sea after being rigged with a flotation system to test the manufacturer's claim it could 'swim.' Like a rock, maybe," he said.

Most importantly, the troops wanted an armored turret on top with a .50-caliber machine gun. Claymore mines strapped to the sides would blast a hail of steel balls to brush off guerrillas during any ambushes.

"MACV and the Army weren't interested. Spraying gallons of Agent Orange and other defoliating chemicals was cheaper and easier all around. Engineers driving bulldozers continued beating back the bush on the ground," Craven said.

In spite of the 221st's coverage of the Tree Crusher and its taking a backseat to Agent Orange, the unit continued to take pride in its work, although another incident might have been detrimental to that pride.

"By the late summer of 1967, men of the 221st were beginning to admire the considerable progress being made in their race to establish a working base camp with basic living amenities and buildings for supplies, operations, living quarters, latrines, and motor pool maintenance."

Laying concrete foundations and erecting fabricated aluminum buildings in around-the-clock shifts gave way to building sandbag-protected mortar bunkers beside every building.

"The complex of portable, interconnected mobile shelters, manufactured by Kellett, for photo and motion-picture film lab processing and production plus other audiovisual functions, was in full operation to support fledgling efforts of unit photo assignment teams, and theater units in over-the-counter operations," Craven recalled.

"Unit morale was improving. Everyone felt we were now able to begin full-scale operations and prove the essentiality and importance of our mission. That feeling was about to be tested. The 221st was tasked to provide a work detail of 99 men from October 18, 1967 to November 1, 1967 to support operations at Newport docks, a facility constructed by the Army transportation corps and used by Army barges, tugs and Navy vessels to offload war supplies, men, and materiel. The Army needed help to off-load ships filled with vital war supplies during the build-up ordered by MAC-V commanded by General Westmoreland. Westmoreland knew the political significance of Khe Sanh, a cluster of small Marine and Army outposts, primarily firebases, near the DMZ dividing North and South Vietnam. The North Vietnamese Army sought a propaganda victory over this small area of rugged terrain, and amassed a large number of artillery guns in the high ground surrounding the small American military encampments.

"It was a test of wills of the two sides, and the difficult task of resupplying and reinforcing the beleaguered outpost was a legendary feat of ingenuity and resolve showed by the USAF and its skilled pilots.

"To meet the massive resupply, ships were arriving at Newport so frequently that port labor was backlogged and crews were overwhelmed."

In order to alleviate the situation, he and a colleague of Craven, Lieutenant Charles Masters, were tasked with organizing their soldiers, taking care of transportation to the port, and acting as liaisons to the port officials who integrated the soldiers into work shifts.

"The work was hard manual labor, but Chuck and I spoke to the formation before we departed for the port. We knew this could be viewed as a test of our mettle by our in-country parent unit who passed the task intact to 221st solely to avoid interfering with mission integrity of the 160th Signal Group. After all, we were just boys with toys, not serious regular soldiers., To Signal soldiers working in strategic and tactical communications jobs we were Signal Corps weenies," Craven said bitterly. "This stereotype, if not countered and if area commands came to believe we were Long Binh post's 'gopher unit,' could be devastating to the morale of our soldiers.

"Using mission exigency as the reason why the job was critical, Masters and I told our taskforce we were selected to help the war effort and the worst thing we could was to sulk, misbehave, or act unprofessionally."

The NCOs of the 221st followed right in line and reinforced the wishes of the command of the unit and, at the same time, were keen to watch for what Craven termed "any signs of disaffection." All of which surprised the 160th command and relieved the 221st's HQ staff, according to Craven, who further said the 221st teams did not create a single problem. "Our soldiers performed magnificently without complaint. They were told their contribution was invaluable to meeting off-loading deadlines."

The 221st's mission on the Newport docks did not go unnoticed by the commanding general of the 1st Logistics Command either. He wrote a letter that circulated down through the chain of command, in which he said, "Of particular importance was the conscientious and industrious manner with which they [the 221st] approached their assignments at Newport. Their pleasant, friendly, and cooperative spirit greatly assisted the 71st Transportation Battalion (Terminal Services) in reducing the congestion in the Saigon Port Complex."

While it was not what the 221st Signal Company was trained for and might have disturbed the soldiers and garnered many a complaint, pride in accomplishment overcame any negativity.

"Clearly, it was a distraction to our unit mission, but it was also the beginning of a new attitude. We had been tested as soldiers, not camera jockeys. Soon, we would succeed in every challenge thrown our way. Ground combat troops and their commanders we worked with were the first to express their admiration when they saw us share the same risks to do our job, and that we kept pace and never shirked our duties."

Craven is quick to point out that while the 221st got the accolades it deserved, that did not mean that he himself, as an officer, was immune from getting into some degree of trouble. Luckily, it happened only once.

"I was aware of a cacophony of unintelligible noises in that semi-conscious state between sleep and awakening," he remembered. "Was I dreaming it? Groggy, I finally became aware of cadences and barked orders as I tried in the early dawn to get my eyes to focus on the dials of my olive-drab military-issue watch. 0430. What could be happening? I left my hooch cot to find the origin of the shouting and grunting."

It was the first morning after Craven's team arrived at the base camp of the vaunted South Korean "Tiger" Division to film combat operations of an allied country unit. The noise was coming from hundreds of Tiger Division soldiers performing organized unit calisthenics, followed by impressive Tae Kwon Do drills at the ungodly hour of 4:30 in the morning.

"That should have tipped me off that this project would not be ordinary. It kicked off a few weeks of impressive practices and operations of a division possessed of pride, élan, and high-morale. Every Korean soldier we encountered, officer and enlisted, was professional and all-business. We had arrived just in time for the next scheduled search-and-destroy operation not far from the base camp, which was located near Qui Nhon, South Vietnam, The Tiger Division had a reputation as fearless fighters. Even local villagers outside the division perimeter gave way to division soldiers."

"The usual bevy of mama-sans who came onto American bases to shine shoes and wash GI laundry were absent. Children didn't hang on perimeter fences begging for chewing gum, as was the custom outside US encampments. Local villagers kept their distance. I wondered why."

He stopped wondering when he saw calling cards and flyers produced by the division for villagers and visiting guests alike. They featured a division Tiger logo jumping out of a division crest, and the words, "Beware, if you mess with us, the Tiger will eat you," inscribed in Vietnamese.

Since it was a common occurrence throughout South Vietnam during the war for some Vietnamese workers who were permitted on the base to do manual labor, as well as hang out at the perimeters, to be Viet Cong, one could surmise that to be the case at the Tiger Division base camp.

Whether that was indeed so or not, Craven reveals that he very quickly came to understand and respect what he called "disciplined warriors."

"As the division prepared to move to the assigned objective, a four- to five-mile march over rough, hilly, rocky terrain, I gathered our team members to go over some points on the customs and practices of our hosts. We had brought some C-rations, but I decided now it might insult our hosts and make us appear to be aloof, just the opposite of our desire to establish a relationship of goodwill and camaraderie. I informed the team we would march alongside them and eat their staple of unpolished rice, which they ate at breaks, up to five times a day in the field, just to get enough nutrition. Just rice. Not rice with chicken. No rice and gravy. Plain, unpolished rice. The kind that you boil in a canteen cup after adding water, and you eat in clumps because it sticks together," he said, never forgetting the graciousness and concern of the South Koreans for the Americans' welfare at breaks.

Mid-morning stop: "Ah, you take breakfast?"

Noon: "Ah, you take lunch?"

Mid-afternoon: "Ah, you take food?"

Evening: "Ah, you take dinner?"

"Soon, we were starving from lack of nutrition and carbs, but we hungrily ate it all, with a steel spoon the size of an entrenching shovel. The Korean soldiers nodded in approval at our love of rice, but laughed when we couldn't master eating with chopsticks. This went over well with Tiger soldiers, and the gesture gave us acceptance and access to capturing their story on film, as well as offers of extra helpings ... of rice."

Craven expanded on the mission with the Tiger Division.

"We met up with a Tiger Cavalry squadron and hitched a ride on top of the armored personnel carriers with the Tiger logo painted on the armor-plated front. We traveled across rice fields and meadows, stopping at quaint thatched-roof huts to search for VC who were villagers by day. Huts often contained weapons caches hidden under mounds of drying rice.

"One of our team members was hurt when he was taking pictures from atop his Tiger APC, but not enough to be evacuated. He had been thrown off when the APC abruptly stopped to negotiate one of the many rice paddy levees. It was hard to find something to hold and brace himself as well as take pictures, and when his APC stopped suddenly, he was launched forward, down into the muck."

"During breaks, I was able to get in some practice with my .45 pistol when Koreans were testing their weapons or calibrating their gun sights in anticipation of a firefight. I built an impressive record for 'killing' coconuts, dislodged from their palm tree hosts."

"The battalion we were assigned to the next day began sweeping a steep tree-lined hill. The public information liaison with us explained that South Koreans were tenacious. When Air Force B-52 'Arc Light,' or carpet-bombing missions against enemy, occurred in the valley below us, often the intelligence supplied by US sources was days-old. The enemy would move to the wooded steep hills to escape certain death and hide in the rocky crevices until danger passed.

"Similarly, when Koreans swept these hideouts, the enemy were alerted and would hide until the Koreans grew tired and moved on. Unlike American forces, the Tiger units would return multiple times over the span of a few days and surprise them in close ambushes. Tenacity. Patience."

"I asked our Korean ROK PIO host about rumors some Korean soldiers liked to kill enemy with their bare hands, and then take a body part as a souvenir. We had heard that a favorite practice was to cut off a dead enemy's ears. He was rattled by my questions, but finally told me that the division did not condone the practice of removing enemy body parts, but it still occurred occasionally. He explained that some South Koreans came from sects in rural regions of South Korea and followed quaint religious and mystical practices. Some believed that dismembering an enemy left the dead spirits to roam and to wander forever, the ultimate disgrace to his family because the spirit could not reunite with the body and ever find peace. I had heard some ARVN (South Vietnamese Army) cultural tribes believed the same thing and held to the same practices."

"We stopped for a water break and smokes midway up a heavily forested steep hill. My team consisted of four photographers, including one Specialist/5 who was a holdover from the Korean conflict. He was overweight and frequently lagged behind. Breaks were his favorite activity, and he hung two canteens of water on his pistol-belt to rehydrate from his profuse sweating. Instead of walking stealthily toe-to-heel, my team NCO clomped, causing the ROK soldiers to wince in disbelief.

"Suddenly, shots rang out just as the platoon we were with lined up for a headcount before we moved out. More shots, and we then understood we were under attack. The Koreans ran down the hill to find defensive positions from which to return fire. We tried to keep up. I noticed my team NCO was gasping and grabbing his knees after a 20-yard sprint, then zigzagged down the hill. He was the only team member I could see, as the younger members were fast and fleet of foot. I knew this out-of-shape soldier was in no position to take pictures of the Koreans maneuvering and attacking, so I began shooting pictures, as I hopped, ran, and low-crawled tree to tree, ripping off a few frames each time. I was beside the platoon command element, which allowed me to get great shots of leaders and soldiers organizing a defense, then attacking and returning fire."

"The experience was exhilarating. After we returned to Long Binh, I sent our Tiger Division PIO liaison copies of many of our photos to help division morale and to contribute to its war-fighting history.

"After the film was processed, we readied for the next mission, this time a 30-day embedment with a green, untested [unit], Thailand's palace guard, officially called the Royal Queen's Cobra Regiment. It was seeking to earn its first Vietnam battle streamer for the unit guidon. That would be tough to do because it was clear to us the Thais were risk-averse by official edict in the first months after arrival. They didn't conduct many patrols far from base and when they did, emphasis was placed on minimizing casualties. They dug tunnels for living quarters, but the soldiers were eager and high-spirited. They made excellent hosts. That all changed when they were ambushed one night after we had ended our assignment. VC sappers were in the perimeter double-concertina wire, then the main unit. They threatened to overwhelm the base camp but were slaughtered when the nearby 105mm artillery guns were cranked almost level, loaded with deadly "bee-hive" rounds. Each round contained hundreds of small fish-hook 'flachettes.' The results were devastating. We learned General Westmoreland came to observe the dead caught in the wire and to celebrate the Thais' first sizeable victory, accompanied by press who wanted a body count.

"Then, someone from our company headquarters told me that I had been summoned to report to MAC-V headquarters information office to explain why I was credited in a double-truck (left and right inside-facing pages) photo feature in *Pacific Stars and Stripes*. I was bewildered and had not seen the day's edition. I scurried around and found the answer in our mission coordinating agency, SEAPC, Southeast Asia Pictorial Center. Someone there volunteered that a photo editor came from the *Stripes* Saigon bureau to look over photos from recent missions.

"He liked several of mine that I had turned in with my caption sheets from the Tiger Division project. He wasn't aware of the unwritten Army tradition that officers lead, not perform as technicians. At the bottom of the published pictures was my rank, name, and unit credit: 'Photos by 2LT Sonny Craven, 221st Signal Co.' they read. It was a long ride over the short distance from Long Binh to Saigon. When I arrived, I was told to wait, which dramatically ramped my anxiety, dread, and anticipation.

"Finally, someone directed me to report to a lieutenant colonel. I could feel sweat break out on my back but I mustered a crisp salute, saying 'Lieutenant Craven reporting as ordered, sir.'"

The colonel explained to Craven then that his name had been mentioned in the daily high-level staff meeting by some general who demanded to know why the "Army has a lieutenant with an allied unit running around the battlefield taking pictures."

According to Craven, "As the lieutenant colonel swore oaths and pronouncements and threatened to visit violence upon my head, I gulped, and thought to myself that when my photographic effort was described in that manner, it sounded preposterous even to me."

Craven explained as humbly as possible that he was leading his men, but when no one else was present to accomplish a mission, that it was his responsibility to decide what to do, or risk failing his unit, the team, and its hosts.

"He went quiet for a minute, to think about the righteousness or foolhardiness of my deed. Actually, as an information officer, I think he needed to explain the reasons behind my transgression so he could spin it in a way that turned a negative to positive," Craven said.

"With a stern face that turned into a forced smile, he 'let me off' with a warning. As I walked back to my jeep, I breathed for the first time since I had left Long Binh, it seemed. When I returned to the unit, I told of the experience to company officials who had cited 'reasons' why they couldn't accompany me to my first and only ass-chewing of my nearly 30-year career."

Craven feels he was left with two ironies.

"Photo Assignment Team officers who were assigned in later years were schooled and trained in the photo arts and expected to take photos.

"During our project with the Thai Army, our hosts offered an invitation to eat their rations. 'Ah, you take dinner?' The team looked at each other with fake smiles. It would be a long 30 days of another rice diet. The difference was the occasional small strip of water buffalo steak—and always the red curry powder that excreted the rice from our alimentary canal accompanied by the noise and shaking of a space shuttle launch. When I returned stateside, I welcomed a return to my wife's Southern cooking. Except for rice, which I wouldn't eat again for 20 years."

Craven's thoughts quickly shifted from rice to the infamous Tet Offensive of 1968, which he feels fooled the US civilian media but did not fool American forces in Vietnam.

"On the verge of the Tet Offensive of January 1968, officers of various unit intelligence shops in the Long Binh area could not escape the sense that the enemy was about to attack somewhere, and soon," he said.

"The 221st received information that the 199th Light Infantry Brigade was moving out to search for Viet Cong troop buildup in the area around the Parrot's Beak, a narrow distance between Saigon and the Cambodian border, and in the jungles and rice fields near Long Binh. The Viet Cong often marshaled hit-and-run attacks in this zone, then withdrew to the safety of Cambodia knowing that US forces were forbidden to cross or even fly across the international boundary," Craven said.

During the Tet Offensive, the 199th defended Bien Hoa airfield together with the Long Binh post complex and the headquarters of II Field Force Vietnam. The 199th sustained more than 3,200 casualties during its stay in South Vietnam.

"My team and I received permission from the brigade operations folks to accompany the brigade on the sweep looking for VC. We traveled alongside a seasoned Infantry company with good officers and NCOs.

"The first days were uneventful, but our photography of infantry patrols, and units fording jungle streams, attracted attention because of the 'thunk' sound made by the shutters of our Beseler Topcon 35mm cameras. Each time we depressed the shutter release, a noisy 'ka-thunk' was produced by the mirror as it flipped up to allow the curtain shutter to expose an image. In dead-quiet triple-canopy jungles, this noise was amplified and could travel hundreds of yards, heard by anyone in close proximity. This cheap camera was another result of the lowest-bidder government procurement system and the downside of ordering off-the-shelf equipment untested for noise, durability, or even the ability to withstand the effects of high humidity and temperatures in tropical environments."

"We had learned to carry our personal cameras as backup. Nikon F models were preferred, but I carried my Pentax SLV1, a dead ringer for the later popular Spotmatic series, except for the external exposure meter clipped to the hotshoe mount.

"On the evening of the second day, we were deep in the jungle and had not detected any VC. We had the feeling, however, of being watched.

"Suddenly, a crack echoed around the jungle floor, and everyone hit the ground. A fusillade of gunfire broke out. We soon learned that the shooting was mostly return fire from our own infantry in the confusion and mayhem, as no one actually saw the enemy. A VC sniper had wounded the unit point man in the thigh as he walked 20 yards in front of the column.

"The company radio-telephone operator (RTO) called for a medical 'dust-off,' and in 15 minutes a Huey with white and red crosses on the nose and doors appeared and spotted our location through the yellow plume billowing from the smoke grenade thrown by someone. It marked the spot and signaled wind direction for a suitable landing spot.

"Once the 'dust-off' landed, a number of soldiers established a security perimeter around it, facing outward toward the tree-line. The chopper crew chief jumped to the ground, jerked open the door, then motioned for the four infantrymen waiting in the protective tree-line to run to the chopper with their wounded buddy, holding four sides of a poncho liner.

"Then, the chopper blades spun up RPM, and lifted slightly to perform a hover-check, a standard operating requirement in Vietnam due to the effects of high heat and power-robbing thin-air thermals. It performed a running start nose-down just feet above the ground to attain transitional lift. The unarmed helicopter banked right over the trees and circled the perimeter to allow the pilot and crew to survey the jungle's edge for snipers before safely gaining altitude and flying into the horizon.

"As we were ready to again get underway, the newly appointed point man looked for the tracker dog that typically accompanied point. The Doberman was missing, and no one saw him after the chaos. Tracker dogs are invaluable to the unit because of their keen sense of smell. In a humid jungle where there is little air movement, human scents hang for hours and dogs' acute hearing alerts them to the faintest sounds long before humans can detect them. Thus, the VC hated tracker dogs, and had standing bounties on them.

"Nothing the soldiers did, including whistling, summoned the dog. The troops surmised the gunfire scared the dog into the jungle or he was wounded and crawled off and died."

The unit remained on alert for a firefight into the night.

"Two companies, configured abreast of each other, put out double, overlapping perimeters. We took incoming random probing fire but our hosts recognized it as efforts to provoke a reaction so that our strength, gauge, and employment of types of weapons could be defined to identify unit size. We became used to such probes, and marveled when there were no casualties," Craven said, remembering that one morning, while searching his ruck sack, he found a can of cola with a bullet hole through it.

"The next morning, we were just waking, making coffee when a shot rang out from one perimeter. In an undisciplined moment, two companies opened up and laid down a base of suppressing, overlapping fields of fire. It was two minutes of danger, when finally, unit radios crackled and commands were given the order to ceasefire.

"Our team members were already maneuvering to cover the action, and low-crawling to find cover. Word was passed that noise at one perimeter spooked a sentry who fired into the jungle toward the sound."

Amazingly, the noise was coming from the lost tracking dog running around that sector in an attempt to come home.

"We were pretty unnerved for a few hours at how dangerous it had been, and a flashpoint for a real attack. After four days, we were running low on water. Excessive hill climbing and hacking trails had drained it. We weren't due to be resupplied at a planned water point for another two days.

"The first sergeants of the two companies walking abreast decided to call for a water resupply by chopper. They agreed on a rendezvous point a few hours away up on higher ground from which we could defend during a vulnerable stand-down. We climbed up a steep, large hill and when the units arrived, there was no suitable clearing for a helicopter re-supply effort because the small mountain-top was ringed by tall trees up to 70 feet high. A Huey UH-1 wouldn't fit in the small opening. One unit called for an LZ kit, consisting of axes, ropes, and chainsaws. A chopper arrived in a half-hour, hovered and the crew chief slowly dropped the kits past the skids using thick ropes, then the helicopter lifted from the area.

"It took two hours and a quantity of C4 explosives to blow a rough landing zone, then unit troops hacked and cut the trees down. Once cut to manageable size, the logs were pulled to the side of the clearing with hemp ropes by 7–10 troops; very back-breaking work. There was a debate whether the clearing was big enough to allow a helicopter to land without entangling the blades, which, if enmeshed, would put the rotor blades out of balance causing the chopper blades to flail and wildly oscillate and shake themselves until they broke apart, a not uncommon occurrence of Army aviation in Vietnam. Such situations, temperatures and troop-frustrations often determined their course. Troops were exhausted, weary, and very thirsty."

It took several attempts by different types of helicopters all day and into the night, but the water was finally delivered to the grateful troops. Filming the action of the day was another matter altogether. In that sense, the 221st was always at war with the elements.

"If needed, we could double our film sensitivity and compensate for tricking the real exposure value in what is called 'push-processing,' which involved adjusting film developing time and chemistry temperatures. The consideration created color shifts and introduced graininess in the finished film. But that was an acceptable risk we took. And, we didn't want to look like we were standing around when everyone was working so hard to acquire water.

"The next day, the decision was made to extract the companies. Word came to wind down our search and to move to a helicopter extraction point one mile away. Unit leaders knew our location was being telegraphed to nearby enemy trackers by the noise generated on the small mountain top in blowing the primitive landing zone and helicopters swarming to drop water. An order went out to avoid existing paths and trails along our route, and have recon out in advance.

"As we moved closer to our destination, a large clearing, unit commanders suspected that paths were mined or an ambush awaited us. We would blaze our own trail through the jungle until we reached sight of the clearing. Cutting virgin jungle brush, bushes, and vines is hard, slow work. It's also noisy and increases body sweat to perfume the air. It prevents, however, L-shaped formation ambushes because the unit isn't following a traditional trail or road.

"We finally broke out into a huge clearing late in the afternoon. At one time, this had been a rice field; now it was a meadow of dry tall grass. Unit commanders decided to camp in the center of the open field, put in place our observation points, roving sentries, and a tight perimeter. As an added precaution, the unit providing fires inside our artillery fire plan were requested to fire H&I [Harassment and Interdiction] rounds throughout the night. This measure randomizes impact zones and times to discourage sappers and dissuade enemy buildup for an attack. It was a surprising technique to us, and we had a hard time trying to fall asleep at the first sounds of 155mm artillery landing on the edge of the jungle that had just disgorged us. The sound of shells just over our heads before impact, then the explosion, was an effective deterrent. Added to that, every eighth to twelfth round was a parachute flare that lit up the sky like daylight until it fizzled and fell to earth. Each one lit the jungle perimeter and us as well."

Ever concerned for the safety of his troops under these circumstances, there was one troop in particular that Craven worried about.

"I remember fretting for the safety of our old, seasoned, grizzled first-sergeant who grabbed the PRC-25 tactical backpack radio to adjust fires and stood up, back-lighted by flares, and hoisted the radio above his head to get enough height above the terrain to make contact with the artillery fire center. When the flares popped, he was a conspicuous target for any sharpshooter. We admired him for his guts."

After a delay of a few hours because the troops came upon some abandoned American ammo, and then after F-100 Super Saber jets strafed the extraction point, the unit's transportation out of the bush arrived in what Craven called "textbook formation for extraction." They boarded the helicopters and flew back to Bien Hoa Air Base, HQ of the 199th.

"All the searching turned up nothing. No enemy contact. No sightings. Yet, we knew they were there, watching us. But they were disciplined enough to follow their overarching order not to give away what ultimately was in store for US forces. They were saving that for a few weeks later," Craven said.

Despite the 199th's mission—with the 221st in tow to photograph it—into the bush because of an impending sense of a massive enemy attack, the 1968 Tet Offensive did arrive and stays with Craven even today.

"Early in the morning of January 31, a main force of VC fired 122mm rockets at Long Binh, and the main base of the 199th Light Infantry Brigade. Sappers managed to penetrate the ammo dump near the 90th Replacement Battalion. I still relive the memories of Tet 1968, and the accompanying attacks by communist forces throughout South Vietnam. The surprise attacks were a desperate effort by North Vietnam to shock America (i.e. the media) into believing that it had enough capacity left to conduct a coordinated surprise attack on major US facilities and South Vietnamese provincial capitals," Craven said in agreement with many historians.

"In pure military terms, when the fighting ebbed after a week, the Tet Offensive was a disaster for the communists. They achieved no major physical objectives and incurred tens of thousands of casualties. The Viet Cong were decimated in the kind of open, conventional fighting that guaranteed their demise. Basically, the communists had abandoned their hit-and-run attrition tactics in favor of an all-out battle of firepower and maneuver, exactly the kind of fight at which the US Army excelled. The communists paid a heavy price in the process."

If it had any destructive effect at all, most historians believe it was on the will of the American people to continue the war; Tet stimulated the sentiment that the war in Vietnam was unwinnable.

"The furious offensive seemingly negated all the optimistic talk about an imminent end to the war. It seemed to many Americans that, on the contrary, the war was only beginning," Craven feels.

"My Army combat photography team performed the still and mopic photo documentation of a battle stemming from the infiltration and attacks by VC and NVA in the Long Binh area that covered a fierce three-and-a-half-hour firefight. It was around a major Army regional headquarters and across the road leading to Saigon from a village built by the South Vietnamese government for widows of South Vietnam soldiers. For me, it began with explosions of a nearby ammo dump and our unit siren activated by the duty officer, a survivor buddy today. Immediately, I began preparing to go cover the action, finding as many team members and others gathered near the company headquarters who were ready to move out on a moment's notice. Once I was given the clearance, my team and I piled into two jeeps and headed to the post's main gate adjoining the highway that led to Saigon. I had to convince them our job required us to be in the thick of the action and we were allowed to pass through because no one from Long Binh post was allowed to exit by gate security and Army military police except fighting forces and our team, and military police road patrols.

"We didn't make it far before encountering highway roadblocks configured of MP jeeps topped with sandbags, as a large firefight was in progress between friendly and enemy forces adjacent to the II Field Force headquarters, a major three-star command in charge of area fighting forces.

"We ditched our jeep on the roadside and ran in a crouch to avoid being hit by enemy and friendly crossfire, all the while snapping still pictures and rolling our hand-held motion-picture film camera. The team and I eventually became pinned down in a narrow ditch for what seemed like hours.

"My team and I, mopic cameraman PFC Norman Buchman, still photogs SP/4 David Wilhite, PFC Michael Epstein, did our best to follow the action from both sides of the road and still remain in the ditch with our heads down. Buchman had already tried to run in a zigzag fashion between sandbagged observation bunkers inside the Field Force perimeter to get action shots, stopping and dropping occasionally for cover, or to just pancake on the ground to escape withering volleys of small arms fire exchanged between enemy and US ground forces protecting the II Field Force headquarters compound."

Craven went on to describe the intensity of covering the Tet Offensive very up close and personal.

"The firing became too intense as VC and American security forces engaged in a prolonged firefight. From behind their parked jeeps layered with sandbags in front of their windshields, MPs were shouting to us to stay down. I borrowed one team member's backup Filmo as he continued to pop up and squeeze off a few still shots with his 35mm Topcon interchangeable lens camera. We were all school-trained and knew that using the wide-angle lens was perfectly suited to this situation. Exposing oneself to enemy direct fire by having to perform critical focus wasn't a factor because a characteristic of a wide-angle lens is its ability to resolve focus to infinity mere inches from the lens surface. One only needed to point the camera in a general direction above the head and press the shutter release button. The wide field of view almost guaranteed encompassing, in-focus shots of the battle.

"The battle raged for what seemed like eternity before AH-1 Huey Cobra attack helicopters from the 101st Airborne aviation unit arrived overhead and began strafing the village. VC embedded in the hooches and ditches of the village tried to escape but were driven out and caught in the open brush by the overhead stream of fire from the Cobra's chin-turret Gatling guns and stubby wing-mounted 2.75 inch rockets."

Craven feels a debt of endless gratitude for what the helicopter pilots did.

"Our butts were saved by the unrelenting air assaults of heroic Army pilots flying these newly introduced Huey Cobras. This suppressing fire made it possible for us to document the actions of elements of Colonel (later, Major General) George S. Patton's 11th Armored Cavalry Regiment as they conducted relief and mopping-up operations in the village and surrounding area. Several of us were wounded in the effort.

"As we entered Widows' Village behind the Cavalry, we filmed mopping-up actions. Mech infantry soldiers, joined by Army military police, were pulling enemy wounded out of ditches and cuffing their hands behind their backs with thick plastic ties. Someone called out to be careful as some wounded VC lying by their roads and in ditches were still alive and carrying weapons and grenades. We heard the warning but we were too busy filming the action in the chaos for it to register."

Soon Craven was told that one of the 221st troops was wounded.

"When another team member informed me that PFC Norman Buchman was injured, I ran over to check his condition, but combat medics following the 11th Cavalry troopers in case of battle injuries had already swarmed Buchman and loaded him for transport in the medical 'meat-wagon' to nearby 24th Evacuation Hospital."

PFC Buchman had apparently fallen backwards over a wire fence as he was looking through the mopic camera eye-piece, according to reports.

"It was the last we'd see of Norman. The team was never told his disposition and a rumor circulated back at the 221st that his injury was serious enough to warrant medical evacuation to Okinawa. I concluded he suffered a broken or severely injured spine," Craven said.

"I returned to taking action shots as tracked armored personnel carriers whirled around the village providing fire support if needed from its top .50-caliber machine gun. I filmed one prisoner standing on one leg, with the other in shreds and partially missing. Army troopers systematically searched prisoners and stripped them of grenades. Unexploded aerial ordnance from the Apaches—mostly rockets—was everywhere.

"Then out of the corner of my right eye, I caught sight of a black-clad VC looking at me, but he appeared dazed and dying. I walked a few steps past him. Then, a loud, ear-splitting explosion; I was knocked to the ground by the concussion and lost consciousness. I don't know for how long. When I came to, my ears were ringing, and sound was muffled and distant like you see in war films as the actor stumbles around disoriented and mortally wounded. I felt something warm oozing down my neck on the right side and saw copious amounts of blood on my jungle fatigues. I put my right hand to my ear and neck and felt blood, lots of it. I had no pain, and no feeling. I panicked for a moment with the thought of being badly wounded, disfigured and half the right area of my head blown off. Was I dying and just didn't know it?"

Next, Craven heard a muffled, distant voice shouting at him, "Are you okay?" It was someone from his team, possibly a trooper by the name of Wilhite, who, Craven recently found out, was also wounded.

"I asked him for an assessment of my wound, as I feared the worst—a piece of my head on the right side was missing. After checking me thoroughly, and then a medic giving me a compression bandage to stanch the bleeding, he pronounced my head was still on my shoulders though a large piece of shrapnel was lodged behind my ear lobe. The medic removed and replaced the compression bandage and offered to transport me to 24th Evac," Craven said.

He told Craven that he might have more injuries that would be found when he removed his uniform.

"His advice was prescient, as I would learn later. I promised I would get there on my own if I could get back to our jeep. When I arrived at the field hospital, it was hectic, a beehive of frenzied activity. Wounded were triaged and waiting to be fully diagnosed and treated. More serious cases were attended to in surgical rooms where doctors in bloody gowns worked to save their patients still lying on stretchers because gurney tables were taken. One doctor had his hands in a patient's chest. There were no attempts to close flaps dividing wards and everyone waiting could see heroic efforts in progress."

Looking around the 24th Evac Hospital at the carnage doctors and nurses were attempting to control put things in proper perspective for Craven.

"It was enough to convince me to leave without treatment. I was embarrassed to even inform anyone of my light shrapnel wounds. Then, I turned to leave and saw wounded VC stacked upright against the wall, most still wearing bandages applied by Army field medics.

"When I got back to the 221st compound, I pushed by the clamor of comrades who wanted to know details 'from the front' and what happened when they saw my bloody uniform. In my hooch, I stripped down to gauge my wounds from the blast. My chest, stomach, and upper thighs were peppered with dozens of very small pieces of shrapnel and explosive powder. My face was tattooed in a perfect oval pattern around my nose exactly where my camera had been when I was sighting. The crappy old Beseler Topcon had prevented shrapnel from entering my brain and probably saved my life. I had picked it up and placed it in the jeep to bring it back because I knew it would have to be declared a 'combat-loss' to properly account for it." A "by-the-book man to the end," Craven said of himself.

And the US Army was acting by the book as well when Company Commander Major Tom DeYoung awarded Craven the Purple Heart for his wounds in the orderly room, offering him "Congratulations."

Craven remembers not only his wounds but the "wounds" that his camera suffered.

"It was a bloody mess, and the lens was shattered right where shrapnel entered the center which, if not stopped, would have traveled to my face. The unit supply officer would not let me keep it as a souvenir. I regret my honesty in divulging it, but I was honor-bound to tell the truth," he said.

Taking a stance on the fierce response to the Tet Offensive that the media at the time did not acknowledge, at least in the beginning, Craven lauds the gut-wrenching efforts of his fellow soldiers.

"The outcome of Tet attacks was never in doubt, but the carnage was evident throughout our sector of coverage, from Long Binh, the Army's largest encampment in Vietnam, to Newport Docks, near Saigon, where war supplies were unloaded. The devastation unleashed by the Viet Cong, who infiltrated from Cambodian sanctuaries near Saigon, on villages and the population in the provincial capitals, was documented by our various Army combat photography teams from Saigon to Hue.

"But for a young second lieutenant on that day and the next, I learned again about real fear—being scared when lots of people are shooting at you in real combat. Fear you've never known before or can experience in any other way. From that day forward, you fear little else.

"Recently, I relived that fateful day when I saw my team's footage in the 'Vietnam in HD' series on cable. The documentary was unmistakably clear. The surprise attack failed miserably and in most places, US forces regained the initiative with superior numbers and firepower. But, despite heavy losses by the enemy, the media shamelessly portrayed this as a defeat for America because the president had been reporting 'light at the end of the tunnel,'" Craven added.

"Roger Hawkins, a photo assignment team officer in our unit, who served at a later time than me, wryly said, 'I have thought of getting a T-shirt that says, "I shot women and children in Vietnam." On the back it would say, "'In 16 and 35mm."' But a lot of people wouldn't understand the irony," Craven said of Hawkins' statement.

And while Hawkins' words would not be lost on anyone who wielded a camera in Southeast Asia, photographers and photojournalists whose MOS required them to tell the stories of their respective branches and shoot the film did have to take weapons along for their "ride through the jungle."

The AR-15 was standard issue for officers and enlisted soldiers when traveling administratively between area units and to the Saigon or Long Binh local area. "The .45-caliber semi-automatic pistol was the sidearm carried by officers and enlisted when away from base camp on photographic missions in hostile zones, and, in particular, accompanying ground combat units. Our 'hosts' insisted on assuming security responsibility when we accompanied patrols, sweeps, and search operations. We were expected to keep our weapons holstered and cameras at the aim."

But according to Craven, if the need ever arose for the 221st's still and mopic photographers to use those weapons, they were always ready to do so. He speaks very highly of the men to this day.

"In an all-out firefight where and when every life is threatened, or leaders have been killed, neutralized or incapacitated, or chaos has seized disciplined and orderly tactical lines, and every unit member is caught up in the moment, I had no doubt our team was prepared to switch roles and fight like infantry, and as an integral member of the host team, not a Rambo episode.

"We had a great mix of dedicated soldiers, but the hardships of startup and fielding an untested unit with a sophisticated mission and high expectations made them strain to be all they could be. Taking into account the various ways of personnel assignment of soldiers with occupational skills specialties required by the 221st mission after it was reactivated as a photo unit and its flag unfurled, the unit was blessed on the one hand with a mix of motivated soldiers with the right attitude, determined to serve their country and on the other hand those who were part of a sweep of stateside and overseas commands, who, in some cases were excess to unit needs and authorizations. As expected, commanders availed themselves of the opportunity presented to divest their units of chronic disciplinary cases, and soldiers who lacked requisite standards of soldiering."

Having said that, Craven realizes full well that differences in the unit between those who were committed to the cause and those who may have had questions about their service in the unit were not always solvable. Nevertheless, the picture he paints is one of positivity, the likes of which the media, and certainly films about the war that came after it, rarely portrayed.

"The necessity of deploying the unit rapidly meant that there wasn't time to resolve these differences, which included officers who harbored questions about their mandatory commitment and their conscientious support of the war. Yet two unforeseen events occurred that acted as a crucible for a mental adjustment once the packets were serialized. The packets were all small and members bonded quickly. Most were motivated to do the right thing and pull together, mainly the result of these tight bonds and not some abstract concept of doing it for duty or country.

"Starting from scratch when they arrived in Vietnam, they faced a bleak outlook because nothing was prepared for them or made easy. The tasks were always more numerous than available manpower resources, causing all to 'lean forward in the foxholes.' They were faced with having to build a base camp of operations complete with facilities and living accommodations. This required officers and men to work together around the clock, without regard to rank or job title, to meet deadlines in order to become mission-ready. The levels of respect and cooperation necessary to accomplish this enormous feat, without rancor, pettiness, or in-fighting, were achieved without difficulty. In fact, harmony and cooperation came from teamwork.

"This bond was strengthened, and unit resilience was tested again by an external task requiring nearly 100 men to offload ships at a sea port carrying war supplies for front-line units. Instead of sapping the morale of these skilled photographers, their mutual bonds and relationships with their NCOs bound them together. They got the task done in an impressive manner, formally noted by a general officer responsible for port operations who praised their professionalism and hard work.

"I believe these experiences undergirded our fledgling efforts to build and mature the unit from scratch, enabling the unit to also simultaneously perform our main photographic mission, And it built men … real soldiers in the process. The psychological 'windowing' of soldier development that began at Ft. Monmouth to the initial challenges faced in Vietnam may have helped ultimately to prepare our soldiers for the hardships and risks they would encounter in the tough jobs associated with documenting combat operations."

That was true, no matter the branch of service the 221st was ordered to accompany onto the battlefield.

"There was never a formal attachment letter order. We requested permission to accompany a unit and remained an integral part of our home unit during my era. Formal attachments were certainly a consideration for detachments later deployed because they were too far for the home unit to routinely or efficiently support rations, quarters, and, perhaps, administer Uniformed Code of Military Justice. It was not unusual to not omit consigning UCMJ and administrative custodianship of personnel records in attachments to other units in order to retain control of the detachments, especially in subject areas of infrequent needs. Travel to and from Long Binh using Army and Air Force aircraft was routine when needed.

"Keegan Federal, who later became a noted Atlanta judge, and still has an active practice, was given quarters at 221st, but he was the legal officer for the parent unit, 160th Signal Group. He frequently traveled to dispersed 160th unit sites to handle legal matters. Although my team had the distinction of working with Asian allied units, we worked with Air Force pilots flying combat airstrike ground support missions in the course of our Army combat assignments. There was a 221st PAT team dedicated to the Navy Delta Riverine Force during my time."

In addition, the 221st performed various civic actions in addition to their standard missions.

"Reports contained in the 221st History Report indicate that there were humanitarian and training assistance efforts carried out by the unit. My team was involved in documenting dozens of MEDCAP (Medical Civic Action Programs) as a matter of course when working with combat units. Medical sections of large US Army units routinely scheduled health and welfare checkups of villages in combat zones. They provided basic dental extractions, pre-natal, and disease prevention checkups. They performed minor surgeries, and carried out routine immunizations and vaccinations. In one case, we filmed an entire operation in a remote village performed by an American surgeon from New York under very rustic conditions."

And while some combat correspondents and photographers crossed paths in equally rustic conditions with the civilian media, during Sonny Craven's time in Vietnam that was the exception rather than the rule.

"In my tour, we rarely saw a civilian journalist and then only if we crossed paths in Saigon, where they clustered," he said.

And while some combat correspondents and photographers in uniform admired their counterparts who reported and photographed for the press, the same cannot be said for Sonny Craven.

"Many working reporters of the American news bureaus were sloth, with notable exceptions. They hung around their hotels, the Rex and Caravelle, and checked in with MAC-V JUSPAO. That's the Joint Public Affairs Press Office, which 'credentialed' reporters (issued official press ID cards), and conducted the 'Five o'clock Follies,' meaning daily briefings of military reports, news and progress reports, referred to as the 'body-counts.' The irreverent phrase, 'body-counts,' was purely a press invention because they were so dependent on JUSPAO for what was happening daily in South Vietnam and reports of enemy movements. They needed a measurement of effectiveness, or MOE, to gauge military claims of progress toward winning the war. They hated the dependency, but to strike out on their own to gather news was too dangerous; they had few working relationships with combat units, and the limits of tactical communications (Army switchboards and telephone trunking) were barriers to making cold calls to develop leads.

"Conversely, Army unit commanders were wary of direct press contact that might result in negative stories that would end their military careers. They distrusted the press corps, which they linked to unfavorable US news reports they received from loved ones. Commanders I knew or talked with often complained of bias and press distrust of the military.

"So, many of the working press mostly remained collected around the bars, killed time by visits to the steam and cream shops of Saigon's Tu Do Street's collection of bars and 'sin-dens.' They had fancy walking suits tailored-made and traveled to Bangkok frequently for fun and relaxation.

"Occasionally, JUSPAO would arrange for some reporters to visit units where they received boring, self-serving command briefings, but the press rarely remained long enough to accompany small units to the field in 'Charlie Country,' where they would have developed deeper knowledge of units they covered. JUSPAO would order up helicopters to ferry them to accompany General Westmoreland when he visited units the day after a big battle, especially when there were many bodies to count. Like piranhas, the press would jockey to get pictures. But anytime I witnessed this obscene gawking gaggle, it was done in daylight hours, and they would eagerly seek to depart before nightfall.

"The problem was exacerbated by young combat-arms captains detailed to be information officers without benefit of any formal training or requirement to attend the Defense Information School. At that time, many IO officers, as they were called, were unit rejects or deemed unpromotable. Not all, mind you, but enough to be noticed, and some of them resented babysitting the press which, in their view, had one aim: undermine the American people's faith in the US military."

However, Craven did have communication with one member of the civilian press.

"Years later, CBS correspondent Sam Ford told me that when the term 'military information officer' was mentioned among civilian media colleagues they immediately thought of an aging, overweight, cigar-chomping hack who had reached his terminal rank."

Still, Craven insists there were exceptions in the Saigon press corps.

"To be fair, there were many good reporters from time to time, but the unit commanders would tell you that the reporters invited from their unit hometowns were best. This was particularly true for Reserve and Guard units activated and deployed to Vietnam. Hometown reporters had credibility, were accountable to their editors, and were part of the Reserve or Guard community where they lived and worked. The results were informed stories with detail and depth, rich in texture, focused on accomplishments of the hometown boys fighting the war. Commanders loved and trusted them, and took them with them and taught them how to understand soldiers and the art of war."

One of those, in Craven's opinion, was Joe Galloway, UPI correspondent known for putting down his camera and joining in the fight against the North Vietnamese Army regulars at the battle of the Ia Drang Valley, and, years later, co-author, along with the late Lieutenant General Hal Moore, of the book *We Were Soldiers Once … and Young*, which also became a film starring Mel Gibson.

"Galloway was such a reporter, and was integrated with [then] Lieutenant Colonel Hal Moore's battalion. He often picked-up weapons to protect himself and others, especially in the Ia Drang Valley battle."

Craven has a different outlook on the Asian media than he does on the majority of those in the American media.

"I had great respect for the Asian press, mainly those who worked for the foreign press services. We found them embedded with Special Forces A teams in the Highlands. We knew they were tough, low-maintenance, and grizzled. They seemed to always be missing a few fingers and they had three cameras around their necks that showed bare-metal from scuffs and hard use," he said.

Asian media aside, his disdain for the American media persists.

"The problem, in part, was created by 'hot-dogs,' young naive men who may or may not have had any journalism skills or training. The bureaus found it difficult to attract reporters with established reputations from their New York operations who would agree to a full-time war zone assignment, a minority because they had families, eschewed the military role in Vietnam, or didn't want the risk. Others were looking to make a name as a 'war correspondent.' There were exceptions, such as CBS reporter Morley Safer, but his name was made in Vietnam.

"So the news bureaus succumbed to hiring Gonzo journalists, those who flew to Thailand at their own expense, crossed the border and were hired on the spot. Many had apprentice-level skills. But few were deeply subscribed to upholding the canons of journalism. Many were graduates of liberal universities and their J-schools. They were often only a year out from attending anti-war and campus peace rallies. Now, they were prepared to inform Americans back home about how the American military was faring.

"Then there were the knuckleheads," Craven said. "Sean Flynn, actor Errol Flynn's son, was a so-called photojournalist. [Flynn had actually come to Vietnam to star in a movie about a combat correspondent in Vietnam and then became a real one]. He listened to few people, didn't heed safety warnings and one day took off [with fellow journalist Dana Stone] with no escort, down a road in an area in Cambodia controlled by VC [and Khmer Rouge cadres], despite being warned. They disappeared and have never been found.

"During Tet, a member of another photo team which covered the Saigon attacks told me he was offered a lot of money by a network news reporter for his film of the street fighting. He explained it was too dangerous for him and his crew to be in the streets. They were warned by military police to stay sheltered, especially after the assault on the US embassy in Saigon.

"I think what bothered many of my team members—and was widely known around the 221st—was a JUSPAO practice to curry favor with the press. MAC-V JUSPAO issued press cards with priority authorization for press to use military transport to fly or travel by ground transportation in pursuit of assignments. In effect, it meant any civilian member of the press credentialed by JUSPAO could bump us, if seats were scarce. We can never forget that insulting practice. I had to return to Saigon from Ban Me Thuot in the Central Highlands but was told that military air was on a space-available basis because a New York-based news crew had priority. It had 'bumped' me."

Craven was fortunate, however, to have worked with military intelligence and CIA personnel in the Highlands, and they arranged a seat back to Saigon in an old Air America C-47 after hauling Hmong fighters.

"One day, one of my fellow officers and I drove to Saigon for a meeting. We walked past the compound wall surrounding the VNAF [South Vietnamese Air Force] Officers Club and heard talking as if someone was giving a report. We walked closer to the wall and peered over. It was an American news reporter and his cinematographer. He was practicing his stand-up report to be shuttled by DHL to his New York news headquarters, as was the practice then, and, we assumed, would be used as news from South Vietnam. We watched him stoop down, pick-up some dirt and rub it on his face. He practiced a couple of takes until he was satisfied he had reported the day's news from the Vietnam War front to the American people. And that's the way it was," Craven said sarcastically.

His bitter feelings about how the media reported the war in Vietnam did not stop Craven himself from seeking employment in the very same institution once his Army service, in which he had achieved the rank of colonel, came to an end.

What he termed "Army career follow-on assignments" as a public-affairs officer of major Army installations and senior commands helped him make that transition to civilian work. These career positions included chief of Army news teams and commander of the Defense Department's largest overseas live satellite radio and television network—AFN-E (Armed Forces Network-Europe)—serving an audience of nearly 500,000 military, government, civilian employees and families in Belgium, Netherlands, West Germany, and West Berlin through a system of 12 studio station affiliates,

"After retirement from active duty, I was interviewed and offered the position of general manager of the Northwestern Public Broadcasting system, based in Bemidji, Minnesota. After my visit, I reluctantly declined the offer but felt satisfied my Army skills and experience were competitive."

It was an assignment after his command of the Army broadcast network that proved most helpful to his future civilian career as an educator and proved a culmination of his experiences.

The Army selected him for battalion command of what had formerly been the Army audiovisual school at Ft. Monmouth, charged with training not only MOSs used by 221st soldiers, but anyone entering the photo sciences, television production, engineering and illustration career fields. He was able to take his own training from that same school at the beginning of his Army career, along with his other audiovisual enterprise assignments, to improve the skills of soldiers destined for worldwide Army assignments. Best of all, it gave him the authority as schoolhouse commander to attempt to formally preserve the Army audiovisual career fields and doctrine. He hopes, in some way, it inspired creation of two combat photography companies in the Army structure today, capable of deploying to combat zones.

Craven was recommended by faculty friends of his undergraduate school alma mater, Florida State University, to build a modern film and television school for the seven campuses of Miami-Dade College. With its 125,000 faculty, staff and students, it remains the largest college in the nation, according to Craven, who became the first dean of the college's new film and television schools. With Craven's tutelage and guidance, the department sought to be a strategic partner of the Miami film and television industry, and to manage a school for journeymen and women professionals. He taught courses at the college as well. "In three years, graduates were so in demand," Craven proudly says, "that the television school achieved a 100 percent hiring rate.

After spending time in the restaurant business, an Army friend of Craven's who was chief of staff of Virginia Military Institute, implored him to become director of communications and marketing for VMI, one of the nation's premier and oldest military colleges. "In all of these jobs, I extensively used the skills and experience from my education and Army background reaching back to my time in the 221st," he said.

"In all of this, it must said that the story of 221st was more than combat photography. It was a time when young men of disparate, diverse backgrounds were pulled together to meet their military service requirements, draftees and enlisted alike. The common purpose of deploying to war and building a unit from scratch on a dirt parcel of unimproved land took the human homogenization of young people in their formative years, most without having fully formed a philosophy of life. What a remarkable feat. They were asked to do something noble without knowing how or if their efforts would someday be important and, maybe, even shape history. Long after the unit flag was furled, we remember details of the experience less, but we can never forget our comrades, even the few knuckleheads, or our own mistakes."

One doubts there were many of the latter.

221st Signal Pictorial Company, US Army combat cameraman Sonny Craven (left) and crew testing an early-model ENG chip-based video camera. A technical representative from the Sacramento Army Depot is holding the camera. (Sonny Craven collection)

Photography Became His World: Robert Frank

Robert Frank grew up on a small dairy farm in Norman, Oklahoma, and had put himself through five years of college there at the University of Oklahoma, from which he earned a degree in business management, as a professional still photographer and lab technician for both black and white and color. He earned all his expenses for high school and college working more than 55 hours a week between 1957 and 1963. So he could pay for everything, his work involved all sorts of photography and lab tasks, including fraternity house living costs, even acquiring a 1954 Porsche 1500 coupe, which he raced at weekends.

"But I could not graduate *summa cum laude* like my future wife—who had fewer work duties," he laughs.

He was commissioned through Air Force ROTC and entered active duty in August 1963 as a supply officer. As such his expertise, along with the photography skills he had learned in high school, would serve him well as a member of the USAF's 600th Photographic Squadron.

"I learned black-and-white photography and lab work in high school as part of a science fair project. I learned color photography and color lab work while working for the University of Oklahoma Photographic Service during college," he said.

But in reality, photography had become his world while he was still in high school, when he got a photography job in 1958 working for the *Norman Oklahoma Transcript* newspaper.

"I used 4×5 Speed Graphic and Rolliflex equipment and a high-performance strobe flash. My special assignments usually were to cover high-school sporting events on Friday nights all over Oklahoma and make sure high-quality photos were taken, developed, printed, and ready for editors to select for Saturday and Sunday papers. It usually took all evening and all night for that type of assignment depending on how far I had to drive the newspaper vehicle and return from the games."

His commission, starting as a 1st lieutenant and later as captain, took him from January 1967 through December 1968 to the 69th Military Airlift Support Group at the Philippines' Clark Air Base. While there, he was responsible for supply support to the Military Airlift Command missions at all AF bases during the major base build-ups in 1967–68. But one month later he was assigned to the 600th Photo Squadron at Tan Son Nhut Air Base in Saigon.

"I spent more than half of my time away from Clark in Thailand and Vietnam coordinating and managing critical supply support matters for Military Airlift Command. A key reason why I was able to be highly successful in the 600th Photo Squadron position was because I was extremely well acquainted with how to get around in Southeast Asia and who to contact when needing logistics assistance for MAC units."

Unlike most Air Force officers who reported to Vietnam for a one-year assignment and were disoriented and depressed by the confusing and hectic war-zone environment, he already knew a great deal about the AAVS (Aerospace Audiovisual Service) missions and had time to prepare before arriving for what to do about the complex logistics problems facing the 600th in 1969.

"As a result of the two years of prior Southeast Asia experience and my college professional photographic experiences, I was uniquely prepared to quickly lead our support teams in positive directions. It would be nice if I could report that the genius of the Air Force or AAVS identified my unique combination of college photographic expertise and my prior two years in Southeast Asia support duties. But, no, it was more likely a minor miracle with divine help for all concerned."

Surviving a daily changing routine regularly was also a result of Frank's time in Southeast Asia.

"There was no such thing as a daily routine. There was one emergency after another. I spent very few days during 1969 in my office at the 600th. I had my combined materiel staff, and the field unit commanders prepared for what to do when I was urgently needed to initiate support actions beyond their local base and unit capabilities."

In order for the limited support staff to properly function, Frank had to be what he called "on the go" between photo units. This often meant emergency flights to major business centers in the western Pacific, such as Hong Kong, Tokyo, Taipei, and Bangkok to buy or deliver items for repair.

"A couple of times I had to travel to the support depot in Salt Lake City to negotiate better stock levels and demand improved response times for the complex mix of parts and supplies.

"I was able to accomplish that as a captain with only five years of service. Normally field-grade officers are the ones who might have the experience and skills to deal with such high-level military organizations and commercial companies, but I had been well trained by senior officers and NCOs while at my initial, three-year supply officer duty assignment at Travis Air Force Base, California.

One of Frank's special assignments while at Travis was to personally negotiate with senior civilians (GS-12 through GS-15) for special levels of critically short expensive aircraft parts coming from such military depots as those at Salt Lake City, Oklahoma City, and Warner Robbins, Georgia.

"I had previously learned at Travis how to use an extremely high mission priority such as assigned to the 600th Photo Squadron to negotiate fast and reliable response actions from the complex depot organizations. And I had learned how to send the kind of official electronic correspondence to depot command sections using the proper protocol to get the kind of quick actions needed when something failed to work and the 600th had a mission impact."

Frank went on to become the Chief of Materiel/Logistics/Supply for the 600th Photo Squadron as a captain in 1969. He remembers that year very well.

"There was fantastic work being done by the USAF in Southeast Asia in 1969. The 600th support personnel at 17 USAF locations in Vietnam and Thailand were exceptionally effective at keeping the fighter aircraft gun cameras, strike documentation camera systems, combat camera Aeries and Naira audio recording systems, Forward Air Command (FAC) Pilot Intel cameras (motor driven, zoom-lens Pentad Spermatic kits), as well as motion picture labs and base photo labs working in that horrible Southeast Asia combat environment."

And Frank was the ideal logistician to be assigned to support and augment the 600th photographers, aircraft servicing personnel, and lab workers.

"They never had to argue with me on their requirements, and my job was to effectively interpret what had to be ordered, see if better options might be available if there were problems with acquiring the items, and see that they always got what they needed, as soon as possible."

It was difficult, Frank recalls, for the 600th to do all of the USAF combat documentation in the war zone under combat conditions and jungle environments. But he knows that they performed their missions as flawlessly as possible.

"I am confident that all of the front-line photographers and video documenters would agree that the 600th support folks performed near-miracles every day so that the operational/documenters could do what they had to do while producing exceptionally high-quality results to send back to the States.

"Imagine how hard it was to reliably maintain the mopic and still lab processing chemicals up to top quality while maintaining vat temperatures within +/- a few degrees, 24/7/365, in such places as Saigon, Karat, and so many other places. Imagine how hard it was for young airmen to control the storage environments of the backup chemicals so they were effective when the time came."

Frank's thoughts turned to Major Norma Archer, Chief of the 600th Photo Squadron Combat Operations.

"Imagine the guts it took for Major Archer to fearlessly lead her younger operational members when having to carry a sidearm while doing their documentation duties riding in the backseats of combat fighters, slow FACs, Fast-FACs, C-130 Specters, and so many USAF missions.

"Norma and her team were highly vulnerable—they could not be as well prepared for being shot down over Southeast Asia as the air crew members."

Frank called Major Archer "that extremely rare woman in charge of combat operational support in 1969. "What could she do if her aircraft was shot down and she had to escape, evade, be rescued, or be captured by the enemy?" Frank asked. "I never heard her talk about such things, but no doubt it had to be a worrisome consideration every time she flew a mission."

In Frank's opinion, Major Archer deserved far more credit than was ever given her.

"She was an outstanding, remarkable example of a combat operational professional as well as a unique female officer in combat surrounded by men of all types who could not miss the fact she was both an attractive person, a totally professional Air Force officer, and the unit's leading combat photographer."

Despite the praise he has for Major Archer, Frank insisted he did not know her well because of his being the only logistics/supply officer in the unit, and being frequently TDY in various locales in Southeast Asia.

"There may be few of us fellow officers or NCOs still living who can report first-person about some of Norma's and other Ops and Support team accomplishments. And I have no idea if Norma Archer or the squadron administrative officer, Captain Mary Dowd, are still alive.

"Major Archer would assign the relative priorities to each critical equipment, pars and chemical shortage, and I had to travel continuously to places like Thailand, Hong Kong, Japan, and the States to personally acquire critical items for the various units. It was not feasible to try order-by-phone and then wait for complex transportation shipping through Southeast Asian ports and inadequate postal services.

"Imagine how hard it was to find a company that could repair a Naira III tape recorder after being dropped in rice paddy water. It had tubes and belts and stuff that were never supposed to be immersed in any liquid. Repair was required by going to Hong Kong. Buying a replacement required travel to the East Coast or Europe. It was amazing we could get it fixed, but we did."

Robert Frank, like so many servicemen and women who served in Southeast Asia, can tell a plethora of stories. Here is one:

"The 600th was tasked by a Lieutenant General George Brown, 7th Air Force Commander, to find a way to save the Specter Gunship from being cancelled by Congress. As crazy as that sounds, it is a fact, and I witnessed the details directly. It involved a combination of the professional photographic expertise of a number of highly experienced 600th Photo Squadron officers and enlisted professionals, plus a lot of raw courage."

In the year Frank spent in Vietnam, between January and December 1969, Frank got a chance to pitch in as an officer to support the raw courage of the enlisted personnel.

He was responsible for supply, maintenance, and logistics support for 17 USAF units in the Vietnam and Thailand combat zones. The units were responsible for using commercially available, off-the-shelf equipment and trailer facilities to take and develop photos and video, write the scripts, narrate the videos, edit the final results, and produce finished products reporting on USAF combat results.

"The mission included photo processing services to all air bases, weapons systems, and support services to all USAF aircraft operational forces—except USAF airborne reconnaissance units. In addition to hundreds of unit members, there were thousands of air crew members, intelligence officers, and still/motion picture photographers supported by the 600th.

"Some of the weapon system-installed combat photography devices maintained included fighter-aircraft gun cameras, fighter-bomber aircraft strike cameras, which recorded bomb damage via belly-mounted panoramic cameras, combat photographers flying along on combat missions, and intelligence camera systems used by Air Force forward controllers designating targets for the fighter aircraft."

The 600th photo squadron was unquestionably one of the busiest combat camera units in the Indochina Theater.

"Among many other major tasks, the 600th Photo Squadron units produced weekly combat reports of USAF operations for the Secretary of Defense and the President, and released information to the media. Consistently high-quality results from its high-tech, commercially acquired AF systems were mandatory. But, that was extremely difficult to accomplish with such state-of-the-art sophisticated equipment, film, and chemicals by often inexperienced men and women in nasty environments of high heat, high humidity, unreliable power, thick jungle, and combat."

Although Frank is quick to shift any kudos to those under his command and the USAF's 600th Photo Squadron as a whole, for his own efforts, he was awarded the Legion of Merit (LOM) by General Brown, for exceptionally meritorious conduct in the performance of outstanding services.

No doubt, those who served under Robert Frank would approve of General Brown's pinning that award on Frank's uniform.

US Air Force Captain Bob Frank checking out camera equipment with a fellow Air Force combat cameraman from Support Team 3, Vietnam, 1969. (Bob Frank collection)

Gunner with a Camera: Ron Gorman

Denver, Colorado resident Ron Gorman was not technically a US Navy photographer when he was sent to Vietnam in January 1968. But he did take a lot of pictures of the conflict that surrounded him about the time of the infamous Tet Offensive.

"Most of the pictures I took were centered on the unit I was stationed with. They were of Navy and Army personnel and the various ships and river boats that were attached to my unit. I also took a lot of scenic shots of various places in the Mekong Delta, though as far as I know, none were ever published. They were mainly for my use."

Gorman used a 35mm single lens reflex Pentax camera. "Never had any problem with it at all," he said.

Later in his Navy career, when he was stationed with a photo unit, he continued to use the same Pentax camera as a backup.

When he first arrived in Vietnam, Gorman was with the Navy Mobile Riverine Force (MRF) Task Force 117, Tango 91-10 (the boat he was on). Though far from being tasked to shoot film, his job was as a 20mm gunner on a river boat that transported Army and ARVN troops to various missions.

"The 20mm cannon I manned was probably the most exposed place on the boat. The guy I replaced was either killed or wounded badly while manning the it."

The boat also had two 50mm guns that were just below Gorman and to the left and right in the rear of the boat. There were also two 30-caliber machine guns on each forward side in the well deck by the ramp.

"When we weren't out on an operation, we mainly did a lot of maintenance on the boat and our guns. During our free time we wrote letters to our families and friends, played cards, ate and, of course, slept whenever we could. Sometimes we were able to watch a movie on the ship we were tied up next to."

For Gorman, taking pictures was an escape from the horrors of the war.

"I really enjoyed taking pictures. It was a good way to pass the time, and I wanted to set up a photo album of the time I spent in Vietnam. Taking pictures was my 'stay healthy pill.' I also thought it would be good experience for when I got back to the States because I wanted to be a Navy photographer."

As such, Gorman never embarked on a mission without what he called his "trusty camera."

"It was like another limb that was attached to my upper body. I never knew when there would be something I wanted to take a picture of. I wanted to be prepared if something was going to happen. There were times when I didn't have my camera handy and something came up, and I couldn't take a picture. It didn't take long for me to learn to always have a camera nearby."

There was no average day aboard Tango-10, whether it was patrolling or tied to the pontoon alongside the mother ship.

"I woke up. Had a bite to eat, usually C-Rations, and I was at the mercy of our boat captain. We did whatever duties he wanted us to do. It was 95 percent pure boredom interlaced with 5 percent sheer terror," Gorman said.

There was one fairly constant aspect to Gorman's tour aboard T-10 as it traversed the Mekong River close to the city of My Tho, which was near the Army's 9th Infantry Division base at Dong Tam.

"We usually ran up and down the Mekong Delta, sometimes close to the Cambodian border, and some of the smaller rivers, taking the Army wherever they needed to go. I can count the times on my fingers that my feet touched land. Usually I went from the boat to the flat barge that was between our boats and the Navy troop ship. The only other time when my feet touched land was when I was at the Army base or was on R&R in Hawaii."

That meant Gorman and his shipmates saw an awful lot of hazardous duty.

"If memory doesn't fail me, I was in a total of 19 firefights during the 12 months I was in Vietnam. Some were worse than others. The one that sticks in my mind the most was when we were coming back on a narrow channel after dropping off the Army troops that were going on an operation. We got caught in an ambush. The tide was low and ground was about 8–10 feet above us. No way could we shoot our guns because all we could see was river bank to the left and right of us. We were sitting ducks. I heard the sound of AK47s, B-40s and RPG rockets all around our boat. I thought my number was up. I was really scared as there was nothing I could do other than sweat. Luckily, we made it back to the main river without our boat or crew being hit. We were just plain ass lucky that day. Somebody was looking out after us. I will never forget that as long as I live."

Though a photo enthusiast, Gorman is realistic when it comes to being asked if he ever had occasion to shoot film during an incident rather than his weapon.

"No. I didn't have time to think about my camera. I was too busy shooting my gun," he said.

His dream of becoming a Navy photographer persisted, though he's not certain now who or what influenced him to think the way he did about what one might call his military avocation.

"I was always hoping to be a photographer. I was told in no uncertain words that they had something for me to shoot but not a camera. I knew what they were talking about. Even before I went to Vietnam I wanted to be a Navy photographer. It was number one on my bucket list."

Although his tour in Vietnam ended without him switching his rate to that of Navy photographer, he carried that hope with him as he continued to serve while the war raged on.

"Ever since I raised my hand and said, 'I do,' I knew that was what I wanted to be. It was a year after I got back to the States. Around the latter part of 1969. That's when everything started to click for me.

"After my tour ended in December 1968, I got orders to a ship, the USS *Tallahatchie County*, which was home ported in Naples, Italy. We supported an Air Base in Souda Bay, Crete. The ship had a Navy photographer and a small photo lab. I had a talk with ship's photographer and explained to him I wanted to be a photographer's mate. Even though I had another job on the ship, I was able to spend some time in the photo lab. The photographer worked with me and told me what I needed to do. I followed his instructions to the tee and eventually became a photographer. I was at the point where I was so determined to become a PH [photographer's mate], I would do whatever necessary to follow my dreams.

"The ship was de-commissioned and, as luck would have it, I got orders to my next duty station, the Naval Air Station with the Atlantic Fleet Combat Camera Group (AFCCG) in Norfolk, Virginia."

Later that year, he also attended the US Navy's Photo "A" School in Pensacola, Florida. After that, he was also on flight duty as an aircrew.

Gorman received his orders to the AFCCG in September of 1969 and soon traveled TAD (Temporary Additional Duty) to England, Spain, France, and Germany, and to the Leica camera factories in Norway and Italy.

He was also tasked with another still photographer and mopic photographers to Colombia, South America aboard the USS *Sanctuary* hospital ship for the purpose of documenting US Navy medical personnel who were caring for the needs of the people of the small and depressed town of Buena Ventura, where medical facilities and medical care were lacking. The hours were long and, in addition to his regular duties, he "got volunteered" to do the ship's cruise book (the equivalent of a school yearbook).

He also spent some time in Port Au Prince, Haiti.

"I was taking pictures of Haitian President Jean Claude "Baby Doc" Duvalier and some of his high-ranking military thugs at his palace, which had a very intimidating canon in the front yard. There was an additional contingent of highly armed military that were constantly on patrol on the premises. What a scary experience that was. But I had a job to do and did it to the best of my ability."

Even though Gorman's service in Vietnam as a 20mm gunner aboard T-10 was behind him, the war was becoming increasingly unpopular. There were protests, not only in the States but also in Europe where Gorman was then stationed TAD for six months at the detachment in Naples, Italy, which the AFCCG supported.

"There were two incidents that happened to me. The first was when I went on assignment. During a break, I went to the Spanish Steps in Rome to take in the sights. This is where American hippies and draft dodgers hung out waiting for money to be sent to them at the nearby Western Union office. I was sitting on the steps minding my business when one of the hippies sat next to me and started a conversation. I didn't like the direction it was going. I eventually asked him what he was doing there. He told me he had run out of money and was waiting for his parents to send him some so he could get home. I thought to myself how pathetic that he was giving me a hard time, calling me 'baby killer,' talking to me like I as the mud off the bottom of his shoes when he didn't even have enough money to get home. Not wanting a public argument with him, I got up, shook his hand, said good luck and left."

The next time Gorman was faced with anti-war sentiment was in Norway.

"We were at a bar enjoying ourselves. The table next to us had a group of young communists. They saw we were in the military and tried to provoke us. It got kind of hairy for a few minutes. Some of the guys I was with were kind of drunk and wanted to kick their asses. But sounder minds prevailed. We bought them a mug of beer and left."

Though the bulk of Gorman's time as a Navy photographer was spent taking pictures, processing, and printing, as always no two days were ever alike.

"Every day was different. Most of the pictures I took were published in the base newspaper. Guys getting awards, being congratulated for something by an officer. Some of the pictures I took were sent to the Navy PAO [Public Affairs Office] in Washington, D.C. I don't know what they did with them after that. I did see some that were published in the Navy's *All Hands* magazine."

In addition to his work appearing in *All Hands*, Gorman's photos also ran in the *Navy Times*.

"I was also TAD to the *Virginia Pilot Ledger Star*, the local paper in Norfolk, for a month for additional training. I had a lot of stuff published in that paper with a byline. Also did my own processing and printing of pictures. This was great training for me. It gave me an opportunity to see what it was like to work for a large civilian paper, working under deadlines and the pressure that goes with it. I really enjoyed that opportunity and learned a lot."

That was also true of the time Gorman spent on Coronado Island at the Naval Air Station, San Diego, where he was a staff photographer with COMNAVAIRPAC PIO (Commander, Naval Air Force, Pacific Public Information Office) between

December 1974 and May 1976, during which he also worked as a photographer and writer for the base newspaper. This was a full year after the fall of Saigon and the definitive end to American involvement in Southeast Asia.

"Took a lot of grip and grins, did some writing, worked in the darkroom," he said.

While on Coronado, he also wrote a story called "A Day in the Life of a Dog," about a dog that used to hang out at the base boat house. It and pictures he took of the dog ran in various publications, both Navy and civilian.

"It sparked a lot of interest from other civilian papers. It was also used in a children's book. This was a fun article for me to do. I had full control of the photography and writing, and it made me feel good when it was published.

"I enjoyed the work I was doing on Coronado. It gave me the opportunity to do a lot of interesting photo jobs before receiving my honorable discharge."

When Gorman was discharged from the Navy in 1976 as a PH-2 (equivalent to an Army sergeant), after spending eight years on active duty, he rid himself of most of his cameras and photography equipment with the exception of the 35mm Pentax camera, which he had had with him all through his eight years in the Navy.

"Discarding all the other equipment was a big mistake on my part. But I wanted to look at other job opportunities. Being a vet, I knew I could land a government job. After looking around, I decided the post office was the place for me. The pay and benefits were the deciding factor."

Six months into his job at the US Postal Service, Gorman learned that they had a union that published a newsletter called the *Mountaineer*. So he joined the union and got a part-time job as the associate editor.

"When the union president interviewed me, I told him I was a Navy photographer for six and half years, that many of my pictures were published and that I also did a limited amount of writing. He told me I was the person he was looking for and hired me on the spot. I believe if it wasn't for the experience I gained as a Navy photographer, I would never have gotten the job, which I'm still doing to this day, years after being honorably discharged."

Today, Ron Gorman is involved with three veterans groups: the National Association of Naval Photographers, the Mobile Riverine Force Association, and the Vietnam Veterans of America.

"The eight years, six and a half of which I was a Navy photographer, I will always carry with me. I had the opportunity to travel to a large part of the United States, Asia, all over Europe, into parts of South America and the Caribbean. I had some of the best training anybody could have. This helped me to become a better photographer and human being. The friends I made I will never forget. Many of them I'm still in contact with. If I had it to do all over again, there isn't much I would change with the exception of, instead of only spending eight years, I would have made the Navy my career."

Although Gorman's time in Vietnam was officially spent manning a ship's cannon, he wishes to reach out to those who were tasked, while in uniform, with bringing the war home to the American public.

"I would like to thank all of the military combat cameramen, photographers, and journalists for the great work that they did while serving in Vietnam. If it wasn't for you," he says, "there would be no images of the day-to-day life of our troops who served in the Republic of Vietnam. Thanks for a job well done and welcome home."

Ron Gorman in a US Navy flight suit. Ron spent his tour in Vietnam manning a 20mm canon aboard a Riverine Tango Boat in the Mekong Delta but took pictures on the side and was designated a photographer's mate after his service in Vietnam. (Ron Gorman collection)

Never Ambushed: Larry Letzer

All Larry Letzer has ever done is photography. Even at the young age of 12, he carried camera bags for a photographer in Atlantic City "just for the experience," as he puts it. That eventually led him to a job with the *Atlantic City Press* as a staff photographer, a job he held until he went into the Army in July 1956. His reason for joining up? To go to still-photography school.

After graduating, Letzer, originally from Brigantine, New Jersey, was assigned to be a photographer in Korea. How he got there is a story he enjoys regaling people with.

"In 1957, as a private, I was sent to the Ft. Lewis [Washington] Replacement Center to await a ship to take us to Korea. Even then I knew that the Army abhors inactive soldiers and would find lots of busy work during the days awaiting our vessel," he said.

And Letzer knew how to make the Army feel that he was doing busy work.

"Even when on detail before basic training, when I was only 17 years old, I got hold of a clipboard and while others were busting their ass, I walked around making notes on the clipboard. Not one person questioned me. Hence, I was busy and they were happy."

But not liking details, Letzer got the idea to avoid "this meaningless travail," as he called it.

"I called the post photo lab and told them I was a school-trained photographer and was volunteering to work there while at the REPO Depot. They took me up on that, and every morning a post taxi would transport me from north post to main post, where I would work as a staff photographer. After work, I would be taken back to my barracks. Just before my ship arrived, the Post Signal Officer asked me if I wanted to stay at Ft. Lewis instead of going to Korea. I said no, as I thought this would be my only chance to go overseas."

Letzer's next assignment was then to Ft. Monroe, Virginia, where he became the photographer for General Bruce C. Clarke.

In 1959, Letzer was discharged and returned to the *Atlantic City Press*. He even turned down a job offer to become a photographer at Colonial Williamsburg to be back at his old job.

However, his time out of uniform would be short-lived.

After working as a photographer in Atlantic City for four years, he realized he missed the Army and re-enlisted. He went back through basic training, infantry school and OCS (Officer Candidate School). He was then assigned to the HHC (Headquarters and Headquarters Company), 1st Military Intelligence Battalion.

While in Combat Developments Command, he was sent to Officers' Basic Photography school. "After two days there, I was made an instructor," he said. "I went back to Combat Developments Command as chief of the photo branch, which had 32 employees, including three civilians. I only left there to attend the officers' advanced course as my mom was suffering terminal cancer. As the school was also in New Jersey, the Army allowed me to be near my mom during her last days."

Then in December 1965, Letzer found himself in Vietnam with the HHC 1BN and a very important mission to fulfill.

"Although our primary mission was to process aerial imagery shot by the Air Force and give it to our integrated image interpreters for evaluation and immediate notification to Army intelligence, we obtained a UH-1H (Huey) helicopter with a Tyler mount and the dual Pentax cameras coaxially mounted for photographing prescribed areas."

But that was not the end of his or the 1BN Military Intelligence's mission.

"After photographing, we would process the two 100-foot rolls of Ansco Shellburst film, make prints and give this to our IIs for interpretation. We had five units assigned to our battalion with the same mission except I had the only dual Pentax setup. I photographed in the II Field Force area."

While Letzer's counterparts in the Air Force had several different aircraft at their disposal to perform the USAF's photographic tasks in Vietnam, the 1BN was somewhat more limited in how they got aloft, Letzer explained.

"The Air Force flew several different reconnaissance aircraft such as RF-4C Phantoms and RF-10 Voodoos. I only flew in the Huey because the Tyler mount [the contraption used to stabilize a camera for aerial photography] would not fit in anything smaller."

With the Tyler mount in place in the Huey, Letzer was able to use two separate lenses—a 50mm and a 1,000mm—to take the photos the 1st Battalion needed. Their capabilities covered different uses.

"The 50mm lens was used to establish a general area because it has a short focal length lens and covers a broad area. The 1,000mm lens photographed the optical center of the area covered by the 50mm lens and had great magnification," he said.

No matter the scope of the lens, Letzer's mission during his first of two tours in Vietnam was to photograph and give the imagery to interpreters for immediate evaluation. When asked how much of Vietnam he covered, he said, "I worked only in the Second Field Force, but the 1st MI Bn covered all of South Vietnam."

One would have thought that a photographer like Letzer might have gotten the pilot bug with all that time aloft. He did, and eventually received a pilot's license but never had the chance to put it into practice in Vietnam. "Although I hold a Single Engine

Land Commercial Certificate with Instrument Rating, I did no flying in Vietnam other than being allowed to handle the controls occasionally. Not often," he said.

Of course, with a war on, Letzer's job was not always problem free. During one mission aloft, the Huey pilot had to evade a 51-caliber antiaircraft gun that had targeted them. Luckily, the pilots heard the projectiles' whine in their headsets and were able to maneuver the helicopter out of range.

The end result of Letzer's unit's work involved turning over their images to what he called the IIs, who then used what was known as a TIFF (Tagged Image File Format) van to store the images Letzer had shot. They would then manipulate the photos in a way that would benefit the troops on the ground. But that is where Letzer's connection to the valuable work he did stopped.

"Intelligence was very closely held. After we turned over our work to our intelligence interpreters, we were not allowed to get follow-ups, so I don't know the value of our work."

Letzer left Vietnam in December 1966 still unaware of whether his work had helped our troops, but experienced enough to be tasked with being the photo lab chief of Combat Developments Command. He soon was promoted to branch chief for the unit. In the coming years he also took the Signal Officer Advanced Course and then, in July 1969, returned to Vietnam. This time he was with SEAPC, the Southeast Asia Pictorial Center.

"With SEAPC, I was an operations assignment officer assigning photo missions to still- and motion-picture photographers and sound people. I only went on two jobs as a still photographer because my boss, Lieutenant Colonel Colville, wanted me to stay close to the flagpole. He repeatedly told me that we had people to do those jobs."

Letzer always considered himself first and foremost a photographer, so, naturally, he enjoyed photographing, and secondarily flying. Assigning photographers to do the job he wanted to do bored him.

"I assigned interesting assignments to photographers. Often we assigned them to general areas and it was up to them to develop assignments. Targets of opportunity."

In spite of that, Letzer considered it an honor to work with Lieutenant Colonel Colville, who would become his boss for four years when the two worked together for DASPO, the Department of the Army Special Photographic Office, in Panama beginning in 1970.

"He was the commander of the US Army Audio-Visual Agency. One interesting fact: he had 12 kids, and so did the Vietnamese head of their pictorial group, a lieutenant colonel."

After four months with SEAPC, where he had been selected for company commander, Letzer was transferred to Company B, 125th Signal Battalion, 25th Infantry Division.

"We were the forward area signal company supporting the front-line units, indeed if there was a front line in Nam," Letzer says sarcastically. "The rest of the battalion was at Cu Chi. I had half the company spread all over the II [2d] Field Force. I spent half the month visiting every soldier at fire-support bases and on top of Nui Ba Den, Black Virgin Mountain. The only purple hearts my soldiers received were from an assault and mortar attack on the mountain."

But life was far from mundane for Letzer and those whom he tasked with photographing the war.

"After I left SEAPC, we had four photographers killed when their helicopter was downed. I was on the same mission invading Cambodia, but I was with Bravo Company, 125th Signal Battalion of the 25th Infantry Division. We provided communications for the 1st Brigade, the forward brigade of the 25th ID. I had a company of 230 men, 90 of which were in three–four man teams on fire-support bases and on the Black Virgin Mountain providing multi-channel (telephone) communications for the tactical battalions. Almost every day my driver and I would visit these soldiers by driving by ourselves in a jeep on back roads. A week before completing this tour, the Army mandated that any time a vehicle left the main supply route in Vietnam, it would have to be part of a three-vehicle-minimum convoy with an automatic weapon in the first and trail vehicles. I guess it was dumb luck we were never ambushed. Once it was kind of hairy as we had a flat and got back to the Tay Ninh compound after dark. Pucker factor time."

Letzer left Vietnam for the last time in July 1970, but he was not through with the Army. He soon found himself with what he termed "the best job in the Army." His nearest boss was the Pentagon, and he found himself in Panama, as he went to work for DASPO, which had a team there.

His memories of his time there remain just as prevalent today as his time in Vietnam.

"I got to travel all over Central and South America for four years. We covered Army assistance to host countries during disasters, plus coverage of Army activities with military groups in almost every country."

The only country Letzer did not visit was Chile because the country was embroiled in a civil war that lasted almost the entire time he was in South America.

After DASPO, Letzer went to Ft. Hood, Texas, and was promoted to major with the 16th Signal Battalion. He was then assigned as chief telephone officer at Ft. Hood, where he ran a platoon-sized photo outfit.

Letzer retired in 1980 and devoted his time to Camera Artistry Photography, a business he began in 1974 and which today is run by his son. Today Letzer rides his own Honda Goldwing motorcycle.

"As my photography swan song, I am going to photograph buildings throughout my town and give the images to the city and the school district as a thank you for making a good living in this city for 44 years.

"*No más!*" he says.

A Magic Slice of Life: David Sommers

In the summer before his senior year of high school in Flint, Michigan, David Sommers borrowed his World War II veteran, police officer father's camera.

"It looked sophisticated to me. The first roll of film I shot was returned scratched and printed backwards. I decided I could do better and literally walked into a local camera shop and asked them to sell me the stuff I needed to develop pictures. This led to an interest and hobby that, pardon the pun, developed."

For his high-school graduation in June 1967, his grandparents chipped in to help buy Sommers a Nikon F 35mm camera.

He was good at math and science in high school and planned to study engineering in college, which he began at Flint Community College, where he also helped out with the yearbook photography. That led him to changing his major to art with an emphasis on photography.

"I decided photography was my calling," Sommers said. However, due to a low GPA and dropping a class, he lost his II-S student deferment, and shortly thereafter received notice to report for a draft physical on April 1, 1969.

"April Fools' Day. Not a good omen," he said.

Eventually, Sommers received his notice to report for military service. He'd been drafted but was not excited about making a career out of being an infantryman, so he enlisted in the USAF.

"I technically was a draft dodger," Sommers believes, "but figured I was in the military and the worst they could do is come and get me and stick me in the Army or Marines."

Before Sommers' student deferment ran out, during his sophomore year in college, he got a scholarship to do photography for the school paper.

"I was doing great photography and was hired to do some work for the local paper, *The Flint Journal*, under the tutelage and mentorship of Bill Gallagher, who won the 1953 Pulitzer Prize for the Adlai Stevenson hole in the shoe photo. Gallagher would soon be very proud of his protégé's work as a full-time photographer.

Once in the Air Force, Sommers did basic training at Lackland Air Force Base in San Antonio. He was told he could choose one of four job groups.

"I chose general, which meant I could be a cop, cook, or even a photographer."

Sommers and other enlistees took tests to determine what USAF job they were best qualified for.

"I greatly embellished my photography resume. Eight weeks after entering the Air Force I was at Hanscom Field in Massachusetts doing exactly what I had been doing in college."

And not too long after, Sommers landed a part-time job at the Lawrence *Eagle Tribune* as their weekend photographer. "My photo lab and squadron commanders thought that was pretty cool."

His work at the *Eagle Tribune* would be interrupted, however, in December 1969, when he received orders for Vietnam as a combat photographer.

"I was to be sent to a month-long Combat Documentation camera school at Lowery AFB in Denver. It was a big training base for the Air Force."

But Sommers was first sent to an altitude chamber at Otis Air Force Base, Massachusetts, because he was expected to be on flying status in Vietnam.

"Part of this training was to teach us what would happen if, flying at high altitude, we lost our oxygen supply. Since I was the most junior member in the class I was 'volunteered' to go off my oxygen supply at a simulated altitude of 45,000 feet. I passed out in about 15 seconds, as expected."

In January 1970, Sommers was sent to Lowery for the month-long Still Photo Combat Camera class. "At that time there was a strong push to teach photographers to shoot in a photojournalistic style."

"I found the class a blast, as all I had ever done was news photography photojournalism. We were give assignments and then set loose to do them. I was at the top of my class and often used as an example on how to cover an assignment. I was 20, getting paid to do photography."

But he also developed the attitude, "I'm going to Vietnam. There is nothing worse they can do to me," he added.

Sommers left for Vietnam in March 1970. Before arriving, however, he endured a week-long Jungle Survival school in the Philippines.

"This was for all air-crew members. We spent three or four days in a classroom. The entire course was classified SECRET. We were taught things like what to eat if we were shot down over the jungle. How to escape and live in the jungle and evade capture. How we would be rescued if possible. What to expect if captured, what the POW camps were like. How to communicate as prisoners."

Then they spent two days in the field putting what they had been taught to use.

"We lived in the jungle, sleeping on the ground and eating what we could gather. For the final, we were turned loose with only some water and a survival knife. We were expected to evade the locals looking for us overnight. In the morning we were to assemble at a location and call in a helicopter to hoist us out. I remember laying in the grass as locals came by and didn't see me. They walked within feet of me. I remember watching a full moon come up. The rats chewing on my boots woke me several times."

Sommers was assigned to Detachment 16 of the 600th Photo Squadron at Phu Cat Air Base. Later, he was assigned to Pleiku Air Base to document the base turnover to the Vietnamese. He did this for about three months and was the only photographer on base.

He returned home in March 1971, but not before he'd been aloft taking pictures for the USAF on many occasions.

"I got to fly a lot. If I remember correctly, I had combat time in 15 different types of aircraft. My MOS—the Air Force called it something else—was Still Photographer; in Vietnam is was Still Combat Photographer."

Among the aircraft Sommers hitched rides on was the C-7 Caribou.

"We had a resupply group at our base and often went with them as they flew supply missions into advance Army and Marine bases. We would document the crews. We wouldn't spend much time on the ground. There were times when there would be crashed planes at the end of the runways we were going into. I remember one airstrip we landed at was only 1,000 feet long with crashed planes at both ends."

Among his assignments was to document the base rescue helicopter group. In addition, he flew with the C-119 gunships on night missions and had some F-4 backseat flights documenting the fighter pilots.

"Some of this took days to set up and get permission. When I flew I took the space of the regular backseat crew member and had to be trained."

He also flew in the O-2 Cessna Skymaster, a Forward Aircraft Control (FAC) plane calling in air strikes in support of troops on the ground.

"I would get a call from the FAC's squadron that they had something going on, or that there was something going to happen, and there was a need for last-minute surveillance photos. I enjoyed flying with these guys. It was like flying with your older brother, and I got a lot of stick time actually flying the plane."

"A lot of the FAC photography involved ground surveillance, last-minute intelligence gathering. We would often go out and photograph an area from the air, providing information for an attack the next day. It was interesting what you could see from the air, hidden trails, etc.

"Several times we were looking for other FAC that never returned. I do remember one day walking out to the plane, dressed in flight suit and survival vest, pistol, and cameras. A true Tom Cruise *Top Gun* moment. The pilot said, 'Let's see if we can find someone to shoot at us.' I remember thinking, 'This probably not a good idea', yet we went out like that a lot. I was only 20 years old," said Sommers, who, in addition to flying, also covered security police at a remote observation post.

While on TDY at Pleiku Air Base covering the turnover to South Vietnamese forces, Sommers would often go out with Civil Affairs units to the local villages and give the villagers items.

"I remember eating a dinner in our honor in a thatched room, with dog, eel, and water buffalo on the menu. Everyone had a great laugh at my inability to eat with chopsticks. I went with them to a leprosarium [leper colony]. I am the only person I know who has been to one," he said

Sommers' tour in Vietnam also included a stint in Cambodia, where American personnel was evacuating civilians.

"It was a very primitive setting in the jungle. We were on the ground some 80 miles—my guess based on flying time—inside the country. The president was saying US troops were no more than 20 miles inside."

Sommers is quick to point out that the missions he went on were not the stereotypical ones of combat laced with slogging through the jungles and rice paddies.

"We flew in and assisted those on the ground. It was still hazardous. Remember," Sommers cautioned, "most of the POW's were USAF."

Sommers also had air-to-air combat photography experience though he admits it was not very easy to accomplish.

"Air-to-air combat photography was somewhat difficult because we had to be a camera platform photographing the other planes while avoiding getting shot and not in the way of the other planes," he said.

Still, certain missions seem seared in his memory.

"We were working a ground attack—troops in contact—where we had the FACs marking targets for the fighters, F-100's in this case. I was able to take some pretty amazing photos of both the FACs and fighters with napalm drops.

I was also able to do some F-4 attacks. The air-to-air photos of flying to the target were pretty straight forward, but we were at 25,000 feet, and in a loose formation. As a chase plane, we could move around. Once we started to roll in on target, a chase plane could fly alongside, but that presented two targets for the enemy and we had to coordinate how we would escape, or leave the target, so we didn't collide. If we were the attack plane, there wasn't much to photograph. Sort of like photographing a commercial airliner while a passenger."

Photographing C-7 Caribous in formation was far less problematic, according to Sommers. "Really pretty easy as we could lower the rear tailgate and photograph the other plane from that vantage point."

Whether his missions were easy or difficult, one thing that stands out in Sommers' mind is the communication he had with the pilots.

"It was certainly a unique situation and didn't conform to usual military standards. We hung out with many of the pilots. They were all officers, mainly lieutenants and captains, and just a few years older than we were. They were sort of like big brothers. We couldn't really hang out in the officers' quarters, but they would come over to the photo squadron barracks and drink and barbecue."

Although not during resupply missions, when Sommers was flying in the likes of the 02s and F-4s he was part of the crew.

"We had full knowledge of everything the pilots did," he said.

"In the 02s we talked a lot. I got to have control of the plane. The pilot would say, 'Do you want the plane?' I would reply, 'Affirmative,' and the pilot would say, 'It's your airplane.' How very cool. I actually had control of an F-4 on a combat mission before I was 21 years old. I don't think you could do that now. I wanted to know how to fly and the pilot encouraged it. If something happened to the pilot, we had a reasonable chance of getting back if I knew how to control the plane."

When asked if he could define the average day for him in Vietnam, Sommers notes that every day was different and explains why.

"My photo detachment covered all photographic aspects at the base. As a still photographer, I did a little bit of everything, including the combat documentation. We would do portraits for officer promotions and hometown news releases. We would do passport photos. If there was an award ceremony, we covered that. When a pilot completed his last mission, there was a celebration and we covered that also. When there were plane crashes, either on or off base, we documented that. If there was damage or deaths from enemy attacks on the base, we covered that."

Sommers specifically remembers when a security police officer stepped on a land mine and was blown up. He was tasked with photographing the pieces of the policeman's body.

In what would have to be described as one of the strangest twists of fate in war time, Sommers photographed the autopsy of a dead pilot who bore the same name as Sommers.

There were some similarities, as he wrote in the *Saginaw News*, between Vietnam and Gulf War I in Iraq in 1991. That war caused him deep reflection, which he expressed brilliantly in a piece for his newspaper.

"As I sit in my living room, I can hear the noise and feel the vibrations as Air Force jets light their afterburners. I can even smell the jet exhaust. Watching television coverage of the air war over Iraq brings back vivid memories of another conflict, an unpopular war more than 20 years ago," he wrote.

"On the day of a mission I woke and showered, being careful not to use deodorant or aftershave the enemy could smell if we were shotdown. Flight suits were made of Nomex, a new fabric at the time. They didn't breathe much; inside, I was almost constantly sweating. I picked up my camera equipment, my pistol, and ammunition, and my flight gear including an anti-G suit, helmet, and survival vest.

"I would load my .38-caliber pistol—every other round a tracer—and stashed another 60 rounds or so in a lower leg pocket. I filled two small canteens with water and stored them in the lower leg pockets, and checked two survival radios in my survival vest to make sure they were working. If had to eject, this would be all I had other than the survival pack I would sit on. Then I checked to make sure I had loaded film into my cameras. I always carried two."

When he was in Vietnam, Sommers did not have the opportunity to cover any celebs who came through, though he did work some USO shows. "I don't remember any politicians, but if they did come through, we covered them," he says.

The big wigs would come later when he was the photographer for the Thunderbirds, the Air Force Demonstration Team equivalent to the US Navy's Blue Angels. While covering them, he photographed "all kinds of politicians and military officials, from the President, Secretary of Defense, Air Force Chief of Staff, governors, etc. During my time at the newspaper, I even had a close-in pass to cover the pope," he said. "My military experience gave me the ability and confidence to work with any person."

His tenure with the Thunderbirds came six months after he had left Vietnam for a temporary duty at Clovis Air Force Base in New Mexico.

"I was one of about 100 who applied. My Vietnam flying gave me the edge up for the position. They were delighted to get a photographer with time a F-4, the plane the team was flying. I didn't get sick flying, like the previous two or three photographers. I was fully trained and made my first team flight only two weeks after joining the team."

He spent just under two years with the team before he left the Air Force in May 1973, after serving one day shy of four years and retiring as a staff sergeant.

"By the time I left the team, I had been to all 50 states," he said.

And for the time he served in Vietnam, Sommers had received an Air Medal and an Air Force Commendation Medal. Perhaps equally important to Sommers is the fact that his unit, the 600th Photo Squadron, received the Presidential Unit Citation with a V for Valor.

"During my tour I spent many hours flying over Vietnam in more than 15 types of aircraft, from cargo planes to jet fighters. With very few exceptions, I never was concerned about not coming back. I was confident that I was immortal," he wrote in the *Saginaw News*.

Two weeks after his discharge, he went to work taking pictures for the Dow Chemical Company working out of the public affairs office at its corporate headquarters in Midland, Michigan. He spent six years with them doing still and video photography. In 1979, Sommers accepted a position as a staff photographer at the *Saginaw News* and put in almost 30 years. He spent several years as the department head and photo editor.

"I helped bring the paper into the color and digital age," he said. "When the economy soured I took a buyout and retired."

Today, Sommers serves his community as trustee on the Thomas Township Board and as an assistant chief in the volunteer fire department. He's been in the

US Air Force photographer David Sommers about to board a jet for a photo mission. (David Sommers collection)

department for 20 years. He also commands the Sheriffs' Department Dive Rescue (scuba) Team and Marine Division. He's also president of his Lake Association.

"I always found photography a wonderful career. It gave me the chance to see, experience, and share many facets of life that I would not have been able to do in another career. It was like a magic slice of life and I feel so fortunate to have had such a wonderful career," Sommers concluded.

"My last official work day was a Friday the 13th. How ironic that the start of my 'official' working career, my draft physical, was on April Fool's Day," he adds.

No Photography on Night
Patrols ... Just Ambushes: Terry Lang

One day, Terry Lang's 9th-grade science teacher in Alexandria, Minnesota, had all the students pick a subject to do extra-credit work; Lang picked photography because his teacher had a darkroom at school and Lang liked the idea that he could see the results of his projects just by processing film and making contact prints.

By the time Lang was in high school, his family had resettled in Pullman, Washington, where he graduated in June 1963. The following September, he enlisted in the Navy. Though his family moved west to Bremerton, Lang remained in eastern Washington that summer while waiting for his induction, delivering furniture for a local store and helping a friend and his friend's father install a new roof on their home.

By 1964, Lang had graduated from PH (Photo) "A" school and been sent to his first duty station, Naval Station Keflavik, Iceland.

"I received orders to a reconnaissance squadron in Sanford, Florida, and while home on leave I received a telegram cancelling those orders and re-directing me to Naval Base Coronado for training *en route* to Vietnam. I was one of six or seven Navy photographers who were ordered to the NAG [Navy Advisory Group] and the training cycle that PBR [Patrol Boat-River] crewmembers were going through. This was early 1966 and PBRs were just being sent to Nam. I don't remember the names of the other PHs in the group, but we had a PHC [Photo Chief], at least one PH1 (Robinson), a couple of PH2s (Dick Dreher was one) and me, a PH3. I was also the only designated air crewman in the group."

The training they went through included classroom time, firing range at NAS [Naval Air Station] Miramar learning and qualifying on everything from the .45-caliber pistol to the .30-caliber carbine, M-1, M-16, AK-47, Grenade launcher, .30-caliber and .50-caliber machine guns and the BAR (Browning Automatic Rifle).

"And we had a week of SERE [Survival, Evasion, Resistance and Escape] training at NAS Whidbey Island, Washington," Land said. "Washington in March tends to be wet and cold and the week in SERE was miserable."

When Lang arrived in Vietnam, he was attached to the Command, Naval Forces and Naval Advisory Group Vietnam with headquarters in Saigon.

244 • VIETNAM *BAO CHI*

"Because I was the most junior and the youngest of the photo crew, I was given more field assignments, so I had open-end TDY orders with all-encompassing flight orders. I traveled into the Rung Sat Special Zone plus Da Nang, Hue, the Central Highlands, and with various Navy and Marine Corps-related activities including Junks, PACVs [Patrol Air-Cushioned Vehicles], PBRs, PCFs [Patrol Craft Fast, otherwise known as Swift Boats], Coast Guard cutters, ANGLICO [Air Naval Gunfire Liaison Company], as well as Army and Air Force units in support of Naval activities in-country. A lot of my field time was spent with [1965-instituted operations] *Market Time* (PCF and Coast Guard cutters) and *Game Warden* (PBR) units." [These were operations successful in stopping the flow of enemy troops and materiel into South Vietnam by sea, coast, and river. They lasted until 1970.]

"At one time or another, I spent days with US Army ground forces, helicopter units, USMC units, and flying with various USAF aircraft," Lang added.

In spite of spending much of his time on the water in Vietnam, Lang was able to maintain his land legs as well.

"I lived in a hotel in Saigon, the Metropole Annex, and roomed with two Army specialists. I owned a Honda 90 motorcycle and would drive it to the Navy compound on Phan Dinh Phung Street, where I would find out if I was going into the field or process film in the photo lab. The photo lab was in the Naval Advisory Group compound, in the back near the armory. I can't prove my suspicions, but I always suspected that the photo lab was once the stables for the compound."

Lang sometimes took his repast a short walk from the NAG compound at the famed Cercle Sportif, where the well-to-do French and Saigonese families of South Vietnamese Army officers, high-ranking American officers, and visiting dignitaries often availed themselves of the swimming pool and tennis court.

"It was there that I ran into Nancy Sinatra one day, literally. I was talking and walking and not looking where I was going and bumped into her. She was very gracious and even asked my name and outfit," Lang remembered.

"Most of the time in Saigon [eating food entailed] a quick bite at the 'mom and pop' store across the street from the NAG compound. It was there that I learned to drink and like '33' beer or 'Bah-me-bah' [a lose transliteration for the number 33 in Vietnamese: ba-muoi-ba] as most American GIs called it."

"After work, it was back to the hotel to change into civvies and then head to downtown Saigon and meet up with friends for dinner and drinks. My favorite place was the Caravelle Hotel because of the European ambiance."

Because of Lang's rank, he was often tasked with running errands for the more senior personnel, including officers. That usually involved delivering messages to various units, or picking up supplies, in and around Tan Son Nhut Air Base.

"I usually drove a jeep but once in a while a 'deuce and a half,' a 2½ ton truck. We went through a lot of film and chemicals while I was in-country. I look back now and wish I had kept track of the number of rolls of Kodachrome film, the primary film that I was issued, I used."

Lang was required to devote a lot of time waiting for airplanes at Ton Son Nhut to ferry in-coming or out-going passengers between there and the NAG compound.

When he wasn't doing that, he was spending a lot of time at the air base waiting for airplane or helicopter transportation to other American bases in-country.

"In the field, my days depended on the unit I was with, but since I was extra-personnel, I pretty much had the day to myself to decide what I should be photographing. I was not a PAO photog, but my work was intelligence type, gathering plus documenting what was a typical work day for US Navy personnel."

When Lang was in the field, he had to find his own billeting and food, which meant spending part of each day making sure that he had a bed and a place to eat.

"I also got to see much of Vietnam while most people in-country stayed at one spot for their tour. I once flew out from Da Nang to Dalat, then to Saigon and on to Can Tho in one day, going from Marine to Army to Air Force to Navy units on the way.

"Field work was exciting to someone who was only 21 years old (my 21st birthday was in Vietnam) because I never knew what I would be involved in from day to day. I usually had an idea of the units and their missions before I left Saigon, but due to the changing atmosphere, every day was something new. I was in Nha Be to ride missions with the PBRs when the PACVs came to Vietnam for their six-month tour. Man! To watch those things spool up and move out was really exciting. And noisy! I got some good photos of them on land and on the water, but their OIC didn't want any extra personnel aboard, so I couldn't get a ride."

Because Nha Be, where PBRs and PCFs operated, was the closest Navy base to Saigon, many visiting dignitaries and journalists were often escorted by enlisted sailors, such as Lang, in convoys from Phan Dinh Phung Street in Saigon to the base at Nha Be. That happened whenever they wanted to have a look-see at US Navy operations of riverine warfare in Vietnam.

"Two that I remember were Chet Huntley of NBC and the publisher of the Seattle *Post-Intelligencer* newspaper, a Mr. Star."

Another visitor was Lang's senator from Washington state, Henry "Scoop" Jackson. "But, I only met him in the admiral's office. I'm sure his escorts were officers and helicopter crews," Lang explained.

Among the other in-country locales Lang had the pleasure of visiting when he had down time was the well-known coastal town of Vung Tau, where servicemen and women, including Navy personnel, were able to enjoy R&R.

"Rumor had it that Vung Tau was not only a US recreation area but also a recreation area for the Viet Cong. I do know that the Australians were stationed in Vung Tau, and I was able to get to know some of them. It had really good restaurants as well as many other recreation facilities and was very cheap. Thus it was very popular with US military personnel."

Back in Saigon, Lang once met a Philippine Navy ship that pulled into Saigon for a Navy-to-Navy visit. He was tasked with meeting the ship at the port of Saigon and seeing if their photographer needed any film, chemicals, or paper."

As part of his duties, Lang visited almost all of the US Navy bases in Vietnam from Rach Gia to Da Nang during his tour. He also made a quick trip to An Thoi on Phu Quoc Island to photograph US Coast Guard cutters.

"That was the southernmost post in my travels," Lang said.

"I spent a lot of time at Nha Be to document riverine operations with CTF 116 [Commander Task Force 116 Mobile Riverine Force] during Operation *Game Warden* and any other operations that I felt should be photographed."

Lang never technically photographed a firefight; however; he was involved in a couple of incidents with the PBRs while on patrol.

"Most of the time, the easiest patrols for riding along were night patrols, which really put a stop to any photography, but it was also at night that most of the ambushes happened. A couple of times, the patrols that I was on came under enemy fire from the shore, but we were usually in deep water and the coxswain just pushed the throttles to the firewall as we returned fire and we were out of harm's way. I was very impressed by how fast a PBR could go from very, very slow to maximum speed in such a short time. If you weren't paying attention, the sudden increase of speed could throw you around."

The inability to shoot film at night notwithstanding, Lang had the opportunity to carry a bevy of still-camera equipment on his person during his tour in Vietnam.

"I started out carrying a Nikon F because that is what the public affairs officer bought for the photo lab on a supply trip to Japan. I was given a 50mm lens and a "new" lens of 43–86mm called a "baby zoom." It was a soft-focus lens, so I stopped using it after my first job. We also changed to Leica M3 cameras because the Army found out that the shutter on the Nikon F sounded like a Viet Cong AK-47 being locked and loaded. The Nikon was a great camera to learn 35mm photography on; up to that point, I had been using the standard US Navy camera: the 4×5 Speed Graphic. The Nikon F had bayonet-mounted interchangeable lenses, so it was easy to switch, and was an SLR, so you could see what you were shooting, especially close-up."

His Leica was another matter altogether.

"The Leica M3 was a viewfinder/rangefinder type camera, but the shutter and the advance mechanism were 'quiet.' And the Leica required you to completely take off the bottom plate, thread the film into a spool, put the spool back into the camera and then reattach the bottom simply to change film," he said, seemingly more approving of his Nikon.

"The Nikon was a breeze. You'd simply drop the new roll into the supply side, then thread the take-up end onto the take-up reel, close the door, advance two times, and begin shooting."

However, his superiors seemed to come down on the side of the Leica, and for a very good reason.

"The Leica produced exceedingly sharp images, and the chain-of-command really liked sharp images. Because of that fact and that the camera was very quiet, I carried two bodies and a couple of lenses. Plus, I usually ended up carrying about 25 rolls of film. I never ran out of film while in the field, but I had also figured out how to talk nice to helicopter crews going to and from Saigon to carry or bring me film."

As with all combat photographers, cameras and their equipment were not the only thing that weighed Lang down.

"I also carried two canteens, a small backpack with a few underclothes and socks, a .45-caliber pistol and a .30-caliber carbine. One of the wonderful things that I remember about Vietnam is that no matter where I went, there was always some place to get my clothes washed at either a laundry or by house girls or houseboys."

And since he traversed so much of the county during his tour between 1966 and 1967, in addition to the tense times aboard the PBRs and the like, Lang also had his share of funny times.

"I had rented a room near Tan Son Nhut and had to get to the Navy compound before sunrise one morning to pick up equipment and get back to the airport for a flight out. There were no taxis or cyclos around, but along came a line of American tanks, and I was able to hitch a ride with them. So, I bragged about my 'tank time' while I was in Vietnam."

Another incident happened to him on Tu Do Street.

"As I was coming out of a bar, a soldier grabbed me and wanted to shake my hand. It was Michael Berglund, with whom I had gone to grade school and up to freshman year of high school when we moved from Minnesota. Mike and I had dinner together at the Caravelle. All the while, all I could think about was breaking his leg in fourth grade when I tackled him during a football game," Lang recalled.

But the memories of Vietnam Lang has are not all memories that make him chuckle.

"I was onboard a USCG cutter when a trawler belonging to the VC was run aground in the Rung Sat south of Soc Trang. It was the largest haul of weapons captured up to that point in late 1966.

And his memories are not restricted to blue or brown water or land either. Many times Lang's orders took him aloft.

"I flew on many different types of aircraft during my time in Vietnam, but the oddest flight was from Pleiku to Saigon. The Caribou was full of body bags. Needless to say, the smell was atrocious. I lost my lunch numerous times during that flight."

When Lang returned from Vietnam in 1967, he was nowhere near being through with the US Navy. In fact, he carried on for the next 30 years building a most impressive résumé. His last duty station was during 1990 to 1993 at the Fleet Imaging Command Pacific, NAS North Island, California, where he was a Command Master Chief, the rank at which he retired after 30 years of devoted service to the US Navy.

Terry Lang, US Navy combat photographer, standing by with weapons and camera Nha Be, Vietnam, 1967. (Terry Lang collection)

Robert Capa Was His Hero:
Dick Durrance

Dick Durrance knew by the time his draft notice arrived that he wanted to be a photographer. Among his heroes at the time was Robert Capa, Hungarian-born photojournalist and iconic war photographer, who was killed when he stepped on a land mine during the French Indochina war in 1954.

"Naturally," says Durrance, who was raised in Colorado and Germany, "I wanted to be a combat photographer as well."

He decided to keep a photographic journal of his two years in the Army and began photographing the moment he reported for duty at Ft. Hamilton, New York. He was lucky enough to serve under a company commander in basic training who gave him permission to photograph his unit's journey through basic, and again when he went through AIT (Advanced Individual Training). Then he was fortunate enough to make his way to DASPO.

As Durrance remembers his TDYs in Vietnam, his sentiment about what the United States was doing there pretty much ran the gamut.

During his first TDY, a six-week tour in July and August 1967, "the feeling I got from the guys I photographed was that we were 'winning the hearts and minds' of the South Vietnamese, and that we were helping them fend off the communists. On this tour I felt comfortable prowling the streets of Saigon and the villages. That illusion was shattered early in my second tour, January through March of 1968, during the Tet Offensive, when battalions or larger forces were able to surprise attack 80-plus cities. You can't hide that many fighting men in that many cities without the support of the people who live there. Clearly, we were not winning the hearts and minds of the South Vietnamese. As a result, I no longer felt safe alone on the streets."

It's safe to say that members of the civilian press shared Durrance's fear after the Tet Offensive. He had the chance to share that feeling with a college classmate of his from Dartmouth College, Robert Wildau, whom he ran into at the Da Nang Press Center. Wildau was then a correspondent for *Time* magazine.

And though they had shared the same trepidation, Durrance knows that their missions were not the same.

"Our missions were different: DASPO photographers were telling the Army's story; members of the civilian press corps were covering the war."

In pursuit of covering the Army's story, Durrance photographed a 1st Air Cavalry patrol in the Que Son Valley in January 1968.

"I went out with a small patrol, elements of A Company, 5th Battalion, 7th Cavalry, 1st Air Cavalry Division, known as 'The Eyes and Ears of the 1st Air Cavalry,' on a scouting mission to try and locate a large unit of North Vietnamese Army forces reported to be in the area. The tension never let up. What made the patrol particularly unnerving was that, in spite of fierce fighting that was occurring in that area, normal life seemed to be going on for the Vietnamese farm families we passed: kids tending their water buffalo and women irrigating their rice paddies."

They didn't know if the men working the fields were farmers or fighters or both. In spite of really intense interrogations, the farmers didn't talk. Durrance and the patrol he photographed learned nothing about the NVA from them.

"On the chopper, flying back to Da Nang, I thought about the patrol and began to understand that the Vietnamese were caught in an impossible bind. Whether their loyalties were with the North or the South, anything they divulged to us might have harmed family members or friends."

Of course, the NVA forces that Durrance's platoon never encountered were indeed out there. They attacked at 3:30 in the morning the very next day, 31 January 1968, the first day of the Tet Offensive. They blasted through perimeter fences and set the fuel tanks at the Da Nang Air Base ablaze.

Later that same day, Durrance photographed an ARVN Ranger unit forcing the NVA out of the villages that surrounded the air base.

"The civilian casualties were appalling," Durrance said. "After the Rangers headed out into the rice paddies, Robert Wildau and I started walking back through the village to the air base. We were about halfway when we realized that the streets … and the houses … were empty. The village was eerily quiet. Were the enemy soldiers in tunnels under the village instead of being out in the rice paddies? We didn't know … But you have never in your life seen two guys walk so fast, trying to look casual," he mused.

In March 1968, Durrance joined soldiers from D Company, 1st Battalion, 27th Infantry, and B Troop, 3/4 Cavalry, both of the 25th Infantry Division. They were operating out of their HQ base near Cu Chi, known for being the nexus 25 kilometers northwest of Saigon of a series of multi-level subterranean tunnels where Viet Cong cadres carried on their lives when they weren't above ground attacking our troops.

On this occasion, Durrance photographed a search-and-destroy mission in the village of Tan Thoi Nhut, between Cu Chi and Saigon's Tan Son Nhut Air Base.

"Following the Tet Offensive the area, which was known to house the HQ for the Viet Cong in tunnels, was the site of fierce and almost daily fighting. Shooting erupted shortly after I joined the soldiers. At one point, one of the infantrymen to my left got hit and I dashed over to help him get to the medics who were located in a trench about a 100 yards behind the action. In helping him, I lost most of the film I had shot during the firefight. It fell out of my jungle fatigue's pocket. Happily, he was not seriously wounded. Unhappily, we will never know what was on that film."

The Viet Cong and North Vietnamese were not Durrance's only enemies in Vietnam. He also had to fight the elements. During his first tour in the An Loa Valley, Durrance experienced his first unpleasant introduction to elephant grass.

"Not only did it slice and dice exposed skin, it hid enemy that might be waiting to ambush us. Very scary stuff ... The terror was slightly alleviated by the unit commander circling above in a helicopter, helping spot any NVA or VC units waiting for us."

And that was not the only element Durrance had to contend with. During that same first tour, in the Run Suc Swamp of the Mekong Delta, he recalled that it "sucked. Figuratively and literally, the seemingly bottomless muck sucked us in up to our thighs, as in really unpleasant. The fear factor was high here, as we were sitting ducks chugging up or down canals in little boats called Monitors that RPGs could penetrate, and then we were easy pickings when we got out of the boat and sank into the muck."

Durrance was relieved, therefore, when, not much later, he arrived to photograph a Special Forces camp in Thailand. "Everything was quiet when we were there," he said.

When Durrance reflects on his time photographing the war in Vietnam, it rests in special quarters of his memory.

"Photographing combat was unlike anything I had done before ... except in this one regard: like skiing a downhill race, I was so focused on being alert to the danger and, at the same time, concentrating totally on capturing pictures that I thought of nothing else."

He was aided in that endeavor by the fact that, though he always carried a .45-caliber pistol with him into battle, he never once had to give his camera a backseat in a firefight and put it down in favor of shooting his weapon.

Truth be told, at least some of the chops photographing combat may have actually taken root before he even set foot in Southeast Asia.

"Between my junior and senior year in college, I was one of two photographers photographing an expedition to canoe the Danube River from Germany to the Black Sea that *National Geographic* helped support. But because of the Iron Curtain, N-Geo couldn't get their photographers and writers into Eastern Europe, although we were able to secure student visas. The magazine published the pictures as a 45-page cover story," he remembered.

The association with *National Geographic* also served him well after he came home from Vietnam.

"Right after being discharged from the Army, I joined two guys from the Danube trip to do another story for *National Geographic*, hiking the Carpathian Mountains of Romania. Following that story, I was asked to join the magazine's photographic staff."

When asked to compare combat photography and his work with *National Geographic*, Durrance says, "In combat, on *National Geographic* assignments, and indeed whenever I raise a camera to take a picture, my goal is to tell a story about people or things in this time and place."

Dick and his wife, photographer Susan Drinker, whom he met several years later while taking a photography class, now run a photography-based company called Drinker Durrance Graphics from their home in Carbondale, Colorado.

"We still share a passion for photography." According to Durrance, his wife now devotes more time to videography than still photography, and he now spends the majority of his time as a motivational speaker.

"I speak to a wide variety of audiences, from corporate executives to corporate sales teams, from association executives to medical professionals and students. The point I stress with the Vietnam War pictures is the importance of connecting with and caring about people."

US Army combat cameraman Dick Durrance, DASPO, filming the rubble in Cholon, the Chinese quarter of Saigon, after the Tet Offensive of 1968. (Dick Durrance collection)

Followed Directions and Kept His Mouth Shut: Bob Douville

Bob Douville's journey to Vietnam as a Coast Guardsman is ironic to say the least. He has said that the reasons he ended up in the US Coast Guard in January 1961 were unemployment and the probability of being drafted into the Army—an Army that would soon be embroiled in a battle in the jungles of Southeast Asia. He also told the website that he made "utterly ignorant assumptions about how easy Coast Guard boot camp would be," and chided himself for being "very naive and completely scammed by the recruiters."[1]

"I was a year and a few months out of high school and back home again, having been unsuccessful in my initial effort to spread my tiny wings and fly the nest. I knew my local draft board would soon send me greetings. I also had learned from the local group commander, a hard old combat veteran of World War II North Atlantic convoys, that the Coast Guard was a part of the Armed Forces. He looked like I had slapped his face when I asked him if the Coast Guard fulfilled the military obligation. But he controlled himself and said through a clenched jaw, 'It certainly does, son. It certainly does.'"

Soon after that, Douville saw a brief classified ad stating that a USCG recruiter would be in town, so he went to talk to him. He asked the recruiter whether the Coast Guard had journalists.

"Sure, see here?" said the recruiter, pointing to a section of a recruiting brochure.

"I thought I had made no commitment but the Chief OIC of the Recruiting Office in Green Bay, Wisconsin, called in early January. He put on a great show of being very upset because I had not presented myself at his office earlier that day. In retrospect, I am certain it was all an act to stampede a gullible kid into their quota. They knew a fish when they saw one. I thought I had done something wrong."

He soon found himself in Forming Company at the Recruit Training Center in Alameda, California. To say that Douville was surprised by how "easy" USCG boot

---

[1] www.togetherweserved.com

camp would be is an understatement. "At graduation I was three inches slimmer in the waist and 5lb heavier."

Before being shipped to Vietnam, Douville was attached to the Fleet Home Town News Center, a joint Navy, Marine, and Coast Guard tenant organization of the Naval Training Center in Great Lakes, Illinois.

"FHTNC was in my day a fleet public-affairs support activity that took event info about an individual or similarly situated group, e.g., completed recruit training, together with some bio data and generated one to any number of 'news' releases sent to newspapers—dailies, weeklies, and shoppers' advertorials—with a pic if available in the new sailor's hometown."

Douville provides the following example, which he says is "made up from memory with a sarcastic dollop:"

"GREAT LAKES, Ill.—(Date)—John Deaux, son of Mr. and Mrs. Jim Deaux, of 1200 Crawfish Dr., Baton Rouge, graduated (date or less desirable, 'recently') after 10 weeks of basic training at the Naval Training Center (NTC) at Great Lakes. He has been assigned to Gunner's Mate primary ('A') school, also located at NTC Great Lakes and may be expected to report for duty to Riverrine Force X in S. E. Asia as a boat machine gun operator (where we hope he does not get his ass shot off)."

Then in 1965, it was off to "Vietnam, Republic of" ... but not directly. Before that, Douville did something in virtue of which he labels himself a prima donna and over which he wishes to clear the air.

He became frustrated with his CG role, had too much to drink, then went AWOL for five days and financed his absence with proceeds from a part-time on-base job. He thought the better of it after a while and turned himself in. After a pre-trial agreement before a "Special Court Martial," which assured Douville that he would not be kicked out of the Coast Guard, he spent 54 days locked up in the brig at the former Naval Station on Treasure Island in San Francisco Bay. He also lost two stripes.

At the time, defense counsel did not necessarily have to be an attorney. As such, Douville was defended by a Lieutenant Douglas Currier. Douville's and Currier's lives would cross several times after that, including the former's retirement. However, in May 1965, when Douville reported for duty with the newly commissioned Squadron One at what is now Coast Guard Island, Alameda, California, the lieutenant was also present in the role of prospective commanding officer of one of the Squadron's 82-foot patrol boats.

With his defense still in recent memory, Currier quietly informed the Squadron commander of Douville's record. Later the Squadron commander told Douville they sent only him from the admin staff to SERE [Survival, Evasion, Resistance and Escape] training hoping that he would "bilge" out, i.e., fail to complete the course. This would be a basis for leaving him behind when the Squadron moved on to Vietnam. But Douville completed SERE training, so the attempt to get rid of him failed. Ironically the attempt actually worked to his favor. The Squadron commander, reassured by Douville's completion of SERE training, and responsible performance since, assigned him to a special project involving access to the communications center, the support ship's most restricted area.

"It was a first step in overcoming my prior bad behavior and salvaging a career," Douville reflected.

In a first-person "hometowner" that Douville wrote for his former employer, the *Evening News* of Sault Ste. Marie, Michigan, he informed his (then) fellow Michiganders (he lives in Mandeville, Louisiana today), that there were initially 17 patrol boats, designated "WPB" (W for some reason the Naval designation for a Coast Guard ship and PB for patrol boat) hurried to Vietnam, all fitted with .50-caliber machine guns and .81-caliber mortars.

He can still explicitly define the weaponry aboard ship 52 years later.

"Initially there were nine WPBs in Division 11 and eight in Division 12. Five .50-caliber MGs and one 81mm mortar were standard heavy weapons on all the boats. The mortar was hydraulic for recoil, mounted centered on the deck forward of the superstructure. A single .50-caliber machine gun was mounted above the mortar in an over/under configuration. Two .50-caliber machine guns were mounted amidships at the port and starboard rails and two more aft at the transom port and starboard. Three of them could be fired broadside simultaneously; the bow arrangement meant only one of these weapons could be used at a time, either the mortar or the .50-caliber machine guns."

"There were also small arms. For example, M1 and M2 carbines, clip-fed Thompson submachine guns, and various types of hand grenades, .45-caliber pistols. Later, after my time, the Coast Guard got more modern weapons: M-14 and M-16 rifles and M-60 machine guns, the latter being mounted on the rails at either side of a tiny deck abaft the wheel house."

The talk shifts from the weaponry to his partial role as a Coast Guard journalist.

"I recall taking pictures after a firefight between a WPB and a 25–30-foot [Viet Cong] junk. I was not aboard for the firefight but went out later for the daylight examination of the enemy craft. There were perhaps 600 steel cores from .50 API [armor-piercing incendiary rounds] in the bilges of the junk, half-sunk now in shallow water. API was possibly every fourth or fifth round. A bit of math and one can understand the rain of death and destruction these young untested Coast Guardsmen unloaded in the darkness after the junk's occupants foolishly opened fire, with bolt action ChiCom (Chinese Communist) carbines on the patrol boat. Have you seen bodies struck by a single .50-caliber round? Just devastating. The divers found two bodies, as I recall."

"In their last moments, the VC must have been stunned by the volume of return fire; it was likely the first encounter for both sides, involving an American WPB of Division 11."

The anecdotes roll on.

"I heard a story of one WPB called in close to the shoreline to provide flanking fire support for a Special Forces position under heavy assault. The enemy broke off its attack. The next day the slope up which the enemy assaulted was found to be chewed up by heavy machine gun and mortar fire. Blood trails and bits of flesh were found. Fire from one WPB machine gun was so heavy the barrel was glowing red in the darkness. A gunner's mate changed the barrel (with special gloves) and dropped the ruined one over the side."

Douville was along for a raid on a VC base at Hon Mot, northeast of Phu Quoc Island. "I well recall the dispatch of the cutter's [all Coast Guard ships are called 'cutters,' by long tradition] small boat to shore and return with the still sweat-beaded body of Staff Sergeant James Pruitt and a wounded trooper from the CIDG [Civilian Irregular Defense Group, a program begun by the CIA to counter Viet Cong efforts in the Central Highlands]. I photographed Pruitt's body and the wounded trooper, feeling conflicted and certain that I would get an ass chewing for doing so. But no one said anything to me about it. I recall the cutter's chief boatswain's mate with tears running down his face. That sad event brought home to me the reality of the war. Years later, I looked up the sergeant's name during a visit to the Vietnam Memorial Wall."

Douville's role in the Squadron, despite his primary clerical and administrative duties, did allow him to make patrols aboard the Coast Guard cutters, but infrequently. "I don't recall any set schedule. I was not in a 'JO' billet. I was only assigned to the squadron because I had been a yeoman.

"One of my most memorable experiences was a three-day TAD (TDY) interlude at a Special Forces A-Team camp at Duong Dong, the Phu Quoc district town. My mission was to type copies of a list the Special Forces had compiled of VC suspects in the area. Other than mimeograph machines the only way to make copies in those days was by typewriter and carbon paper.

"It turned out that the A-Team was short-handed because a couple of troopers were out on a recon patrol. So, they pressed me into service, manning a .30-caliber MG position if there was an enemy attack. I also went out at night with a couple of troopers as observers on a harassing fire mission executed by the local regional forces equipped with two 4.2-inch mortars. The Special Forces called the Vietnamese 'Ruff-Puffs' and it was clear from their cynical remarks that they did not hold them in high regard. They were anxious about the lack of security as the night wore on, with the Ruff-Puffs apparently arguing among the leaders about something. Finally, my Special Forces compadres set up a .30-caliber assault MG in our open-bed truck, which for some reason they instructed me to man! My instructions were, should we be ambushed, to get on the machine gun and start firing while they (knowing the way) drove to escape, and ended on a note that has vividly remained with me ever since. One of them said, 'And don't worry about them f**kers (meaning the Ruff-Puffs). If they get in the way shoot them too!'"

When he returned to the Squadron, Douville recalled he was "pretty pumped up" by his sojourn with the Special Forces. He enthusiastically related his adventures to his boss, who sourly remarked, "G*d dammit Douville! Do you know how much paperwork we'd have had to do if you'd been shot?"

Douville recalls making at least one other patrol with a WPB of Division 13.

"I also made a largely uneventful interdicting patrol in the Rung Sat Special Zone (RSSZ) with a Division 13 WPB. We almost had a friendly-fire engagement with a SEAL Team we had not been told was in our patrol area. And we picked up a Marine Corps squad that had spent the night in the swamp deployed in ambush. They gathered in our tiny mess, where they wolfed anything not nailed down. One of them dropped his rifle in the waterway when he was trying to climb aboard. It was not recovered (at least by us)."

He relished those patrols because they saved him from the "numbing boredom of admin flunky work as embarked squadron staff on the mother ship and later in Saigon." On one such occasion, when he was tasked with being a "Remington Raider," his sense of humor kicked in.

"After moving to Saigon, I was told to and did compose and type up a lot of personal decoration citations, all of them for officers and some made up completely from my imagination," he said.

"If you timed it well, you could go on patrol for five days or so on a WPB with a really great cook and eat much better than on the mother ship."

His transfer from Phu Quoc to Saigon, where he wrote those citations, occurred in February 1966.

"We enlisted admin personnel were transferred there when a captain was sent by the Coast Guard to command the expanding squadron. While Division 12 was based at Da Nang, Division 11 was at the other end of the country at An Thoi, Phu Quoc Island, beyond the Ca Mau peninsula in the Gulf of Thailand. A new Division, 13, was taking up station out of Cat Lo, near the South China Sea resort of Vung Tau, or as known in French, Cap St. Jacques. I never got to Division 12 or saw anything of them again after they left Subic Bay, in the Philippines."

"There were two Coast Guard Squadrons in Vietnam, One and Three. One was composed of 82-foot "Point Class" WPBs. Three, which came after my time, was made up of high-endurance cutters (WHEC) both old and, at that time, new. The WHECs kept their homeports, the WPBs did not."

In time, they were all turned over to the Republic of Vietnam Navy, according to Douville.

"The Coast Guard also had an explosive loading detail in-country, a priority LORAN [Long Range Navigation] chain, with some of it located in Vietnam and some in other Southeast Asian countries. A buoy tender worked there as well. There were also some Coast Guard aviators, flying SAR [Search and Rescue] helos in an Air Force/Coast Guard exchange program."

When asked to describe a typical day for a Coast Guard journalist, Douville does not hold back.

"Boring, dull, with brief interludes of busy and interesting times," he states. "I only remember bits and pieces, like showering in the monsoon rains on the open main deck of the initial support ship, an old LST [Landing Ship Tank] with constantly failing fresh water-making evaporators; being transported by launch to a support ship for showers; carrying out resupply by UNREP (underway replenishment); being called to sickbay for plague shots, by weight in the butt; not having 'sea' legs and standing on a ladder with a laden mess tray, trying not to spill down the neck of the guy waiting on the next step down; the rattle of dice at 2am against the aft bulkhead of the forward ladder vestibule adjacent to our sleeping compartment and the excited Tagalog chatter of the stewards gambling; being roused out at 3am to type one or another message or can't-wait letter; hearing the GQ [General Quarters] alarm go in the night and the mothership's Navy CO, repeatedly screaming over the P.A., 'SLIP THE CHAIN!' He meant the anchor detail was to allow the bitter end of the deployed anchor chain (normally fixed to a sturdy place in the chain locker) to fall into the sea whilst he desperately backed away to get his ship out of range of an enemy 'attack' from the shore that later proved to be a false alarm. The next few days were spent trying to find and retrieve the anchor and chain from the harbor floor."

He also remembered, "An afternoon at Division 11 of R&R at one of numerous small uninhabited islands in the area. A gunner's mate, filled with an excess of exuberance (and beer) fired off a burst of Tommy gun fire into the air. We momentarily thought we were being ambushed. He got a slap on the wrist later."

But it wasn't always routine and boredom that filled Douville's time in Vietnam.

"This is funny now but was deadly serious when it happened. After moving to Saigon, my billet was in a small hotel. It housed a few dozen enlisted military personnel of various services. One of them was a SK1 [Storekeeper] also assigned to Ron One staff at what was then Naval Advisory Group (later NAVFORV) HQ on Phan Dinh Phung Street. There was at that time a good deal of tension brought on by demonstrating Buddhist monks, who protested against whatever by horrific public self-immolation. Although garrison troops in the city were not allowed to carry personal weapons, the SK, an older guy, carried a .45-caliber pistol in his briefcase. It was after the workday. I was in the hotel near the stairs having a brew in the room of another guy. The room door was open so those passing in the adjacent hallway could see us. I was wearing a custom-tailored pair of black pajamas, modeled on the clothes worn by countless peasants throughout Vietnam. And, not incidentally, by lots of VC. The SK1 was an alcoholic who fortified himself with numerous Ba Muoi Ba ["33," a Vietnamese beer] to face the peril of the journey from Phan Dinh Phung Street to our hotel. We waved as he stumbled past the open door.

Moments later he reappeared in the doorway, now unsteadily aiming his pistol at me," Douville recalled.

"'Get out of them VC clothes,' he ordered. I quickly did so. 'Now put on some Coast Guard clothes,' he said. I carefully explained they were in my room nearby. He marched me at gunpoint down the hall where I put on my dungarees and chambray shirt. 'Don't let me catch you in them VC clothes again,' he said, at the same time working the slide on the pistol and a round ejected. He was weaving and laid the pistol on my bed while trying to retrieve the round on the floor. As he lurched down to pick it up, I dove across him and got the gun. Meanwhile someone had called the MPs, who arrived and took custody of my fellow Coast Guard warrior and his pistol. I don't think he remembered any of it the next day. I wrote nothing and recall hearing nothing about it after."

Though the Coast Guard is widely regarded as having first been deployed to Vietnam in 1965, Douville did attempt, many years later, to substantiate that the USCG had actually been deployed to Vietnam two years before. He did so through an unexpected source's recollections that involved an apparently classified deployment of 40-foot UTBs and a small cadre of Coast Guard crewmen and support personnel circa 1963.

"I sought to find corroborating facts from the Coast Guard, Navy, and next-of-kin, but came up with nothing definitive. I decided to go with what I had, having neither the means nor ambition to pursue this intriguing lead further. I believe my source's recollection; he became rather reticent in a follow-up interview, believing that he might get in trouble for revealing a clandestine operation more than half a century ago. I found no facts that were contradictory to his story, only tantalizing hints of corroboration being somewhere in archive files."

When asked to reflect on his career as a "JO" in Vietnam, Douville sums it up this way:

"I was a frustrated and failed writer who mostly took pictures, was too junior and anxious about my future to exercise any initiative. I was issued a Yashica twin lens 110 camera and a vintage Bell and Howell 8mm movie camera with a booklet of instructions," he says.

"I wasted a lot of film through the movie camera. What CGHQ [Coast Guard Headquarters] did with the pix and such written copy as I may have sent back, I don't know. I think I also wrote some dispatches that were published internally in the old *Commandant's Bulletin.*"

Douville, who retired from the US Coast Guard at the end of June, 1997, after 36 years and five months of continuous active duty, with the rank of commander (O-5), also feels a need to put his performance as a JO in Vietnam in context.

"I was a junior petty officer not thought of as a JO but as a yeoman, an admin clerk, by the officers for whom I worked; officers who were extremely stressed, not only to perform but to do so despite any personal considerations and to excel. I had no USCG public affairs officer pro, no JO leading chief, hardly any contact with Coast Guard Public Information back in the States, and virtually no public-affairs guidance. From where I was, well below the salt and coming to the assignment with a bad reputation, I needed to follow directions and keep my mouth shut."

US Coast Guard journalist Bob Douville getting his land legs back while locals look on, Ha Tien, South Vietnam. (Bob Douville collection)

Vietnam Seemed Just Fine: Mike Stokey II

"I may be the only freak from Beverly Hills who ever volunteered for service in Vietnam," said Mike Stokey II. Stokey, born of what he called "Hollywood parents"— Mike Stokey, Sr., producer and gameshow host of *Pantomime Quiz*, *Stump the Stars* and *Beat the Odds*, and movie actress Pamela Blake, who starred alongside the likes of John Wayne in *Wyoming Outlaw* and singing cowboy Tex Ritter in *The Utah Trail*—carried on the artistic tradition in his family by writing of his experiences as a US Marine in the battle for Hue during the Tet Offensive of 1968 in his book *River of Perfumes*.

Of his upbringing, Stokey said, "Born in Hollywood, California. Divorced parents. Spent time with both, but mostly with my mother growing up in Las Vegas."

Few Marine recruits ever heard the words "combat correspondent" when they signed up, according to Stokey, who went through boot camp at MCRD (Marine Corps Recruit Depot) in San Diego.

"I remember writing my dad a letter in boot camp saying that I wanted to be a Recon Marine. When our platoon graduated and they announced my MOS, the D.I. had no idea what a 4312 was. I don't know if my father panicked and pulled covert strings, or if I just got lucky from my test scores on English and typing," Stokey recalled.

In addition to his English and typing skills, Stokey came to writing at a young age.

"I had always written plays to force the neighborhood to watch," he said. But, other than being good in literature classes and being well read, he had not taken formal writing courses. And unlike many other combat correspondents, Stokey never attended DINFOS [the Defense Information School] then at Ft. Benjamin Harrison, Indiana.

"Never gave them the time," he said.

Stokey was sent to Camp Lejeune, North Carolina, after ITR [Intensive Training Regiment], which he hated. His only reprieve was being able to get away to what he called "J-Ville [Jacksonville, Florida]."

"I hated it [Camp Lejeune]. After two or three months I told them I wanted a transfer. Of course, they laughed."

Stokey recalled the humorous encounter he had with higher-ups when he requested that transfer:

"What's so funny?" I asked.

"You don't pick where you're going. This is the Marine Corps."

"How about Vietnam?"

"Sign on the dotted line."

"Wasn't so hard, after all," he said.

Stokey got to Da Nang in January 1967. After wandering around the Da Nang Air Base for an hour, he hopped a ride to the 1st Marine Division, ISO (Informational Service Office). His first impression of Vietnam?

"Nothing but monsoon rain and red muck. And that buzzing in the stomach wondering what would happen next," he said.

What happened next was that Stokey wound up writing stories about his fellow Marines throughout all of I Corps, chiefly with the 5th and 7th Marines, but also with the 1st Marines and other units in three consecutive tours between January 1967 and April 1969. With the MOS 4312, his mission was to be a writer, but he also carried his personal Minox camera with him into battle. And since every Marine is a rifleman, in addition to notebook and pen, Stokey slugged an M-14 over his shoulder through all of 1967.

"Turned it in before my first 30-day leave in January 1968. From that point on I carried a .45," he said.

The first time he ever used his M-14 was during Operation *Arizona*. It was a heavy battle which included tanks.

"Nobody clicks a ballpoint in the middle of a firefight. You either fire, maneuver, or help with the casualties. Photogs are different. That's their job."

Stokey would fire his M-14 a number of times after that until he surrendered it and picked up the .45, which he rarely fired. Exceptions were in Hue during the Tet Offensive and during Operation *Meade River* in December 1968.

Operation *Meade River* was what the 1st Battalion, 1st and 3d Marine Regiments, called a "County Fair" mission. It employed a technique that allowed the Marines to cordon off an area to search and clear it inward, literally foot by foot, to counteract the common Viet Cong practice of infiltrating villages. Operation *Meade River* was the largest mission using the County Fair technique during the war.[1]

Meade River was at the top of Stokey's list for his worst experience in Vietnam.

"Everything about combat is relative. There are 'moments' from various operations, but one that encompassed both lunacy and terror was *Meade River*."

His description of the events of that mission leave no doubt as to how enthralling and worthy of reading his book *River of Perfumes* is.

"I joined Lima company, 3d Battalion, 5th Marines, operating in the Dodge City area, where several hundred NVA and VC troops had amassed. The company had already been hit and their commanding officer, a captain, had been wounded and medivac'd. I was dropped in on a resupply chopper and headed for the command post to get briefed by a lieutenant, the new CO. They were setting in for the day, but intel had been notified of possible enemy movement a couple hundred meters away. A four-man fire team was dispatched and I asked if I could catch it.

---

[1] George A. Hill. *Heart of the Third Sector, Hill 55.* George A. Hill, 2005.

"We headed through a wooded area that opened up on a large plateau blanketed with elephant grass. Not long after, enemy snipers opened up from a tree line. One grunt fell, a bullet graze in the neck, and we pulled him back, returning fire, wending our way out of the thick grass.

"Finally back with the company, at chow time I got word that the lieutenant wanted to see me. He extended his thanks for my accompanying the unit, then told me the fire team leader I was out with said I was smoking and that's why we got ambushed."

Stokey remarked to the CO, "The team leader was six foot four, his head a full six inches above the elephant grass, and he blamed me for the ambush?"

"But I was on the radar," he said.

A couple more incidents of volunteering with four-man probes also come to mind for Stokey. He recounted one firefight in particular that was sheer terror.

"No grunts volunteer for these things. With combat correspondents, it's different. It doesn't matter if you've been in-country one or two years, and the grunts only a few months. Each time out with a new infantry unit you have to earn your due. Probes, and pulling watch, were always a way to do it, even if you were a sergeant," he said.

"A couple of days later all hell broke loose. The company was scattered, fighting to reassemble under heavy enemy fire, and we ended up in small pockets. An hour into it came a sudden lull in the chaos, one of those holes in the universe that happen during battle. Both sides stopped firing and revised their tactics. I was with an undermanned squad, a lieutenant and staff sergeant, sitting outside a small, old brick French bunker. There was a small, sloping mound where a couple Marines kept watch just below the military crest. Near us, at the base of the mound, a two-foot opening and a ladder leading down into a large underground bunker beckoned jeopardy. One guy had already thrown a grenade down there. Looking in, the darkness was large and wide, no telling how far it stretched.

"Most of us sat in a circle, checking mags, helmets off despite the slight rain. Adrenaline was heat enough. A few minutes into it, a grunt across a small open area called to me, the only one within his view. He hollered about a pack he had dropped in the open, a few meters from our position when he had tried to cross. Somehow he scrambled back without it. 'Could you grab it for me?' he yelled.

"It was closer to me, and I only had to go a few meters into the open to retrieve it. He'd pick it up when he and his squad rushed over.

"Was he nuts? It was a stupid pack, for Chrissakes. But, there again, could I grab it, *would* I grab it for him?" Stokey's fellow Marine asked.

"Jesus. There was no reason for it, and I shook my head, but rose, hunched over. I got about ten steps, about to reach for the pack, when a mortar exploded dead center in the circle I left.

"I flattened on the deck as black debris and smoke erupted. Then, the always predictable dreaded sound of casualties and bedlam roiled past. I shuddered. Automatic fire from both sides flared up and I was back where I left the group at the bunker.

"Most of the guys were crammed inside the brick bunker. The lieutenant was badly hit and the staff sergeant was cowering in a corner, hollering for his helmet.

"The black guy I had been talking to most was splayed out on the ground, his head hanging over the edge of the hole to the underground bunker. I scrambled to his side, eased behind him, and stepped down the rungs of the ladder. His head was a mess as I tried to plug the holes in his skull. Through the chaos, I thought I heard something shuffle below me and all I could think about was a gook shoving a fixed bayonet up my rectum.

"I moved up the ladder and pulled the black guy toward the brick bunker. Almost everyone inside was wounded, the staff sergeant still in full panic and yelling for his helmet. I saw mine on the ground outside, crawled for it and threw it to him. The men were frozen at the sight of one of their leaders cracking. It shut him up and everyone got their bearings again.

"For the first time I noticed the men on the crest of the hill were gone. They must have been crammed inside the brick house with the rest of us and I thought we were going to be overrun.

"We started punching a hole in the rear brick wall, finally large enough to move the casualties through, one by one. A couple grunts knelt at the small door, keeping a watch out. We signaled the line of grunts behind us that we needed cover and started carrying the wounded across the open paddy while the grunts poured out fire. We got them behind the lines and a few of us went back again for the others.

"By the time we got them to a casualty collection point, big twin-rotor CH-46 Sea Knight helicopters started coming in for medevacs. A few of us carried the casualties inside, returning for a second round, when the helicopter started taking fire. Still inside, it started rising off the ground as I hustled to the rear ramp ready to jump off. The chopper lurched to the left as the ramp came up and the next thing I knew I was dangling from the ramp, too far from the ground to let loose. It was like one of those mad moments in an old Harold Lloyd movie, my feet dangling as bullets snapped past me, hitting the belly of the chopper.

"A couple guys pulled me in and we were finally high enough in the air where I could take a breath. Marines never had much use for helicopters compared with the Army. There was no Air Cav to the rescue in the Marine Corps. Basically, they were taxis we didn't much respect.

"But we were high aloft and heading back to Charlie Med … I hoped. Then suddenly we were turning. I asked the door gunner where we were going.

"'Going back in for more casualties,' he said. It was the second time that that day I thought someone was crazy. The guy didn't react to my expression, but I'm sure my eyes bulged. And here came that respect.

"Now what? I had made it through all that shit and we were heading back in and going in hot. I could just stay inside and wait it out. Then the ramp went down and I was out the rear, helping on-load another batch of casualties."

At chow call that night, the CO called Stokey over to his quarters. They talked about writing, which the CO had long wanted to do. "It was a quiet moment," Stokey said.

The CO informed him that the lieutenant that had been wounded at the brick fort wanted Stokey to get a medal.

"It wasn't heroic or altruistic or any gooey-sap a Berkeley poet would espouse, but I told him he should give it to one of his own men. Those were the guys who were at his side. And, in my own mind, like almost everyone who was still around and made it this far, I didn't feel special, just grateful to be alive. Besides, the Marine Corps wasn't a career for me."

No matter Stokey's feelings about receiving a medal for his actions in the *Mead River* mission, two months later, he was looking at a Bronze Star with V for valor. Lieutenant General Ormond R. Simpson, 1st Marine Division's Commanding General, pinned it on him.

"An unexpected final twist: General Simpson's new aide was the captain who had commanded Lima Company and who was medivac'd just before I arrived," Stokey said.

Stokey's time in Vietnam did not leave him without wounds unfortunately. The first time he was wounded was in September 1967, with Lima Company, 3d Battalion, 7th Marines.

"It was a dinky operation and I was the first one hit. A simple rice-harvesting operation where we were to establish a perimeter to protect the villagers and prevent the VC from coming in to exact taxes. Except the VC were already there, and already knew we were coming. As Ian Adams wrote for an article in Canada's *MacLean's* magazine in February 1968, "They [the VC] even said so the night before over a portable loudspeaker that moved up and down the river: 'Soldiers of the American Imperialist Army, we know you are coming across the river tomorrow. We are ready for you. If you do not want to die, surrender with your arms and you will be treated well.'"

In spite of the Viet Cong knowing that Lima Company was in the area, the company moved into position the following day. They cordoned off the area. Stokey takes it from there.

"Ian Adams and I accompanied a fire team of five Marines to check out a village across an open rice paddy 100 meters away. A sniper had just shot and apparently killed a VC moving in one of the huts. We made it across the paddy. Nobody, just a scared old man and a woman. They shook their heads as they always did when the VC were watching, and we took them with us back to the unit. We waited for the South Vietnamese Popular Forces to move up on our flank—they were too scared to move off the beach—when, as Adams wrote: 'there comes that vicious, fast pop-popping of some AK47s. Stokey goes down with a sharp grunt, a round through his right leg. "I'm hit," he says matter-of-factly.'

"And that was pretty much it, for me," Stokey said. "In and out before things got hairy."

Mike Stokey left Vietnam in April 1969 and two weeks later he was out of the Marine Corps. He probably didn't know it in 1969, but that would not be the last time he would set foot on Vietnamese soil. In 2016, he and a group of other Snuffies, including director/writer/actor Dale Dye and former *Los Angeles Times* editor Bob Bayer, and several Marine Corps combat correspondents, went back to Vietnam under the auspices of the Greatest Generations Foundation, which chiefly arranges for World War II veterans to return to their areas of operation, Stokey found himself once again in Vietnam.

In a piece he shared just as stirring as his description of Operation *Meade River* and called "The Great Snuffy Trek Home," Stokey wrote, "I may have been the only one who didn't anticipate a trigger. My face-downs with terror came in the bush. Except for smells, what was there to find? In Hue I escaped unscathed, physically and psychologically, and had no ghosts in waiting. But the funny thing is, I think mine came first [in 2016], on our second day in Da Nang.

"We were taken to a tiny bar called Tam's in the midst of the teeming ramshackle jungle of Da Nang. I don't know why it hit me so hard. Like the time I was struck by the first round fired before there was the urgency to duck. It smacked me like a shockwave," he said.

Stokey recalls the visit to Tam's in the most eloquent of writing.

"Gilding the walls were hundreds of photos of the war and soldiers who fought for the South. It was like a blast furnace sucking me into the heat. Photos everywhere, on the walls, the furniture, the shelves. Snapshots of Marines in villages, soldiers on the hump, soldiers holding babies. There were old, rotted military fatigues and gear, canteen cups, and jungle boots. They still had a smell to them. Grunts know it: a mixture of dirt and chlorophyll, sweat and blood. A dank, sick sweetness. There were old dog tags. I picked one up to take a look when Tam, the owner, pulled me down to talk."

Tam endured much suffering, which all started when, as a young girl, some Viet Cong attempted to use her as a human sacrifice by ordering her to take a bomb fashioned out of a Coke can to the security gate of the 1st Marine Division.

"Rounding the hill and out of sight, she struggled with pidgin English to tell the guards it was a bomb. She pleaded with them to safely explode it nearby. The explosion was important—proof to the VC that she had delivered the device. There were other tests, but in time the Americans left and the communist armies swept south. Declining to join the exodus of boat people, she was ushered to one of the notorious re-education camps," Stokey learned from her.

But her troubles were not over after she was released from the camp.

"She eventually opened her pub. As more photos went up, more pressure by the state was applied. Through the years she had been closed down, maligned by the press, jailed for treason and unremittingly threatened. Even today it wasn't completely safe. But things were looking up and opening up."

Today a technical advisor to such films as *Casualties of War*, *Born on the 4th of July*, *Tigerland*, *Jacob's Ladder*, *The Thin Red Line*, *Snow Falling on Cedars*, and the HBO Steven Spielberg/Tom Hanks Production documentaries *Band of Brothers* and *The Pacific*, Stokey continued, "I listened and looked around again. Then I saw another photo … of a buddy I wasn't able to save. It wasn't him, but it looked like him, enough to send me plummeting.

"I needed air, and it all flooded back, the staggering memories, the hurt and despair, overwhelmed again by the carefully buried loss and futility. It was a 30-second shutdown, another 30 to stop the tears and shakes. My brothers stood guard … but left me alone. In a flat minute I was collected again because there's no point being stuck on a battlefield. And through it all Vietnam seemed just fine."

There but for the Grace of God Go I: Eddie Carroll

"Every cameraman has been in combat, some closer than others," said former USAF photographer Eddie Carroll. "Our positions were shelled almost every night whether we were in Saigon or in the boonies. You never left a camera unattended because it would be stolen and we were warned never to let our products fall into the wrong hands."

Carroll still remembers how it felt to carry two cameras around his neck. And he still remembers his US Air Force Combat Documentary Photographer ID card number: 591.

But a photographic "baptism under fire" did not necessarily begin in Vietnam. His future as a photographer was actually set in stone when he turned eight.

"On my eighth birthday, I received three cameras from my family," the Wharton, Texas native recalls. "I studied photography all through undergraduate work and took a degree in photographic sciences with a minor in journalism in 1967 from Sam Houston State Teachers' College. I was sent on what is called a Direct Duty Assignment right out of college to bypass technical schools."

That same year Carroll enlisted in the Air Force and reported to his first duty station, Vandenberg Air Force Base, where he was attached to the 1369th Photo Squadron, a MAC (Military Airlift Command) detachment and part of the Air Force Audio Visual Services Group (AAVS).

"I was assigned as a still photographer. Vandenberg AFB was the training and launch center for the United States missile system. The base averaged a launch every 3.5 days through the year. The 1369th provided cameramen, photographers, and film crews around the western United States and all through the Pacific Theater."

Not long after that, the USAF made sure that Carroll put several survival schools on his military résumé. They included Water Survival, Eglin AFB, Florida; Jungle Training and Survival, Panama, Canal Zone; Aircrew Escape and Evasion Training, Course 1, Winter/Arctic Survival and Course 2 at Fairchild AFB, Washington; and Jungle Survival Training, Clark AFB, the Philippines.

Many of the courses could have been stamped with the word "Vietnam" on every page of the coursework because that is exactly where Carroll ended up. He was attached to the 600th Photo Squadron there.

"I went to Saigon twice on TDY, each tour for 90 days in 1968, PCS (Permanent Change of Station) in February of 1969, and departed Vietnam on April 2, 1970. In addition to in-country assignments, the 600th Photographic Squadron supplied crews into Korea to cover the capture and release of the USS *Pueblo* which was captured by the North Koreans in early 1968."

His AFSC (Air Force Specialist Code) was still-photographer, but he was also cross-trained in 16mm film work when an assignment required only single operators. For example, filming air-to-air when only one seat was available in aircraft. He also worked in the photo processing lab at Ton San Nhut Air Base when he was not doing day-to-day assignments.

"We had detachments all over South Vietnam where I would go when assigned. Our work required top-secret clearances because much of the documentary work was presented to senior officers both in-theater and at US headquarters."

When asked to describe the day-to-day missions that occupied most of his time with the 600th, Carroll said, "We all lived by 'The Board.' Our assignments and future requirements were posted each day, many times well in advance of a need, so we could find jobs through other organizations such as the Australian Air Force, Republic of Korea Air Force, our own Marine detachments, or, an especially easy one, with the Navy. If AAVS had photo or filming jobs for that day or that week, we would prepare the equipment by cleaning and making sure all batteries were either charged or declared unusable. When we were 'out' and equipment failed, we were out of luck and didn't get a lot of second chances to document an event. I have seen a lot of movies and stories showing guys spending time sitting around and shooting the breeze; we never had the luxury of time to do that."

Very often missions for the 600th Photo Squadron entailed being aloft.

"All of us were on flight status and trained as aircrew members for the specific aircraft on which we operated. I had a total of 107 sorties in Vietnam and flew in several different aircraft types, both fixed wing and rotor."

The list of aircraft Eddie Carroll boarded is extensive: AC 119, AC 123, AC 130 and AC 141 gunships as well as F101, F105, F104, F106 and F4 fighter aircraft. His time in helicopters included the "Jolly Green Giant" Sikorsky; the Huey, which he called the "Pack Horse of the Army"; and LOACH (Light Observation Aircraft).

"And one which I have forgotten the nomenclature of, but it was lovingly called 'The Bullshit Bomber' because propaganda and warning documents were carried into habitable areas and dropped, warning the locals that all hell was going to come to their area sooner rather than later," he said.

Much of the 600th's work at altitude, Carroll says, was done at night.

"I operated on several late-evening flights where the aircraft mission was to provide very specific coverage of a ground operation that was in trouble. We called it '[being] in the shit.'"

In support of American troops, a gunship would make low passes at the target area to observe any movement by the enemy. Commonly, a million-candle watt floating flare was kicked out of the aircraft and suspended on a small parachute that ignited and then floated down for several minutes. That way, "we got a fix on the bad guys," he said. "Once the gunship was cleared by the troops we were supporting, the mini-cannons would open up. It became a wall of lead and tracers and the noise was unimaginable. The on-board commander would direct the firing as needed and where needed for as long as we stayed on-target.

"Each time we returned, the crew chief's first assignment was to determine the number of 'post production perforations' in the aircraft. That's bullet holes."

"On more than one occasion, the commander would peel off target to determine how much damage was done, and to determine if any of the air crew had been injured. It happened from time to time."

"Our assignment [also] included documenting the discipline of our troops and the resolve with which they did their respective jobs."

Though the bulk of Carroll's Air Force missions entailed still photography in Vietnam, he also experienced mopic photography elsewhere.

"I had never operated a motion-picture camera until we were deployed to Osan AFB, Korea. The squadron commander requested a stills-qualified cameraman to film his crew chief re-enlisting as they flew upside down at Mach 1 over the South China Sea. Our mopic guy gladly gave me the assignment and a quick review of the operation of the camera. That led to me using ultra-high-speed cameras in air-to-air coverage at Sandia Labs, White Sands Missile Range, in my final Air Force assignment," he recalled.

It could be said that his work at Sandia Labs was as critical as his missions in Vietnam.

"My final assignment for Sandia Labs was at Kirtland AFB, New Mexico. They were developing smart-bomb technology and I was blessed to be able to fly almost every day. My training in motion-picture cameras became essential as our instrumentation photography was critical to studying cause and effect in ordinance release from aircraft."

It would almost seem that photography and Eddie Carroll's life are inextricably interwoven,

"I have never lost my love for photography and continue to be astounded by the world of digital photography," he says.

As regards Vietnam though, Carroll looks upon his time as an Air Force photographer as *a* point in his life and not *the* point in his life as many Vietnam veterans do.

"In my post-military work, I have encountered many fellow veterans who could just not 'let go' of the past, particularly if they had served in Vietnam; I had some issues separating myself from that part of my life, but with some counseling and a very grounded faith/belief, I moved on and became successful at my life's occupation, working with a very small software company helping to make it very large and successful."

He does talk to people about his time in Vietnam, but it is clearly not the focus of his life. "I served, I healed and I moved forward," he said.

One of those with whom Carroll has talked about his service is his son Gary, a captain in the US Army, who has just left for his third tour of duty in nine years to the Middle East.

"We have talked about both of our experiences over the years. He came back from his first deployment as almost a mirror image of my own; angry, depressed, unappreciated, and defensive. He did not fare better than did I with the anger. It cost him his 17-year marriage. I am very proud of him as he moves forward with his life. He's an engineer, and way too often is in harm's way."

Carroll has also spoken to many others who wore the uniform as a volunteer hospice counselor for veterans facing their deaths at Envoy Hospice, Inc. in Ft. Worth, where he has helped over 200 of them and their families.

"Many of the men with whom I work at end-of-life consider themselves to still be 'in the shit.' Some just can't let it go and live in the moment. I have one current client who is three months my junior, served in the Army in 1968 and, according to his counselor, lost several buddies there [in Vietnam]. He is totally, completely unable to see anything other than those horrible events. He has been in counseling for years at the local VA and is not on any medication other than for high blood pressure. He will talk with me about his experiences and will cry sometimes as he struggles with survivor guilt. Vietnam is *the* sole focus of his life. His name ought to be on the Wall; he is a victim of the Vietnam War. I refuse to stay there and beg him to leave the shit behind and breathe the free air of today. He just can't do it. There are thousands just like him." Carroll believes.

Carroll also believes there is a marked difference between providing hospice care to veterans and non-veterans.

"My first year of working with hospice taught me that most people do not recognize their own mortality even when greeted with the notion that they are terminally ill. I found former military guys and, from time to time, women [who served], face things differently. There is more resolve among veterans as end-of-life becomes evident. The veteran is far more likely to immediately begin taking care of issues that must be attended to: last will and testament, burial instructions, VA benefits, if any. Once the hard facts are on the table, veterans deal with them, especially when they have family. Veterans take steps to insure as much is being done for their families so that they do not have to make decisions in a vacuum: Where to be buried? Cremated?

Military services? My oldest veteran was a female Navy WAVE [Women Accepted for Voluntary Emergency Service], age 97. She was buried with full military honors at DFW Memorial Cemetery last year. My youngest veteran was a 28-year-old Iraq war veteran, a multiple amputee who ended his own life. Very sad."

In spite of his feelings on how many veterans do not or cannot get beyond their time in battle as he has, Eddie Carroll, who worked for CBS News for four years after he was discharged from the Air Force, called his time in Southeast Asia "a fantastic journey."

"I had a front-row seat in one of the most defining eras in history. I was educated, experienced and survived a time in our nation's history when I thought, more than once, that the whole nation was going to crash and burn. I was spat upon, ridiculed and shunned by people with whom I had grown up. As life moves forward, I have mellowed and realized that God had something much greater in store for me. He did, and I continue to draw on those experiences as I minister to fellow Veterans who are struggling."

* * *

In the course of interviewing Eddie Carroll for this book, he sent me the following letter, which I include in its entirety, since its message, I hope the reader will agree, is so very powerful.

Marc:
I have deliberated about sharing this with you. After our son left yesterday, I thought about all the guys I knew who did not come back whole. One such gentleman was Bradford Smith Ellsworth. He was a SSgt who arrived in-country on September 30, 1969 and joined the 600th Photographic Squadron as something of a squad leader … .we did not break down to squad groups; we worked as a crew. That system was what we inherited when I got there and it worked great as far as I knew.

I mentioned earlier that all of us carried Combat Cameraman ID cards which were sort of a priority pass to board virtually any aircraft, room allowing, to perform our missions. On October 11, 1969, I was manifested on an in-country flight aboard a Caribou 123 STOL [Short Take-off and Landing] craft operated by the Australian Air Force. It was essentially a mail-drop flight where they would do pilot training, make several stops on the all-night assignment and kick out mail bags for the troops assigned to the various bases and camps. I needed a couple hours and was trying out some new low-light techniques with black and white film.

About 45 minutes before the flight, SSgt Ellsworth walked into the ready room and announced that I had been bumped from the flight in his favor. It got confrontational as I challenged his using rank to get on this flight and showed him my ComDoc card. He told me, in very harsh terms, what I could do with the card and reminded me that as a career man he could certainly "take care of the paperwork" another time. He never had that opportunity.

The flight crashed on take-off. There was talk that it took small-arms fire during the run up but the aircraft was completely destroyed and all aboard were burned beyond recognition. They had to be identified by dental records.

That experience taught me several things, Marc: Never, never argue with anyone who wants to take your seat on an airplane and never, never take for granted how fragile life is. I carry a small print-out of Brad Ellsworth in my briefcase as a reminder that "There but for the Grace of God go I."

Brad is listed on The Wall on panel 17W, Line 65.

Rest in peace, Brad. My life has been so filled with joy and I never forget how many like Brad lost it all.

Eddie

The War as Reported and Photographed by the Civilian Press

The majority of the combat correspondents and photographers I interviewed for this book had the utmost respect for the men and women who covered the war for the civilian media. Though their missions were different—the military writers and photographers told the stories of their respective service branches, while the civilian journalists and photographers reported on the war—their paths would often cross, whether in the rear, on the field of battle, or at firebases during respites in the fighting which both were sent to record and report. It's with that in mind that I felt it appropriate to finish the book with profiles of three such civilians, who, in turn, had the utmost respect for their counterparts in uniform (some of them having worn a uniform previously in fact). These came from magazine articles I wrote for *Stars and Stripes*, *Vietnam* magazine, *News Photographer* magazine, and *American Veteran*, from which a finale is included about the civilian "Bao Chi" and were also in my first book, *Distant War: Recollections of Vietnam, Laos and Cambodia* (published by Navigator Books).

A One-way Ticket, $100 and Leica: Catherine Leroy

The late Catherine Leroy never wore the uniform, but she had the respect of hundreds who did. It's fitting then that she should find a place in these pages. I had the honor of interviewing her for the US military newspaper *Stars and Stripes* and, later, for *Vietnam* magazine. Sadly, Catherine succumbed to lung cancer in 2006.

"Excuse me Catherine," said a Secret Service agent from behind French photojournalist Catherine Leroy as she waited at the Pentagon for press credentials several years after the Vietnam War ended. "I'm sure you don't remember me, but I'll never forget you." He had first encountered Leroy after being wounded. He was getting off a Huey at a firebase somewhere in Vietnam, headed for fresh bandages, when their paths first crossed. Leroy, who had been getting on the chopper just he left it, had tossed him a can of Coke.

Looking back on that incident, and the sequel that happened years later, Leroy said simply, "That's war. You meet someone for a few seconds and you remember it for all your life." Now 55 and a resident of Los Angeles, Leroy has had an adventuresome career that has taken her into combat around the world, covering the civil war in Beirut, the Iranian revolution that brought Ayatollah Khomeini to power, upheavals in Mozambique and Somalia, and the 1992 Los Angeles riots.

But she got her initial combat experience in Vietnam. In 1966, Leroy arrived in Saigon as a blonde, pony-tailed 21-year-old with the stub of a one-way ticket, $100, and a Leica camera. The only picture-taking experience she had up to then, she admitted freely years later, was of her cat and scenes of her native France. "I wanted to be a photojournalist, and Vietnam seemed like a good place to achieve that," she said.

Achieve it she did. In a short time, her images of the bloody conflict in Southeast Asia found their way onto the pages of *Life*, *Look*, *Time*, *Newsweek* and *Paris Match* through her assignments as a stringer for the Associated Press and Black Star. A May 1967 *Time* magazine piece even profiled Leroy, describing the petite young woman this way: "She has size four feet stuffed into size six combat boots."

By the time Leroy's profile was published, she had earned the honorary title of "Bao Chi" (correspondent) and parachuted into combat with American airborne troops—a highly unusual feat for a reporter, let alone a woman. Trained as a sky-diver, she had already logged 85 jumps by the time she talked her way onto one of the Lockheed C-130s from which was launched the first American airborne assault in Vietnam. Leroy joined troops of the 173d Airborne Brigade as they jumped over Tay Ninh province during Operation *Junction City* in February 1967, just after the Vietnamese Tet (New Year) holiday that year. She jumped from the back of the C-130 like the paratroopers.

Leroy had worked hard to be able to hitch that ride with the 173d. She had previously established a sort of father–daughter relationship with Brigadier General John R. Deane, Jr., who had become the brigade commander just before the mission. She frequently joined him in the officers' mess as a dinner guest. "I asked him, 'Just in case there were to be a jump, when do you think it might be?' He strongly hinted what I needed to do, saying, 'Well, Cathy, if I were you, I would make an official request.'"

So Leroy traveled back to Saigon to make that request, "just in case there were to be a jump." Leroy later recalled that approval was a long time coming: "It took about a month of red tape in Washington at the Pentagon. Then the answer came back: 'If she's qualified and the CO says yes, we don't see any reason why not.'"

Even before parachuting into Tay Ninh, she commanded respect not only from her fellow correspondents but also from the GIs, who for the most part treated her as an equal. "I never looked like Marilyn Monroe, so I never really had a problem," she joked years later.

Fortunately, Leroy was already field-tested by the time she participated in *Junction City*, an operation that resulted in three months of combat in the bush for American troops, who were in contact with Viet Cong as well as North Vietnamese Army regulars. *Junction City* had been orchestrated to stop communist forces from retreating into the jungles of Cambodia. At the same time, the troops were supposed to search out what was purported to be an elaborate headquarters setup for VC and National Liberation Front cadres. In addition to the 173d's troops, the mission was carried out by elements of the 1st, 4th, 9th, and 25th Infantry Divisions, the 11th Air Cavalry Regiment, 196th Light Infantry Brigade, and the 503d Airborne. What the troops actually found was a beat-up old desk and an antiquated radio in the "Parrot's Beak" region on the Cambodia–Vietnam border. They also captured large quantities of food and supplies.

The jump into Tay Ninh was no picnic. "It clearly had no strategic value," Leroy recalled. "It was really a morale booster for the troops. But it was scary. I had never parachuted into a war zone before. I knew people could get killed. On the other hand, I knew that there was not much danger because there had been so much prep. My only concern was not to land in a tree because I would have become the laughing stock of the operation." She didn't. That embarrassing honor went instead to a 173d paratrooper.

A year later, Leroy's courage was tested again when she was captured by NVA troops. She and fellow French journalist François Mazure, of Agence France Presse, were apprehended while heading into the fray of the 1968 Tet Offensive on a tandem bicycle outside Hue in February that year. But Leroy eventually managed to talk the NVA out of holding her and Mazure captive, promising them that she would publish photos of the NVA unit if released—a promise she was able to keep.

Looking back on the incident, she recalled: "It was very frightening. We didn't know if we were going to be killed or not. But they didn't shoot first, which was a good sign." The communists took their cameras, tied their hands behind their backs and transported the pair to a room in a commandeered villa occupied by a Frenchman, his Vietnamese wife, and their children. Hours later, a young North Vietnamese officer arrived on the scene. "We were very lucky because the Frenchman's wife translated for us," Leroy recalled.

Right after that, they were untied and their equipment was returned to them. Then something happened that still makes Leroy laugh when she thinks about it today: "There were cigars there, so we all started to smoke. Then, amazingly, the officer asked me, 'Are you sure you have all your equipment?'" After that, Leroy photographed the NVA troops as promised, and she and Mazure were off.

In fact, the French correspondent's capture was cited by American negotiators at the opening session of the Paris Peace Talks as proof that NVA troops were in the South—a fact that the communists continued to deny. Yet Leroy recalled vividly how, during the interview and photo shoot that helped her and Mazure and later graced the pages of *Life* and *Look*, her captors freely admitted they were Northerners. 'Where are you from?' I asked them. 'I'm from Vinh,' said one. 'I'm from Haiphong,' said another. They were all from the North. There was no reason for them to lie to us then."

Vietnam for Leroy represented a kind of metamorphosis. She witnessed the horrors of war, yet also experienced the brotherhood that sometimes comes with it. "It was a unique comradeship," she recalled, "one that was based on life and death, not money and power. I learned that war is not a normal circumstance. It's the biggest game of all; one that only those who survive can talk about."

Leroy herself nearly did not survive. While covering the Marines on Hill 881 near the DMZ at Khe Sanh in 1967, she was wounded by shrapnel during a mortar barrage. She was transported to the hospital ship USS *Sanctuary* for a two-month convalescence.

Raymond Ramirez, a veteran of the 173d Airborne Brigade, once voiced the view that it was the journalists who lost the Vietnam War for the United States. Yet Ramirez exonerated Leroy and some other reporters whom he had seen in action, blaming higher-ups for what he felt was faulty journalism. "The reporters in the field were our friends," said Ramirez. "They hung out with us and attempted to tell our story. It was not their fault. It was the editors who sat on their asses back in Saigon or New York who changed the news. They edited it, putting on a different spin."

It allegedly proved impossible to edit the tongue of the feisty Leroy, who often shocked paratroopers as well as officials with her no-holds-barred commentary. She was banned from I Corps for six months after shouting down the Marine Corps top brass. She got her credentials back just in time to shoot frame after frame of the battle at Hill 881, where she received her shrapnel wound. Experiences like that made Leroy the tough reporter she became.

"When I got to Vietnam, I spoke three words of English," she recalled. "I slept in the same shitholes as the GIs."

"And she took her English lessons from those GIs," added Ramirez, laughing as he remembered her frequently salty speech. "Cathy is fluent in 10 languages," he added, "but she can cuss in 15."

Asked if she felt she had acted courageously, Leroy responded with a question: "Courage for what? I'm a survivor. The person who survives the ghetto has courage. The soldiers in World War II had courage."

Leroy decided to stop covering wars, "because when I photographed war, it went from dying soldiers to dead civilians. In the wars of one little world against another, one sees the senseless violence." Instead of seeking out battlefields around the world, she took on a very different kind of assignment, shooting images of high-fashion models for an Internet project called Pièce Unique.

Looking back on her lengthy career as a war correspondent, Leroy said simply, "I feel as though I captured my own death. It should be about being alive."

Everything Is Okay Now: Nick Ut

Fifteen-year-old Huynh Cong Ut was playing cards with his 23-year-old sister-in-law Arlette, in her family's house on Tran Hung Dao Street in Saigon one night in 1965 when she drew a black king, to her an unlucky omen. Soon, a messenger from the Associated Press's bureau knocked on the door to let her know that her husband, AP photographer Huynh Thanh My, had been killed covering a skirmish between South Vietnamese Army Rangers and the Viet Cong in the Mekong Delta near Can Tho.

Ut's life changed forever that night, just as shortly thereafter his first name also changed. He became Nick, which derived from "Nik Nik," a name given to him by his dear friend, French-Vietnamese photographer Henri Huet.

After his brother My's death, Nick was taken under protective custody, not only by the AP's chief photographer Horst Faas, but also by everyone in the AP's Saigon bureau, because Nick soon endeavored to follow in his much beloved brother's footsteps.

"My brother was also a very famous actor. A lot of media came to his funeral," Nick said, tears welling up in his eyes at the recollection.

In fact, the entire Saigon press corps was reported to have shown up at My's burial at the Mac Dinh Chi Cemetery, according to the book *Requiem: By the Photographers Who Died in Vietnam and Indochina*, compiled by two combat photographers who made it home: Faas and Tim Page.

Out of a sense of loyalty to My and the family, AP staffers would not let Nick go beyond the darkroom, in which his sister-in-law had asked Faas to allow Nick to work because the family was now in need of a bread-winner.

Faas had originally turned her down owing to Nick's age. "He's too young," he told Arlette.

But she persisted and Faas agreed to hire him.

"I had never been a photographer before but the darkroom was so easy. Nothing to learn but loading the film and developing. I learned everything in three minutes … and loved it," Ut recalled recently from the AP's Los Angeles bureau at which he recently celebrated his 40th anniversary of employment with the wire service.

Forty years earlier, Ut began a career in which he rose from humble surroundings in Long An, in the Mekong Delta, to a Pulitzer Prize-winning war photographer.

"To me, Nicky continues to serve as an inspiration—proof that you can always improve. I've watched him go from a so-so shooter to a museum-quality photojournalist," said Steve Stibbens, a former Marine, who came to know Nick during his second tour in Vietnam as a reporter for *Leatherneck Magazine*. His first had been in uniform with *Stars and Stripes*, his third with the AP.

"After my brother died, I had no one to learn from," Nick remembered.

That would soon change as he developed hundreds of images of AP shooters—images of the war in which Vietnam was by now embroiled.

"Horst Faas told me how his own beginning in photography was in the darkroom at the Keystone Agency 50-plus years ago and he was able to learn what makes a good photo by seeing the work of others. I think that same beginning worked for Nicky," said Stibbens.

"One day I picked up a camera and began to shoot pictures of my girlfriend. Many girls wanted copies of the photos I took of them," Nick recalled, the welled-up eyes of earlier now turned to the broad, baby-faced smile that has earned him continued affection from those who have known him.

Pictures of beautiful young Vietnamese girls soon gave way to a much different assignment when then AP correspondent Peter Arnett, years later of cable TV channel CNN, was writing a story about the bar girls and shoe-shine boys that often congregated around the Rex Hotel in Saigon's District 1.

Nick was able to win Arnett's confidence and shoot the photos for his piece.

"Peter told me, `this is good photography Nicky.'"

His images were so good in fact that they soon earned him front-page slots in newspapers such as *Stars and Stripes* and the *Saigon Post*.

Stibbens and Arnett were not alone in noting Nick's work behind the lens. Admiration for his talents grew, and it also quickly earned him the respect of most of the Saigon press corps.

"Nick, for me, reinforces the belief that the best work out of a war comes from people who open themselves to the agony around them and feel the pain of the subjects they photograph," said Jim Caccavo. Caccavo himself went to Vietnam as the photographer and writer for the Red Cross between 1968 and 1970, and also shot photo assignments and filed reports for *Newsweek* magazine during that time.

"Larry Burrows and Henri Huet were photographers of that standing. They were known to—at times—show emotion when talking about the children they had photographed in the war," Caccavo said.

That is a fact not lost on Nick Ut, the photographer of the most famous of Vietnamese children taken during the war, Phan Thi Kim Phuc, otherwise known as "the Napalm Girl."

It was June 8, 1972, in the Cao Dai village of Trang Bang that the incident occurred that would forever bind Nick with Kim Phuc.

He had been covering operations with the ARVN early in the morning of the second day of a three-day combined NVA/Viet Cong attack on the village. He had hitched a ride in the AP van, ordered the driver to stay by the side of the road, and got out.

He had witnessed plenty of attacks in his, by then, seventh year of shooting for the AP, but sensed there was something different about the one pending.

"I saw the ARVN surround the Cao Dai temple and knew if I stood there, I would be dead," said Nick, who had previously been wounded twice covering the war in Cambodia, and once in Vietnam.

As he and other reporters moved further down the road to take a more secure position, they observed black smoke rising outside the temple. Suddenly, one of the ARVN troops popped a yellow smoke marker.

Nick pointed his camera up to focus and caught, in his viewfinder, a Korean War era A-37 just at the instant that it dropped four bombs on the village right where the smoke had revealed itself.

Within seconds an A-1 Sky Raider dropped four additional bombs on Trang Bang—but these were napalm.

"I had seen napalm before, but never dropped on a village. I was shooting in black and white. I wished I'd had color," Nick recalls, not for any reason other than to show the full effect of what napalm could do.

He started shooting "like crazy. I told myself, 'I hope there was nobody in the village.'"

Unfortunately, that was not the case.

Soon he saw a woman, her body badly burned, with four or five kids. She was a grandmother holding her dead grandson, the skin peeling off his torso, and was asking Ut and the other reporters, "Cuu con toi!" ("Please help!").

Ironically, when Nick got back to the AP office and developed the photo of the grandmother, everybody initially thought that was *the* shot, but what happened next turned out to be the photo that would change his life—and Kim Phuc's—forever. "I saw a little girl running. She had torn off all her clothes. She was yelling 'Nóng quá! Nóng quá!' ("Too hot! Too hot!")."

The little girl was the nine-year-old Kim (the others he had just seen were, in fact, members of her family, all of whom had sought refuge in the temple). He shot a series of photos, the most famous of which would garner him both the Pulitzer Prize and World Press Photo Award for 1973.

But recognition was far from his mind when he laid his camera on the side of Highway 1 and came to Kim Phuc's aid.

"Her back was burned so badly," Nick said. "I didn't want her to die, so I poured cold water on her."

However, her cries of "Nong qua! Nong qua!" continued because, unbeknownst to him and other journalists who tried to cool her skin with water, liquid spreads the napalm gel around.

"Then I borrowed a poncho from an ARVN 25th Division soldier because I didn't want her to be naked."

As she began to weaken, Nick began to carry her, but the pain was unbearable for Kim and she asked him to put her down. Together, he, Kim and her uncle made it to the AP van and drove to Cu Chi Hospital.

"The traffic was crazy. There were dogs and water buffalo everywhere," he remembered.

"She kept saying, 'Chắc con sắp chết! Chắc con sắp chết!' ('I think I'm dying! I think I'm dying!')," Nick recalled. As she was going into shock, he felt time was running out.

When they arrived at the hospital they saw many ARVN soldiers, some dead, some dying. Nick realized a nine-year-old girl's wounds would not take precedence over a soldier's, and his adrenaline kicked in.

"I showed my media pass and I threatened, 'If she dies, I will tell the story of this hospital!'"

That apparently shook the staff into action and Kim's life was saved.

"I think most photographers would have headed back to Saigon with their film and left Kim to local authorities," Caccavo said. "What Nick did is called 'getting involved,' which most journalism schools frown on, but I think he changed that inhumane attitude forever."

Whether or not that attitude was changed that day was no one's particular concern in early June 1972 however.

Whether to send the photo out at all was the debate at the AP Saigon bureau. Not because it showed the horrors of war on par with Eddie Adams' photo of Brigadier General Nguyen Ngoc Loan shooting Viet Cong Nguyen Van Lem in the head at point blank range, or with Malcolm Browne's photo of the Venerable Buddhist monk Thich Quang Duc immolating himself on the streets of Saigon in 1963.

The issue was the frontal nudity.

AP higher-ups thought the photo should not run, according to Nick. But Horst Faas overruled them, emphatically stating, "Move it now!" And, after it endured some degree of touch up, the photo was transmitted to New York via Tokyo.

The image had immediate impact around the world.

Eddie Adams' and Malcolm Browne's photos indeed spoke to the horrors of the war. Ut's image of Kim Phuc did as well, but it also had something more: Kim's outstretched arms reached out to envelope the viewer.

"Even today, Vietnam veterans come up to me and say, 'Thank you Nicky. Yours is the photo that stopped the war.'"

Many of his friends and colleagues agree.

"His image stands alone in its mega impact, becoming an iconic anti-war statement and will be forever more," said Tim Page, renowned British photojournalist and combat photographer in Vietnam, now teaching a new generation of photojournalists at Griffiths University in Australia where he is working on his Ph.D. It was "further sway to end that nightmare," Page added.

Author Marvin Wolf (*Buddha's Child: My Fight to Save Vietnam* with Nguyen Cao Ky), public information officer for the 1st Air Cavalry stationed at An Khe in the Central Highlands, concurs with Page.

"It had enormous impact … the photo served to influence public opinion around the world. Unfortunately, few who saw Nick's photo bothered to read the original caption, which explained that the napalm had been dropped by a VNAF [South Vietnamese Air Force] aircraft. Most people still believe it was an American plane."

Nevertheless, many Americans, Vietnam veterans and others, continue to feel that it was because of photos like Nick Ut's, Eddie Adams' and Malcolm Browne's that the United States lost the war in Vietnam. They believe the photos so turned public opinion against the war as to sway those in Congress to cut off funding, thereby making the war unwinnable.

Not surprisingly, many of the photojournalists who took these very photos disagree wholeheartedly. Steve Stibbens is one of them.

"It is such nonsense and reveals their ignorance," he said.

Marvin Wolf elaborated: "I'm more than a little bummed out by this kind of simplistic jingoism. That the communists capitalized on US policy blunders and military mistakes is hardly the fault of the media," he said.

Meanwhile for Nick Ut, Pulitzer Prize in hand, the war was over, as it was for all of his fellow South Vietnamese, when Saigon fell on April 30, 1975.

And as Saigon was falling, the AP evacuated Ut and put him up in a nice hotel in Los Angeles. But his surroundings, indeed life in L.A. itself, were so foreign to him that he opted to relocate with the first wave of Vietnamese refugees to the Tent City erected on their behalf just north of San Diego at the Marine Corps' Camp Pendleton.

Among his first assignments, once settled in southern California, was to photograph a Los Angeles Dodgers baseball game. Ironically, not only had Nick never seen a baseball game in his life, he knew nothing about the sport. Regardless, that day, he shot some of the most compelling sports frames ever.

But while he went about the day-to-day routine of a wire service "photog," thoughts of Vietnam and the young nine-year-old whose life he had saved years before persistently haunted him.

Then in 1989, his friend Jim Caccavo received an assignment from *Los Angeles Times Magazine* to photograph a reunion between Nick and Kim Phuc in Havana. Correspondent Judy Coburn wrote the story. The three were granted 24-hour visas and departed for Cuba.

"When I saw Kim, I couldn't believe it was her," Nick said.

The nine-year-old girl was now a grown woman.

"It was obvious from the moment their eyes met that there was a special bond between them," Caccavo recalled.

Following their meeting in a hotel, overseen in typical communist fashion by minders, one Cuban, one Vietnamese, and a two-hour "undisturbed" interview in a restaurant—which Kim later told Ut, Caccavo and Coburn, was secretly taped—Nick recalled how Kim expressed to him that nobody would marry her because of her severely burned body.

Until then, Kim's life had been one of constant pain, suffering through several reconstructive surgeries in West Germany, years as a poster child in a now reunited communist Vietnam, and additional years in Cuba studying pharmacy and Spanish (in which she is fluent even today).

In the years that followed, Nick would hear news of Kim through her family still back in Vietnam.

Once, he even got a letter postmarked Mexico City charmingly telling Nick, "Uncle, I want to come to America. Can you wait for me at the border in San Diego?"

Then, mysteriously, in 1992, while away on assignment, he got a message at the AP from "somebody in Toronto." Not knowing a soul in Canada, he was non-plussed.

Until the caller called again. It was Kim. She'd married fellow Vietnamese student Bui Huy Toan in Havana. While returning from their honeymoon in Moscow and during a refueling stop in Gander, Newfoundland, they'd simply walked off the plane, leaving all their luggage aboard, and requested political asylum. This was granted them by the Canadian government.

Today, Phan Thi Kim Phuc is a UNESCO goodwill ambassador for culture and peace, and Nick Ut sees and talks to her whenever the two can connect.

In late April 2005, 30 years after the fall of Saigon, Nick was back in what had been renamed Ho Chi Minh City. He was among the deans of the former Saigon press corps at a reunion atop the Rex Hotel.

According to Caccavo, who was present, an American woman approached Nick and told him how much she appreciated the photo of Kim Phuc. Through tears, she expressed how much it had affected her.

Nick, trying to console her, very humbly said, "Thank you so much, but everything is okay now. Kim is married ... in Canada. She has two healthy boys."

Indeed everything is okay now for this gentle and most respected shooter among war photographers. He may have gone on from his experiences covering Vietnam, but they are never far behind him. He wouldn't forget them even if he could.

Nick Ut retired from the Associated Press after 51 years on the job at its Los Angeles bureau in April 2017.

A Moment of Truth: Eddie Adams

A photo of USMC Private First Class Thomas N. Bresnan holding a large crucifix in front of his face during Good Friday services at the Marine Corps compound in Da Nang on April 16, 1965 is intentionally juxtaposed opposite a grainy photo of Army of the Republic of [South] Vietnam soldiers preparing 24-year-old, blindfolded Viet Cong guerilla Le Dau for execution in the same city one day before.

Deeper into the book, two photos face off. The first, almost surrealistic, is of motor bikes afire while citizens trash the office of the Saigon-based newspaper *Nha Bao Song* in protest at Premier Nguyen Cao Ky's regime. The other, across the fold from the first, shows hundreds of Vietnamese women dressed in their traditional alluring *ao dai* and *non la* (conical) hats marching peacefully across a bridge in Hue protesting the same regime.

Such was the Vietnam War, and such is page after page of the telling, stark and gut-wrenching imagery of Umbrage Editions' new book *Eddie Adams: Vietnam*, the effort of the late Associated Press photographer's widow Alyssa, who edited the work, and Hal Buell, former AP worldwide photo editor, who was responsible for the narration.

Staring at the black-and-white images, one after another, I'm reminded of the Eddie Adams I had the honor of hearing lecture at a gathering of members of the American Society of Media Photographers at the Hollywood Roosevelt Hotel in Los Angeles several years ago. Adams was every bit the storyteller as he was a photographer. But why should that be surprising? His photos remain among the images, like those of Malcolm Browne, Larry Burrows, Henri Huet, Nick Ut, and others, that best defined the Vietnam War for the American public back home as well as the rest of the world.

Adams abhorred the fact that he was chiefly known for taking his most famous photo, the one of former Saigon police chief Brigadier General Nguyen Ngoc Loan executing a flannel-shirted Viet Cong Nguyen Van Lem on a street in the Saigon's Chinese quarter called Cholon. Adams felt equally bad that he was directly responsible for ruining Loan's life—or as he would often say, "Two lives were ruined that day"—with the Pulitzer-Prize winning photo. The photograph, Adams felt, relegated Loan to the life of a pizza parlor owner in Virginia. But Loan did not share that sentiment, and Adams and he remained close until Loan's death in 1998. Adams himself died of Lou Gehrig's Disease in 2004.

On February 1, 1968 Adams and a TV crew from NBC News had heard that there was going to be, as his memoirs indicate, "a little battle" near the An Quang Pagoda. But no one had any idea what was going to happen. Adams thought the captured VC was perhaps going to get roughed up and carted away. He knew from instinct that whenever you as a photojournalist see police leading away a perpetrator from a crime scene, it's your job to follow the action. Which he and the NBC crew did.

Then he saw General Loan reach for a ladies' model snub-nosed .38-caliber Smith & Wesson and point it at Lem's head. Even then Adams did not flinch because he knew threats are often issued at the point of a gun.

"When somebody goes for their pistol, they normally threaten the prisoner," Adams wrote in his memoirs. "I've taken pictures like that. Somebody threatens somebody … You're going to do this or I'm going to shoot you. And nothing ever happens."

But then, in an instant, something did happen: General Loan fired his gun. NBC captured Lem falling to the ground, all the while blood erupting from his head, something Adams turned away from and refused to watch.

"The bullet was inside that VC's head before I snapped that picture," he told those in attendance at the American Society of Media Photographers meeting. He also went on to stress the fact that what most of the world did not know at the time was that very same VC had, moments before, executed at close range the entire family—including the wife and children—of one of Loan's lieutenants, a close friend. Adams, a Marine during the Korean War, who unlike most journalists covering Vietnam believed in American foreign policy, badly needed and wanted that understood.

Adams went on to tell the ASMP gathering that he viewed his camera as protection from harm, and that, somehow, he felt safe behind the viewfinder. That sentiment was echoed again in *Eddie Adams: Vietnam*.

"The camera is like a shield and I will go into situations unarmed. I've never carried a weapon. I feel that the camera's going to protect me, you know, and I think that's a part of the survival too."

Another part of survival for Eddie Adams was, apparently, his ability to use the "f" word with the second-person singular pronoun attached to it when those two words were called for. He regaled for the ASMP attendees a story that still brings a chuckle.

He and a reporter had gone to Havana in 1984 on assignment to interview and photograph Cuban President Fidel Castro for *Parade* magazine. Both were kept holed up in their hotel rooms for two weeks without any signal that the interview would proceed. When Adams had had enough, over the protestations of the reporter, he uttered the two words and flew back home to New York.

Weeks later, in the middle of the night, came a knock on his door, he recalled. It was a representative from the Cuban Mission at the United Nations, who told him, "El Presidenté would like to see you now." Said Adams, "Fuck you! I waited two weeks down there. They kept me in my hotel, and he never showed up!"

"No, no, señor. He really wants to see you now," insisted the emissary from the mission.

So Adams grabbed the reporter and off the two went again to Havana, where the interview did occur this time, Adams shooting frame after frame. All at once, interview over, Castro got up to leave.

"But Presidenté," interjected Adams, "I don't have any photos."

Castro's retort came in the near perfect English that, though a lot people don't know it, Castro speaks: "But Eddie, what have you been doing with your camera?"

"Well, I want to get you in your element. What say you and I go jogging down on the beach?"

"But Eddie, Havana has a lot of beaches. I have a better idea. I'll take you to my favorite lake where I go duck hunting. But you'd better not tell the CIA where it is!" Castro warned him.

When Adams returned to New York, he found in his exposed film, a photo of the two of them by the lake with dozens of dead ducks at their feet. He took it upon himself to mail it to Castro with dim hopes of receiving the dictator's autograph and even dimmer hopes of ever seeing the photo again. But see it again he did, and it was signed with the following inscription: "To my friend Eddie: I shot all the ducks. Your friend, Fidel."

Anecdotes are plentiful throughout the 223-page book. They come from the likes of many of Eddie Adams' colleagues in Vietnam: the late David Halberstam, writer of a plethora of non-fiction, who covered the war for *The New York Times* and was tragically killed in an auto accident on his way to a lecture at Berkeley in 2007; former CNN field reporter Peter Arnett, who, like Adams, worked for the AP in Vietnam; their fellow AP correspondent George Esper; UPI, and later White House, photographer David Hume Kennerly; CBS News's Morley Safer; Bob Schieffer, who originally went to Vietnam as a print reporter for the Ft. Worth *Star-Telegram*; and others.

Inescapably, many of their anecdotes focus, at least in part, on the photo Adams despaired having taken.

"How ironic that Eddie's most famous photo was also his cruelest," David Halberstam wrote. "How strange that a man whose extraordinary body of work celebrates the richness and complexity of the human family is best remembered for an image he captured detailing the ultimate act of inhumanity."

The photo of General Loan "was one of the most shocking moments in journalism in the last hundred years. It was taken at a point when the country was already pretty disillusioned about the war, and the politicians were also becoming disillusioned. In a sense, it was a nail in the coffin of Vietnam," the late Morley Safer wrote.

Said Peter Arnett: "I told Eddie that what he captured was a moment of truth about the war. The picture was a tangible reality that came to characterize the whole conflict … but Eddie, Mr. Patriot, just would not accept that. He enjoyed winning the Pulitzer Prize as well as the fame that came with it, but in his heart, he felt that he had let the country down."

Eddie Adams yearned to be known and appreciated for more than just the photo that his friends—indeed an entire generation who lived through the Vietnam War—will never forget. With *Eddie Adams: Vietnam*, that will be entirely possible.

Bringing the War Home: Requiem

"We all left a bit of our souls in Southeast Asia," said renowned British photojournalist Tim Page, former UPI shooter whose Vietnam War images made the covers and pages of a plethora of worldwide periodicals and his own books. "We don't want to lose that."

In 1997, Page, who was wounded four times in Vietnam—the last time almost fatally—delivered his unique perspective on photographing the war before a Washington, D.C., assemblage of correspondents who were alongside him there, as well as in Cambodia and Laos.

They had gathered at the Freedom Forum's Arlington, Virginia "Newseum" to commemorate the shooters who did not return. And the correspondents also celebrated the publication of *Requiem*, which features the work of 135 photojournalists—American, British, Australian, French, Swiss, German, Austrian, Japanese, Singaporean, Cambodian, South Vietnamese, and even North Vietnamese—who died attempting to bring both the French Indochina and American Vietnam War experiences home. The book was the brainchild of Page, and Associated Press photographer Horst Faas, until he retired recently, Chief of Photo of the AP's London bureau.

Vietnam haunts millions for various reasons. Civilian media who reported and photographed the war are no different. The late David Halberstam, former *New York Times* correspondent, was one.

"Who would have thought when we arrived 35 years ago, virtually boys, that Vietnam would be the spine of our professional lives; that we would still be getting together at the turn of a new century, drawn by this painful bond; that we would be the custodians of that most precious thing, the memory of war," he said in 1997.

"It was the first and last war covered without the accustomed censorship," Page wrote in the book's eulogy. "Sometimes you got lucky; got caught in the right place at the wrong time and came back with exposed rolls of film. Other times it was just another long, hot plod through a hostile, demanding countryside that could grab your limb or your life."

In Cambodia, in fact, it did grab the life of one of Page's closest friends, Sean Flynn (son of actor Errol Flynn), who had come to Vietnam very much the pin-up star acting out the role of a combat photojournalist for *Paris Match*. He had never shot a serious frame.

Indochina soon got inside Flynn's veins, and his real images, like Page's—and those of Black Star Photo Agency's Robert Ellison and *Life*'s Larry Burrows—were soon face-up on the coffee tables of America wreaking their effect on those at home.

Page's baptism under fire came while he bicycled through Laos in the mid 1960s. He was sitting in café in Vientiane with the likes of a Kodak Instamatic when a Buddhist uprising occurred.

Like his soon-to-be friend Flynn, Page had never spent much time looking through a viewfinder. Nonetheless, he began clicking away and soon found himself in Saigon shooting for UPI for a nominal existence.

The 1997 gathering of journalists was MC'd by CNN commentator Bernard Kalb, himself a network TV reporter in Vietnam. Besides Flynn, Ellison and Burrows, many others were remembered that evening.

They included: CBS cameraman Dana Stone, who with companion Flynn motor-biked into Cambodia in 1970, was caught and held captive by the NVA for two years before being turned over to the Khmer Rouge and never seen again; Kent Potter, Henri Huet, and Keisaburo Shimamoto, all fatally shot down in 1971 in a chopper with Larry Burrows over a Laos portion of the Ho Chi Minh Trail covering Operation *Lam Son 719*, the failed attempt to interdict communist cadres and materiel headed for South Vietnam; Bernard Fall, famed author of *Street Without Joy* and *Hell in a Very Small Place*; and both François Sully and Kyoichi Sawada, who also lost their lives.

"I believe their spirits are with us here tonight," said Page.

They certainly live on in the pages of *Requiem*.

Their colleagues who survived the war have shouldered much more than their camera bags in conviction, guilt, and incomprehension over what they themselves witnessed and photographed. The shooters agree that their telling photos no doubt swayed public opinion in the United States; they point out that the so-called "TV War" should really have been dubbed the "Still Photo War."

Susan Moeller, author of *Shooting War*, tends to agree. In an interview during A&E Network's presentation *Vietnam: The Camera at War*, she said, "Still images [of Vietnam] lingered in the memory. People could go back to them. They couldn't linger on the TV [footage] in the same way."

A case in point occurred in 1963. Protesting Catholic Ngo Dinh Diem's regime's anti-Buddhist actions, an elderly Buddhist monk named Thich Quang Duc immolated himself in the middle of a busy Saigon intersection. Correspondent Malcolm Browne had been tipped off that something would happen and was there to take the shot.

"That photo was the first time Americans began to take the war seriously," insisted Faas. "We did our jobs to put the war on the map."

Nick Ut—the Vietnamese photographer of the Pulitzer Prize winning photo of Phan Thi Kim Phuc, the young Vietnamese girl running naked down the road after having been severely burned by napalm—concurs.

Recalling the 1972 strike by the South Vietnamese Air Force on the village of Trang Bang, Ut said, "I pointed my camera up to focus and saw a Sky Raider drop four napalm bombs. Then another dropped four. I saw a grandmother running down the road with her dead grandchild and took her picture. Then Kim and the others came toward me yelling 'Nong qua, nong qua' ('too hot, too hot')." Ut snapped that frame as well, and then helped her get to the hospital in Cu Chi.

In the A & E special, former AP shooter and US Marine Korean War veteran Eddie Adams recalled snapping the equally horrific photo of General Nguyen Ngoc Loan, chief of South Vietnam's national police, pointing his pistol at the head of a flannel-shirted Viet Cong in the streets of Saigon. The press had been alerted to the possibility of action at the An Quang Pagoda nearby. According to Adams, "We saw the South Vietnamese grabbing this guy. I thought he [Loan] was just going to threaten him. I had no idea that he was going to shoot him. The bullet was in his head when that picture was taken."

Though their distinctive experiences in Vietnam have haunted them through the years, Adams, Ut, Page, and their fellow photographers all share the endless memory of capturing the conflict. That experience, however, was not unique to press photographers. Sergio Ortiz, a US Marine Corps combat correspondent in Vietnam from 1969 to 1971, and Jim Caccavo, the chief Red Cross photographer in Vietnam between 1968 and 1970 who had previously served in the US Army in Germany and with the 1st Air Cavalry on the DMZ in Korea, also knew and felt the conflict deeply.

A lance corporal at the time, Ortiz ran a two-man press center in Chu Lai. When he wasn't covering his fellow Marines at Khe Sanh or medevac units, the Malibu resident could be found taking photographs from the second seats of Skyhawks, Phantoms, OV-10 Broncos, and even a two-seater Cessna Bird Dog with the South Korean Marines.

"The Bird Dog would draw fire," he explained. "Then we would call in the 'Big Boys' upstairs."

While Ortiz's job was to snap the action in Vietnam, Jim Caccavo saw his own job as one of photographing those most affected by the war: civilians. "To capture faces always felt personal, as if I were intruding into their lives, pain, and suffering of their very tragic moments. I felt appreciative of what they were going through."

He had respect as well for the soldiers he photographed. One time he gladly put down his focused camera when a wounded lieutenant asked him to. The young officer did not want his family back home to see him in that condition. "I never felt any picture was worth causing discomfort to anyone's suffering," he said.

Still, Caccavo, like others who photographed the war, knew he was risking his life each time he boarded a helicopter at Tan Son Nhut's Hotel 3 helipad. "Every time we went out, we never knew what would happen."

Glossary

0-2	Cessna aircraft
0-5	Commander in the Coast Guard
1/10 Air Cav	1st Squadron/10th Cavalry, U.S. Army
1/4	1st Battalion, 4th Marine Regiment
1/501	1st Battalion/ 501st Regiment, U.S. Army Airborne
1/5	1st Battalion, 5th Marine Regiment
105	Half-ton U.S. Army trailer
11 Bravo	Military Occupation Specialty for U.S. Army Infantryman
1BN	1st Battalion
1stMarDiv	1st Marine Division
2/17	2nd Battalion/17th Regiment, U.S. Army Airborne
2/327	2nd Battalion/327th Regiment, U.S. Army Airborne
2/4	2nd Battalion, 4th Marine Regiment
2/502	2nd Battalion/502nd Regiment, U.S. Army Airborne
3/1	3rd Battalion, 1st Marine Regiment
3/4	3rd Battalion, 4th Marine Regiment
4312	Combat Correspondent Military Occupation in the Marine Corps
A&E Network	Abbreviation for American cable TV channel, the Arts & Entertainment Network
A-1 Skyraider	Aircraft built by Douglas Aircraft
A-10	Aircraft built by Fairchild Republic, also known as the "Warthog"
A-2C	U.S. Air Force Airman Second Class
A-37	Light Attack Aircraft Known also as the "Dragonfly" and built by Cessna
AARG	Aerospace Rescue and Reconnaissance Group, U.S. Air Force
AAVS	Aerospace Audio Visual Service Combat Camera
ABC	American Broadcasting Corp.
AFCCG	Atlantic Fleet Combat Camera Group
AFN-E	Armed Forces Network-Europe
AFRTS	Armed Forces Radio and Television Service
AFSC	Air Force Specialty Code
Air Wing	U.S. Air Force Unit of Command
AIT	Advanced Individual Training

AK-47	Gas-operated Russian rifle used by the Viet Cong, invented by Mikhail Kalashnikov in 1947.
ANGLICO	Air Naval Gunfire Liaison Company
AO	Area of Operation
APA	Army Photographic Agency
AP	Associated Press
APC	Armored Personnel Carrier
APD	U.S. Navy Destroyer converted to haul troops
AR-15	Rifle made by Armalite
Arc Light	B-52 bomber strikes
Arty	Nickname for artillery
ARVN	Army of the Republic of South Vietnam
ASA	Refers to film speed or sensitivity to light
ASMP	American Society of Media Photographers
ASOPD	Army Special Operations Pictorial Department
AWOL	Absent without leave
B-52	U.S. Air Force bomber built by Boeing
Bao Chi	Vietnamese word for journalist or journalism
Bat 21	Call sign for downed pilot Lt. Col. Iceal Hambledon
BEQ	Bachelor Enlisted Quarters
Boonie Rat	grunts, fellow soldiers on the front lines
BOQ	Bachelor Officer Quarters
Bronze Star with Combat V	Medal awarded U.S. military personnel for bravery in a combat zone
C-119	Aircraft built by Fairchild and referred to as the "Flying Boxcar"
C-130	Aircraft built by Lockheed and often referred to as "Hercules"
C-141	Aircraft built by Lockheed and often referred to as the "Starlifter"
C-4	Explosive
C-5	Transport aircraft built by Lockheed
C-7 Caribou	Aircraft built by de Havilland
CA	Combat Assault
CAR-15	Type of carbine rifle
CBS	Columbia Broadcasting System
CG	Commanding General
CGHQ	Coast Guard Headquarters
CH-46	Sea Knight helicopter manufactured by Boeing
ChiComs	Chinese Communists
CIA	Central Intelligence Agency
CIDG	Civilian Irregular Defense Group
CINCPAC	Commander-In-Chief, Pacific Command
CM-16	Beckman and Whitney movie camera
CNA	Chief Naval Operations

CNN	Cable News Network
Coasties	Slang for Coast Guardsmen and women
CO	Commanding Officer
COIN	Counterinsurgency
Commo Wire	Wire used for communications
COMNAVAIRPACPAO	Commander, Naval Air Force, Pacific, Public Information Office
COMNAVFORV	Commander, Naval Forces, Vietnam
COMSEVENTHFLEETDETACHMENT	U.S. Navy 7th Fleet Command
Conex Container	Cargo storage container
CONUS	Inside the continental United States
C-Rats	Otherwise known as C-Rations, canned food for GIs
CTF	Navy Commander Task Force
CVA-33	Mid Class Aircraft Carrier
D.I.	Drill Instructor
DASPO	Department of the Army Special Photographic Office
De Oppresso Liber	Special Forces Latin expression meaning "Free the Oppressed"
DEROS	Date Expected Rotation Overseas
DFW	Dallas/Ft. Worth, Texas
Di di	Vietnamese expression for "go quickly"
DINFOS	Defense Information School
DIYGI	Do It Yourself GI
DMZ	Demilitarized Zone
DOD	Department of Defense
Dust Off	Casualty evacuation
E-5, 6, 7	Non-Commissioned Officer ranks
EC 47	Electronic Warfare Plan
EIR	Equipment Improvement Recommendation
ELD	Explosive Loading Detachment
ESPN	Entertainment and Sports Programming Network
ETS	Expiration Term of Service
F/V	U.S. Coast Guard acronym for Fishing Vessel
F-100	Fighter jet manufactured by North American Aviation
F-4	Fighter jet manufactured by McDonnel Douglas
F-8U-1P-Crusader	Jet aircraft manufactured by Vought
FAC	Forward Air Control Plane (used to scout areas before bombers unleashed their payloads)
FANK	Khmer National Armed Forces (Cambodia)
FAPL	U.S. Navy Fleet Air Photo Lab
FHNC	U.S. Coast Guard Fleet Hometown News Center
FHNTC	Fleet Headquarters Naval Training Center
Flechette	Shrapnel in an anti-personnel bomb

FULRO	Front for the Liberation of Oppressed Races (Montagnard rebel group)
G-1	Personnel and Administration Staff at Corps and Division Levels
GED	General Education Diploma (precursor to a high school diploma)
GI	Literally Government Issue, a term used for those in the U.S. Military
Grunt	Marine or soldier who has experienced combat
GS	Government Service Rating
Gunny	Marine Gunnery Sergeant
H&I	Harassment and Interdiction
H-13	Helicopter manufactured by Bell Helicopters
H-21	"Flying Banana"-helicopter used early in the Vietnam War and manufactured by Piasecki
H-34	Helicopter used by the Marines in Vietnam and manufactured by Sikorsky
HAHO	High-Altitude High-Opening Parachute Jump
HALO	High-Altitude Low-Opening Parachute Jump
HD	High Definition
HH-43	Rescue helicopter referred to as the Husky and manufactured by Kaman
HH-53	Helicopter often referred to as the "Jolly Green Giant" and manufactured by Sikorsky
HHC	Headquarters and Headquarters Company
HMAS	Her Majesty's Australian Ship
HQ	Headquarters
Huey	UH series helicopter used by all the armed services in Vietnam, manufactured by Bell
I, II and III Corps	Tactical Zones in Vietnam
IBS	U.S. Coast Guard Inflatable Boat Small
ISO	Marine Informational Services Office
ITR	Intensive Training Regiment
JO1 & 2	U.S. Coast Guard Ratings for journalists
JUSPAO	Joint United States Public Affairs Office
KIA	Killed in Action
LAW	Light Anti-Armor Weapon
LCU	Landing Craft Utility
LMAFS	Lookout Mountain Air Station, in the Laurel Canyon neighborhood of Los Angeles
LOACH	Light Observation Aircraft
LOM	Legion of Merit medal
LORAN	Long-range navigation
LSM	Landing Ship Medium
LST	Landing Ship Tank
L-T	Slang for the rank of lieutenant

LZ	Landing Zone
M/V	U.S. Coast Guard acronym for Motor Vessel
MAAG	Military Aid and Assistance Group
MAC	Military Airlift Command
MAC-V	Military Assistance Command-Vietnam
MCRD	Marine Corps Recruit Depot
MEDCAP	Medical Civic Action Program
MG	Machine Gun
MIA	Missing in Action
MiG	Soviet jet fighter built by the Mikoyan Design Bureau
MI	Military Intelligence
Montagnards	Indigenous hilltribes from the Central Highlands of Vietnam. The name literally means "mountain people" in French
Mopic	Motion picture
MOS	Military Occupation Specialty
MP	Military Police
MRF	Mobile Riverine Force
MSTS	Military Sea Transportation Service
MTO & E	Modified Table of Organization & Equipment
NAG	Naval Advisory Group
NAS	Naval Air Station
NATO	North Atlantic Treaty Organization
NAVFORVHQ	Naval Advisory Group Headquarters
NBC	National Broadcasting Corp.
NCOIC	Non-Commissioned Officer in Charge
NCO	Non-Commissioned Officer
NDP	Night Defensive Position
NSA	Naval Support Activity
NTC	Naval Training Center
NVA	North Vietnamese Army
OB	Order of Battle
OCONUS	Outside the Continental United States
OCS	Officer Candidate School
O-Dark 30	Slang for after midnight
OIC	Officer in Charge
OPCON	Operational Control
PACV	Patrol Air-Cushioned Vehicle
PAO	Public Affairs Office
PAT	Photo Assignment Team
PAVN	People's Army of North Vietnam
PBR	Patrol Boat River
PCF	Patrol Craft Fast
PCS	Permanent Change of Station

PFC	Private First Class
PH1,2, 3	Ranks for Navy photographers
PHC	Navy Photo Chief
PHCS	Navy Photo Senior Chief
PH	Navy Photographer's Mate
PID	Public Information Detachment
PIO	Public Information Office
PJ	U.S. Air Force Pararescue Specialist
Pog	Marine terminology meaning "Personnel Other than Grunt"
POL	Preserve, Oil Lubricant Depot
POR	Preparations for Overseas Redeployment
POW	Prisoner of War
PRC-25	Tactical Backpack radio (Portable Radio Communication)
PT 76	A type of tank
PTSD	Post Traumatic Stress Disorder
PX	Post Exchange
R & R	Rest and Relaxation
Recon	Reconnaissance
Repo Depot	Unit of replacement troops
RF	A series of jets manufactured by the McDonnel Douglas Corp.
RIT	Rochester Institute of Technology
ROK	Republic Of Korea
ROTC	Reserve Officers' Training Corps
RPG	Rocket Propelled Grenade
RPM	Revolutions per minute
RSSZ	Rung Sat Special Zone
RTAFB	Royal Thai Air Force Base
RTO	Radio Telephone Operator
Ruff-Puffs	Derogatory term for South Vietnamese soldiers
RVN	Republic of South Vietnam
S-2	Intelligence Office
S2	Type of Nikon camera
S-5	Civil Affairs Office
Sandy	A-1E Attack jet manufactured by Douglas Aircraft
SeaBees	Naval Construction Battalion
SEALS	Sea, Air and Land Combat Team
SEAPC	Southeast Asia Pictorial Center
SEATO	Southeast Asia Treaty Organization
SERE	Survival, Evasion, Rescue and Escape School
SFG	Special Forces Group
SK1	Store keeper in the Coast Guard
SLR	Single Lens Reflex camera clarification

Snuffy	Any U.S. Marine at a rank of sergeant or below who served as a combat correspondent in the 1st Marine Division between 1966–70. Snuffies identified closely with the cartoon character "Snuffy Smith"
SOF	*Soldier of Fortune* magazine
SPEC-4, 5	Specialist 4th or 5th Class, ranks in the U.S. Army
SP	Shore Patrol duty for Navy and Coast Guard
SP	Type of Nikon camera
STOL	Short Take Off and Landing aircraft
STRAC	Squared Away
Swift Boat	Small shallow draft water Navy vessel
T-39	Aircraft manufactured by North American Aviation, often referred to as a "Scatback"
TAD	Temporary Additional Duty
T-AGS-29	Pathfinder Class Oceanographic Survey Ship
TDY	Temporary Duty Station
TIFF	Tagged Image File Format
TO & E	Table of Organization & Equipment
TOC	Brigade Tactical Operations Center
UCMJ	Uniform Code of Military Justice
UDT	Underwater Demolition Team
UNESCO	United Nations Educational, Scientific and Cultural Organization
UNREP	Underway Replenishment
UPI	United Press International
USAF/PA	United States Air Force Public Affairs
USAR-V	United States Army-Vietnam
USCG	United States Coast Guard
UTB	40-foot Utility Boat in the U.S. Coast Guard
VCMJ-1	Marine Composite Reconnaissance Squadron
VC	Viet Cong Communist cadres
VMI	Virginia Military Institute
VNAF	South Vietnamese Air Force
VOCG	Verbal Order of Commanding General
VVAW	Vietnam Veterans Against the War
WAVE	Women Accepted for Voluntary Emergency Service in the U.S. Navy
WESTPAC	Western Pacific
WHEC	High Endurance Coast Guard Cutter
WLB	Coast Guard Buoy Tender, Seagoing
WPD	82-foot Coast Guard Cutter/Patrol Boat
WSO	Weapons Systems Officer
XO	Executive Officer
Yarmulke	Jewish skull cap

Select Bibliography

Adams, Alyssa and Hal Buell. *Eddie Adams: Vietnam* (Brooklyn, New York: Umbrage Editions Books, 2008)

Anson, Robert Sam. *War News: A Young Reporter in Indochina* (New York: Simon and Schuster, 1989)

Barden, Thomas E., ed. *Steinbeck in Vietnam* (Charlottesville, Va.: University of Virginia Press, 2012)

Burrows, Russell. *Larry Burrows: Vietnam* (New York: Alfred A. Knopf, 2002)

Durrance, Dick. Where War Lives: A Photographic Journal of Vietnam (New York: Noonday Press, 1988)

Faas, Horst and Tim Page, eds. Requiem: By the Photographers Who Died in Vietnam and Indochina (New York: Random House, 1997)

Fawcett, Denby and Ann Bryan Mariano, Kate Webb, Anne Morrissy Merick, Jurate Kazickos, Edith Lederer, Tad Bartimus, Tracy Wood, Laura Palmer. *War Torn: Stories of War from the Women Reporters Who Covered Vietnam* (New York: Random House, 2002)

Jones Griffiths, Philip. *Dark Odyssey* (New York: Aperture Foundation, 1996)

Kennerly, David Hume. *Shooter* (New York: Newsweek Books, 1979)

Page, Tim. *Tim Page's Nam* (New York: Alfred A. Knopf, 1983)

Pyle, Richard and Horst Faas. *Lost over Laos* (Cambridge, Mass.: Da Capo Press, 2003)

Schanberg, Sydney. *Death and Life of Dith Pran* (New York: Elizabeth Sifton Books and Penguin Books, 1985)

Scotti, Paul. Coast Guard Action in Vietnam: Stories of Those Who Served (Ashland, Ore.: Hellgate Press, 2000)

Siemon-Netto, Uwe. *Duc: A Reporter's Love for the Wounded People of Vietnam* (San Juan Capistrano, Calif.: Self-published, 2013)

Stibbens, Steve, ed. Knights over the Delta: An Oral History of the 114th Aviation Company in Vietnam, 1963–72 (Ft. Rucker, Ala.: 114th Aviation Company Association, 2002)

Stokey, Michael. *River of Perfumes* (North Hills, Calif.: Warriors Publishing Group, 2011)

Yablonka, Marc Phillip. *Distant War: Recollections of Vietnam, Laos and Cambodia* (San Diego: Navigator Books, 2011)

Yablonka, Marc Phillip. *Tears Across the Mekong* (Los Angeles: Figueroa Press, 2016)

Index